Glory, Grace, and Truth

Glory, Grace, and Truth

Ratification of the Sinaitic Covenant according to the Gospel of John

ALEXANDER TSUTSEROV

☙PICKWICK *Publications* · Eugene, Oregon

GLORY, GRACE, AND TRUTH
Ratification of the Sinaitic Covenant according to the Gospel of John

Copyright © 2009 Alexander Tsutserov. All rights reserved. Except for brief quotations in critical publications or reviews, no part of this book may be reproduced in any manner without prior written permission from the publisher. Write: Permissions, Wipf and Stock Publishers, 199 W. 8th Ave., Suite 3, Eugene, OR 97401.

Pickwick Publications
A Division of Wipf and Stock Publishers
199 W. 8th Ave., Suite 3
Eugene, OR 97401

www.wipfandstock.com

Scripture quotations taken from the New American Standard Bible®, Copyright © 1960, 1962, 1963, 1968, 1971, 1972, 1973, 1975, 1977, 1995 by The Lockman Foundation. Used by permission. (www.Lockman.org)

Scripture quotations taken from the Revised Standard Version of the Bible, copyright 1952 [2nd edition, 1971] by the Division of Christian Education of the National Council of the Churches of Christ in the United States of America. Used by permission. All rights reserved.

Scripture quotations taken from the English Translation of the Septuagint Version of the Old Testament by Sir Lancelot C. L. Brenton, 1844, 1851, published by Samuel Bagster and Sons, London, original ASCII edition Copyright © 1988 by FABS International (c/o Bob Lewis, DeFuniak Springs, FL 32433). All rights reserved. Used by permission. Copyright © 1998–1999, by Larry Nelson (Box 2083, Rialto, CA, 92376). Used by permission. Repr. Big Fork, MT: BibleWorks, LLC, 1998.

ISBN 13: 978-1-55635-976-7

Cataloging-in-Publication data:

Tsutserov, Alexander

    Glory, grace, and truth : ratification of the Sinaitic covenant according to the Gospel of John

    xvi + 272 p. ; 23 cm. Includes bibliographical references.

    ISBN 13: 978-1-55635-976-7

    1. Bible. N.T. John—Criticism, interpretation, etc. 2. Covenants—Biblical teaching. I. Title.

BS2615.52 T51 2009

Manufactured in the U.S.A.

to Ben Witherington III,
   through whom God ignited, sustained, and realized this vision

to Richard Bauckham,
   for sharing the wisdom of God

Contents

Foreword by Richard Bauckham / ix
Abbreviations / xi

Introduction: The Revelations of God at Sinai and as Jesus / 1

1. Allusions to Exodus 34:6 / **39**
2. Terms of John 1:14–18 / **90**
3. Allusions to Exodus 33:12—34:10 LXX / **140**
4. Exegesis of John 1:14–18 / **162**
5. The Covenant of the Presence of God / **179**

Conclusion / **243**

Bibliography / **257**

Foreword

It has quite often been suggested that when the prologue to John's Gospel says that the Word incarnate was "full of grace and truth" (1:14) it is alluding to the Old Testament's definitive characterization of God as "abounding in steadfast love and faithfulness" (Exod 34:6), but decisive evidence that John's Greek phrase (which is not that of the LXX in Exod 34:6) is a recognizable translation of the Hebrew phrase in Exodus has been lacking. Now, for the first time, Alexander Tsutserov has provided a full and thorough lexical and literary study that demonstrates the allusion conclusively. He explains convincingly not only that John does translate the Hebrew of Exodus 34:6, but also why he does so in the way that he does, departing from the Septuagint translation.

If Tsutserov had done no more than this, his work would be important, but there is much more. The phrase "full of grace and truth" is only one of the ways in which the last five verses of the Johannine prologue echo the Torah's account of the revelation of God at Sinai (Exod 33:12–34:10). Throughout these verses John is relating that revelation to the revelation of God in Jesus. Tsutserov offers a frequently original interpretation of these verses, denying that there is any contrast between the two revelations. Rather the content is the same (the divine character), but the revelation in Jesus surpasses the Mosaic revelation in quality. The essential identity of the two covenants gives Tsutserov's work a distinctive perspective on the much-discussed issue of this Gospel's relationship to Judaism.

The relationship of the prologue to the rest of the Gospel has often been regarded as highly problematic, not least because the term *charis* (grace), so important in these concluding verses of the prologue, never appears again in the Gospel. Tsutserov argues, however, that while the word is absent, the concept it stands for in the prologue is unfolded throughout the Gospel. He also argues that the term *doxa* (glory), another key term in 1:14, takes its Johannine meaning from its use in the account of the Sinai revelation. In this case both word and meaning recur throughout the Gospel.

In tracing the themes of 1:14–18 through the Gospel, Tsutserov identifies a central theme of the Gospel as the bestowal God's presence and God's character on believers. Thus, Tsutserov offers a fresh way into the theology of the Gospel, which highlights much that other approaches have missed in this richly allusive text.

It is a great pleasure to welcome this Russian contribution to Johannine studies. Tsutserov's work combines meticulous scholarship with original insight. He is well abreast of current Johannine studies, but he is never afraid to strike out on a path of his own. I am happy to be able now to commend it to all readers who wish to work at the detailed interpretation of a passage packed with meaning.

Richard Bauckham
Emeritus Professor of New Testament Studies
St Andrews University, Scotland

Abbreviations

AB	Anchor Bible
ABD	*Anchor Bible Dictionary*
AGJU	Arbeiten zur Geschichte des antiken Judentums und des Urchristentums
AnBib	*Analecta biblica*
ANF	*The Ante-Nicene Fathers*
AnLex	*Analytical Lexicon of the Greek New Testament*
AOAT	Alter Orient und Altes Testament
ASV	American Standard Version
ATANT	Abhandlungen zur Theologie des Alten und Neuen Testaments
BAGD	Bauer, Walter, W. F. Arndt, F. W. Gingrich, and F. W. Danker, *A Greek-English Lexicon of the New Testament and Other Early Christian Literature*
b. Ber.	*Berakot* (Babylonian tractate)
BBE	Bible in Basic English
BDB	Brown, Francis, S. R. Driver, and Charles A. Briggs, *A Hebrew and English Lexicon of the Old Testament*
BDF	Blass, F., A. Debrunner, and Robert W. Funk, *A Greek Grammar of the New Testament and Other Early Christian Literature*
BETL	Bibliotheca ephemeridum theologicarum Lovaniensium
BHS	*Biblia Hebraica Stuttgartensia*
BJRL	*Bulletin of the John Rylands University Library of Manchester*
BNTC	Black's New Testament Commentaries
BSac	*Bibliotheca sacra*
BT	*The Bible Translator*
BTB	*Biblical Theology Bulletin*
BZ	*Biblische Zeitschrift*
CBC	Cambridge Bible Commentary
CBET	Contributions to Biblical Exegesis and Theology
CBQ	*Catholic Biblical Quarterly*
CD	*Damascus Document* (Cairo Genizah)
Chr	Chronicles
Col	Colossians
Cor	Corinthians
CSEL	Corpus scriptorum ecclesiasticorum latinorum

Dan	Daniel
DBY	Darby Bible
Deut	Deuteronomy
DRB	Douay-Rheims Version
EBib	Etudes bibliques
En.	*Enoch*
Eph	Ephesians
Esdr.	*Esdras*
Esth	Esther
ESV	English Standard Version
ETS	Erfurter theologische Studien
Exod	Exodus
ExpTim	*Expository Times*
Ezek	Ezekiel
FRLANT	Forschungen zur Religion und Literatur des Alten und Neuen Testaments
Gal	Galatians
Gen	Genesis
GLXX	Septuagint (Göttingen)
GNV	Geneva Bible (1599)
HALOT	*Hebrew and Aramaic Lexicon of the Old Testament*
Heb	Hebrews
Hos	Hosea
HSM	Harvard Semitic Monographs
HTKNT	Herder's theologischer Kommentar zum Neuen Testament
HTR	*Harvard Theological Review*
IBHS	*An Introduction to Biblical Hebrew Syntax*
Int	*Interpretation*
Isa	Isaiah
Jas	James
JBL	*Journal of Biblical Literature*
Jer	Jeremiah
JETS	*Journal of the Evangelical Theological Society*
Jos. Asen.	*Joseph and Aseneth*
Josh	Joshua
JSOT	*Journal for the Study of the Old Testament*
JSNT	*Journal for the Study of the New Testament*
JSNTSup	Journal for the Study of the New Testament, Supplement Series
JTS	*Journal of Theological Studies*
Judg	Judges

KD	*Kerygma und Dogma*
KEK	Kritisch-exegetischer Kommentar über das Neue Testament (Meyer-Kommentar)
Kgs	Kings
KJV	King James Version
L&N	Louw, Johannes P., and Eugene A. Nida. *Greek-English Lexicon of the New Testament: Based on Semantic Domains*
L.A.B.	*Liber antiquitatum biblicarum* (Pseudo-Philo)
Lam	Lamentations
Lam.	*Lamentations*
LASBF	*Liber annuus Studii biblici fransciscani*
LD	Lectio Divina
Lev	Leviticus
LXE	Septuagint (Brenton's translation)
LXX	Septuagint
Macc	Maccabees
Mal	Malachi
Matt	Matthew
Mic	Micah
MRD	Murdock, James, *The New Testament, A Literal Translation from the Syriac Peshito Version*
MSU	Mitteilungen des Septuaginta-Unternehmens
MT	Masoretic Text
NA^{27}	*Novum Testamentum Graece*, Nestle-Aland, 27th ed.
NAB	New American Bible
Nah	Nahum
NASB	New American Standard Bible
NCINT	The New International Commentary on the New Testament
Neh	Nehemiah
NIB	New International Version (British Edition)
NIGTC	New International Greek Testament Commentary
NIV	New International Version
NJB	New Jerusalem Bible
NKJV	New King James Version
NLT	New Living Translation
NovT	*Novum Testamentum*
NovTSup	Supplements to Novum Testamentum
NPNF$^{1/2}$	*The Nicene and Post-Nicene Fathers*, Series 1/2
NRSV	New Revised Standard Version
NT	New Testament

NTAbh	Neutestamentliche Abhandlungen
NTOA	Novum Testamentum et Orbis Antiquus
NTS	*New Testament Studies*
Num	Numbers
OBT	Overtures to Biblical Theology
OED	*The Oxford English Dictionary*, 2nd ed.
OG	Old Greek
OT	Old Testament
OtSt	*Oudtestamentische Studien*
Pet	Peter
PG	Patrologia graeca
Phil	Philippians
Phlm	Philemon
PNT	The Bishops' New Testament 1595
Pr. Man.	*Prayer of Manasseh* (Psuedepigrapha)
Prov	Proverbs
Ps/Pss	Psalm/Psalms
Pss. Sol.	*Psalms of Solomon*
QH	*Hodayot* or *Thanksgiving Hymns*
QpHab	Pesher Habakkuk
QS	*Serek Hayaḥad* or *Rule of the Community*
RB	*Revue biblique*
Rev	Revelation
RLXX	Septuagint (Rahlf's)
Rom	Romans
RSR	*Recherches de science religieuse*
RSV	Revised Standard Version
RWB	Revised Webster Update
Sam	Samuel
ScEs	*Science et esprit*
SCS	Septuagint and Cognate Studies
Sir	Sirach
SNTSMS	Society for New Testament Studies Monograph Series
SSS	*Semitic Study Series*
T. Jud.	*Testament of Judah*
T. Zeb.	*Testament of Zebulun*
TDNT	*Theological Dictionary of the New Testament*
TDOT	*Theological Dictionary of the Old Testament*
Thess	Thessalonians
Tim	Timothy

TNT	Tyndale's New Testament
TOB	*Traduction Œcuménique de la Bible*
Tob	Tobit
TWOT	*Theological Wordbook of the Old Testament*
TUGAL	Texte und Untersuchungen zur Geschichte der altchristlichen Literatur
UBSDict	Newman, Barclay M, *A Concise Greek-English Dictionary of the New Testament*
UNT	Untersuchungen zum Neuen Testament
VT	*Vetus Testamentum*
VTSup	Supplements to Vetus Testamentum
WBC	*Word Biblical Commentary*
WEB	Webster's Revision of the KJV
Wis	Wisdom of Solomon
WMANT	Wissenschaftliche Monographien zum Alten und Neuen Testament
WUNT	Wissenschaftliche Untersuchungen zum Neuen Testament
YLT	Young's Literal Translation
Zech	Zechariah
Zeph	Zephaniah
ZNW	*Zeitschrift für die neutestamentliche Wissenschaft und die Kunde der älteren Kirche*

Introduction

The Revelations of God at Sinai and as Jesus

THE RELATIONSHIP BETWEEN THE REVELATIONS OF GOD AT SINAI AND as Jesus is a key issue in the dialogue between Judaism and Christianity. Scholars discuss the relationship in terms of *replacement, fulfillment,* and *continuity.* Clear differentiation of scholarly views on the issue is hardly possible. First, these three approaches do not necessarily have to exclude one another. For example, neither replacement nor fulfillment has to essentially undermine the continuity between the revelations. Second, these three approaches may overlap or combine with each other. For instance, replacement and fulfillment can potentially coexist. Third, these three approaches lack strict definitions of the terms. For example, "replacement" and "fulfillment" are occasionally used as close synonyms, or even interchangeably. With this in mind, we will now set the scene for examining relationships between the revelations of God at Sinai and as Jesus as depicted in the Gospel of John.[1] We will first look at this issue from the perspective of the Gospel as a whole and then specifically in John 1:14–18.

---

1. Hereafter, "the Gospel" refers to "the Gospel of John."

Views of Their Relationship from the Perspective of the Gospel of John as a Whole

The Revelation of God as Jesus *Replaces* the Revelation of God at Sinai

In the first view, the revelation of God as Jesus *replaces* the revelation of God at Sinai. To begin with, adherents of this approach argue that Jesus is not only "a prophet," who would fit in the line of the OT prophets, but "the Prophet" par excellence, in the sense of Deuteronomy 18:18–19: as Marie É. Boismard summarizes, "Formerly God spoke to Moses, putting in his mouth the words intended for his people. Today, God is going to speak through Jesus; it is by his mouth that he is going to address his people and to give them a new law."[2] Moreover, grace in the NT is generally opposed to the Law, as in Paul's "you are not under law but under grace" (Rom 6:14).[3] Furthermore, Mount Sinai, which had been the preeminent location of theophany in Israel's formative period, was, during the Israelite monarchy, superseded in dominance by Mount Zion. From the time of David on, psalmists, prophets, historians, and apocalyptic writers saw Zion as the most prominent place of divine self-disclosure.[4] Emphasis on seeing the Lord was gradually replaced[5] in prominence by hearing the word of God. Where there were accounts of seeing God, their main concern was to provide the setting for the revelation of the Word.[6] When God appeared, it was not primarily for the sake of the theophany, but in order to send a prophet to pass on God's word. Judaism became a religion of God's word, which was either heard or to be heard. Seeing God was envisioned as an eschatological event, which was to take place when Yahweh would come to Zion.[7] In

---

2. Boismard, *Moses or Jesus*, 6, 39.

3. To render a Hebrew/Greek text in English, this study utilizes the NASB for BHS, MT, OT, and NA^{27} NT; LXE for the Proto-canonical corpus of the LXX/OG; RSV for the Deutero-canonical corpus of the LXX/OG (unless otherwise noted). Versification in the OT is given according to MT (unless otherwise noted).

4. Hiebert, "Theophany in the OT," 508.

5. The vision of God was perceived as something exceptional and dangerous (Gen 19:26; 32:31; Exod 3:6; 33:20). Absence of images of God in Israel contributed to a lessening of the Sinaitic emphasis of seeing God (Kittel, "*akouō*," 1:217–18).

6. Isa 6:1; Ezek 1; Amos 9:1; cf. also Exod 3:1.

7. Kittel, "*akouō*," 1:218.

the Evangelist's view, eschatology characterized by seeing God is now realized. Yahweh has come to Zion as the Word incarnate, Jesus. Finally, according to the Gospel, Jesus replaces various OT institutions, such as the temple and festivals. By implication Jesus replaces the OT Law with (the new law of) the Gospel as well.[8]

Opposition in the Replacement of the Revelation of God at Sinai with the Revelation of God as Jesus

Some of those who argue that the revelation of God as Jesus replaces the revelation of God at Sinai envision an *opposition* between the revelations. Some scholars feel that such contrast is expressed by Jesus who, in their evaluation, contradicts either the written or oral Law. Jesus is alleged to be a lawbreaker or sinner in various ways; for example, he is called a "sinner" for breaking the Sabbath (cf. 5:16; 7:21–23; 9:13–16)[9] and a "blasphemer" because he is calling God his own Father, making himself equal with God (cf. 5:17–18; 10:31–36; 19:7).[10] Jesus is judged by some of the participants to be a false prophet who is leading the people astray, and therefore, an enemy of the nation (cf. 7:12; 11:47–50). Opponents of Jesus appeal to the Scriptures when they question whether Jesus can be the Christ (7:40–42) and/or the Prophet (7:52) because he is from Galilee. When interrogated on such charges, Jesus can only witness to himself (cf. 5:31; 8:13, 17). Jesus offers his blood to drink, which contradicts the Law (6:53–56).[11] Jesus is accused of teaching without having been trained (7:14–15); technically, he breaks the transmission of the chain of oral traditions, which, according to ʾAbot 1:1, went back to Moses, who had received the oral Law from God.[12]

---

8. Motyer, *Your Father the Devil?* 43, 128, cf. 197. Along these lines see also Lincoln, *Truth*, 232–33.

9. Here and following, chapter and verse references without a book title are for John's Gospel.

10. Cf. Deut 13:1–5.

11. See Lincoln, *Truth*, 232; Pancaro, *Law*, 9–125.

12. Manns, *John and Jamnia*, 35.

Denigration in the Replacement of the Revelation of God at Sinai with the Revelation of God as Jesus

Some of those who argue that the revelation of God as Jesus replaces the revelation of God at Sinai discern a degree of *denigration* of Moses and/or the Law. They argue that the Gospel uses the OT revelation as a negative foil by which to portray the revelation as Jesus as immeasurably superior.

Numerous scholars discover a degree of such denigration in particular episodes of the Gospel. Frédéric Manns maintains that just as Moses conveyed the Law at Sinai, so now Jesus gives a new and better law, symbolized by wine, at Cana.[13] Charles H. Dodd and Anthony T. Hanson believe that the water from the well, which the Samaritan woman offers, is contrasted as "dead" water to the living water that Jesus provides; the "dead" water means the Torah.[14] William L. Petersen interprets the bread from heaven episode as denigrating Moses.[15] To begin with, the expression "the food which perishes" (6:27) is believed to be a reference to the Law as the disciples of Moses understood it. It is not Moses who provided the bread from heaven but Jesus's Father. God is now acting to give Israel the true bread, as opposed to the manna, which was much less than "true" in comparison with Jesus. Moreover, the superiority of the revelation as Jesus is accentuated by the present tense of the verb in the phrase, "it is My Father who gives [*didōsin*] you the true bread out of heaven" (6:32). Furthermore, the true bread from heaven gives life not just to Israel, but now to the whole world (6:35, 38, 48–51). Finally, the conventional notion of a sign as an act performed to prove something else, as with Moses, is replaced by the notion that Jesus himself is the sign.

Manns finds a degree of such denigration in the Evangelist allegedly presenting Jesus no longer as a Jew but an adversary of the Jews.[16] Jesus speaks of "your Law" (8:17; 10:34) and "their Law" (15:25). The same distance is found in Jesus addressing the Jews in terms of "your

---

13. Ibid., 63–67. Along these lines also is Lincoln, who remarks, "the water jars employed for purification under the law are now filled with the wine that represents the life and joy of the *new order*" (Lincoln, *Truth*, 233).

14. Dodd, *Interpretation*, 311–14; Hanson, *Prophetic Gospel*, 63 (with the reference to Num 21:17–18).

15. N. Petersen, *John*, 35, 71, 96, 103, 121.

16. Manns, *John and Jamnia*, 30.

fathers" (6:49), as if Jesus was rejecting his Jewish origins.[17] The Evangelist also uses expressions like "the Jewish custom of purification" (2:6), "the Passover of the Jews" (2:13; 6:4; 11:55), "a feast of the Jews" (5:1; 7:2), "the burial custom of the Jews" (19:40), and "the Jewish day of preparation" (19:42), all of which have the flavor of the Evangelist distancing himself from the institutions associated with "the Jews."

Manns also observes that the Evangelist reminds the Jews who stress the Law of Moses that religious history does not begin with Moses. Circumcision is not from Moses but from the fathers (7:22). Before Moses, the patriarchs—Abraham[18] (8:39-40, 56), Isaac (1:29, 36), and Jacob (1:51)—bore witness in favor of Jesus. Thus, *pre*-Mosaic traditions are as important as Mosaic Law.[19]

Norman R. Petersen argues that the message of the Gospel should be interpreted as a conflict in which Jesus and his disciples are given a positive value and Moses and his disciples are assigned a negative one.[20] According to this scholar, the central Christological affirmations of the Gospel appear almost without exception to be derived by antithesis to traditional assertions about Moses. The Evangelist persistently contrasts Moses with Jesus and subordinates the former to the latter. The writer, in other words, does not so much invent exaggerated Christology as simply (or, often, quite elaborately) invert the beliefs of Moses's disciples.[21] Moses did not see God, but Jesus has made the face of God visible. Moses only went up and down the mountain; he did not go up to *heaven*. Jesus, by contrast, comes down from heaven and returns there (3:13; 6:38, 42, 62). Moses was merely the friend of God,[22] but Jesus is the only Son of God. Moses typologically lifted up the bronze serpent, but the Son of Man is himself being lifted up (3:14). Moses served as an

---

17. Ibid.

18. Manns deduces that the Evangelist affirms that Christians are the true sons of Abraham because they do the works of Abraham and because there is no contradiction between faith in Abraham and faith in Christ (ibid., 51). Schoneveld agrees: "the Law (the Torah) is embodied in Abraham" (Schoneveld, "Torah in the Flesh," 84).

19. Manns, *John and Jamnia*, 36, 39.

20. N. Petersen, *John*, 5-6, 35, 45, 70-71, 88, 94, 96, 111-12, 115.

21. See also Fortna, review of *Gospel of John*, 563.

22. Exod 33:11.

intercessor for the people.²³ Jesus inverts this role and makes Moses into the people's accuser (5:45).

Stephen Motyer²⁴ maintains that the Gospel appeals, "Don't put faith in the failed formula, the illusory promise that the Torah life-style can still bring freedom! There is no deliverance from sin and death by that way."²⁵ Jesus reaches the lame and the blind, for whom cult and the Torah offer no hope. Jesus challenges those who regard him as a prophet to accept what he says.²⁶ He then puts his word on a level with the Torah in offering freedom—an Exodus image—to all who will commit themselves to following him. Jesus's word, rather than the Torah, becomes the focus of discipleship and the yardstick of truth. It is not as Moses's but as Jesus's disciples that "the Jews"²⁷ will experience freedom (8:31–32). Jesus denies that this Torah lifestyle can deliver people from *sin*. Because the people were slaves to sin, they were expelled from "the house"; but Jesus is truly able to deliver (8:34–36). Hence, Jesus's words *alone* are the means of liberation from sin. Motyer argues that in 8:31–59 the Law is "positively" used as testimony to Jesus, both by undermining the action of his opponents as lawless, and by testifying to his own rightness. "Negatively," Jesus sets himself in the place of the Law in 8:31–59. Motyer suggests that Jesus's claim, "I have come from God" (8:42), already sets Jesus implicitly in the place of the Law. Moreover, 8:41b–42a alludes²⁸ to the Shema. The expressions "we have one Father: God" (8:41) and "He is our God" (8:54) connote the central Jewish confession of faith, "The Lord is our God, the Lord is one," with its accompanying command to "love the Lord your God with all your heart" (Deut 6:4–5). Jesus's response to the Jew's allusion to the Shema is very pointed: "If God were your Father, you would love Me" (8:42).

23. Exod 32:11–14, 30–35; Num 21:7.

24. See Motyer, *Your Father the Devil?* 123, 169, 170, 183, 192, 193, 195, 214.

25. Ibid., 214.

26. For Motyer, "Recognition of Jesus as a prophet, and continuing loyalty to Torah, do not necessarily entail each other" (ibid., 166)

27. According to Motyer, "the Jews" refers to "a distinct group within Judaism, the Judea-based, Torah-loyal adherents of the Yavneh ideals, the direct heirs of pre-70 Pharisaism" (ibid., 213), except the handful of places where it has a purely ethnic force, particularly in the phrase "King of the Jews"; see 18:20, 33, 35; 19:3, 19, 21.

28. Throughout this study, the term "allusion" is utilized to refer to statements intended to remind an audience of a text or tradition they are presumed to know (Michael Thompson, *Clothed with Christ*, 30).

Furthermore, *Targum Neofiti* systematically replaces the expression "love the Lord" in the book of Deuteronomy with the formula "love the teaching of the law of the Lord." On the basis of these observations Motyer deduces,

> The motivation for loving the law was, of course, precisely that it had "come from God" (42b): love for God was not *replaced* by loving the law, but *expressed* by it. Jesus makes precisely this claim in relation to himself, stepping into the place of the law as the self-expression of God.[29]

Finally, Motyer concludes that the Gospel "emphatically claims that *Jesus alone* is the source of such revelation (1:17f.; 1:51; 3:13f.; 6:62f.)."[30]

Ongoing Value of Moses/the Law in the Replacement of the Revelation of God at Sinai with the Revelation of God as Jesus

Some of those who argue that the revelation of God as Jesus replaces the revelation of God at Sinai also acknowledge that the Gospel *recognizes* the ongoing value of Moses and/or the Law in various respects.

First, several scholars propose that it is the issue of adherence to the *oral* Law that is at stake. Manns[31] interprets the Gospel from the perspective of the break of Christianity from Judaism after the destruction of the temple; the Gospel is a call for Jewish Christians to leave the synagogue for the new church. The Evangelist points out how Jesus, the Son of God, fulfilled and even surpassed all that Jewish Christians had ever had in the Law of Moses. The Spirit now reminds Christians of Jesus's teaching. In Manns words, "Since Christians have their teacher [the Spirit; the *Tanna*, who repeats the words of the Teacher], they should not have any complexes before the teachers of the Jamnia academy."[32] Hence, "To define Jesus as the *way,* is to define him as the *halaka*, which Christians must follow."[33] Also along these lines, Jacobus Schoneveld suggests that in the Gospel, "Jesus—and after his glorification the Holy Spirit (the Paraclete)—provides the Oral Torah. . . . The Johannine

---

29. Motyer, *Your Father the Devil?* 192.
30. Ibid., 195.
31. Manns, *John and Jamnia*, 34, 45, 48.
32. Ibid., 34.
33. Ibid., 48. Manns seems to suggest that the Evangelist reacts to the decisions adopted at Jamnia to accept only the *halaka* of the Hillel school (ibid., 45).

community sees the issue between itself and other Jews as: Which Oral Torah is the valid one and is to be adhered to? It rejects the Pharisaic Oral Torah in favor of the Oral Torah given by Jesus, saying: 'Lord, to whom shall we go? You have the words of eternal life' (6:68)."[34]

Second, several scholars take typology into consideration. For example, Severino Pancaro concludes that "the revelation of Jesus replaces the Torah—the new reality is prepared for by the old, but goes so far beyond it that . . . [the Evangelist] hesitates to speak of it as a 'new Law.'" Pancaro's major argument is that the Evangelist does not want to present the "work" of Jesus as giving origin to a new law, and that "the 'Law' is a concept, which is too laden with overtones for the Jewish adversaries of . . . [the Evangelist] to allow for any such thing (the Law is 'their' Law!)."[35] Rather, he states, "The teaching of Jesus is a 'new' revelation, not to be found in the Law. As such it supersedes the Law. The Law is subservient to the teaching Jesus brings and not vice versa."[36] Yet Pancaro concludes,

> What is the nature of the contrast Moses—Jesus, teaching of Moses—teaching of Jesus? Is it one of opposition? From a certain point of view, yes. . . . The New Covenant is superior to the Old, the Gospel is superior to the Law. Jesus is greater than Moses, his revelation more perfect than that Moses gave (that given through Moses). However, there is no disparagement of Moses, he rather is presented as the "type," the forerunner of Christ.[37]

Third, several scholars—Boismard,[38] Gerhard Kittel, Schoneveld, and others—advocate Jesus as "the New Torah," a "Torah in the Flesh" approach. For example, Schoneveld argues that "in the prologue of John, *Logos* is to be equated with *Torah*."[39] Kittel writes, "Christ is not just a teacher and transmitter of the Torah. He is Himself the Torah, the new Torah."[40]

---

34. Schoneveld, "Torah in the Flesh," 90.
35. Pancaro, *Law*, 542.
36. Ibid., 116.
37. Ibid., 471.
38. Boismard, *St. John's Prologue*, 126.
39. Schoneveld, "Torah in the Flesh," 77.
40. Kittel, "*legō*," 4:135.

The Revelation of God as Jesus *Fulfills* the Revelation of God at Sinai

In the second view, the revelation of God as Jesus *fulfills* the revelation of God at Sinai. Adherents of this approach observe that the notion of fulfillment is generally inherent in the Gospel. Numerous OT quotations in the Gospel emphasize this sense of fulfillment.[41] John the Baptist indicates his position in the history of salvation by a quotation (1:23). Jesus confirms that the Scriptures point to him (5:39, 46-47). Jesus makes use of quotations to show that his ministry is in agreement with the Scriptures (6:45; 7:38; 13:18; 15:25). An action of Jesus reminds the disciples of a word from the Scripture (2:17). Jesus and his opponents, in their disputes on the question concerning who Jesus really is, both use quotations to support their diverging points of view (6:31; 7:42; 8:17; 10:34; 12:34). The Evangelist adduces quotations to establish that what he tells his audience about Jesus—especially about the end of Jesus's ministry—agrees with the Scriptures and constitutes their fulfillment (12:15, 38, 40; 19:24, 36, 37). Jesus himself acknowledges the fulfillment (17:12) and longs to fulfill the Scripture (19:28) in his ministry.[42] The Passover pervades the entirety of the ministry of Jesus. Jesus is presented as the one who fulfills the meaning of the feasts of Israel—Passover, Tabernacles, and Dedication.[43] The Evangelist's pointers to the death of Christ as the fulfillment of Passover are clear and especially significant (2:13; 6:4; 11:55; 19:31-36).[44] On the basis of this notion of fulfillment evident in particular motifs of the Gospel, some scholars would generalize that the revelation of God as Jesus fulfills the revelation of God at Sinai as well.

Moreover, advocates of this approach pay special attention to the role that the Law plays in fulfilling the destiny of Jesus. Manns emphasizes that in the controversy with the Jews, the Evangelist returns continually to the fundamental affirmation that the Law leads to Jesus (5:17; 7:21-24). The Jews who condemn Jesus, therefore, violate the

---

41. Throughout the study, the term "quotation" is used to refer to instances in which the writer uses direct quotation with an explicit citation formula, such as, "as the prophet Isaiah said" (1:23) (see Michael Thompson, *Clothed with Christ*, 30).

42. See Menken, *OT Quotations*, 12-13.

43. Beasley-Murray, *John*, lix.

44. Ibid., 352; Kysar, "John," 917, 927.

Law (7:17; 7:19; 7:24). Even at Jesus's trial, the Law is still present but it is incapable of assuring Jesus's condemnation. On the one hand, the Jews appeal, "We have a law, and by that law He ought to die because He made Himself out *to be* the Son of God" (19:7). On the other hand, the Jews not only "are not permitted to put anyone to death" (18:31), but also are unable to condemn Jesus according to the Law (8:46). The Jews are incapable of condemning Jesus according to "their" Law. They turn to Pilate and false accusations, and Pilate sentences Jesus to fulfill the Scriptures. Thus, the Jews try to accuse Jesus of violating the Law, but Jesus dies because the Law requires his death for a different reason; his death is the fulfillment of the plan of salvation announced in the Law.[45]

The Revelation of God as Jesus *Continues* the Revelation of God at Sinai

In the third view, the revelation of God as Jesus *continues* the revelation of God at Sinai. allusions to the OT in the Gospel are abundant.[46] For the Evangelist, the Scriptures are oriented toward Christ. God created the world through the Word. The Word becomes incarnate in Jesus (1:14). God breathed a soul into Adam; Jesus breathes the Spirit upon the apostles (20:22).[47] Abraham rejoiced to see the day of Jesus (8:56). Isaac served as a prototype of the sacrificial Lamb. Jesus is depicted as God's Passover lamb (1:29, 36). Jacob's vision of a ladder with angels ascending and descending prefigured angels ascending and descending upon the Son of Man (1:51).

The revelation of God as Jesus is profoundly associated with the exodus, the major event with regard to the revelation of God at Sinai. The serpent lifted up presaged the elevation of Christ (3:14). Manna is a prototype of the bread of life. Water, which sprang from the rock, heralded the gift of the Spirit (7:39). Miracles of the exodus foreshadowed those that Christ performs. The imagery of the wrath of God was characteristic of theophany[48] and so is depicted in the Gospel (3:36). The Psalmist[49] recalls memories of God coming in a powerful theophany

---

45. Manns, *John and Jamnia*, 36.
46. Cf. NA^{27}, 770–806.
47. See Beasley-Murray, *John*, 380–81; Manns, *John and Jamnia*, 39.
48. Fichtner, "*orgē*," 5:407.
49. Ps 77:16, 19; cf. Job 9:8.

over the waters to the aid of his people at the exodus.[50] The Evangelist depicts Jesus walking on the sea and appearing to his disciples with the words *egō eimi* (6:16–21); the writer portrays Jesus as the revelation of God coming to his disciples in distress—in the second exodus.[51] Yahweh first reveals himself to Moses in a blazing fire.[52] In the wilderness wanderings, the presence of the Lord with his people is manifested in the pillar of cloud by day and the pillar of fire (i.e. light) by night. It saves the people from their persecutors[53] and guides them through the wilderness.[54] Jesus is portrayed as the light of the world (8:12–20). The celebration in the lighting of the lamps[55] is also "associated with recollection of the nation's experience at the Exodus and the hope for a second Exodus."[56] Numerous scholars—George R. Beasley-Murray,[57] Boismard,[58] John Bowman,[59] George J. Brooke,[60] Thomas F. Glasson,[61] Joachim Jeremias,[62] Robert Kysar,[63] Manns,[64] J. Louis Martyn,[65] Wayne A. Meeks,[66] Motyer,[67] Nicol,[68] Pancaro,[69] Petersen,[70] Günter Reim,[71] and

---

50. Exod 14:19–20, 24–25; 15:1–8.
51. Beasley-Murray, *John*, 89.
52. Exod 3:2.
53. Exod 14:19–25.
54. Exod 13:21–22.
55. As with the water-drawing ceremony.
56. Beasley-Murray, *John*, 127.
57. Ibid., xl, lii, lv, lix, lxxxii, 14–15.
58. Boismard, *Moses or Jesus*, 11–23, 56–57, 59, 66–67.
59. Bowman, "Samaritan Studies," 298–308, 310f.
60. Brooke, "Christ and the Law," 110.
61. Glasson, *Moses*, 62–64.
62. Jeremias, "*Mōusēs*," 4:872.
63. Kysar, "John," 920, 925, 927.
64. Manns, *John and Jamnia*, 39.
65. Martyn, *History*, 125–28.
66. Meeks, *Prophet-King*, 46, 56, 162–64, 290–91, 294.
67. Motyer, *Your Father the Devil?* 134 n. 33, 135–36.
68. Nicol, *Semeia*, 48–94.
69. Pancaro, *Law*, 137, 492–99, 515, 520.
70. N. Petersen, *John*, 92–95, 155 n. 27.
71. Reim, *Studien*, 119–29, 132–40.

12   GLORY, GRACE, AND TRUTH

Gilbert van Belle[72]—maintain that the Gospel resembles both the book and the theme of Exodus.[73]

Moreover, Jesus, his disciples, and the Evangelist refer to the Law and the Prophets. Brooke maintains that in chapters 7-10 of the Gospel there are allusions to each of the Ten Commandments (Exod 20:1-17): you shall have no other gods before Me (10:30), you shall not make for yourself an idol (10:33), you shall not take the name of the Lord your God in vain (10:25), remember the Sabbath day (7:23; cf. 5:18), honor your father and mother (8:49; cf. 5:23), you shall not murder (7:19; 8:40, 44; cf. 5:18), you shall not commit adultery (8:41), you shall not steal (10:1, 8, 10), you shall not bear false witness (8:14),[74] you shall not covet (8:44).[75] He reasons that "the appealing use of the decalogue . . . might have been sufficient to convert some, once they had admitted

---

72. Belle, *Signs Source*, 87-90, 119, 125-27, 156-58, 249, 260, 276, 281, 297-99, 349, 376.

73. Compare Exod 3:6 and John 1:18; 6:46; Exod 3:6-10 and John's theme of Jesus being sent by the Father; Exod 3:12 and John 13:19, 14:29, 8:28; Exod 3:12 (cf. Deut 18:21-22) and John 13:19; 14:29; 8:28; Exod 3:13-16 and John 17:6, 11-12; Exod 4:1, 2-9, 17 and John 4:48; Exod 4:10 and John 7:46; Exod 4:11 and John 9:1-3, 39; Exod 4:10-16 (cf. Deut 18:18) and John 3:34; 7:16-18; 8:26-27, 31, 47; 12:44-50; 14:24b; 15:10, 15; 17:8, 14, 19-20; Exod 4:22 (cf. Deut 6:4; 14:1-2) and John 1:34; 8:41; Exod 6:15 and John 6:31; Exod 7:1 and John 5:18; Exod 12:10, 46 and John 19:36; Exod 12:22 and John 19:29; Exod 13:21-22; 14:19-25 and John 8:12; Exod 16:4-36 and John 6:27-33; Exod 17:1-6 and John 7:37-38; Exod 17:8-13 and John 19:17-18; Exod 19:3, 20, 24; 24:1, 9, 12, 13, 15, 18; 32:30; 34:2; 4 (*anabainō*, cf. Exod 9:12; 34:3) 19:10, 14, 21, 24, 25; 32:1, 7, 15; 34:29 (*katabainō*, cf. Exod 19:11, 18, 20; 20:22; 34:5; cf. also Exod 24:16; 33:9 LXX) and John 3:13, 6:38, 42, 62; Exod 19:5 and John 1:11; Exod 19:10 and John 11:55; Exod 19:9; 37:11 and John 9:29; Exod 19:16-25 (cf. Deut 4:11-12, 33) and John 5:37; Exod 20:15 (cf. Deut 5:9) and John 9:2; Exod 20:19 (cf. Deut 18:16) and John 5:37-38 (cf. Deut 18:19); Exod 28:41 and John 17:19; Exod 32:11-14, 30-35 (cf. Num 21:7 LXX) and John 5:45; Exod 32:30-32 and John 5:45; Exod 33:11 and John 9:28-29; 15:14; Exod 33:13 and John 14:21; Exod 33—34:6 and John 1:14-18; Num 16:28 and John 8:28-29; 14:10, 7:16b-17; Num 21:9 and 3:14-15; 8:28; 12:32, 34; Deut 1:29, 31 and John 13:1; 14:1ff.; Deut 13:1-6 LXX and John 5:18; 7:12, 47; 10:33; 19:7; Deut 18:15 and John 1:21, 45; 5:46; 6:14; 7:40, 52, cf. 1:21; Deut 18:18-19 and John 12:48-50; 9:26ff.; 17:8; 5:30-47; 7:16-18; 17:7-8; Farewell of Moses and Prayer of Jesus (John 13-17); miracles depicted in the book of Exodus and in the Gospel; the theme of Passover in Exodus and in the Gospel (John 1:29, 36; chap. 6; 2:13; 6:4; 11:55; 1:29, 36; 19:31-36); the theme of tabernacles and John 7.

74. Motyer here adds also 8:44 (Motyer, *John and "the Jews," Your Father the Devil?* 130).

75. Brooke, "Christ and the Law," 103-8.

that Jesus and his followers had neither broken nor abrogated the law."[76] Manns observes that even though Jesus distances himself from the Jews by speaking in terms of "your Law" (8:17; 10:34), "their Law" (15:25), and "your fathers" (6:49), still the bonds between Jesus, the synagogue and the temple are being stressed (6:59; 18:20).[77]

Furthermore, numerous approaches affirm continuity in the revelations of God at Sinai and as Jesus, while implying that a) the revelations belong to different dimensions, or b) the former one serves as the prototype for the latter, or c) the latter revelation incorporates the former, or d) the concept of Law in the Gospel is altogether peculiar.

First, some of the scholars envision a continuity between the revelations of God at Sinai and as Jesus that implies a *contrast* between them. For example, Richard J. Bauckham explains, "Moses could only *hear* God's word proclaiming *that* God is full of grace and truth. He could not see God's glory. But in the Word made flesh, God's glory was *seen* in human form, and grace and truth (according to John 1:17) happened or came about (*egeneto*)."[78]

Second, several scholars argue the case for a continuity between the revelations of God at Sinai and as Jesus that assumes a *comparison* (such as lesser/greater, limited/full, etc.) between them. Beasley-Murray believes Jesus is depicted as "the One who fulfills the hope of a second Exodus by carrying out the function of God's passover Lamb, so achieving a *universal* redemption for the world."[79] He concludes, "The concept of Jesus as the new (or rather, greater than) Moses, bringing about a second Exodus for *life in the kingdom of God* is a major theme of the Evangelist's."[80] Martyn argues that the feeding sign goes far *beyond* a mere repetition of Moses and the manna.[81] Petersen stresses the notion of obtaining *eternal* life in Jesus's appeals (4:13–14; 6:27).[82] Motyer perceives *freedom* (8:31–38) from the slavery[83] of *sin* (8:12, 31–38) and

---

76. Ibid., 112.
77. Manns, *John and Jamnia*, 30, also n. 3.
78. Bauckham, *God Crucified*, 74; emphasis on "hear" and "seen" added.
79. Beasley-Murray, *John*, lii; emphasis added.
80. Ibid., 223; emphasis added.
81. Martyn, *History*, 125–28.
82. N. Petersen, *John*, 103.
83. The motif "the Lord, who brought you out of the house of bondage (slavery) with a mighty hand" appears (with variations) nine times in the books of Exodus and

death (11:42–42) as the advantage gained in Jesus.[84] Nahum M. Sarna advocates that it is going beyond just the covenant with the nation of Israel, consummated by the theophany at Sinai, that constitutes the continuity and development in the revelations (10:16).[85]

Third, some of the scholars argue for continuity between revelations of God at Sinai and as Jesus through a *peculiar concept of the Law*. On the one hand, Pancaro holds that the Gospel "presents a view of the Law, which is neither contradictory nor inconsistent."[86] There are two different understandings of the Law—that of the synagogue and that of the church. The Law, as interpreted by the synagogue, is opposed to Jesus.[87] The Law, as perceived by the church, should lead to the recognition of Jesus and is violated by those who condemn Jesus.[88] Jesus is not opposed to the Law and does not deny the divine authority of the Law, but claims that his authority is "equally divine" and that it stands "above the authority of the Law."[89] What is attacked and condemned by the Evangelist, concludes Pancaro, is "a false understanding of the Law, which would oppose the Law and Jesus: observance of the Law and faith in Jesus."[90] The Evangelist avoids speaking of Jesus abrogating or not keeping the Law—because *nomos* for the Evangelist has this double meaning. By saying "your Law" or the "Law of the Jews," the writer means to dissociate Christians from the attitude, meaning, and value that normative Judaism continues to give it. The Law retains its Christian meaning and value as a prophetic and pedagogical tool to prepare the people to accept the Revealer of God. The Law is impotent to condemn Jesus but was given by God to find its fulfillment in the death of Jesus, which comes about as a result of the Father's will, not because Jesus is proven guilty. For this reason, the Evangelist considers the Law "neither with hostil-

---

Deuteronomy, including twice in the "false prophet" passage (Deut 13:5, 10; see also Deut 13:6, "That prophet or dreamer must be put to death, because he preached rebellion against the Lord Your God, who brought you out of Egypt and redeemed you from the house of slavery"). See Motyer, *Your Father the Devil?* 136 n. 42.

84. Motyer, *Your Father the Devil?* 136–37, 169–70.
85. Sarna, "Exodus."
86. Pancaro, *Law*, 2.
87. Ibid., 523.
88. Ibid., 508.
89. Ibid., 492.
90. Ibid., 527.

ity nor with detachment."⁹¹ According to Pancaro, the Evangelist does not mention the question of the relationship of faith in Christ and the observance of the Law because the Evangelist's community

> is formed by Jewish-Christians who observe the Law, but who differ from their Jewish brethren because of the faith they have in Jesus as the Christ, the Son of God and, consequently, in the attitude they assume towards the Law. While they follow it, they do not agree that their relationship to God is determined by their relationship to the Law, that God has revealed himself and his will exclusively in the Law.⁹² They claim that a Jew, however faithful to the Law of Moses, cannot be saved unless he believes in Jesus as the Christ and becomes a member of the community he formed, which has a "law" of its own: that of brotherly love and faithfulness to the "word" received from Jesus.⁹³

On the other hand, Manns argues that by playing on the double meaning of a word, the Evangelist gives a different meaning to the term "Law," depending on whether it is a question of the synagogue or the Johannine community. For the Johannine community, the Law is not the *oral* Law but doing the will of the Father; it is keeping the Word, doing good works. For the Jews, the Law is, first of all, the *written* Law, a legal norm, which they use and interpret against Jesus;⁹⁴ but it is also the *oral* Law. Manns argues that in the Gospel the term *graphē* refers to the Scripture as a common inheritance of Jews who have believed in Christ; the term *nomos* designates either the Jewish Bible (10:34; 15:25; 12:35), the criminal legislation of the Jews (7:51; 8:17, 31; 19:7), or the Law as a distinctive sign of the Jews (1:17; 7:19, 49), and concludes that "this vocabulary distinction reminds the Johannine community of its Jewish roots and, at the same time, expresses the rejection of *oral law* by the Christians."⁹⁵

---

91. Ibid., 520; see also 137, 492–99.
92. Cf. ibid., 51.
93. Ibid., 530.
94. Manns, *John and Jamnia*, 36.
95. Ibid. 34; emphasis added. Manns adds, "one is tempted to say that *graphē* is the written law."

The Revelation of God as Jesus *Complexly Related* to the Revelation of God at Sinai

The complexity of the relationship between the revelation of God at Sinai and as Jesus as depicted in the Gospel has caused scholars to allow a degree of fusion of the concepts of fulfillment, replacement, and continuity between the revelations. Petersen creatively envisions "the *contrast* in 1:17 between the Law that came through Moses and the Grace and Truth that came through Jesus."[96] He contends that "the assertions made about Jesus in . . . [1:17-18 are] . . . to *qualify* the traditional value of the Law . . . the Law [is to] be *evaluated* from the perspective of what came through Jesus, rather than have what came through Jesus be evaluated from the perspective of the Law."[97] He speaks of the Evangelist "making both Moses and the Law *witnesses* on Jesus' behalf."[98] He also points to "Jesus' *revision* of the interpretation of the Law"[99] and asserts that "Jesus is . . . *superior* to the Law because as the incarnate Word he has *displaced* it."[100]

Andrew T. Lincoln blends an even greater number of concepts:[101] the opposition employs essentially wrong criteria for judging.[102] Instead of judging "with righteous judgment," they judge "according to appearance" (7:24) and "according to the flesh" (8:15). Therefore, "Jesus' witness is now the criterion of true judgment, and this requires a totally *new assessment* of the law."[103] Lincoln believes that "this perspective is apparent from the start. In the prologue, not only are the grace and truth previously associated with the glory of Yahweh in the covenant with Moses (cf. Exod 34:6) now associated with the glory of the incarnate *Logos* (1:14), but the prologue also makes an explicit contrast: 'The law

---

96. N. Petersen, *John*, 111, see also 21, 97–99, 121; emphasis added.

97. Ibid., 98–99.

98. Ibid., 105–8; emphasis added.

99. Ibid., 121; emphasis added.

100. Ibid., 122; emphasis added. Perhaps the options have become blended partly because Petersen summarizes the findings of Jeremias, "*Mōusēs*"; Glasson, *Moses*; and Meeks, *Prophet-King*. As Petersen acknowledges, "I do not think that I have found any Moses material in John that these critics have not observed" (N. Petersen, *John*, 155 n. 15).

101. Lincoln, *Truth*, 231–42.

102. Ibid., 231.

103. Ibid., 232; emphasis added.

indeed was given through Moses, grace and truth came through Jesus Christ' (1:17). This is not a denial that, before the coming of the Logos, *the law was previously an expression of Yahweh's grace and truth*. It is, rather, an assertion by the community, which has seen the fullness of grace and truth in the Logos's glory, that *these qualities are not now to be found in the law*."[104] According to him the way of knowing God through Jesus, the only God (1:18), becomes the criterion by which the previous way through the Law is to be judged, and not vice versa. This theme is developed through "the depiction of what were previously symbols of the law, such as water, bread, and light as having their true *realization* in Jesus; of the festivals prescribed in the law as having their significance *fulfilled* in Jesus; of the terminology associated with obeying the law as now being *appropriate* for use in connection with believing in Jesus." Lincoln exemplifies, "the water jars employed for purification under the law are now filled with the wine that represents the life and joy of the *new order*. . . . the temple, whose regulations were based on the law, is to be *replaced* as the locus of God's presence by the body of the risen Jesus."[105] He further states, "If, in the overall pattern of thought, the Mosaic law leads to the sentence of death on Jesus and yet the overall judgment in the lawsuit is a vindication of the one who was sentenced to death, then this positive verdict is also a *negative verdict on the law*."[106] He concludes that Jesus is "an *exception* to the law . . . *not a subject* to the law but instead *fulfills* all that the law previously stood for."[107]

> The law, then, is to be judged in the light of Jesus and his mission and not the other way around. Both of the previously mentioned strategies—exploiting aspects of the law itself and seeing Jesus as an exception—are compatible from this perspective. Once Jesus' unique identity is accepted by faith, then various parts of the law can be seen to be fulfilled by him, but his unique identity also means that he fulfills the law by *transcending* it.[108]

---

104. Ibid.; emphasis added. Cf. Pancaro, *Law*, 537–40.
105. Lincoln, *Truth*, 232–33, based on Pancaro, *Law*, 368–487.
106. Lincoln, *Truth*, 232–33; emphasis added.
107. Ibid., 234–35.
108. Ibid., 235.

Views of Their Relationship from the Perspective of John 1:14–18

The prologue is mostly perceived as an overture to the Gospel. John 1:14–18 is widely recognized as the crux of the prologue. To set the scene for the discussion of the issues related to 1:14–18, we will 1) discuss the range of meanings of terms *doxa, charis, alētheia,* and *nomos* utilized in 1:14–18, 2) contour the frame of reference for 1:14–18, and 3) examine 1:14–18 verse by verse.[109] In doing this, we will set out the disputed points of interpretations as given by scholars.

JOHN 1:14–18: THE RANGE OF MEANINGS FOR *doxa, charis, alētheia,* AND *nomos*

The broad range of meanings of terms *doxa, charis, alētheia,* and *nomos* utilized in 1:14–18 complicates the interpretation of the passage. At this point we will simply list the full scope of possible meanings of these terms with a view to eventually eliminate those connotations that are impossible for 1:14–18. Various lexica and dictionaries[110] list four to six different connotations for *doxa*, generally as follows:[111]

1) a manifestation of light, "radiance, brightness, splendor"
2) a manifestation of God's excellent power, "glory, majesty"
3) an excellent reputation, "honor, glory, praise"
4) a state characterized by honor, power, and remarkable appearance, "glory, splendor"
5) a person created in the image of God, "reflection, glory"
6) angelic powers around God, "angelic beings, majesties, dignities"

Various lexica and dictionaries[112] list four to six different connotations for *charis* as follows:[113]

---

109. Due to limitations on the volume of this study we will only consider aspects directly relevant to it. In this examination we utilize the following studies: Barkhuizen, "A Short Note"; Blumenthal, "Charis anti charitos"; Carson, *John*, 131; La Potterie, "*Charis*"; Edwards, "*Charin anti charitos*"; and King, "Prologue."

110. See *AnLex*, 01464; Kittel, "*doxa*"; L&N, 01751; UBSDict, 01657.

111. Here, following the *AnLex*, 01464 categories.

112. See *AnLex*, 05609; L&N, 06874; UBSDict.

113. Here, following the *AnLex*, 05609 categories.

1) a quality that adds delight or pleasure, "graciousness, attractiveness, charm"
2a) a favorable attitude in what is felt toward another, "good will, favor"
2b) as a religious term for God's attitude toward human beings, "kindness, grace, favor, helpfulness"
3a) exceptional effects produced by God's favor, "ability, power, enablement"
3b) practical proofs of good will from one person to another, "kind deed, benefit, favor"
3c) "collection" for the poor, "generous gift"
4) an experience or state resulting from God's favor, "state of grace, favored position"
5) a verbal thank-offering to God, "gratitude, thanks"
6) as contained in formulas that express greetings or farewell in letters, "good will, favor, blessing"

Various lexica and dictionaries[114] list four to six different connotations to *alētheia* generally as follows:[115]

1) what has certainty and validity, "truth"
2) the real state of affairs, especially as divinely disclosed "truth"
3) the concept of the Gospel message as being absolute truth, "truth"
4) true to fact statements, "truth, fact"
5) what is characterized by love of truth, "truthfulness, uprightness, fidelity"
6) reality as opposed to pretence or mere appearance, "truth, sincerity"

The meaning of the term *nomos* in the phrase *ho nomos dia Mōuseōs edothē . . . hē charis kai hē alētheia dia Iēsou Christou egeneto* (1:17) is debated; suggestions are "a distinctive sign of the Jews,"[116] "Torah in its comprehensive sense, as the authoritative basis of the whole religious life and thoughts of the Jewish people,"[117] "the body of teaching revealed

---

114. See *AnLex*, 00233; Bultmann, "*alētheia*"; L&N, 00238; UBSDict.
115. Here, following the *AnLex*, 00233 categories.
116. Manns, *John and Jamnia*, 34.
117. Dodd, *Interpretation*, 77; Pancaro, *Law*, 517.

to Moses which constitutes the foundation of the whole social-religious life and thought of Israel,"[118] etc. Scholars also discuss the difference between the Johannine and Pauline usage of the term. Paul uses the word *nomos* to designate: 1) the Decalogue and the Mosaic Law in the "strict" sense—as a body of legislation, 2) the Pentateuch, and 3) the OT as a whole. In this respect, Pauline usage corresponds to the usage of the word *tôrā^h* in the consecrated Jewish sense. However, Paul also uses *nomos* in an "extended" or "improper" sense (from a Jewish point of view) and speaks of "the law of sin and of death," "the law of the Spirit of life in Christ Jesus," "the law of Christ," etc. In such cases, *nomos* takes on the meaning it has in the Greek tradition. Johannine scholars argue that in the Gospel, *nomos* never "strays away from the Jewish into the Greek field of meaning." The Evangelist uses *nomos* only in the consecrated Jewish sense covered by *tôrā^h*.[119]

John 1:14–18: The Frame of Reference

During the first half of the twentieth century Rudolf Bultmann,[120] Dodd,[121] Ernest F. Scott,[122] Robert H. Strachan,[123] and other scholars sought to interpret the Gospel mainly against a Hellenistic background. In the second half of the twentieth century scholars increasingly recognized the Jewishness of the Gospel.[124] It has been studied from such Jewish perspectives as the temple/synagogal liturgy,[125] rabbinic exegesis/patterns of

---

118. Pancaro, *Law*, 515.

119. See Dodd, *Interpretation*, 76; Pancaro, *Law*, 514.

120. Bultmann, *John*.

121. Dodd, *Interpretation*. Dodd particularly links the Gospel with the Hermetic Corpus and Philo. He already mentions, though, that *charis kai alētheia* "corresponds with the Old Testament expression *rab-ḥesed we'ĕmet*" without a particular reference to Exod 34:6 (ibid., 175).

122. Scott, *Fourth Gospel*.

123. Strachan, *Fourth Gospel*.

124. Beasley-Murray, *John*; Boismard, *Moses or Jesus*; Edwards, "Charin anti charitos."

125. Guilding, *Fourth Gospel*.

thoughts,[126] the Torah,[127] the Prophets,[128] and the Wisdom traditions.[129] The matter of the OT quotations in the Gospel has been widely discussed.[130] Associations of characters of the Gospel with their counterparts and prototypes in the OT—Moses,[131] David,[132] and others—have also been investigated.

Scholars have particularly stressed the attention the Gospel pays to the matter of the Law and the glory of God. The place where the glory of the Lord dwelt and where the people went to obtain expiation for their sins no longer exists.[133] The Law without the temple has become the centre of Jewish religious life. It is therefore urgent to interpret the Law given during the exodus.[134] Therefore, scholars reason that the Gospel pays much attention to the matter of the Law. The theme of the glory of God dwelling among the people of Israel, in and upon the tabernacle, is one of the most prominent themes of Exodus. Hence, researchers argue that already in 1:14 the language concerning the Logos being among the people (*eskēnōsen en hēmin*) echoes[135] the dwelling of the glory of the Lord among the people of God in the wilderness.[136]

Scholars have intensely debated the matter of the frame of reference for John 1:14–18. The relationships between John 1:14–18 and Exodus 32–34 are often considered to be the key to the revelations of

---

126. Borgen, "Some Jewish Exegetical Traditions"; Evans, *Word and Glory*; Le Déaut, "Targumic Literature," 265–83; Motyer, *Your Father the Devil?* 44 (especially); Thyen, "Heil," 174.

127. Beasley-Murray, *John*; Boismard, *Moses or Jesus*.

128. Lincoln, *Truth*.

129. Witherington, *John's Wisdom*.

130. See Menken, *OT Quotations*.

131. Meeks, *Prophet-King*; Boismard, *Moses or Jesus*.

132. Daly-Denton, *David*.

133. Most scholars assume that the Gospel is written after the destruction of the temple in 70 C.E. Robinson, however, argues that the theology of the Gospel, particularly the pre-existent Christology as developed by the prologue, is old, since Paul and the letter to the Hebrews knew of it already (J. A. T. Robinson, *Redating*, 254–311).

134. Manns, *John and Jamnia*, 51; Pancaro, *Law*, 2, 492, 508, 523, 527.

135. Throughout the study, the term "echo" is employed to refer to cases where the influence of a text or tradition upon the writer seems evident, but where it remains uncertain whether the writer was conscious of the influence at the time of writing or dictating (see Thompson, *Clothed with Christ*, 30).

136. The Evangelist repeatedly uses the terminology of the "wilderness" (1:23; 3:14; 6:31; 6:49; 11:54).

God at Sinai and as Jesus. Exodus 33—34:6 depicts the revelation of God at Sinai. Moses requests to see God's glory (Exod 33:18). The Lord does not allow Moses to see God's face and explains that "no man can see Me and live" (Exod 33:20). The Lord promises to place Moses in the cleft of the rock, cover him with his hand as he passes by, and then take his hand away so that Moses can see God's back (Exod 33:22, 23). Then the Lord descends, passes in front of Moses, and proclaims, "The Lord, the Lord God, compassionate and gracious, slow to anger, and abounding in lovingkindness and truth" (Exod 34:6).

A relationship between John 1:14–18 and Exodus 33–34:6 was first proposed by Brooke F. Westcott in 1887.[137] In 1953, the idea was further developed by Boismard, who focused specifically on the connection between John 1:14 and Exodus 34:6.[138] In 1985, Gérard Rochais claimed that the idea of a connection between John 1:14 and Exodus 34:6, "has since then become well known and, it seems, commonly accepted."[139]

Scholars distinguish five important points of convergence between John 1:14–18 and Exodus 33—34:6:[140]

> 1) The general contrast between Moses and Jesus presupposes the giving of the Law at Sinai, "For the Law was given through Moses; grace and truth were realized through Jesus Christ" (John 1:17).[141]

---

137. Westcott writes that the "[*plērēs charitos kai alētheias*] combination recalls the description of Jehovah, Exod. xxxiv. 6 (Ps. xxv. 10); and is not infrequent in the Old Testament; Gen. xxiv. 27, 49, xxxii. 10; Ps. xl. 10, 11, lxi 7 (*ḥsd wʾmt*)" (Westcott, *John*, 1:24). His commentary was apparently written mostly between 1883 and 1887, but published posthumously in 1908.

138. Boismard, *St. John's Prologue*, 69f.

139. Rochais, "La formation du Prologue," 32.

140. As listed in Evans, *Word and Glory*, 80–81. Several scholars deviate from this paradigm. Leon Morris sees the parallelism as follows: "Moses used to take the tent and pitch it outside the camp. . . . Whenever Moses entered the tent, the pillar of cloud would descend" (Exod 33:7, 9) = "the Word became flesh, and dwelt [tabernacled] among us" (1:14); "all the people saw the pillar of cloud" (Exod 33:10) = "we saw His glory" (1:14); "the Lord used to speak to Moses face to face" (Exod 33:11) = "the law was given through Moses" (1:17); [The Lord said to Moses] . . . , "You cannot see My face" (Exod 33:20) = "No one has ever seen God" (1:18); [The Lord says to Moses] . . . "you shall see My back, but My face shall not be seen" (Exod 33:23) = "the only Son, who is in the bosom of the Father, He has made Him known" (1:18) (Morris, *John*, 103 n. 87; cf. also Mowley, "John 1:14–18").

141. Of course, there are exceptions. Brueggemann and Daly-Denton envision

2) Moses's request "show me Your glory!" (Exod 33:18; cf. 40:31) is presupposed by the prologue's declaration "and we saw His glory" (John 1:14).

3) The prologue's statement "No one has seen God at any time" (John 1:18) echoes God's response to Moses that "You cannot see My face, for no man can see Me and live!" (Exod 33:20; cf. 33:23).

4) The prologue's assertion that the unique God (or Son) existed "in the bosom of the Father" (John 1:18) contrasts with Moses's fleeting glimpse of God's "back" (Exod 33:23).

5) The prologue's "full of grace and truth" (John 1:14), echoed in John 1:17, is likely an allusion to Exodus 34:6: "abounding in lovingkindness and truth," though according to the Hebrew (*rab-ḥesed we'ĕmet*), not the Septuagint (*polueleos kai alēthinos*).[142]

Scholars who envision a relationship between John 1:14, 17 and Exodus 34:6[143] differ in their interpretation of it. Bauckham explains, "Moses

---

David in the phrase *hē charis kai hē alētheia* (behind which, in their opinion, stands the Hebrew *ḥsd w'mt*). Daly-Denton argues from the Jewish tendency to draw comparisons between Moses and David: "If Jesus was to replace Moses, he would do so as 'David.'" In light of this, "it seems quite possible that a contrast between Moses and David may lie behind Jn 1:17." Following Brueggemann, Daly-Denton writes that "if we refer to the Hebrew behind the Greek *hē charis kai hē alētheia*, we find a formula which sounds very Davidic and is present in 2 Sam 7:14-16 concerning David—*ḥsd* and *'mt*" (Daly-Denton, *David*, 101-2). It should be noted that Brueggemann does not actually mention 1:17 but only 1:14 in that regard, and further claims that "it is grace and truth (*ḥesed we'ĕmet*; *charis kai alētheia*) that causes David to pour out water in solidarity (2 Sam 23:14-17; 1 Chron. 11:15-19). It is grace and truth that leads David to recognize that all gifts are given back to the real giver of all (1 Chron. 29:14)" (Brueggemann, *David's Truth*, 115). Notice, though, that 2 Sam 7:14-16 does not actually employ the noun *'mt* but the verb *'mn*. Moreover, in the context of 2 Sam 7:14-16 the verb *'mn* does not represent a personal quality, but rather it vaguely (if at all) relates to David as a person, and scarcely (not at all?) corresponds with God's quality of *ḥsd* (2 Sam 7:14-16).

142. Carson and Mowley suggest *kai pōs gnōston estai alēthōs hoti heurēka charin para soi egō te kai ho laos sou*, "and how shall it be surely known, that both I and thy people have found favor with thee" (Exod 33:16) behind *plērēs charitos kai alētheias* and *hē charis kai hē alētheia*. See Carson, *John*, 130-31; Mowley, "John 1:14-18."

143. Barrett, *John*, 167; Bauckham, *God Crucified*, 74; Boismard, *Moses or Jesus*, 96; Borgen, *Bread from Heaven*, 150-51; Beasley-Murray, *John*, 13; R. Brown, *John (I-XII)*, 14; Bruce, *John*, 41-42; Bultmann, "*alētheia*," n. 37 (Bultmann cautiously claims: "I think it possible that in 1:14 there is a play on the *ḥesed we'ĕmet* of Ex. 34:6, but this is not very likely"); Carter, "Prologue," 40, 46, 54 n. 45; Dodd, *Interpretation*, 175; Dumbrell,

could only hear God's word proclaiming *that* God is full of grace and truth. He could not see God's glory. But in the Word made flesh, God's glory was seen in human form, and grace and truth (according to John 1:17) happened or came about (*egeneto*)."[144] Beasley-Murray comments, "*charis kai alētheia*, 'grace and truth,' = the common *rab-ḥesed we'ĕmet* . . . frequently rendered in the Septuagint . . . to describe the covenant mercy of God (cf. Exod 34:6). This 'gracious constancy' of God is manifest in its fullness in the Logos-Son."[145] Boismard concludes that the *rab-ḥesed we'ĕmet* of Exodus 34:6 "is found again in the phrase *plērēs charitos kai alētheias* which, in John 1:14, characterizes the incarnate Logos, or the Only-Begotten."[146] Hanson argues that the "grace and truth" of John 1:14 is a reflection of God's essential nature as described in Exodus 34:6.[147] Lester J. Kuyper believes that the phrase *plērēs charitos kai alētheias* is employed to attest the full deity of Jesus.[148]

Pancaro observes, "in Jn 1,14.17 . . . [the Evangelist] predicates *charis kai alētheia*—which correspond to *ḥesed we'ĕmet*—of Jesus. . . . In the OT . . . it is God who is full of *ḥesed we'ĕmet*. . . . [the Evangelist] would be affirming that Jesus is full of *ḥesed we'ĕmet* . . . like God himself."[149] Schoneveld concludes that, "the glory of the Torah was seen when the Torah emerged as flesh, as a human person in Jesus Christ. Through him emerged the grace-and-truth which is inherent in the Torah; as Psalm 25 says, all the paths of the Lord (on which He leads people through His Torah) are 'grace and truth.'"[150] Ralph L. Smith reasons that

---

"Grace and Truth," 115 (as an option); Evans, *Word and Glory*, 81; Glasson, *Moses*, 97 (as an option); Hanson, *Grace and Truth*, 5–6; Hanson, "John I. 14–18 and Exodus XXXIV"; Hanson, *Prophetic Gospel*, 6 (Hanson also suggests that Ps 85:7–10 is "a secondary scriptural source for this passage [1:14–18]"; Hooker, "Johannine Prologue," 53 (referring to Boismard with approval), 136–40; Lincoln, *Truth*, 232; Lindars, *John*, 95; Kuyper, "Grace and Truth," 3; nab, 1:14 n. 1; NA[27] (by providing a reference to Exod 34:6 in the margin at 1:14); Meeks, *Prophet-King*, 288 n. 2; Pancaro, *Law*, 93 n. 75; Reim, *Studien*, 140; Sanders, *John*, 82; Sakenfeld, *Faithfulness*, 134; Schoneveld, "Torah in the Flesh," 83; Theobald, *Fleischwerdung*, 255; N. Turner, "Style of John," 68.

144. Bauckham, *God Crucified*, 74.
145. Beasley-Murray, *John*, 14; cf. also Sakenfeld, *Faithfulness*, 134.
146. Boismard, *Moses or Jesus*, 96.
147. Hanson, *Grace and Truth*, 5–6, 21.
148. Kuyper, "Grace and Truth," 14.
149. Pancaro, *Law*, 93.
150. Schoneveld, "Torah in the Flesh," 83.

"Jesus is the fulfillment of God's covenant promise to Abraham and Jacob."[151]

Several researchers, though, argue that *plērēs charitos kai alētheias* does not allude to *wərab-ḥesed weʾĕmet*. Elizabeth Harris observes that the "actual combination of *hē charis kai hē alētheia* nowhere occurs in the LXX or in any biblical references in Philo, so that Greek readers would be unlikely to recognize it as a Semitic expression even if they were familiar with the OT in Greek."[152] For Bultmann,

> It [is] possible that in 1:14 there is a play on the *ḥesed weʾĕmet* of Ex. 34:6, but this is not very likely, for we must remember 1. that the LXX rendering is *polueleos kai alēthinos*, and 2. that . . . [the Evangelist] does not bring out the idea of faithfulness which *ʾmt* has in this verse.[153]

These scholars interpret *plērēs charitos kai alētheias* against a background—gnostic, Hellenistic, Platonic, Pauline—that is other than the one of Exodus.

John 1:14–18: Approaches to Interpretation

1:14

A number of major issues relate to the interpretation of *kai ho logos sarx egeneto kai eskēnōsen en hēmin, kai etheasametha tēn doxan autou, doxan hōs monogenous para patros, plērēs charitos kai alētheias* (1:14). First, scholars are sharply divided into two groups over the meaning of *plērēs charitos kai alētheias*. Some assert that the phrase *charitos kai alētheias* denotes subjective qualities of God (in this case it is often suggested that *plērēs charitos kai alētheias* alludes to either *wərab-ḥesed weʾĕmet* or *polueleos kai alēthinos*[154] of Exodus 34:6 MT/LXX). Others maintain that *charis* stands for an object ("gift") and *alētheia* denotes

---

151. R. Smith, *Micah–Malachi*, 59.

152. Harris, *Prologue and Gospel*, 66; similarly La Potterie, "Charis," 258; cf. also Theobald, *Fleischwerdung*, 254.

153. Bultmann, "alētheia," n. 37. On the second point, he says elsewhere that "it is not possible to take *al[ētheia* of] 1.14 in the sense of 'faithfulness' as in the LXX (for *ʾĕmet*) . . . [Exod 34:6]" (Bultmann, *John*, 74 n. 2). On the second point Hodges agrees with Bultmann (Hodges, "Grace after Grace," 38).

154. The symbol "/ " may stand for "translated in LXX/OG"; for example, *ḥēn/charis* means "*ḥēn* translated as *charis* in LXX/OG."

either the Platonic, Hellenistic, or gnostic "divine truth," "the truth in itself, substantially,"[155] or the Jewish-Christian "revelation brought by Christ."[156] Second, scholars intensely debate whether the phrase *charitos kai alētheias* denotes one attribute ("true grace," "gracious truth," "gift of truth," etc.) or two ("grace and truth"). Third, the meaning of *tēn doxan autou, doxan hōs* is widely discussed, with suggestions for *doxa* ranging anywhere from "luminosity" to "character."

1:15

No agreement has yet been reached regarding the interpretation of *Iōannēs marturei peri autou kai kekragen legōn: houtos ēn hon eipon: ho opisō mou erchomenos emprosthen mou gegonen, hoti prōtos mou ēn* (1:15). Scholars disagree even on the context of the statement. Some argue that it opens a new section of the Gospel—the witness of John the Baptist.[157] A vast majority maintains that it is an insertion into the prologue.[158] Most scholars of the latter group effectively skip over 1:15. A typical comment is as follows: "The saying [John 1:16] relates immediately to v 14 (v 15 is parenthetic)."[159] The saying is commonly interpreted from the standpoint of an alleged polemic against disciples of John the Baptist who were supposedly challenging Christianity in the Evangelist's time.

1:16

Regarding the matter of interpreting *oti ek tou plērōmatos autou hēmeis pantes elabomen kai charin anti charitos* (1:16), Ignace de la Potterie concludes, "Nous voilà donc en pleine confusion," (We are thus in complete confusion).[160] To begin with, interpretation of *charin anti charitos* is highly complicated by the lack of occurrences of *charis* and *anti* beyond the prologue. Moreover, scholars disagree whether occurrences of *charis*

---

155. Bultmann, *John*, 74 n. 2; Harris, *Prologue and Gospel*, 50–51.

156. La Potterie, "*Charis*," 258; Panimolle, *Il dono della degge*, 314.

157. Harris, *Prologue and Gospel*; Hodges, "Grace after Grace," 34–36.

158. A few English translations of the Gospel—DBY, ESV, NRSV, RSV—even put 1:15 in parenthesis.

159. Beasley-Murray, *John*, 15.

160. La Potterie, "*Charis*," 263.

in *(hē) charis kai (hē) alētheia*[161] and *charin anti charitos* convey the same[162] meaning or not.[163] Furthermore, no consensus has yet been reached over the meaning of *anti* in *charin anti charitos*. Finally, scholars intensely dispute the interpretation of each occurrence of *charis* in *charin anti charitos*. Five usages of *anti* with regard to *charin anti charitos* are discussed:[164] First, *anti* may mean "in front of" or "opposite."[165] Second, it may imply "in return for."[166] Third, it may mean "corresponding to," in the same way that effect corresponds to cause. In this case, *charin anti charitos* denotes that "the grace which Christians receive corresponds to the grace of Christ"[167] or "the love which corresponds to God's love, filial love which corresponds with His paternal love."[168] Fourth, *anti* may mean "upon," "in addition to." In this case it refers to the inexhaustible bounty of God's gifts, resulting in a constant stream of graces.[169] Normally, adherents of this point of view do not specify

161. Throughout this study, the phrase *"(hē) charis kai (hē) alētheia"* equals *"plērēs charitos kai alētheias and hē charis kai hē alētheia."*

162. La Potterie, "Charis," 270.

163. For example, Schnackenburg maintains that the term *charis* in 1:14 is to be taken in the subjective sense of "der Gnadenreichtum, die Spendergüte" of Logos, but in 1:16 it would have the objective meaning of "das Gnadengeschenk selbst" (Schnackenburg, *John*, 1:248). Sometimes *charis* would be understood in the subjective sense of *agapē* in 1:14, but in the objective sense of the grace of redemption in 1:17.

164. Our study summarizes findings available in Barkhuizen, "A Short Note" (especially church fathers); Blumenthal, "Charis anti charitos," 290 n. 2, 291 n. 4 (especially German scholarship); La Potterie, *Vérité*, 1:142–44, 1:142 n. 60 (especially French scholarship); Edwards, *"Charin anti charitos"* (especially classical Greek and the Hellenistic papyri. Due to limitations on volume, only an illustrative selection of scholars is represented here.

165. Never occurs in the LXX/OG/NT.

166. As a designated penalty in Exod 21:23–24; Matt 5:38; Rom 12:17, cf. 1 Thess 5:15, 1 Pet 3:9.

167. This interpretation originates with Thomas Aquinas and is further supported by Bernard, *John*, 1:29; Bover, *"Charin anti charitos,"* 458; Joüon, "Jean 1,16," 206; J. A. Robinson, *Ephesians*, 223; cf. "grace for grace" (ASV, DRB, GNV, KJV, MRD, NKJV, RWB, TNT, WEB).

168. Lacan, "Prologue," 109 n. 4.

169. This interpretation is adopted by Barrett, *John*; Bruce, *John*; Bultmann, *John*; Conzelmann, "charis," n. 226; GNB; Gnilka, *Johannesevangelium*; Hanson, *John 1:14–18 and Exodus 34*; Hanson, *Prophetic Gospel*, 21; Hoskyns, *Fourth Gospel*; Lindars, *John*; Schnackenburg, *John*; cf. "grace upon grace" (DBY, ESV, NASB, NRSV, RSV); "one blessing after another" (NIB, NIV), "one gracious blessing after another" (NLT), and "grace on grace" (BBE).

exactly what occurrences of *charis* in *charin anti charitos* mean, the generic "grace upon grace" being the most popular translation. Fifth, *anti* may denote "instead of," "in place of."[170] This is the view of the majority of church fathers:[171] Chrysostom,[172] Cyril of Alexandria,[173] Origen,[174] Theophylact,[175] and Jerome[176] think that *charin anti charitos* refers to the replacement of the Mosaic Law by the Gospel. Various views assuming this notion of replacement in *anti* are also prominent among modern scholars. E. Abbott interprets, "from his fullness we all received and grace *in the place of* (*anti*) grace: because [whereas] the Law through Moses was given [by God,] the grace [of God] and the truth [of God] through Jesus Christ came into being."[177] He concludes that

170. Cf. Gen 22:13; Luke 11:11; Matt 2:22; cf. "grace in place of grace" (NAB), "one gift replacing another" (NJB), "grace over-against grace" (YLT).

171. See Edwards, "*Charin anti charitos*," 7.

172. Chrysostom stresses that the Law itself had the nature of a gift: *kai gar ta tou nomou kai auta charitos ēn*, "even the things of the law were of grace" (Chrysostom *Homilies on St. John* 14).

173. Cyril of Alexandria explains that *charis euangelikē*, "the grace of the Gospel," replaces *charis nomikē*, "the grace of the law." Cyril readily recognizes the superiority of the new grace, but nevertheless affirms, that the Law did impart a gift of grace to humankind: *kai charin men anthrōpois kai ho nomos edidou, kalōn holōs eis theognōsian* (Cyril of Alexandria *In Jo. Ev. Lib.* I.101).

174. The views of Origen are complicated and perhaps not entirely consistent. Particularly, Origen comments, "The words 'Of his fulness all we received,' and 'Grace for grace,' show, . . . , that the prophets also received their gift from the fulness of Christ and received a second grace in place of that they had before; for they also, led by the Spirit, advanced from the introduction they had in types to the vision of truth" (Origen *Commentary on the Gospel of John* 6:2, *ANF* 10:560). But Origen further explains that John the Baptist, by saying *ek tou plērōmatos autou hēmeis pantes elabomen kai charin anti charitos*, means "of His fulness both I and the prophets before me received the more divine prophetic grace instead of the grace we received at His hands before in respect of our election" (ibid. 6:3, *ANF* 10:564).

175. Theophylact understands the grace of the new covenant as replacing that of the old lawgiving—*kai charin de elabomen, tēn tēs kainēs dēladē diathēkēs, anti tēs charitos, tēs palaias nomothesias*. Theophylact goes on to contrast the greatness of the gift of grace through Jesus Christ with the lesser gift of grace through the law—*charin megistēn anti mikras charitos* (Theophylact *Enarr. in Jo.* I.518f., PG 123:1164).

176. Jerome comments, "Instead of the grace of the law which has passed away, we have received the grace of the gospel which is abiding; and instead of the shadows and types of the old dispensation, the truth has come by Jesus Christ" (Jerome *Ep.* 112.14, CSEL 55:383, online: www.ccel.org/ccel/schaff/npnf101.vii.1.lxxV.html#fnf_vii.1.lxxV).

177. Abbott, *Johannine Grammar*, 225 [2284].

there is probably in John . . . an intention to suggest the notion of "exchange" rather than that of mere succession. . . . The Law was given to Israel through Moses because (Deut. vii. 7) the Lord "loved" them and "chose" them, that is to say, God gave it as a gift, or grace; but His full grace and truth, latent under that Law, did not come into being till the Word became flesh as Jesus Christ in order to "*take away*" the first grace, *i.e.* the Law of Moses, so as to establish the second grace, *i.e.* the grace of freedom, or sonship,—the grace of the Father as manifested in the grace of the Son.[178]

He further explains that "'the grace' (*including all the grace that reached Israel through the Law*) came through Jesus Christ."[179] Hence, Abbott argues for a continuity between revelations of God at Sinai and as Jesus that implies an incorporation of the former revelation into the latter. Matthew Black suggests that underlying the Greek *charin anti charitos* is an Aramaic word-play, *ḥsdʾ hlp ḥs(w)dʾ*, grace (*ḥisdʾ*) in place of shame (*ḥisûdʾ*, or *ḥisdʾ*), which escaped the translator's notice.[180] Beasley-Murray comments that "fresh grace replaces grace received," and explains, "the salvation brought by the Word thus defined in terms of inexhaustible grace."[181] Boismard[182] and Raymond E. Brown[183] maintain that *anti* means "in place of," but they understand, by the double mention of *charis*, two successive demonstrations of the love of God. Adhémar d'Alès suggests that *charin anti charitos* refers to the "replacement of grace received through Christ by the grace received, after his physical departure from this earth, by the Holy Spirit."[184] De la Potterie evaluates that in 1:16 the Evangelist speaks about "the replacement of the Law of Moses by the truth of Jesus about Christ."[185] Ruth B. Edwards argues, "the Law . . . this former manifestation of God's gracious love

---

178. Abbott, *Johannine Grammar*, 226 [2286]. This scholar adds in n. 5, "Comp. Heb. x. 9 'He *taketh away* the first that he may establish the second.'"

179. Abbott, *Johannine Grammar*, 302 n. 2411e.

180. Black, "Aramaic Tradition," 64, 69–70.

181. Beasley-Murray, *John*, 15.

182. Boismard, *St. John's Prologue*, 83–84.

183. R. Brown, *John (I–XII)*, 4, 16.

184. D'Alès, "Charin anti charitos."

185. La Potterie, "*Charis*," 280. La Potterie believes that only the option of *anti* meaning "instead of," "in place of" is "really based on the philological point of view" (ibid., 263).

and favor has now been replaced by a new, personal and unique manifestation through his Son. . . . this verse [John 1:16] refers to the Law itself as God's gracious gift."[186] Nigel Turner remarks that *charin anti charitos* may refer to the gift of grace of the Spirit, which has stepped into the place of the grace of Jesus.[187]

The variety of options with regard to the meaning of terms in *charin anti charitos* has led to rather eclectic interpretations of the phrase. For example, Warren Carter suggests that in *charin anti charitos*,

> The preposition *anti* can be read as expressing both replacement ('grace in place of grace') and accumulation ('grace upon grace'); it would seem that John wishes to link two manifestations of divine grace—God's presence in Jesus Christ is continuous with the Sinai gift of the law to Moses—while also expressing discontinuity and supercession, since for him, the revelation in the one who has been with God from the beginning (Jesus), surpasses all others. 1.16–17 draws the two figures together yet sets them apart.[188]

1:17

Interpretations of *ho nomos dia Mōuseōs edothē, hē charis kai hē alētheia dia Iēsou Christou egeneto* (1:17) vary drastically and virtually exclude each other.

There is an uncertainty with regard to the relationships between *ho nomos* and *hē charis kai hē alētheia*. One group of interpreters suggests that an *antithesis* or *opposition* between the Law and grace is explicitly mentioned in the 1:17.[189] These scholars—Beasley-Murray,[190]

---

186. Edwards, "Charin anti charitos," 9–10.
187. Turner and Moulton, *Syntax*, 258; as one of the options.
188. Carter, "Prologue," 40.
189. Notice the usage of "but" (GNV, MRD, PNT, TNT), "*but*" (KJV, NKJV, RWB), or "{but}" (WEB) as a means to express such antithesis or opposition.
190. Beasley-Murray writes, "Moses saw no more than God's back (Exod 34:21–23), and out of that encounter issued the revelation of *the Law*; . . . By contrast, however, the only Son, who shares the nature of God (*ho monogenēs Theos*), has given an authentic exposition of *God* to man" (Beasley-Murray, *John*, 15).

Hans Conzelmann,[191] D'Alès,[192] Craig A. Evans,[193] Joachim Gnilka,[194] Ernst Haenchen,[195] Barnabas Lindars,[196] Pancaro,[197] Petersen,[198] Richardson,[199] Walther Zimmerli,[200] and others—assume that the writer is referring here to a contrast or even an opposition between the Law and the Gospel[201] or between Moses and Jesus. Another group of scholars argues for *continuity* between revelations of God at Sinai and as Jesus. To support their view, they point out that there is no adversative—neither *alla* nor *de* in the Greek.[202] Grammatically and structurally the two halves of the verse are exactly balanced:[203] noun phrase (*ho nomos*; *hē charis kai hē alētheia*) > prepositional phrase (*dia Mōuseōs*; *dia Iēsou Christou*) > verb (*edothē*; *egeneto*). Lindars,[204] Jeremias,[205] and others have suggested that the phrase may well be translated, "Just as the law was given through Moses, so grace and truth came through Jesus

191. Conzelmann believes, that in 1:14, 16f, "the word [*charis*] denotes the result of the revelation of the Logos. Paul's antithesis of grace and Law is adopted, but it is not developed" (Conzelmann, "*charis*").

192. D'Alès sees the phraseology of 1:17 as excluding the possibility that the Law could be referred to as grace in *charin anti charitos* (D'Alès, "Charin anti charitos," 385).

193. Evans, *Word and Glory*, 80 n. 2.

194. Gnilka, *Johannesevangelium*, 16.

195. Haenchen, *Johannesevangelium*, 131, or in English translation, *John*, 1:120.

196. Lindars evaluates, "there has been no real gift of grace and truth except in Christ" (Lindars, *John*, 97–98).

197. Pancaro, *Law*, 541.

198. Petersen concludes that "there is an implicit contrast ['in a subordinating manner'] between the Law that came through Moses and the 'Grace and Truth' that came through Jesus" (N. Petersen, *John*, 21; see also 5–6, 43, 111–19).

199. Richardson, *Introduction*, 283f.

200. Zimmerli, "*charis* (OT)."

201. See Edwards, "*Charin anti charitos*," 5. Some commentators suppose that 1:17 represents a case of antithetic parallelism; consider Krasovec, *Antithetic Structure*.

202. Schoneveld, "Torah in the Flesh," 84. Notice the usage of ";" (ASV, BBE, ESV, MRD, NASB, NLT, NRSV, RSV) or ":" (DBY, DRA, PNT) for the purpose of parting the clauses. Edwards also argues, "nowhere else in John or the Gospels do we find a direct contrast between 'grace and truth' and the Law such as has been suggested for v. 17" (Edwards, "*Charin anti charitos*," 8). This is a true statement but an invalid argument because the phraseology "grace and truth" does not occur in the Synoptics, and neither does the term "grace" beyond the prologue.

203. La Potterie, "*Charis*," 273; Edwards, "*Charin anti charitos*," 8.

204. Lindars, *John*, 98.

205. Jeremias, "*Mōusēs*," 4:872.

Christ."²⁰⁶ Rather than choosing between synonymous²⁰⁷ and antithetic parallelism for this verse, it should be classified as "synthetic"²⁰⁸ or "progressive." In this case, even though the new grace is superior to the old, as the church fathers strongly emphasized in their comments on this text, the old covenant was still a gift of grace, that is, a mark of God's gracious favor to his people.²⁰⁹ The Law was also a divine revelation, as is indicated by the divine passive *edothē*.²¹⁰ So Pancaro maintains that the Evangelist is exclusively concerned with the meaning and value the Law has *after* the coming of Christ.²¹¹ To wish to consider the Law as the revelation of God and the way to life *after* Christ's coming means "to have misunderstood it, . . . to reject God's revelation, to remain in sin and to refuse the gift of life. . . . the revelation and life is *now* to be found in Christ, not in the Law. If the Law has a revelatory and salvific function *now* it is only insofar as it leads to Jesus."²¹² In this sense, concludes Pancaro, "there is an element of continuity between the Law given through Moses and the *charis kai alētheia* which came to be through Jesus Christ."²¹³

This variety of issues causes scholars to exercise five approaches in interpreting the whole phrase *ho nomos dia Mōuseōs edothē, hē charis kai hē alētheia dia Iēsou Christou egeneto* (1:17).

The first group of scholars argues that *charis* must be understood in the subjective sense of "love" or "mercy" (in this case 1:17 is often

---

206. Edwards notices that such an interpretation would give *hoti*, "for," its full weight, with 1:17 explaining the force of the previous verse (Edwards, "*Charin anti charitos*," 8). Schoneveld recognizes that there is no contrast involved in 1:17 and, for 1:14–18 employs the terminology, "of the same rank," "analogous," and "as great an order as" (Schoneveld, "Torah in the Flesh," 83–84).

207. Edwards argues that grammatical and structural sameness of the clauses "is not to suggest for one moment that the Law and 'grace and truth' are synonymous, or that Moses and Christ are one and the same, or even that *edothē* has exactly the same meaning as *egeneto*. In spite of the strict parallelism in form, there is a progression of thought in the second part of the verse which could not readily have been predicted from its first half" (Edwards, "*Charin anti charitos*," 8).

208. Jeremias, "*Mōusēs*," 4:872.

209. Edwards, "*Charin anti charitos*," 8.

210. Pancaro, *Law*, 470 n. 50.

211. Ibid., 525. For the Evangelist "it may *have been* legitimate to say God revealed Himself in the Law" but the writer "does not reflect upon this."

212. Ibid., 526.

213. Ibid., 543.

viewed as a parallel to 1:14). For example, Brown translates, "filled with enduring love . . . love in place of love . . . For while the Law was a gift through Moses, this enduring love came through Jesus Christ."[214]

The second approach envisions 1:17 depicting an antithesis[215] between the Law and grace. Concerning the second term of the phrase *hē charis kai hē alētheia*, representatives of this group typically suggest that in 1:17 *alētheia* was added to *charis* under the influence of *plērēs charitos kai alētheias* in 1:14.[216] To explain the alleged variation of meanings in 1:14 and 17, certain scholars postulate two different sources lying behind these usages.

The third group maintains that 1:17 depicts an antithesis between the Law and the truth. This exegesis is typical of the church fathers—Cyril of Alexandria, Jerome, and others.[217] It is to be understood as an opposition of the "foreshadowing" (*skia*) represented by the figures of the OT (the Law), and "reality"—gifts brought by Christ (*alētheia*). Here, *alētheia* is not the equivalent of ʾ*mt* in its sense of a subjective quality, an attribute of the Divine. The term *alētheia* is instead taken in the Greek sense of "reality" but applied in the biblical sense to a typological correspondence between the Testaments. This interpretation also finds a lot of echoes in modern scholarship. For Alfred F. Loisy this "reality" is "la réalité de la grace."[218] According to Paul Marie de la Croix, "the Law fades in front of the grace, the letter in front of the Spirit, the shadow gives way to the light, the signs to the Reality."[219]

---

214. R. Brown, *John (I–XII)*, 4.

215. Several exegetes believe they have uncovered in this text a Pauline antithesis between grace and the Law (cf. Rom 4:16; 6:14,15; Gal 5:4). Some scholars would also make a connection between John 1:16 and Rom 5:17 and speak of the succession of graces, which Christians receive in Christ.

216. For example, Pancaro evaluates, "Jn was using a pre-existent hymn which spoke of the Word becoming flesh and being full of *charitos kai alētheias* . . . . *Charis* was mentioned in both vv. 14 and 16. In adding v. 17 Jn did not see fit to omit *charis*; he takes up the same expression used at v. 14" (Pancaro, *Law*, 541).

217. See La Potterie, "*Charis*," 265 n. 29. Cf. "For the law was given by the hand of Moses; but the reality and grace was by the hand of Jesus Messiah" (MRD).

218. Loisy, *Le quatrième Évangile*, 193.

219. Paul Marie de la Croix, *L'Évangile de Jean*, 85; my translation. Aalen's reading is similar: "What Moses saw and brought to men was not really the truth (in the definitive sense of the word) but only the Law (here understood as a stage in the process of revelation) (John 1,17). . . . The truth is a reality which is sent by God into the world. The truth is in Christ and in his word" (Aalen, "'Truth,'" 11–12). In our view, Aalen tends to be overly eclectic in his interpretation.

The fourth approach envisions 1:17 as depicting the gift of truth, where the phrase *hē charis kai hē alētheia* forms a hendiadys[220] and means "the grace (= the gift) of the truth." Proponents of this approach—most notably Salvatore A. Panimolle,[221] followed by De la Potterie[222]—argue that contrary to Paul, the Evangelist does not refer here to an opposition between *nomos* and *charis*, but instead to an opposition between *nomos* and *alētheia*. Together these terms form, not an antithetical parallelism, but rather, a progressive parallelism. They describe two important stages of God's revelation: the Law was given through Moses at Mount Sinai; in the Eschaton, the gift of the truth was realized in Jesus Christ. In this exegesis the word *charis* denotes the gift (= the grace) given in Christ: this gift is the truth, the plenitude of the revelation. For Bultmann and Harris, the words *charis* and *alētheia* indicate the "being" of Logos, its divine reality (*alētheia*) as far as it is revealed and communicated to us (*charis*).[223] A variation of this hypothesis has been argued by Manns, who insists that the Law mentioned in 1:17 is the written Law. According to him, the Evangelist opposes the exegetical activities of the Pharisees, which aim at deducing the oral Law from the written Law. The Mishnah attempted to show the antiquity of the oral Law in claiming that it went back to Moses: "Moses received the Law of Sinai and transmitted it to Joshua and to the elders, and the elders to the Prophets. The Prophets transmitted it to the men of the great assembly."[224] Manns reasons that the Evangelist could not possibly ignore the activity of the Jamnia teachers. Therefore, the writer proclaims that their efforts were useless, since only a Christological reading of the Scriptures is valid from now on. The only exegetical activity that is valid and useful is that which seeks to show that the Scriptures bear witness to Jesus (5:39).[225]

The fifth approach comprehends *charis kai hē alētheia* as attributes of the divine character. Regarding the phrase *hē charis kai hē alētheia*,[226]

---

220. In the sense of "the co-ordination [by *kai*] of two ideas, one of which is dependent on the other"; see BDF, § 442 (16).

221. Panimolle, *Il dono della legge*.

222. La Potterie, "Charis," 266–67.

223. Harris, *Prologue and Gospel*, 71; cf. 50.

224. ʾAbot 1:1.

225. Manns, "L'Évangile de Jean," 75–78; *John and Jamnia*, 63.

226. For 1:17 only.

Origen suggested, "God . . . made grace and truth through Jesus Christ, that grace and truth which came to man."²²⁷ Boismard later upheld that "grace and fidelity come from God to us, they have been 'made' in us by Jesus Christ, they have become our own possession, qualities of our heart."²²⁸ The NLT translates, "For the law was given through Moses; God's unfailing love and faithfulness came through Jesus Christ."

1:18

Scholars typically interpret *Theon oudeis heōraken pōpote: monogenēs Theos ho ōn eis ton kolpon tou patros ekeinos exēgēsato* (1:18) in reference to their stand taken on 1:14–17 and their view of the message of the Gospel as a whole. For Bultmann, "Jesus as Revealer" is the central feature of the Christology of the Evangelist, and he argues that it shows the Gospel's gnostic background.²²⁹ De la Potterie asks, "What does this revelation brought by Jesus Christ consist of? The parallelism found in vv.14 and 17 (v.14: *ho logos sarx egeneto kai . . . plērēs charitos kai alētheias*; v.17: *hē charis kai hē alētheia . . . egeneto*) already shows that the gift of the truth is strictly connected to the embodiment of the Word. For John, the revelation is essentially the unveiling, the demonstration, of the person of the Word made flesh."²³⁰ Meeks argues that the contemporary understanding of Moses as one who journeyed to heaven, in order to receive heavenly revelations, had influenced John's Christology, and that a polemic against contemporary claims to have made such journeys is found in 1:18; 3:11–13; and 5:37.²³¹ Motyer concludes, "The presentation of Jesus as the Revealer draws not just on prophetic and Wisdom traditions but also on apocalyptic and 'heavenly journey' traditions, especially those associated with the patriarchs. . . . The insistence on the Son of Man as the *sole* Revealer of heavenly things (1:18; 3:13, 31–36; 14:6) is a polemic against such claims made by others."²³² Odeberg interprets the emphasis of the Gospel on Jesus as Revealer against the background of the Jewish *merkabah* mystical

---

227. Origen *Commentary on the Gospel of John* 6:3, ANF 10:353.
228. Boismard, *St. John's Prologue*, 64, similarly 62, 70.
229. Bultmann, *John*, 45–83.
230. La Potterie, "*Charis*," 281; my translation.
231. Meeks, *Prophet-King*, 295–301.
232. Motyer, *Your Father the Devil?* 46.

tradition, and claims that the exclusive emphasis on Jesus as Revealer indicated a contemporary polemic against other sources of apocalyptic revelation.[233] According to John F. O'Grady, Jesus primarily reveals that "religious experience not only involves the mountain tops of mysticism and ecstasy, but also can be found in the dying of Jesus and in one's personal death," and that "God is Father not only to Jesus but to all people."[234] For Pancaro, 1:18 implies that "the perfect unity of Father and Son makes it possible to see the Father in Jesus."[235] Schoneveld advocates "the Torah in the flesh" approach: "Jesus . . . is the Torah in the flesh and as such he 'showed the way' (*exēgēsato*, v. 18) . . . so that it may have a *halakhic* connotation of showing the right way according to the Torah."[236] As there is a vast variety of explanations given for 1:14–17, so there is no agreement over the interpretation of 1:18.

Issues in Their Relationship in the Gospel of John

We have considered views of the relationship between the revelations of God at Sinai and as Jesus, both from the perspective of the whole Gospel and more specifically 1:14–18. Is there a solution that reduces the options of fulfillment, replacement or continuity between the revelations of God at Sinai and as Jesus to a common denominator? To answer this question, the following key issues involved in 1:14–18 ought to be resolved:

First, do the phrases *plērēs charitos kai alētheias* (1:14) and *hē charis kai hē alētheia* (1:17) allude to *wərab-ḥesed weʾĕmet/polueleos kai alēthinos* (Exod 34:6)? The answer to this question should define whether the phrase *(hē) charis kai (hē) alētheia* denotes subjective attribute(s) of the character of God or some objective realities. This is a principal matter. If *plērēs charitos kai alētheias* (1:14) and *hē charis kai hē alētheia* (1:17) do allude to *wərab-ḥesed weʾĕmet/polueleos kai alēthinos* (Exod 34:6), then all the interpretations that are not keyed to the revelation at Sinai referred to at Exodus 34:6—such as Platonic,

---

233. Odeberg, *Fourth Gospel*, especially 94. Cf. also Manns, *John and Jamnia*, 41 n. 41; Dunn, "Let John," 322–25; Motyer, *Your Father the Devil?* 45 n. 40.

234. O'Grady, "Jesus," 164.

235. Pancaro, *Law*, 206.

236. Schoneveld, "Torah in the Flesh," 85.

Hellenistic, or gnostic explanations of this segment of the Gospel—should be discarded as invalid.

Second, do the phrases *plērēs charitos kai alētheias* (1:14) and *hē charis kai hē alētheia* (1:17) constitute hendiadys? The answer to this question will determine the number of attributes that the phrase *(hē) charis kai (hē) alētheia* has in view—either one or two. This is a major issue. If these two phrases do not constitute hendiadys, then all the interpretations that envision such hendiadys—Platonic, Hellenistic, the gnostic "gift of divine truth," "gift of the truth in itself, substantially," the Jewish-Christian "gift of the revelation brought by Christ," "true grace," "gracious truth," etc.—ought to be rejected as invalid.

Third, do the syntax and grammar of the phrase *ho nomos dia Mōuseōs edothē, hē charis kai hē alētheia dia Iēsou Christou egeneto* (1:17) allow one to arbitrarily divide up the phrase *hē charis kai hē alētheia*? The answer to this question should define the relationship between *ho nomos* and *hē charis kai hē alētheia* (1:17). This is a key issue. If the latter phrase cannot be arbitrarily divided up, then all the interpretations that assume such a division—those envisioning an antithesis between the Law and grace or between the Law and truth, etc.—should be discarded.

Fourth, how are the concept(s) of *charis* introduced in the prologue's *(hē) charis kai (hē) alētheia* (1:14, 17) and *charin anti charitos* (1:16) further developed in the Gospel? The answer to this question will evince the unity of the whole Gospel's outlook of the relationships between the revelations of God at Sinai and as Jesus. The major challenge here is that key terms in the prologue—*logos*,[237] "word"; *Christos*, "Christ"; *zōē*, "life"; *phōs*, "light"; *skotia*, "darkness"; *teknon*, "child"; *marturia*, "testimony"; *kosmos*, "world"; *sarx*, "flesh"; *doxa*, "glory"; *alētheia*, "truth"; *monogenēs*, "*the* only begotten"; *patēr*, "father"; *nomos*, "law"; *Mōusēs*, "Moses,"—introduce a concept that will be developed further in the Gospel. Such concepts will use cognates of the term first introduced in the prologue. When it comes to the phrases *charin anti charitos* and *(hē) charis kai (hē) alētheia*, the situation becomes complicated. The term *alētheia* is used in the prologue (1:14, 17); cognates of *alētheia* are widely utilized further in the Gospel (the noun *alētheia* occurs twenty-five times, the adjective *alēthēs* is found fourteen times,

---

237. *Logos* of Jesus does not appear beyond the prologue but nevertheless conveys an important aspect of the Gospel's message.

the adjective *alēthinos* is featured nine times, and the adverb *alēthōs* is utilized seven times). The term *charis*, though, occurs only in the prologue (1:14, 16, 17) and nowhere else in the Gospel. This is a principal matter. Since *charin anti charitos* was *received* and *hē charis kai hē alētheia* were *granted*, then the concept(s) of *charis* must be traceable throughout the Gospel in a rather tangible way; all interpretations that do not evince the concept(s) of *charis* in the Gospel should be discarded as incongruent.

Fifth, how is the concept of *doxa* introduced in the prologue (1:14) further developed in the Gospel? The main difficulty here is that the usage of *doxa* throughout the Gospel is perplexing. Not only various meanings of *doxa* are set alongside one another without restraint in the Gospel (e.g., 12:41–43), but also, whereas the vast majority of NT authors' statements concern the glorification of the risen Lord after Easter,[238] the picture is rather different in the Gospel of John, to the degree that we here find far more references to the *doxa* of the earthly Jesus (e.g., 2:11; 13:31–32; 11:40).[239] Besides, Jesus's report to the Father, "The glory which You have given Me I have given to them, that they may be one, just as We are one" (17:22), remains a riddle. This is a major issue. If the foundational John 1:14–18 alludes to Exodus 34:6, then the concept of *doxa* in the Gospel must be interpreted against the revelation of God at Sinai; all the interpretations that are not capable of accounting for all of the cognates of *doxa* in the Gospel from the perspective of the revelation of God at Sinai should be perceived as incoherent.

The answers to the above questions will clarify the relationships between the revelations of God at Sinai and as Jesus as introduced in the prologue and developed further in the Gospel.

---

238. Rom 6:4; 1 Tim 3:16; Acts 7:55; 1 Pet 1:11, 21. Cf. Luke 2:14; 19:38; Rev 4:9 with Heb 13:21; 1 Pet 4:11; Rev 5:12f. See also Acts 7:2; 1 Cor 2:8; Titus 2:13; 1 Pet 4:13; 5:1; Mark 13:26, etc. The application of the word to the incarnate Jesus is strictly limited. See Matt 19:28; 25:31; Luke 2:9.

239. See Kittel, "*doxa*," 2:249.

1

Allusions to Exodus 34:6

The matter of defining the background for *plērēs charitos kai alētheias* (John 1:14) is crucial because the course of interpretation of the entire Gospel depends on it. The issue is, "How to account for the discrepancy between *wərab-ḥesed weʾĕmet* (Exod 34:6 MT), *polueleos kai alēthinos* (Exod 34:6 LXX), and *plērēs charitos kai alētheias* (John 1:14)."[1] This is where we now turn.

We will first examine an argument against the case that *plērēs charitos kai alētheias* alludes to *wərab-ḥesed weʾĕmet* and dismiss it as fallacious. We will then evaluate a number of attempts to establish the presence of such an allusion and demonstrate that they are flawed or inadequate. Finally, we will provide our own evidence for the case that *plērēs charitos kai alētheias* and *hē charis kai hē alētheia* are allusions to *raḥûm wəḥannûn ʾerek ʾappayim wərab-ḥesed weʾĕmet* (Exod 34:6).

Critique of Accounts of the Discrepancy between *wərab-ḥesed weʾĕmet* (Exod 34:6 MT), *polueleos kai alēthinos* (Exod 34:6 LXX), and *plērēs charitos kai alētheias* (John 1:14)

Bultmann's Argument from the Alleged Incongruity in the Meaning

Bultmann objects to the proposal that *(hē) charis kai (hē) alētheia* is an allusion to *ḥesed weʾĕmet* on the grounds that "Jn. does not bring out the idea of faithfulness which *ʾmt* has in this verse."[2] This assertion

---

1. R. Brown, *John (I–XII)*, 14; Bultmann, "*alētheia*," n. 37; La Potterie, "*Charis*," 258; Sakenfeld, *Faithfulness*, 134.

2. Bultmann, "*alētheia*," n. 37; Hodges, "Grace after Grace," 38 (with approval).

then serves as a basis of looking at the Gospel as reflecting the Platonic or/and the gnostic concept of truth.³ Bultmann's objection is invalid for the following reasons.

First, the profound Jewishness of the Gospel has recently been well recognized. Particularly, scholarship has begun recovering from Bultmann's gnostic and Dodd's Platonic erroneous outlooks on *alētheia* in the Gospel.⁴ This permits the *'ĕmet* meaning behind *alētheia* in the prologue and encourages envisioning connotations of *alētheia* in the sense of *'ĕmet* elsewhere in the Gospel.

The expression *ho . . . poiōn tēn alētheian* (3:21) is a Jewish idiom connoting "the practice of fidelity and steadfastness,"⁵ or "to conduct oneself faithfully, trustworthily."⁶ OT background can be seen behind the Johannine references to the word of God, or the testimony of God or of Jesus, as true in the sense of reliable.⁷ Jesus's plea to the Father, "Sanctify them in the truth [*alētheia*]; Your word is truth [*alētheia*]" (17:17), may well express Christ's request of making the disciples as reliable as the word of God is. Kuyper puts it this way: "To be consecrated . . . through the truth . . . is to possess steadfast devotion by means of the steadfastness of God communicated through Jesus Christ."⁸ It may well be that Jesus and Pilate do not quite communicate because they deal with different—Hebrew and Greek—concepts of *alētheia* (18:37–38). Jesus has come into the world "to testify to the truth [*alētheia*]" and affirms, "Everyone who is of the truth [*alētheias*] hears My voice." Christ wit-

---

3. The Platonic and the Gnostic concept of truth is concerned with heavenly realities or the contrast between a heavenly and an earthly cosmos, within a framework of idealism or dualism respectively. In Hebrew tradition—both the OT and Judaism—the principal criterion of truth is that which can be relied on in life. See Aalen, "'Truth.'"

4. See, particularly, Aalen, "'Truth'"; Beasley-Murray, *John*; La Potterie, *Vérité*.

5. Aalen, "'Truth,'" 6. Cf. Gen 32:10, 47, 29, Tob 4:6; 13:6.

6. Kuyper, "Grace and Truth," 15.

7. 17:17; 5:31–32; 8:13f.; cf. Pss 19:8–10; 119:24, 36, 38, 43, 46 (of the Law). According to the OT, the word is the instrument of revelation, and behind it stands God's truth (Pss 85:11; 118:43 OG), that is, his truthfulness and reliability. See Aalen, "'Truth.'"

8. Kuyper, "Grace and Truth," 17. Aalen interprets the phrase against the OT and Jewish background as a contrast between the truth as a liberating and sanctifying power as against sin as an enslaving power (Aalen, "'Truth,'" 6). Cf. Lev 11:44f.; 19:2; Deut 7:6; Ps 19:8; 51:6–11; 1QS IV.20f.; 1QH XI.7–12; VII.10–14. For the Gospel's contrast between truth and lies, Aalen gives as examples 1QS IV.23; 1QH II.27; IV.20f.; VII.11–14; 1QpHab. III.6.

nesses to the ultimate integrity of God in the redemption of humanity. Everyone who adheres to God—possesses God's character—is capable of grasping Christ's declaration of God *being* with humanity in Jesus. Pilate's question, "What is truth [*alētheia*]?" indicates that the governor operates with the paradigm of *alētheia* denoting an abstract absolute truth, hence he misses Jesus's role conceptually.[9] Ultimately, the Lord is described as *ho Theos tēs alētheias* (the God of the truth) (Ps 30:6 OG) in the OT.[10] Several modern translations have also taken the Jewishness of the Gospel into consideration with reference to cognates of *alētheia*. The NLT translates both *charitos kai alētheias* and *hē charis kai hē alētheia* as "unfailing love and faithfulness" (1:14, 17). The NAB interprets *ho Theos alēthēs estin* as "God is trustworthy" (3:33) and the NIV as "God is truthful." The NAB conveys *ho aph' heautou lalōn tēn doxan tēn idian zētei: ho de zētōn tēn doxan tou pempsantos auton houtos alēthēs estin kai adikia en autō ouk estin* as "whoever seeks the glory of the one who sent him is truthful, and there is no wrong in him" (7:18). The NIV translates *ho pempsas me alēthēs estin* as "he who sent me is reliable" (8:26).

We advance the argument further by drawing attention to other cases where the Gospel conveys the idea of the utmost integrity by utilizing cognates of *alētheia*. To begin with, even expressions that have traditionally been interpreted as true v. false statements are not necessarily so. Jesus himself recognizes that John the Baptist "was the lamp that was burning and was shining and you were willing to rejoice for a while in his light" (5:35). Hence, the Evangelist's assessment of Jesus as "the true [*to alēthinon*] Light" (1:9) may not mean that the *true* light of Jesus implies that John the Baptist's light was *false*. It is just that John the Baptist was a mortal man who died and only a few could enjoy his flickering light, and only for a while; Jesus is the eternal Word and, as such, is the enduring Light (1:5) who enlightens everyone (1:9). In the context of the debate over the food that *perishes* v. the food/drink that *endures* to eternal life (6:27–54), Jesus's statement *hē gar sarx mou alēthēs estin brōsis, kai to haima mou alēthēs estin posis* (6:55) may well be interpreted "For My flesh is reliable food, and My blood is reliable drink."

Moreover, Jesus's integrity is evident in his own *amēn amēn* sayings. Not only is the term *amēn* itself rooted in the OT *'āmēn*, a cognate

---

9. Along these lines Kuyper, "Grace and Truth," 17–18.
10. These examples are available in Aalen, "'Truth,'" 3–23.

of *'ĕmet* = *alētheia*, but also many of these *amēn amēn* sayings come true in a rather tangible way already within Jesus's earthly life span,[11] or soon afterwards.[12] This makes the rest of Jesus's *amēn amēn* accounts[13] and his other predictions (cf. 16:4, etc.) more credible for the audience. The Evangelist recognizes the reliability of Jesus by commenting that Jesus's words are fulfilled (18:9, 32; cf. 2:19, 22). Jesus is also recognized as a reliable witness by John the Baptist (3:32–33). Jesus himself invites others to test his integrity by announcing events in advance (13:19; 14:29; cf. 16:33).

Furthermore, Jesus's integrity is evident because one can certainly rely on him. Some of Jesus's predictions are fulfilled within the Gospel narrative (cf. 4:50/4:51–53; 16:22–23/20:19–20 and 21:12; 16:32/18:36; 12:32/19:20; 6:62/20:17). Readers would recognize others as being fulfilled later (e.g., 4:21). Jesus fulfills expectations (cf. 1:38–39; 5:6–9; 11:23/11:43 and 12:1; 14:16/20:22; 14:18/20:19f.; 16:33/14:27 and 20:19, 21, 26). Jesus is faithful to the mission (4:34; 5:30; 6:38–40; cf. 7:17; 7:18; 9:31), the Scriptures (3:29; 12:38; 13:18; 15:25; 17:12; 19:24; 19:36), and the Father (4:34, 5:36; 17:4; 19:28). Jesus's integrity is manifested in the Christ v. the devil controversy (8:44–55; 14:30).

Finally, adherence to *alētheia* is depicted not in terms of "absolute reality" but as a matter of ethical integrity—whether with reference to Jesus Christ, Nathanael the Israelite, John the Baptist, or even Pontius Pilate.[14] The category of *alētheia* is the opposite of *dolos* "deceit" (1:47); *adikia*, "unrighteousness" (7:18); *arneomai*, "deny" (1:20; 13:38; 18:25, 27); *hamartia*, "sin" (8:46); and *aitia*, "guilt" (18:38; 19:4).

Second, Bultmann's (and others') tendency to assign the meaning of "faithfulness" to *'ĕmet* has been much criticized for pressing the supposed fundamental/etymological meaning of "firmness" for the root *'mt* far beyond what is legitimate. It has also been argued that fundamen-

---

11. 5:25 (raising Lazarus from the dead); 6:26 (feeding of five thousand); 13:21 (betrayal by Judas, the son of Simon Iscariot).

12. 1:51 (angels); 12:24 (multiplication of disciples); 13:38 (Peter's denial); 16:20 (joy of the disciples, cf. 20:20); 21:18 (Peter's martyrdom).

13. 3:3, 5, 11; 5:19, 24, 25 (besides Lazarus); 6:32, 47, 53, 8:34, 51, 58; 10:1, 7; 13:16, 20; 14:12; 16:23.

14. Cf. also Jesus's appraisal of honesty of the Samaritan woman, "You have *kalōs* said, 'I have no husband'... this you have said *alēthes*" (4:17–18).

tally *ʾĕmet* depicts God as intrinsically true.[15] This has made meanings *stemming* from "being intrinsically true"—such as "credible," "reliable," "trustworthy,"[16] "veracious," etc.—rather proper.[17] Besides, cognates of *alētheia* cover the same scope of meanings as *ʾĕmet*.[18] Hence, one may allow any of the OT meanings for *ʾĕmet* for cognates of *alētheia* in the Gospel. Particularly, a translation for *ḥesed weʾĕmet*, *(hē) charis kai (hē) alētheia* may legitimately denote "graciousness and integrity." This drastically increases chances for cognates of *alētheia* throughout the Gospel to correspond with a meaning of *alētheia* in John 1:14, a factor that undermines Bultmann's assertion.

Third, we should observe that translating *ʾĕmet* with *alēthinos*, a cognate of *alētheia*, was considered perfectly appropriate by translators of Exodus 34:6 LXX. In fact, the LXX/OG regularly translates creedal attributes[19] of the *ʾmn* family with *alētheia*. Remarkably, the *ʾmn* family includes not only *ʾĕmet* but also *ʾĕmûnāʰ*.[20] The term *ḥesed* is employed together with *ʾĕmet* in thirty-three verses[21] and with *ʾĕmûnāʰ* in eleven verses.[22] In the LXX/OG, when it comes to the pair *ḥesed* and *ʾĕmet* (*ʾĕmûnāʰ*), the term *ʾĕmet* (*ʾĕmûnāʰ*)—the creedal attribute of the character of God—is always translated with a cognate of *alētheia*.[23] Even when *ḥesed*, *ʾĕmûnāʰ*, and *ʾĕmet* appear in the same verse (Ps 40:11), both *ʾĕmet and ʾĕmûnāʰ* are translated with *alētheia*. Apparently, *alētheia* was deemed to be perfectly capable of conveying the sense of

---

15. Barr, "'Faith' and 'Truth.'"

16. It is exactly *ʾĕmet*—a quality of God's character—that makes people *trust* God.

17. The general range of meanings upheld for *ʾĕmet* is much greater, see elsewhere in our study.

18. Cf. *alētheia* (AnLex, 00233; L&N, 00238; UBSDict) and *ʾĕmet* (Jepsen, "*ʾĕmet*"; Quell, "*alētheia*"; TWOT, 0116).

19. Throughout this study, by "creedal attributes" we mean "attributes of the character of God mentioned in the creed (Exod 34:6 and analogues)."

20. When used of God the difference between the terms is virtually nonexistent (Jepsen, "*ʾĕmet*," 319–20).

21. Gen 24:27, 49; 32:11; 47:29; Exod 34:6; Josh 2:12, 14; 2 Sam 2:6; 15:20; 1 Kgs 3:6; Pss 25:10; 26:3; 40:11, 12; 57:4; 57:11; 61:8; 69:14; 85:11; 86:15; 89:15; 108:5; 115:1; 117:2; 138:2; Prov 3:3; 14:22; 16:6; 20:28; Isa 16:5; Hos 4:1; Mic 7:20; Zech 7:9.

22. Ps 36:6; 40:11; 88:12; 89:2, 3, 25, 34, 50; 92:3; 98:3; 100:5.

23. It is uncertain whether *ḥesed* and *ʾĕmet* denote creedal attributes of the character of God in Proverb 3:3, 16:16.

creedal *'ĕmet* (*'ĕmûnāʰ*) in the LXX/OG.[24] Emanuel Tov rightly concluded, "if a certain Greek word represents a given Hebrew word in most of its occurrences, it has become almost by implication a mere symbol for that Hebrew word in the translation."[25] This certainly is the case with *alētheia*, which, therefore, symbolizes all the connotations of *'ĕmet*.

These considerations completely invalidate Bultmann's argument. It is only natural on the part of the Evangelist to translate *'ĕmet* in Exod 34:6 with *alētheia* in John 1:14, 17.

Piper's Argument from a Stylistic Variation

Our study argues that understanding *plērēs charitos kai alētheias* as the Evangelist's stylistic variation of the Septuagint's *polueleos kai alēthinos* is not a viable option. In the LXX/OG the term *polueleos* is used exclusively of God. This restriction is observed in documents translated from Hebrew and documents that originate in Greek, over a vast geographical area,[26] by a broad variety of authors,[27] and during the vast time span of the third century B.C.E.[28]–50 C.E.[29] The Evangelist—a writer well acquainted with the LXX/OG—must have been aware of this restriction, hence *charis* is not likely to be a stylistic variation of *(polu)eleos* from the viewpoint of the established practice of the LXX/OG. Moreover, cognates of *eleos* never occur in the Gospel. There is no ground to maintain that *charis* is a stylistic variation of *(polu)eleos*. Furthermore, all four

---

24. It is fascinating to read statements like Kuyper's: "of the 92 instances of *'ĕmet*, the Septuagint translated it *alētheia* (truth) 86 times and *pistis* (faith) only six times. A word of the same root, *'ĕmûnāʰ*, is rendered *alētheia* 21 times and *pistis* 19 times.... However, at the beginning of our century, biblical scholarship discovered that *'ĕmet* was not truth as an abstract thought, as found in Greek literature; instead, *'ĕmet* was used to describe a relationship in life. Consequently today our lexicons offer faithfulness, or steadfastness, for this word" (Kuyper, "Grace and Truth," 9). One is only left to wonder just how "at the beginning of our century, biblical scholarship discovered" the meaning that the rather contemporary LXX/OG translators got entirely wrong.

25. Tov, *Greek and Hebrew Bible*, 90. Tov particularly focuses on *kābôd/doxa*.

26. As far as Alexandria, Egypt. See Greenspoon, "Versions, Ancient (Greek)," 794; Anderson, "Third Maccabees," 452.

27. The Pentateuch, Neh 9:17; Pss 85:5; 85:15; 102:8; 144:8 OG; Joel 2:13; Jonah 4:2; *Pr. Man.*; 3 Macc 6:9.

28. The translation of the Torah (Greenspoon, "Versions, Ancient (Greek)," 794).

29. 3 Macc and *Pr. Man.* could have been produced anywhere from ca. 200 B.C.E. to 50 C.E. See Anderson, "Third Maccabees," 452; Charlesworth, "Prayer of Manasseh," 500.

occurrences of *charis* in the Gospel—John 1:14, 16, 16, 17—come in a tight sequence. This makes it unlikely that *charis* is a stylistic variation.

Hanson's Argument from a Hypothetical Version of Exodus 34:6

Hanson postulates that "John must have had *plērēs charitos kai alētheias* in his Greek version of Exod. 34:6."[30] First, this is unverifiable.[31] Second, it is a weak hypothesis. The critical Göttingen LXX confirms that every known variant of Exodus 34:6 features *polueleos*, not *charis*.[32] This unanimity in translating polueleos for *rab-ḥesed* undermines Hanson's proposal of a translation that might have read otherwise. Third, it is the Septuagint that is the source of a large majority of the Evangelist's OT quotations, not only of the three quotations that agree entirely with the Septuagint (10:34; 12:38; 19:24), but also—with varying degrees of certainty—of the other Gospel's quotations.[33] It is not likely that the Evangelist momentarily switched to some other translation only in his quotations of Exodus 34:6. Fourth, even if a detached collection of texts often referred to by the early church[34] had ever existed,[35] Exodus 34:6—as not expressly Messianic—would not likely have been among them. Such evidence, therefore, discourages one from envisioning the

---

30. Hanson, *Grace and Truth*, 6. Hanson finds this argument convincing and applicable generally. He writes, "We may . . . reasonably conjecture that John had in his Greek version of Is. 53.4 *airei* where LXX has *pherei*" (Hanson, *Prophetic Gospel*, 33). Further, he states, "It is possible . . . that John had *thura* in his Greek of Ps. 118.20" (ibid., 33; the OG text has *pulē*, not *thura*).

31. Researchers occasionally advance a thesis that is immune to criticism. See, for example, Charles Goodwin's appeal to lost sources, the freedom or the defective memory of the Evangelist, "This study of John's use of his only explicitly acknowledged source shows that he quoted it *rarely, loosely*, and *confusedly*, often *conflating* two or more passages, *distorting* their *meaning*, and *hiding their context*. We may suspect him of incorporating *alien elements* into them. He appears to have quoted *from memory*, and the attentive reader has seen how elusive are tricks his memory could play . . . It is reasonable to suppose that he would treat his unacknowledged sources in the same manner" (Goodwin, "How Did John Treat His Sources?" 62, 73).

32. Exod GLXX, 375.

33. 1:23; 2:17; 6:31, 45; 7:38; 12:15; 15:25; 19:36. See Menken, *Quotations*, 205.

34. Such as Zech 9–14; Isa 6:1—9:7; 40:1–11; 52:13—53:12; Pss 69, 22, 34, 41.

35. The quotation in 19:37 is sometimes *suggested* as coming from a current early Christian translation of a Hebrew text instead of LXX. For the discussion see Menken, *Quotations*, 168–70, 205.

Evangelist using a hypothetical "Greek version of Exod 34:6" that differs from the Septuagint.

Montgomery's Argument from the Syriac Versions and Christian Palestinian Dialect

Scholars frequently appeal to an earlier study by James A. Montgomery.[36] Boismard points out that "although the word *ḥsd* is usually translated by the Septuagint as *eleos*, its Greek equivalent is rather *charis*, as J. A. Montgomery has well shown."[37] Brown agrees that "J. A. Montgomery . . . has shown that *charis* is an excellent translation for *ḥesed*."[38] Evans states, "J. A. Montgomery . . . has shown that *charis* is a perfectly legitimate translation for *ḥsd*."[39] Zimmerli appeals to J. A. Montgomery in concluding that "the later translators with increasing firmness connect *ḥesed* and *charis*."[40] Hanson refers to "an article by J. A. Montgomery in which he points out that *charis* in the New Testament is regularly translated by *ʾḥsd* in the Syriac."[41]

Our first concern is the texts of the Syriac versions. The earliest gospel text in Syriac was, perhaps, the Diatessaron (ca. 170 C.E.), but no copy of it is extant.[42] The Diatessaron was followed by the Old Syriac version (third or fourth century C.E.).[43] The Old Syriac is useless in evaluating relationships between *ḥesed* and *charis*, as it contains neither the OT nor John 1:14-17. The Syriac versions containing both the Old and most parts of the NT are the Peshitta (ca. fourth or fifth century C.E.), Philoxeniana (507/508 C.E.), and Harklensis (515/516 C.E.).[44] Remarkably, Montgomery does not make clear which Syriac version he is referring to. One can only guess from his remarks dispersed here and there. For example, he writes in one place that "the Syriac translates

---

36. Montgomery, "Hebrew *Hesed*."
37. Boismard, *Moses or Jesus*, 96.
38. R. Brown, *John (I-XII)*, 14.
39. Evans, *Word and Glory*, 81 n. 2.
40. Zimmerli, "*charis* (OT)," n. 65.
41. Hanson, "John I. 14-18 and Exodus XXXIV," 93.
42. See W. Petersen, "Diatessaron," 190; Brock, "Versions, Ancient (Syriac)," 796.
43. NA^{27}, 65*.
44. Ibid.; Brock, "Versions, Ancient (Syriac)," 799.

... at John 1:14, 16, 17, Romans 1:5, 7; 3:24."[45] The earliest Syriac version containing Romans is the Peshitta.[46] He states elsewhere that a "translation has survived here in the late Philoxenian revision."[47] This observation indicates that Montgomery considered the Peshitta and the Philoxeniana for his own research.

Our second concern involves the principles employed in conveying the text of the Greek Gospels into Syriac. By its very design, the Diatessaron cannot be understood as a translation faithfully reflecting the tradition of the Gospel. Tatian harmonized discrepancies found in his source gospels.[48] The Diatessaron only fell out of favor in the fifth century when it was replaced by the Peshitta.[49] But the influence of the Diatessaron upon the gospel text in Syriac was all-pervasive, even when a fourfold gospel form of the Old Syriac versions was adopted. It reveals itself in harmonistic readings and in other variants with theological tendencies deriving from Tatian's views.[50] Hence, the warning of NA[27] does not take one by surprise:

> The various Syriac versions ... are characterized by different translation principles, from a very free, idiomatically correct rendering at the beginning, to a degree of fidelity to the Greek text so extreme that it violates natural Syriac idiom. Any evaluation of these versions as witnesses to the Greek text must bear this in mind.[51]

With these two observations on the Syriac texts and their principles of translation in mind, we will consider Montgomery's argument.

In a five-page article, Montgomery argues that the "Greek *charis* was a happy find for translation" of *ḥesed*. The author adduces two pieces of evidence to support the argument.

First, he appeals to the Syriac:

> The Syriac [translates *ḥesed*] with ... *taibūthā*, ... with the radical meaning of "goodness." With the same word the Syriac

---

45. Montgomery, "Hebrew *Hesed*," 100.
46. NA[27], 66*.
47. Montgomery, "Hebrew *Hesed*," 100.
48. Birdsall, "Versions, Ancient," 790; Brock, "Versions, Ancient (Syriac)," 796–99; W. Petersen, "Diatessaron," 190.
49. Brock, "Versions, Ancient (Syriac)," 799.
50. Birdsall, "Versions, Ancient," 790.
51. NA[27], 65–66*.

translates *charis* in the New Testament, e.g. at John 1:14, 16, 17, Romans 1:5, 7; 3:24.[52]

Second, the author refers to the so-called Christian Syro-Palestinian dialect:

> There is another dialectical quarter of the Aramaic where the word *ḥesed* in the Hebrew sense and = *charis* survived. This is so-called Christian Syro-Palestinian dialect, the dialect in particular of the colony of Christians who fled across Jordan at Vespasian's invasion (Eusebius, H. E., iii:5), with later an emigration into Egypt, where their literary remains have been found. This legacy consists of extensive lectionaries and other ecclesiastical material. In these scanty remains Syriac *ḥasdā* appears to be generally used in translating New Testament *charis*, viz. at Luke 1:30; 2:40, John 1:14, 16 (the last case reproducing the Hebrew of Exodus 34:6), Romans 12:3, Galatians 6:18, Philippians 4:23, Col. 4:18 (the last three cases expressing "the grace be with you"), Hebrews 4:16 . . . Luke 1:28.[53]

Finally, Montgomery concludes:

> What bearing the above rather philological treatise may have on the understanding of grace in the New Testament must be left to qualified students. But the warning may be given that the word is not to be understood primarily from the Greek but from its lively Semitic background; Greek *charis* was a happy find for translation, but it was not the whole of *ḥesed*. Every word has its own personality; a translation is but a mask.[54]

Montgomery's study deserves a thorough critique. His argument from the translation into the Christian Palestinian Dialect should be disregarded from the outset. It cannot be used in the discussion of the principles of the translation of the OT *ḥesed* into the NT *charis*. The translation of the OT into Christian Palestinian Aramaic was made entirely from the Greek.[55] Therefore, from now on this study will deal only with Montgomery's appeal to the Syriac versions.[56]

---

52. Montgomery, "Hebrew *Hesed*," 99–100.
53. Ibid., 100.
54. Ibid., 101.
55. Brock, "Versions, Ancient (Syriac)," 799.
56. One may note, however, that had Montgomery's appeal to the Christian Palestinian Dialect contributed anything to his argument our same critique of Montgomery's

Investigation of Montgomery's argument assures that it does not demonstrate that *charis* was a suitable translation for *ḥesed* by the time of the Evangelist. To demonstrate that "*charis* was a happy find for translation" for *ḥesed* would require the following, at least: 1) to demonstrate that *charis is* a translation for *ḥesed*, 2) to establish that *charis may* serve as a faithful translation for *ḥesed*, and 3) to observe a proper methodology while projecting the findings in documents that postdate the Gospel onto the time of the Evangelist. Montgomery's study meets none of the three requirements. This makes the article's conclusion on the appropriateness of translating of *ḥesed* with *charis* unacceptable.

First, Montgomery's study does not demonstrate that *charis is* a translation for *ḥesed*. Montgomery's conclusion that the "Greek *charis* was a happy find for translation" is fascinating. One can but pause and wonder, "What translation?" None of the OT references in the article gives an example of *ḥesed* translated into *charis*. In a sheer contradiction to the title and the conclusion of the article, *none* of the article's OT references to *ḥesed* are translated with *charis* in the LXX/OG. Neither of the article's NT references rendering *charis* is demonstrated by the author to be a translation from the OT *ḥesed*. Therefore, Montgomery's study does not demonstrate that *charis* is a translation for *ḥesed*.

Second, neither does Montgomery's study demonstrate that *charis may* serve as a faithful translation for *ḥesed*. The author observes that both *ḥesed* and *charis* were translated by *taibūthā* in the Syriac. From this observation the writer concludes that the "Greek *charis* was a happy find for translation" for *ḥesed*. But this conclusion does not really follow from the observation; the logic of the argument is invalid.

An abstract example may clarify the flaw in the article's logic. Suppose that one language uses the term "dog." Another language employs the term "cat." Still another language translates both "dog" in the first language and "cat" in the second language with the term "animal." The third language makes a valid generalized translation because both "dog" and "cat" are animals. But from this translation it does not follow that "cat" in the second language is a faithful translation for "dog" in the first language. The translation of both "dog" and "cat" into "animal" by the third language could have been caused by a variety of factors. The three languages might have belonged to different domains, which

---

appeal to the Syriac versions would have also applied to his appeal to the Christian Palestinian Dialect.

varied in their perception of what "dog," "cat," and "animal" were. The third language itself might have had no equivalents for "dog" and "cat." The local authorities of the third language's area could have issued restrictions on the usage of the terms "dog" and "cat" because they were totems of the local tribes. The translator might not have known the languages well enough to understand the difference between "dog" and "cat." The sponsor of the translation could have been allergic to dogs and cats. Whatever the initial reasons for translating both "dog" and "cat" as "animal," on the basis of such translation one cannot make the conclusion that "dog" and "cat" are the same animal.

Syriac and Greek were languages of different domains. This already makes one especially cautious about drawing any conclusions. There are also too many reasons that might have influenced such translation into the Syriac. The core meaning of the term *taibūthā* is "goodness."[57] Rendering *ḥesed* as "goodness" in the Syriac does not quite seem to fit today's understanding of what *ḥesed* denoted. What if the choice of the terminology of "goodness" was determined by the local traditions?[58] What if the Syriac did not have terminology nuanced enough to differentiate *ḥesed* and *charis*?

The case is not made any more certain with the translation of both the Hebrew *ḥesed* and the Greek *charis* with the Syriac *taibūthā*. Translating both "lovingkindness" and "grace"[59] with "goodness" might have been a legitimate generalized translation. Generic "goodness" may cover both terms, but by no means does it equate "lovingkindness" and "grace." Nor does it with any certainty demonstrate that "grace" may serve as a faithful translation for "lovingkindness." In dealing with the ancient versions, the exegetical translation could be helpful if it was done by making the generalized more specific or by clarificatory additions,[60] but neither is the case with a generic Syriac *taibūthā* rendered for both *ḥesed* and *charis*. Therefore, Montgomery's study does not demonstrate that *charis* may serve as a faithful translation for *ḥesed*.

---

57. Kiraz, *Lexical Tools*, 7 entry 123. Montgomery recognizes this "radical meaning of 'goodness'" for the Syriac *taibūthā* (Montgomery, "Hebrew *Ḥesed*," 100).

58. The orthography of Syriac is based on Standard Literary Aramaic, while its lexicon and grammar are primarily that of the city of Edessa (Kaufman, "Languages (Aramaic)," 175).

59. As in NASB.

60. Birdsall, "Versions, Ancient," 793.

Third, Montgomery's study projects the findings in documents that postdate the Gospel onto the time of the Evangelist *without* following any suitable methodology. Projection of the later sources onto earlier stages is not impossible if properly done.[61] However, Montgomery's study fails to meet the criteria of the methodology. The Syriac versions containing both the OT and NT (fourth to sixth century C.E.) are too late for evaluating the Gospel (ca. first century C.E.). Besides, the Syriac versions could have known the "John 1:14 v. Exod 34:6 LXX" terminological disparity and already tried correcting it.

Thus, Montgomery's argument from the Syriac versions or the Christian Palestinian dialect certainly cannot and does not prove that *charis* was a suitable translation for *ḥesed* by the time of the Evangelist. Accordingly, the appeal on the part of some scholars—Boismard, Brown, Evans, Hanson, and Zimmerli—to Montgomery's study has no credibility.

Boismard's Argument from Modern Comparative Linguistics

Boismard appeals to comparative modern linguistics:

> The equivalence between *rb* and *plērēs* . . . is less obvious, but nevertheless real. The Hebrew adjective means 'numerous, great, powerful', but with important nuances. The translation 'abounding in, full of' is often demanded by the sense of the passage. This is precisely what is adopted by recent French translations of the Bible (TOB and BJ) in Exod 34:6; they translate by 'riche en bonté et en fidélité' (BJ), or 'plein de fidélité et de loyauté' (TOB). Ps 86:15 takes up the same phrase and the BJ translates by 'plein d'amour et de vérité' (full of love and truth). Why could the evangelist not have had the same reaction when translating the Hebrew text of Exod 34:6?[62]

But the twentieth century French translator's vision is not convincing in evaluating the plausibility of a translation from OT Hebrew into Koine Greek. In the LXX/OG, *plērēs* never serves as a translation for the *rb* of the Hebrew Scriptures. Besides, the French translators may have been

---

61. See Evans's four criteria for evaluating the potential relevance of concepts found in a document that postdates the NT writing in question (Evans, *Word and Glory*, 18–19).

62. Boismard, *Moses or Jesus*, 96–97.

aware of the "Exod 34:6 v. John 1:14" terminological disparity and tried to match it. When discussing a translation into Greek, the vocabulary and practices of languages other than Greek generally do not convince. As Ll. J. M. Bebb puts it, "there are no distinctions of gender in Armenian, no neuter in Arabic, no passive voice in Bohairic, no article in Latin, and therefore these versions afford no help where readings involving such points are being discussed."[63]

Boismard himself characteristically demonstrates the uncertainty of the modern comparative linguistics approach. Commenting on "plein de fidélité et de loyauté," (full of fidelity and loyalty [TOB]), the author simultaneously approves the "plein" part, as it fits his argument, and disapproves the "de fidélité et de loyauté" part. He claims, "The translation of the two nouns, especially in the order in which they are given, is unsatisfactory!"[64] Boismard's attempt only demonstrates how insecure and subjective any argumentation from modern comparative linguistics is.

Brown's Argument from Unfaithful Usage

Brown claims, "John's use of Scripture is often not faithful to LXX."[65] Whether Brown's assertion is generally correct or not, it does not make a particular case for the unfaithful usage of Exodus 34:6 LXX in John 1:14. Moreover, recent studies on OT quotations in the Gospel have shown that the Evangelist borrows from the LXX/OG rather accurately.[66] Furthermore, if by rendering "glory . . . full of grace and truth" in 1:14 the Evangelist alludes to Exodus 34:6 LXX, then the writer has a compelling reason to follow the text of the LXX exactly. According to the Hebrew account of Exodus, Moses might not have even been dealing with the glory of the Lord, but, instead, his "goodness."[67] Therefore, Brown's reasoning that "John's use of Scripture is often not faithful to LXX" is not sufficient ground for the Evangelist's deviation from the LXX in this particular instance.

63. Bebb, "Versions," as quoted in Birdsall, "Versions, Ancient," 792.
64. Boismard, *Moses or Jesus*, 96 n. 16.
65. R. Brown, *John (I–XII)*, 14; see also Hübner, *OT Quotations in the NT*, 1104.
66. Menken, *Quotations*, 205–12.
67. Exodus LXX generally exhibits a preference for the term *doxa*. Cf. *gāʾôn*, "excellence" (Exod 15:7); *tahillāʰ*, "praise" (Exod 15:11); and *ṭôb*, "goodness," (Exod 33:19) all rendered with *doxa*.

Dodd's Argument from Hellenistic Judaism

Dodd argues that "in the later stages of the LXX, and in Hellenistic Judaism after the Septuagintal period, *charis* came to be preferred to *eleos* as a rendering of *ḥesed*."[68] However, as Harris points out, "in the four texts in question (Esth. 2.9; 2.17; Ecclus 7.33; 40.17) *charis* means either the favor a woman finds in the eyes of another (her attractiveness), or the kindness and bounty shown by the wealthy to the needy. In these senses it is unlikely to be found in conjunction with *alētheia*"[69] and with God, which is the case in both Exodus 34:6 and John 1:14. Therefore, Dodd's argument from Hellenistic Jewish practices—as it stands—is hardly convincing.

Hanson's Argument from Feeble Translation

Hanson reasons that it is "perfectly possible [that the Evangelist] deliberately translated the phrase from the Hebrew himself"[70] because "the LXX renders the phrase [of Hebrew Exod 34:6] with *polueleos kai alēthinos*, a notably feebler translation."[71] Elsewhere, Hanson observes,

> If it is correct to say that *plērēs charitos kai alētheias* in John i.14 renders *wərab-ḥesed we'ĕmet* in Exod. xxxiv. 6, then *rab* is translated by *plērēs*. For such a translation I can find no parallel anywhere else. From this, however, I would conclude, not that the equivalence is mistaken but that the author of the Fourth Gospel has translated the phrase for himself direct from Hebrew.[72]

These conclusions are not only unverifiable, but also contradictory and circular. Besides, however it looks from Hanson's twentieth century perspective, the simple "feebleness" of *polueleos kai alēthinos* could hardly convince the Evangelist to translate *wərab-ḥesed we'ĕmet* with *plērēs charitos kai alētheias* instead. The writer had compelling reasons to precisely follow the Septuagint. Not only does the Septuagint version of the book of Exodus emphasize *doxa*, but any deviation from the recognizable Septuagint formula *polueleos kai alēthinos* would have

---

68. Dodd, *Interpretation*, 175.
69. Harris, *Prologue and Gospel*, 66.
70. Hanson, *Grace and Truth*, 6; also, *Prophetic Gospel*, 335.
71. Hanson, *Grace and Truth*, 113 n. 1.
72. Hanson, "John I. 14–18 and Exodus XXXIV," 93.

blurred the allusion. These factors should have outweighed the alleged "feebleness" of the Septuagint's *polueleos kai alēthinos*.

Defense of the Proposal that *plērēs charitos kai alētheias (hē charis kai hē alētheia)* Is the Evangelist's Translation of the Creed from Hebrew

Several scholars propose that *plērēs charitos kai alētheias* is the Evangelist's own translation of *wərab-ḥesed weʾĕmet*.[73] Attractive as it is, this suggestion poses three major problems. First, neither is *rab* translated with *plērēs* in the LXX/OG, nor is *ḥesed* conveyed with *charis* anywhere in the LXX. Admittedly, *wərab-ḥesed weʾĕmet* is translated variably already in the Septuagint.[74] But can *plērēs charitos kai alētheias* serve as a legitimate translation for *wərab-ḥesed weʾĕmet*? Second, *wərab-ḥesed weʾĕmet* is a *part* of the creed—*yhwh ʾēl raḥûm wəḥannûn ʾerek ʾappayim wərab-ḥesed weʾĕmet* (Exod 34:6). The creed contains attributes *other* than *wərab-ḥesed weʾĕmet*. Various attributes are *linked* by a *w*. Particularly, the attributes *wərab-ḥesed weʾĕmet* are *preceded* and *linked* by *w*. Why and how would the Evangelist "cut" just the two attributes—*wərab-ḥesed weʾĕmet*—out of the whole creed and "paste" it into John 1:14? Third, the Evangelist writes in Greek for an audience that speaks Greek and is familiar with the Septuagint. The Evangelist generally uses the Septuagint. But the rendering *plērēs charitos kai alētheias* offers a reading different from the Septuagint's *polueleos kai alēthinos* of Exodus 34:6. This rather *blurs* the suggested allusion. Why would the Evangelist bother to make a new translation from Hebrew?

plērēs charitos kai alētheias Is a Valid Translation of *wərab-ḥesed weʾĕmet*

Our research demonstrates that if one follows practices customary to the LXX/OG, then the translation of *wərab-ḥesed weʾĕmet* with *plērēs charitos kai alētheias* is highly unlikely. The creed first rendered in Exod 34:6 is one of the most cited, alluded to and echoed passages in the OT

---

73. So Boismard, *Moses or Jesus*, 96; Hanson, *Grace and Truth*, 6; Hanson, *Prophetic Gospel*, 21; Montgomery, "Hebrew *Ḥesed*," 100–101.

74. So Schoneveld, "Torah in the Flesh," 83 n. 13.

and Pseudepigrapha.[75] In the LXX/OG the phrase *rab-ḥesed* is translated with *polueleos, to plēthos tou eleous,* and *to plēthos tēs dikaiosunēs,* but never with *plērēs* or *charis.* Our challenge then is to demonstrate that *plērēs charitos kai alētheias* can serve as a legitimate translation for *wərab-ḥesed we'ĕmet.*

The Evangelist Can Legitimately Translate *rab* with *plērēs*

There are about six hundred occurrences of the term *rb* in the OT. The critical Göttingen LXX/OG does not attest to a single case of translating *rb* with *plērēs.*[76] Our study argues that the Evangelist can still legitimately translate *rab* with *plērēs.*

There are numerous factors that speak in favor of the legitimacy of translating *rab* with *plērēs.* First, there was no *unanimity* in translating *rab-ḥesed* on the part of LXX/OG interpreters who used *polu*[77] or *plēthos*[78] to convey *rab.* Second, in the OT, the extent of God's *ḥesed* and *'ĕmet* (cognates) was expressed by terms *other* than *rab,* particularly by cognates of *haggādōl,* "great."[79] Third, the extent of God's *ḥesed* was emphasized by various means. The *plural* form of *ḥesed* was used.[80] The extent of God's *ḥesed* and *'ĕmet* (cognates) was expressed *indirectly.* Israel asks Joseph for an enormous favor: "deal with me in *ḥesed*[81] and

---

75. Num 14:18; Neh 9:17 (cf. 9:31); Pss 86:15; 103:8; 145:8; Joel 2:13; Jonah 4:2. The creed is alluded to at 2 Chr 30:9; Ps 77:9–10; in abbreviated form at Pss 111:4; 116:5; and possibly also at Ps 112:4. Cf. Nah 1:3; Deut 7:9–10; 2 Kgs 13:23; Ps 112:4; Isa 30:18; 48:9; 54:10; Jer 32:18; Lam 3:22–23; Hos 2:19–20; Mic 7:18; Sir 2:11; Wis 3:9; 4:15; 15:1; *Pr. Man.* 7; *Pss. Sol.* 9:8–11; *T. Jud.* 19:3; *T. Zeb.* 9:7; *Jos. Asen.* 11:10; Ps.-Philo 13:1; 35:3; 4 Ezra 7:33, 134; CD 2:4; 1QH 16:16. See Bauckham, *Jude, 2 Peter,* 312, 321; Dunn, *Romans 9–16,* 552; Johannes Horst, "*makrothumia,*" 4:376 n. 18; Kselman, "Grace (OT)," 1086.

76. This makes claims like Dumbrell's, "Note the equivalence between *rab* and *plērēs*" (Dumbrell, "Grace and Truth," 53 n. 3), rather unwarranted, to say the least.

77. Exod 34:6; Num 14:18; Neh 9:17; Ps 86:5; Ps 86:15; Ps 103:8; Joel 2:13; Jonah 4:2.

78. Neh 13:22; Pss 5:8; 69:14; 106:7; 106:45; Lam 3:32; Isa 63:7.

79. Gen 19:19; Num 14:19; 1 Kgs 3:6; 2 Chr 1:8; Pss 57:11; 86:13; 108:5; 145:8.

80. Gen 32:11; 2 Chr 6:42; Pss 17:7; 25:6; 89:2, 50; 106:7, 45; 107:43; 119:41, Isa 55:3; 63:7; 63:7; Lam 3:22, 32.

81. Throughout this study, the term *ḥesed* is inserted into a biblical text in English if this occurrence of *ḥesed* is 1) rendered in the singular, and 2) translated with *eleos* in the singular. Exceptions to this pattern are given following "/ " in the text.

ʾĕmet.[82] Please do not bury me in Egypt" (Gen 47:29). A servant acknowledges the source of the success of the long journey: "Blessed be the Lord, . . . who has not forsaken His ḥesed and His ʾĕmet toward my master; as for me, the Lord has guided me in the way to the house of my master's brothers" (Gen 24:27). Jacob appreciates the multiplication of his family and possessions: "I am unworthy of all the ḥăsādîm and of all the ʾĕmet which You have shown to Your servant; for with my staff only I crossed this Jordan, and now I have become two companies" (Gen 32:11). The extent of God's ḥesed and ʾĕmet (cognates) was conveyed by *cosmic imagery*; they extend to the heavens/skies/clouds,[83] the ends of the earth (Ps 98:2–3). Isaiah proclaims regarding the Lord: "For the mountains may be removed and the hills may shake, But My ḥesed will not be removed from you" (Isa 54:10). Indeed, "The earth is full [mlʾ/plērēs] of the ḥesed of the Lord" (Ps 33:5; 119:64). The extent of God's ḥesed and ʾĕmet (cognates) was expressed by *a virtually infinite scope of time*, such as ləʾelep dôr, "to a thousandth generation,"[84] ləʿôlām, "forever,"[85] and ʿôlām, "everlasting."[86] To describe the extent of God's ḥesed, characters of the Scripture often appeal to either *multiple events* or a *generous scope of time*. Moses prays, "Pardon . . . the iniquity of this people according to the greatness of Your ḥesed, just as You also have forgiven this people, from Egypt even until now" (Num 14:19). The leader reassures the people that "God will keep with you

---

82. Throughout this study, the terms ʾĕmet/ʾĕmûnāʰ inserted into a biblical text in English indicate that this occurrence of ʾĕmet/ʾĕmûnāʰ is 1) rendered in the singular, and 2) translated by *alētheia* in the singular. Exceptions to this pattern are given following "/" in the text.

83. Ps 36:6; 57:4, 11; 89:3. Cf. 1 Kgs 8:23; Neh 1:5; 2 Chr 6:14; Pss 103:11; 136:5, 26.

84. Deut 7:9. God keeps his ḥesed to thousands (Exod 20:6; 34:7; Deut 5:10; Jer 32:18).

85. Ps 61:8; 89:1, 2, 29.

86. Isa 55:3. For ʾĕmet cf. Ps 117:2. God's ḥesed is ʿôlām, "everlasting" (1 Chr 16:34, 41; 2 Chr 5:13; 7:3, 6; 20:21; Ezra 3:11; Pss 100:5; 106:1; 107:1; 118:1, 2, 3, 4, 29; 136:1, 2, 3, 4, 5, 6, 7, 8, 9, 10, 11, 12, 13, 14, 15, 16, 17, 18, 19, 20, 21, 22, 23, 24, 25, 26; 138:8; Isa 54:8; Jer 33:11). The ḥesed of God is mēʿôlām wəʾad-ʿôlām, "from everlasting to everlasting" (Ps 103:17). Multiple instances of the ḥesed of the Lord have been mēʿôlām, "from of old," (Ps 25:6) and are shown ʿad-ʿôlām, "forever" (2 Sam 22:51; Ps 18:51). One trusts bəḥesed-ʾĕlōhîm ʿôlām wāʾed, "in ḥesed of God forever and ever" (Ps 52:10). The Lord's acts of ḥesed are many and lōʾ-tāmnû, "never cease" (Lam 3:22). Cf. Jer 31:3; Hos 2:21.

His covenant and His *ḥesed* which He swore to your forefathers" (Deut 7:12). The psalmist asks, "Where are Your former *ḥesed* [pl.], O Lord, Which You swore to David in Your *ʾĕmûnāʰ*?" (Ps 89:50). A Song for the Sabbath day exhorts one "to declare Your *ḥesed* in the morning And Your *ʾĕmûnāʰ* by night" (Ps 92:3; cf. Ps 42:8; 90:14). Surely, the *ḥesed* of God endures *kol-hayyôm*, "all day long" (Ps 52:3; cf. Ps 59:17). The psalmist exclaims, "*ḥesed* [of the Lord] will follow me all the days of my life" (Ps 23:6). The time-oriented references share a sense of *continuity* best expressed in the plea, "Your *ḥesed* and Your *ʾĕmet* will continually [*tāmîd/pas*] preserve me" (Ps 40:11–12). The extent of God's *ḥesed* and *ʾĕmet* (cognates) was articulated by referring to *a substantial number of events*. A sinner pleads, "Do not remember the sins of my youth or my transgressions; According to Your *ḥesed* remember me,... O Lord" (Ps 25:7). Another who is suffering deprivation hopes, "I will rejoice and be glad in Your *ḥesed*, Because you have seen my affliction; You have known the troubles of my soul" (Ps 31:8). Another confesses, "Many are the sorrows of the wicked, But he who trusts in the Lord, *ḥesed* shall surround him" (Ps 32:10). One concludes with assurance that "all the paths of the Lord are *ḥesed* and *ʾĕmet*" (Ps 25:10). The extent of God's *ḥesed* (and *ʾĕmet*) was uttered by referring to a *great number of people*, such as a "great congregation" (Ps 40:11–12), "Israel... the house of Aaron... those who fear the Lord" (Ps 118:2, 3, 4), "the king and his counselors and... all the king's mighty princes" (Ezra 7:28). Sometimes the great number was referred to indirectly. A warrior ruthlessly requests, "in Your *ḥesed*, cut off my enemies and destroy all those who afflict my soul" (Ps 143:12). And the servant of the Lord peacefully acknowledges, "How precious is Your *ḥesed*, O God! And the children of men take refuge in the shadow of Your wings" (Ps 36:8). Ultimately, the Lord is "abundant in *ḥesed* to all who call upon Him" (Ps 86:5).

Moreover, the Evangelist often echoes the book of Exodus, which itself *elaborates* the extent of God's *ḥesed*. The Lord is not only *raḥûm* and *ḥannûn* and *rab-ḥesed/poluĕleos* (Exod 34:6), but also the one "who keeps *ḥesed* for thousands" (Exod 34:7, LXX: *poiōn eleos eis chiliadas*). This sum of *poluĕleos* plus *poiōn eleos eis chiliadas* (Exod 34:6–7; cf. 20:6) could well be equal to the excessive *plērēs* in John 1:14 in the Evangelist's eyes.

Furthermore, the Evangelist's own style of writing has to be taken into consideration. The writer generally tends to use excessive language.

This is evident in the abundance of superlative, correlative, and comparative terminology in the Gospel, such as *epanō*, "over, above, more than"; *megas*, "large, great, greatest"; *meizōn*, "greater, greatest"; *mallon*, "all the more"; *holos*, "whole, all, complete, entire, altogether, wholly"; *hosos*, "as much as, as many as, all, everyone"; *pantote*, "always, at all times"; *pas, pasa, pan*, "each, every, every kind of, all, full, absolute, greatest"; *plēthos*, "multitude, crowd"; *polus*, "many, much, large"; *tosoutos*, "so great, so many, so long," and other relevant terminology.[87] This tendency is especially evident when the author writes of the Divine, in expressions such as,[88] "six stone waterpots . . . containing twenty or thirty gallons each . . . filled . . . up to the brim" (2:6–7); "the Spirit without measure" (3:34); "all who are in the tombs" (5:28); "rivers of living water" (7:38), "a pound of very costly perfume of pure nard . . . the house . . . filled with the fragrance of the perfume" (12:3), "much fruit" (15:5), "a mixture of myrrh and aloes, about a hundred pounds" (19:39), "the great number of fish . . . full of fish . . . full of large fish, a hundred and fifty-three" (21:6–11), and "many other things which Jesus did, which if they were written in detail . . . even the world itself would not contain the books that would be written" (21:25). This overflowing abundance is also clearly seen in the scale of miracles. The man whom Jesus heals has been ill for thirty-eight years (5:5). The crowd Jesus feeds is so great in numbers that "two hundred denarii worth of bread is not sufficient for them, for everyone to receive a little" (6:7). When the crowd is fed, the disciples gather and fill twelve baskets with fragments (6:13). When Jesus raises Lazarus from the dead he has been in the tomb four days (11:17, 39).[89] This tendency to use excessive language is evident from the examination of the scale and vocabulary of the miracle scenes.[90] The Evangelist's tendency to use excessive language while speaking of the Divine might have contributed to translating *rab* with *plērēs*, instead of with the weaker *polu* . . . or *plēthos* as in the LXX.

---

87. Such as *aiōnios*, "eternal"; *teleō*, "(make) complete"; and *teleioō*, "(make) perfect."

88. Cf. 2:6–7; 3:31, 35; 4:11; 5:20; 7:8; 10:10, 29; 11:48; 12:37; 15:11; 16:24; 17:9, 13; 18:20, 36; 19:29.

89. Cf. Mark 5:35–42.

90. Kysar also points out that the wondrous character of Jesus is emphasized in various ways: the healing is done at a distance (4:43–53), Jesus not only walks on the water but immediately effects the landing of the boat (6:16–21; cf. Mark 6:45–52) (Kysar, "John," 917).

Finally, NT authors other than the Evangelist use extraordinary degrees and employ terminology different from that of the standard LXX when speaking of the divine *charis*. Consider, for example, the following: "And with great power the apostles were giving testimony to the resurrection of the Lord Jesus, and abundant grace [*charis . . . megalē*] was upon them all" (Acts 4:33); "But the free gift is not like the transgression. For if by the transgression of the one the many died, much more did the grace of God and the gift by the grace of the one Man, Jesus Christ, abound to the many [*pollō mallon hē charis tou Theou kai hē dōrea en chariti tē tou henos anthrōpou Iēsou Christou eis tous pollous eperisseusen*]" (Rom 5:15); "much more those who receive the abundance of grace [*tēn perisseian tēs charitos*]" (Rom 5:17); "grace abounded all the more [*hupereperisseusen hē charis*]" (Rom 5:20); "so that grace may increase [*hina hē charis pleonasē*]" (Rom 6:1); "so that the grace which is spreading to more and more people may cause the giving of thanks to abound to the glory of God [*hina hē charis pleonasasa dia tōn pleionōn tēn eucharistian perisseusē eis tēn doxan tou Theou*]" (2 Cor 4:15); "and the grace of our Lord was more than abundant [*huperepleonasen de hē charis tou kuriou hēmōn*]" (1 Tim 1:14); "may grace and peace be yours in the fullest measure [*charis humin kai eirēnē plēthuntheiē*]" (1 Pet 1:2; cf. indirectly Titus 2:11); "the wisdom from above is first pure, then peaceable, gentle, reasonable, full of mercy [*mestē eleous*] and good fruits, unwavering, without hypocrisy" (Jas 3:17). So could the Evangelist follow the practices of Christian writers in rendering *rab* with the excessive *plērēs*, instead of the regular but weaker *polu . . .* or *plēthos* as in the LXX/OG. Notably, the NT authors use *various* expressions—*megas*, "great" (Acts 4:33); *mestos*, "full" (Jas 3:17); *pollō mallon . . . eis tous pollous eperisseusen*, "much more . . . abound to the many" (Rom 5:15); *huperperisseuō*, "abound all the more" (Rom 5:20); *pleonazō*, "increase, spread" (Rom 6:1; 2 Cor 4:15); *huperpleonazō*, "overflow, be present without measure" (1 Tim 1:14); *plēthunō*, "increase" (1 Pet 1:2); *perisseia*, "abundance, overflow" (Rom 5:17)—to convey the extent of the divine *charis*. So the Evangelist was not bound to the LXX's *polu . . .* or *plēthos*, but could legitimately use *plērēs* for this purpose of expressing the extent of *charis* in translating *rab*.

The above evidence demonstrates that the Evangelist can legitimately translate the *rab* of Exodus 34:6 with *plērēs* in John 1:14.

The Evangelist Can Legitimately Translate *ḥesed* with *charis*

ḥesed Is Translated with *charis* in the OG

The term *ḥesed* is translated with *charis* in the OG, in the books of Esther and Ben Sirach. The translator of the book of Esther renders *ḥesed* with *charis* in 2:9, so that the sentence "Now the young lady pleased him and found *ḥesed* with him" is translated "And the damsel pleased him, and she found *charis* in his sight." Another case comes in Esther 2:17, where the parent text, "The king loved Esther more than all the women, and she found *ḥēn* and *ḥesed* with him more than all the virgins," is rendered "And the king loved Esther, and she found *charis* beyond all the *other* virgins." At this point the translator either omits one of the occurrences of *ḥesed/ḥēn* or conveys both of them with the single *charis*. With the former option, the interpreter probably keeps *ḥesed* and omits *ḥēn*,[91] and we have a case for translating *ḥesed* with *charis*. With the latter option, both *ḥesed* and *ḥēn* are conveyed with single *charis* in Esther 2:17. This latter option is preferable. First, the author of the book of Esther does not make a distinction between *ḥesed* and *ḥēn* originally. The same writer maintains that "the young lady pleased him and found *ḥesed* with him" (Esth 2:9). Further, "Esther found *ḥēn* in the eyes of all who saw her" (Esth 2:15; see also 5:8; 7:3; 8:5). Second, the translator renders all the other *separate* occurrences of *ḥesed* (Esth 2:9,17) and *ḥēn* (Esth 2:15, 17; 5:8; 7:3; 8:5) in the book with *charis*. Therefore, when *ḥesed* and *ḥēn* occur together in Esther 2:17, the interpreter naturally translates both *ḥesed* and *ḥēn* with a single *charis*. This means that the translator of the book of Esther 1) perceives *ḥesed* and *ḥēn* as synonyms, and 2) deems *charis* as suitable to cover both *ḥesed* and *ḥēn*. The grandson of Ben Sirach translates *ḥesed* with *charis* on two known occasions. The phrase "withhold not Your *ḥesed* from the dead" (Sir 7:33, Patrick W. Skehan's translation) is translated as "withhold not *charis* from the dead" (Sir 7:33b RSV). The exhortation "*ḥesed*, like eternity, will never be cut off" (Sir 40:17, Skehan from the superior

---

91. One may argue this from the absence of a Greek equivalent to *ḥēn* in Esth 5:2 and the presence of a translation for *ḥesed* elsewhere in the book of Esther. This makes it more likely that the translator omits *ḥēn* and renders *ḥesed* with *charis* in Esth 2:17. But it is rather questionable whether one can legitimately take the translator's wide deviation from the parent Hebrew text of Esth 4:17—5:2 as omitting a term of Esth 5:2.

manuscript M) is translated as "*charis* is like a garden of blessings" (Sir 40:17 RSV).⁹² Still missing fragments of Ben Sirach probably contain other occurrences of *ḥesed* translated with *charis*.⁹³

Harris claims that *plērēs charitos kai alētheias* does not allude to *wərab-ḥesed weʾĕmet*. She therefore objects to these OG cases of *ḥesed* translated with *charis*:

> [In] the four texts in question (Esth. 2.9; 2.17; Ecclus 7.33; 40.17) *charis* means either the favor a woman finds in the eyes of another (her attractiveness), or the kindness and bounty shown by the wealthy to the needy. In these senses it is unlikely to be found in conjunction with *alētheia*.⁹⁴

Harris's attempt to overthrow the evidence, however, is invalid. First, in the books of Esther and Ben Sirach, *charis* and *alētheia* are not found in conjunction *by design*. Therefore, it is inappropriate to base the unlikeliness of such a conjunction elsewhere on the basis of usage in the books of Esther and Ben Sirach. Second, the sense of "the kindness and bounty shown by the wealthy to the needy" eminent in Sir 7:33 and 40:7 is indeed a prominent feature of God's character. This sense instead increases the likelihood of finding *ḥesed/charis* in conjunction with *alētheia* elsewhere.⁹⁵ Third, the book of Esther's imagery of marriage is rather appropriate when it comes to God *wərab-ḥesed weʾĕmet*.⁹⁶ At any rate, the likelihood of "*charis* . . . to be found in conjunction with *alētheia*" by no means nullifies the fact that *ḥesed* is translated with *charis* in Esther 2:9 and Ben Sirach 7:33 and 40:17.

---

92. See Wright, *No Small Difference*, 177–78.

93. In Ben Sirach *charis* occurs twenty-seven times. Of these, the parent Hebrew text is extant for thirteen but not yet available for the fourteen other occurrences of *charis*. Since in the thirteen occurrences *charis* does translate *ḥesed* on two occasions then it is likely that among the rest of the fourteen occurrences one finds at least two more cases of *ḥesed* translated with *charis*. And in several of the fourteen, *charis* may well be related to the Lord (Sir 19:25; 21:16; 24:16, 17; 37:21). It may be that the phrase *charin anthrōpou* of Ben Sirach 17:22 has *ḥesed* in the original (Charles, "Ecclesiasticus").

94. Harris, *Prologue and Gospel*, 66.

95. In fact, the terms *ḥēn/ʾĕmet* (*charis/alētheia*) *are* brought together in Ben Sirach. They are even used—though indirectly—of God (Sir 41:14a—42:8). The term *ʾmt* (Sir 4:15; 37:15, translated *alētheia*) may well be related to God.

96. Gen 24:12, 14, 49; Ruth 1:8; Prov 31:26; Jer 2:2; 13:31.

ḥesed Is Translated with *charis* (Cognates) in Theodotion and Aquila, Recensions to the LXX/OG

Theodotion's recension to the LXX/OG was produced in first century B.C.E. to second century C.E.,[97] and Aquila's in 28–128 C.E.[98] As contemporaries of the Evangelist, Theodotion and Aquila are very useful in evaluating tendencies in translating *ḥesed*.[99] Our study has identified[100] numerous occurrences of *ḥesed* translated with *charis* (and cognates) in the OG, Theodotion and Aquila.[101] Thus, an interpreter translates *ḥesed* with *charis* in Esther 2:9, and also, possibly,[102] in Esther 2:17. The grandson of Ben Sirach translates *ḥesed* with *charis* in 7:33 and 40:17. Theodotion uses *charis* to depict *ḥesed* of the Law in Proverbs 31:26.

---

97. The composite nature of the Theodotion text is widely recognized. "Historical" Theodotion lived in the second century C.E., but distinctive "Theodotionic" readings are found in earlier sources. This first "layer" of Theodotion's work appears to be part of a larger burst of recensional activity, from the first century B.C.E. (Greenspoon, "Versions, Ancient (Greek)," 794).

98. Peters maintains that Aquila's version was completed in 128 C.E. (Peters, "Septuagint," 110). Greenspoon places Aquila's activity as a translator in the first quarter of the second century C.E. (Greenspoon, "Aquila's Version," 320). But Aquila's recension should be seen as the culmination of at least a century's worth of translational activity within the Jewish community (Barthélemy, *Les Devanciers d'Aquila*).

99. Symmachus, Quinta, and Sexta—recensions to the LXX/OG represented in the Hexapla of Origen (see Field, *Jobus–Malachias*)—post-date the Gospel. Evans proposes four criteria—antecedent documentation, contamination, provenance, and coherence—that should be considered in evaluating the potential relevance of concepts found in a document that postdates the NT writing in question (Evans, *Word and Glory*, 18–19). By using these criteria one certainly can (and we have done so but omitted this component due to restrictions on the study's volume) demonstrate that Symmachus, Quinta, and Sexta 1) are not biased toward making the LXX/OG sound more like the Gospel, and 2) view *eleos* and *charis* as interchangeable synonyms both suitable for translating *ḥesed* (see, particularly, Pss 33, 89). Evidence found in Symmachus, Quinta, and Sexta can be projected legitimately onto the époque of the Evangelist.

100. Some of them have already been noted by scholars. Cf. Dodd, *Interpretation*, 175, n. 3; Hanson, "John I. 14–18 and Exodus XXXIV," 93; Harris, *Prologue and Gospel*, 66; Schnackenburg, *John*, 1:272 n. 193.

101. An unknown interpreter translates *ḥesed* with *charis* in Ps 109:12, as indicated by an inscription in the margins to Syro-Hexapla (see—in small print indicating uncertainty—Field, *Jobus–Malachias*, 265).

102. *ḥesed* and/or *ḥēn* correspond to *charis* in Esth 2:17. The translator has a slight preference for omitting *ḥēn* and translating *ḥesed* with *charis*. But it is more likely—by far—that the interpreter conveys both *ḥesed* and *ḥēn* with a single *charis* in 2 Esth 2:17.

Theodotion renders *charisma* for the ḥesed of the Lord in Psalm 31:22 (MT).[103] Aquila, perhaps,[104] translates the ḥesed of the LORD with *charis* in Psalm 106:7. Symmachus translates the ḥesed of man with *charis* in 2 Samuel 10:2.[105] Symmachus employs *charis* to express the ḥesed of the LORD in Psalms 31:8, 40:11, and 89:25. Symmachus employs *charis* to express the ḥesed of the LORD in Lamentations 3:32 and, perhaps,[106] also in Psalm 40:12 (MT). Symmachus also renders *epicharis* translating ḥesed in regard to the Law in Proverbs 31:26. Quinta translates the ḥesed of the LORD with *charis* in Psalm 33:5. Sexta conveys the ḥesed of the LORD with *charis* in Psalm 31:17 (33:18 MT).

Our study concludes that evidence from the OG, Theodotion, Aquila, Symmachus, Quinta, and Sexta, with its scope and continuity, definitely supports the case of the legitimacy of translating ḥesed with *charis* at the time of the Evangelist.

The Evangelist Can Legitimately Translate ʾĕmet with alētheia

The Evangelist can legitimately translate ʾĕmet with *alētheia*.[107] Translating ʾĕmet with *alēthinos*, a cognate of *alētheia*, was considered to be perfectly appropriate by the translators of Exodus 34:6 LXX. In fact, the translating of creedal attributes of the ʾmn family with *alētheia* is found consistently throughout the whole of the LXX/OG. This vast scope assures one that the use of *alētheia* for ʾĕmet was entirely proper. Remarkably, the ʾmn family includes not only ʾĕmet but also ʾĕmûnāʰ. The term ḥesed is employed together with ʾĕmet in thirty-three verses and with ʾĕmûnāʰ in eleven verses. In the LXX/OG, when it comes to the pair ḥesed and ʾĕmet (ʾĕmûnāʰ), the term ʾĕmet (ʾĕmûnāʰ)—the creedal attribute of the character of God—is always translated with a cognate of *alētheia*. Even when ḥesed, ʾĕmûnāʰ, and ʾĕmet appear in the same verse, both ʾĕmet and ʾĕmûnāʰ are translated with *alētheia*. This is

---

103. So also Conzelmann, "charisma," 9:403; Martin, "Gifts, Spiritual," 1018; Wetter, *Charis*, 174. Conzelmann observes that *charisma* "denotes the result of *charis* viewed as an action with no sharp distinction from this term." Wetter agrees that "as *charisma* overlaps the field of *charis*, so does *charis* that of *charisma*." See Rom 5:15.

104. Attested by Syro-Hexapla.

105. Symmachus does not translate ḥesed with *charis* in 2 Sam 2:6 (contra Hanson, "John I. 14–18 and Exodus XXXIV," 93; Schnackenburg, *John*, 1:272 n. 193).

106. Attested by Syro-Hexapla.

107. See elsewhere in our study (under the critique of Bultmann's arguments).

particularly true in the case of *'ĕmet* when employed in the known OT occurrences of the creed (Exod 34:6; Ps 86:15). Apparently, *alētheia* was deemed to be perfectly capable of conveying the sense of the creedal *'ĕmet* (*'ĕmûnāʰ*). Tov rightly concluded that "if a certain Greek word represents a given Hebrew word in most of its occurrences, it has become almost by implication a mere symbol for that Hebrew word in the translation."[108] This certainly is the case with *alētheia*, which, therefore, symbolizes all the connotations of *'ĕmet*.

plērēs charitos kai alētheias Reflects Practices Common to the Époque of the Evangelist

Our study further proposes that the choice of *plērēs charitos kai alētheias* reflects practices common to the époque of the Evangelist in alluding to/echoing the OT creed. To begin with, writers immediately preceding and contemporary with the Evangelist allude to and echo the creed. It is evident in their descriptions of Christian virtues—*makrothumia*, "patience";[109] *oiktirmos*, "compassion";[110] and *splanchnon*, "affection."[111] Attributes of God also appear in various passages, such as Luke 1:50, 58, 71; 6:35;[112] 18:7;[113] Romans 2:4;[114] 3:24–25;[115] 9:15,[116] 22;[117] 11:29–32;[118] 15:7–11; Ephesians 2:4–8; James 5:11; 2 Peter 1:3;[119] 1:16;[120] Revelation 3:14; 6:10;[121] *Pr. Man.* 7; Sirach 2:11; 5:4–6. So it is appropriate for the

---

108. Tov, *Greek and Hebrew Bible*, 90.

109. See Longenecker, *Galatians*, 258–59; O'Brien, *Colossians*, 24; Bruce, *1 & 2 Thessalonians*, 123 (*makrothumeō*).

110. Köster, "*splanchnon*," 7:556 n. 50 (Col 3:12); O'Brien, *Colossians*, 192.

111. Köster, "*splanchnon*," 7:556 n. 50 (Col 3:12).

112. NA^{27}, 786; Nolland, *Luke 1:1—9:20*, 300.

113. Catchpole, "Son of Man's Search," 93–98; Nolland, *Luke 9:21—18:34*, 869.

114. Dunn, *Romans 1–8*, 82; Weiss, "*chrēstos*," 9:486.

115. Dunn, *Romans 1–8*, 174.

116. Dunn, *Romans 9–16*, 551–52; Piper, *Justification*, 67.

117. Dunn, *Romans 9–16*, 558.

118. Ibid., 687–8.

119. Bauckham, *Jude, 2 Peter*, 178.

120. Ibid., 215.

121. There is an ongoing discussion regarding whether the expression *ho despotēs ho hagios kai alēthinos*, "Lord, holy and true," (Rev 6:10) stems from Exod 34:6. See Aune, *Revelation 1–5*, 235; *Revelation 6–16*, 378, 388, 406.

Evangelist to allude to Exodus 34:6 in John 1:14. Moreover, writers of the Evangelist's époque are rather flexible in alluding to/echoing the OT creed. So the Evangelist can render the non-Septuagintal *plērēs charitos kai alētheias* for *wərab-ḥesed we'ĕmet*. To demonstrate this point, let us consider several passages dealing with *wərab-ḥesed we'ĕmet* as attributes of the character of God.

Luke writes, *kai to eleos autou eis geneas kai geneas tois phoboumenois auton*, "and His mercy is upon generation after generation toward those who fear Him" (Luke 1:50). John Nolland observes that the thought is that of Psalm 103:17 (102:17 LXX). The Lukan language noticeably diverges from the LXX, especially in the phrase *eis geneas kai geneas*, "to generation upon generation," which is not found anywhere in the LXX/OG.[122]

The Magnificat depicts Mary exalting the Lord in a song of praise (Luke 1:46–55). Modeling the Magnificat after the hymn-of-praise category of psalms suggests that its author is, perhaps, aware of the creedal formula *rab-ḥesed/polueleos* extant in Psalm 103:8.[123] How the sense of grace can predominate is seen in the explanatory *emegalunen kurios to eleos autou met' autēs*, "the Lord had displayed His great mercy toward her" (Luke 1:58).[124] Bultmann indicates that this corresponds to the creedal *rab-ḥesed*.[125] Again, Luke deviates from the LXX/OG terminology of *polueleos* to *emegalunen . . . eleos* in Luke 1:58.

Zechariah prophesies: "To show *eleos* toward our fathers, and to remember His holy covenant" (Luke 1:72). The editorial board of NA[27] lists Luke 1:72 as an allusion to "and He remembered His covenant for their sake, and relented according to the *rōb ḥasdô* [OG: *plēthos tou eleous*]"[126] (Ps 106:45).[127] Remarkably, Luke 1:72 does not convey the

---

122. Nolland, *Luke 1:1—9:20*, 71.

123. Brown is content (with qualification) to assign the Magnificat to the hymn-of-praise category, which includes Pss 8, 19, 29, 33, 100, 103, 104, 111, 113, 114, 117, 135, 136, 145–50. See R. Brown, *Birth*, 355–57; Nolland, *Luke 1:1—9:20*, 62–64.

124. Notice also the notion of the fullness of God's *eleos* in the exclamation "His *eleos* is upon generation after generation" (Luke 1:50).

125. Bultmann, "eleos," n. 96; NA[27], 771. Noticeably, several scholars view canticles of Luke as translated from Hebrew. So the Evangelist could translate according to contemporary custom. See Bichsel, "Hymns," 350–51; R. Brown, *Birth*, 660–62; Nolland, *Luke 1:1—9:20*, 62–64.

126. Kere: *ḥăsādāyw*.

127. NA[27], 787.

extent of God's *ḥesed/eleos* expressed by both the Hebrew and Greek texts of the Psalm (*rb/plēthos*).

One cannot help but think that Paul's appeal, *ē tou ploutou tēs chrēstotētos autou kai tēs anochēs kai tēs makrothumias kataphroneis, agnoōn hoti to chrēston tou Theou eis metanoian se agei*, "Or do you think lightly of the riches of His kindness and tolerance and patience, not knowing that the kindness of God leads you to repentance?" (Rom 2:4), is an echo of three to four creedal attributes of God, only expressed in the author's own terms.

Paul appeals to creedal attributes of the character of God in his exhortation to "accept one another, just as Christ also accepted us to the glory [*doxan*] of God. For I say that Christ has become a servant to the circumcision on behalf of the truth [*alētheias*] of God to confirm the promises *given* to the fathers, and for the Gentiles to glorify God for His mercy [*eleous*]; as it is written, . . . 'PRAISE THE LORD ALL YOU GENTILES, AND LET ALL THE PEOPLES PRAISE HIM'" (Rom 15:7–11). James D. G. Dunn correctly observes that Paul argues from an allusion to Psalm 116:1–2 in the OG, which reads, "Alleluia. Praise the Lord, all ye nations: praise him, all ye peoples. For his mercy has been abundant [*ekrataiōthē to eleos*] toward us: and the truth of the Lord endures for ever [*alētheia tou kuriou menei eis ton aiōna*]."[128] Here the apostle uses the common creedal LXX terminology of *eleos . . . alētheia* and even mentions the *doxa* of God. But Paul does not feel obligated to follow the exact LXX phraseology while dealing with attributes of the character of God (cf. Rom 15:7–11 and Ps 116:1–2 OG).

Paul elsewhere explains,

> But God, being rich in mercy [*plousios ōn en eleei*], because of His great love with which He loved us,[129] even when we were dead in our transgressions, made us alive together with Christ (by grace [*chariti*] you have been saved), and raised us up with Him, and seated us with Him in the heavenly *places* in Christ Jesus, so that in the ages to come He might show the surpassing riches of His grace in kindness [*to huperballon ploutos tēs charitos autou en chrēstotēti*] toward us in Christ Jesus. For by

---

128. Dunn, *Romans 1–8*, 845–50.

129. Notice the resemblance to the Gospel of John's "full of grace and truth . . . God so loved the world."

grace [*chariti*] you have been saved through faith; and that not of yourselves, *it is* the gift of God . . . (Eph 2:4-8)

The pericope of Ephesians 2:4-8 contributes much to the discussion. First, as Bultmann[130] and Lincoln[131] point out, the expression *ho de Theos plousios ōn en eleei*, "God, being rich in mercy," corresponds to the creedal *rab-ḥesed*. But instead of the standard LXX/OG's *polu* or *plēthos* for *rb*, Ephesians 2:4 employs *plousios*. Second, *charis* (Eph 2:5, 7, 8) serves as a synonym for *eleos* (Eph 2:4),[132] while both denote an attribute of God (at least in Eph 2:4, 7). Third, *charis*—an attribute of God—is modified by *to huperballon ploutos*, "the surpassing riches" (Eph 2:7). The combination of *huperballō*, "surpass,"[133] and *ploutos*, "riches, wealth, abundance,"[134] expresses the extreme extent of God's *charis*. Without a doubt, the expression *to huperballon ploutos tēs charitos autou* echoes the OT description of the *rab-ḥesed* of God. But neither *huperballō* nor *ploutos* nor *charis* is employed by the LXX/OG to translate the *rab-ḥesed* of God. Thus, the writer again deviates from the LXX/OG's pattern of conveying *rab-ḥesed*.

James writes that *polusplanchnos estin ho kurios kai oiktirmōn*, "the Lord is very compassionate[135] and *is* merciful" (Jas 5:11). The editorial board of NA[27] lists James 5:11 as an allusion to either Exodus 34:6 or Psalm 103:8.[136] Ralph P. Martin agrees that "such attributions to God here reflect OT teaching (Pss 103:8; 111:4; cf. Exod 34:6)."[137] Helmut Köster claims that "the saying sounds like an OT quotation and is unquestionably a Greek translation of the common OT *raḥûm wəhannûn yhwh* or similar Hebrew formulae" and refers to the creedal Psalm 103:8; 111:4, cf. Exodus 34:6, Joel 2:13.[138]

---

130. Bultmann, "*eleos*," n. 96.

131. Lincoln, *Ephesians*, 99-100.

132. Lincoln acknowledges that "the term *charis* ('grace') (Eph 2:5, 7, 8) is synonymous with *eleos* ('mercy') (Eph 2:4)" (Lincoln, *Ephesians*, 100).

133. In the form of a participle, "immeasurable, tremendous" (UBSDict).

134. UBSDict.

135. NASB has "full of compassion."

136. NA[27], 774, 786.

137. Martin, *James*, 196.

138. Köster, "*splanchnon*," n. 56.

The phrase in James 5:11 is illuminating for our discussion. First, its *polusplanchnos*, "very compassionate,"[139] probably corresponds to *polueleos* and not some other term of the creedal *oiktirmōn kai eleēmōn makrothumos kai polueleos kai alēthinos*. Of all the terms used in the creed 1) *oiktirmōn* is already used in Jas 5:11; 2) *eleēmōn* lacks a modifier of extent, which *polusplanchnos* employs; 3) *makrothumos* and *alēthinos* differ from *polusplanchnos* in meaning; and 4) *polueleos* corresponds with both the meaning and extent (*polu*) of *polusplanchnos*.[140] Therefore, James probably employs *polusplanchnos* . . . *oiktirmōn* to convey the either creedal *raḥûm* . . . *rab-ḥesed* or the LXX/OG's corresponding *oiktirmōn* . . . *polueleos*. In any case, the writer deviates from the LXX/OG's pattern. Second, if James translates *polusplanchnos* for *rab-ḥesed* then the writer is probably *dissatisfied* with the standard LXX/OG translation *polueleos/to plēthos tou eleous*. Third, the LXX/OG never uses *polus-planchnos* for the Hebrew terminology of the creed. The term *polusplanchnos* occurs only once in biblical Greek, in James 5:11. Hence, James does not hesitate to use a *unique* term to depict an attribute of God.[141] Fourth, if *polusplanchnos* . . . *oiktirmōn* translates the creedal *raḥûm* . . . *rab-ḥesed* (corresponding to LXX/OG's *oiktirmōn* . . . *polueleos*), then neither the observance of the traditional *order* nor the *extraction* of just the two attributes of God from their full original list seems to constitute a problem for the writer.

James and Peter are aware of the term *plēthos* used to convey *rb* in numerous occurrences of *rb ḥsd*. Both writers employ the phrase *plēthos hamartiōn*, "multitude of sins" (Jas 5:20; 1 Pet 4:8). The authors probably even use *plēthos* to translate *rb*.[142] But neither James nor Peter uses *plēthos* to convey the extent of *rab-ḥesed* as the LXX/OG does. Instead, James employs *polusplanchnos* (Jas 5:11) and Peter chooses *polu autou eleos*[143] (1 Pet 1:3). Hence, NT authors have preferences in the vocabu-

---

139. UBSDict.

140. The term *polueleos* also has the advantage of covering the meaning of another creedal term—*eleēmōn*—as both stem from the same root.

141. James is aware that the term *plēthos* is used to convey *rab* in numerous occurrences of *rab-ḥesed* (Jas 5:20) and employs *eleos*, the LXX/OG term used to convey *ḥesed* (Jas 2:13; 3:17).

142. Cf. *mērōb ʿăwōneykā/to plēthos tōn hamartiōn sou*, "the multitude of your iniquities/sins," in Ezek 28:18 (Michaels, *1 Peter*, 246).

143. *polu autou eleos* corresponds to the LXX/OG's *polueleos*.

lary to convey the extent of *rb ḥsd* that differ from that established by the LXX/OG. Moreover, Martin rightly observes that the reference to the covering of a multitude of sins in James 5:20 (cf. 1 Pet 4:8) parallels the saving of the person from death and implies forgiveness (Jas 5:11).[144] This concept of a plurality of sins suggests the "extent of the forgiveness"[145] and harkens back to the wideness of God's mercy (cf. Jas 2:13b).[146] It reminds one of rather artistic ways in which the extent of God's *ḥesed* can be conveyed in the NT. This in turn encourages seeing *rab-ḥesed* behind *plērēs charitos*.

Peter exclaims, "Blessed be the God and Father of our Lord Jesus Christ, who *kata to polu autou eleos* has caused us to be born again to a living hope through the resurrection of Jesus Christ from the dead" (1 Pet 1:3). J. Ramsey Michaels points out that the Jewishness of Peter's reference to mercy in this context of blessing can be seen from the OT, particularly Psalm 65:20: "Blessed be God, who has not turned away my prayer nor *to eleos autou ap' emou*."[147] Bultmann believes that the phrase *kata to polu autou eleos* corresponds to the creedal *rab-ḥesed*.[148] In *kata to polu autou eleos*, Peter inserts *autos* between *polus* and *eleos*, so that he deviates somewhat from the LXX/OG's pattern of rendering *rb ḥsd* with *polueleos*.

The *Prayer of Manasseh* is preserved primarily in Greek and Syriac. Many scholars maintain that Greek is the original language; others conclude that it was composed in a Semitic language.[149] It is safe to conclude that the *Prayer* was composed "either in the second or the first century B.C.E., with the recognition that it also could have been composed during the early part of the first century C.E. Therefore this text is appropriate for evaluating the suitability of alluding to the OT creed with *plērēs charitos kai alētheias*. The *Prayer* reads:[150]

---

144. See Martin, *James*, 217. Cf. Pss 32:1; 85:2; Dan 4:24; Rom 4:7.

145. Davids, *James*, 200.

146. Martin, *James*, 219.

147. Ps 65:20 OG. See Michaels, *1 Peter*, 18.

148. Bultmann, "*eleos*," n. 96.

149. See Charlesworth, "Prayer of Manasseh," 625–27; Dancy, Fuerst, and Hammer, *Shorter Books*, 243.

150. The Greek text of *Pr. Man.* as in Odes 12 (IB`) according to GLXX, *Psalmi cum Odis*. The English translation is from the RSV.

> 1 O Lord Almighty, God of our fathers ... 6 yet immeasurable and unsearchable is thy promised mercy [*ametrēton te kai anexichniaston to eleos tēs epangelias sou*] 7 for thou art the Lord Most High, of great compassion, long-suffering, and very merciful, and repentest over the evils of men [*eusplanchnos makrothumos kai polueleos kai metanoōn epi kakiais anthrōpōn*] ...[151] 11 And now I bend the knee of my heart, beseeching thee for thy kindness [*chrēstotētos*] ... 14 and in me thou wilt manifest thy goodness [*tēn agathōsunēn sou*]; for, unworthy as I am, thou wilt save me in thy great mercy [*to polu eleos sou*] ... (Pr. Man. RSV)

The author probably alludes to the "Jonah 4:2/Joel 2:13" version of the creed. Only Jonah 4:2/Joel 2:13 mention the *nīḥām ʿal-hārāʿāʰ* /*metanoōn epi tais kakiais*, "the relenting of evil," attribute of God. The three also observe the reversed—*ḥannûn ... raḥûm/eleēmōn ... oiktirmōn*[152]—order of the attributes.

Comparison of *eleēmōn kai oiktirmōn makrothumos kai polueleos kai metanoōn epi tais kakiais*, "merciful and compassionate, long-suffering, and abundant in kindness, and repentest of evil," (Jonah 4:2; cf. also Joel 2:13) with *eusplanchnos makrothumos kai polueleos kai metanoōn epi kakiais anthrōpōn*, "of great compassion, long-suffering, and very merciful, and repentest over the evils of men," (Pr. Man. 7) suggests that the author of the *Prayer* covers both creedal *ḥannûn*/*eleēmōn* and *raḥûm*/*oiktirmōn* with only the single term *eusplanchnos* and then reproduces the rest of the creed. Similarly, the Evangelist may also cover any two of the three or even all three creedal terms—*oiktirmōn*, *eleēmōn*, and *polueleos* (Exod 34:6)—by the single term *charis* (John 1:14). Remarkably, *eusplanchnos*, employed in Pr. Man. 7 is never used in the LXX/OG to convey any of the creedal attributes. So the Evangelist can initiate the usage of *charis* (1:14) instead of the common *(polu)eleos* (Exod 34:6). The writer of the *Prayer* uses *ametrētos*, "unmeasured, immeasurable, immense, unnumbered, countless," to describe the extent of God's *eleos* (Pr. Man. 6). What is notable is that *ametrētos* has never been used for this purpose in the LXX/OG. So the Evangelist can inno-

---

151. GLXX, *Psalmi cum Odis*, 362, reports a textual variant, which here continues, "Thou, O Lord, according to thy *plēthos tēs chrēstotētos* hast promised repentance and forgiveness to those who have sinned against thee; and *tō plēthei tōn oiktirmōn* thou hast appointed repentance for sinners, that they may be saved" (Pr. Man. 7a RSV). This textual variant is doubtful.

152. Cf. the standard *raḥûm ... ḥannûn* (Exod 34:6).

vate and use *plērēs* to translate *rab* of the creedal *rab-ḥesed*. Finally, the writer of the *Prayer* emphasizes the degree of God's *eleos*. Its force is first expressed by *ametrētos*, then followed by *polueleos* and *polu eleos* (*Pr. Man.* 6, 7, 14). Correspondingly, the Evangelist perhaps renders *plērēs* as a result of dissatisfaction with the inadequate LXX/OG translation of *rab* with either *polu*, or *plēthos*.

No Hebrew parent text is yet available to evaluate the principles of translation of the numerous occurrences of *eleos*,[153] *charis*,[154] *oiktirmōn*,[155] *eleēmōn*,[156] and *makrothumos*[157] in Ben Sirach.[158] Our study confirms[159] that *ḥesed* is translated as *charis* in Sirach 7:33 and 40:17. Our study advances the case by discussing the following findings.[160]

The translator of the book of Ben Sirach is flexible in translating the term *ḥesed* into Greek. On the one hand, the interpreter translates "I will now praise those godly [*ḥesed* pl.] people, our ancestors" with "Let us now praise famous men [*andras endoxous*], and our fathers in their generations" (Sir 44:1). On the other hand, the grandson translates "these were godly [*ḥesed*] people whose virtues will not be forgotten"[161] with "these were men of mercy [*andres eleous*], whose righteous deeds have not been forgotten" (Sir 44:10). Here, the interpreter translates two occurrences of *ḥesed* brought into a close proximity with basically the same meaning and context by, first *endoxous* (Sir 44:1), and then *eleos* (Sir 44:10). Notably *eleos*, besides serving as a translation for *ḥesed*, translates also *yəšûʿāʰ*—God's "saving help" (Sir 35:25, cf. Sir 51:29)—and *rāṣôn*—God's "will" (Sir 50:22).

---

153. Sir 2:7a, 9, 18; 18:5, 11; 13ab; 28:4a; 29:1a; 32(35):26a.

154. Sir 17:22; 19:25; 20:16; 21:16; 24:16; 24:17; 26:13; 26:15; 29:15; 30:6; 35:2; 37:21; 40:22.

155. Sir 2:11a.

156. Ibid.

157. Ibid., 1:23.

158. Our study uses Beentjes, *Ben Sira*; Ben-Hayyim, *Ben Sira*; Barthélemy and Rickenbacher, *Konkordanz zum Hebräischen Sirach*; GLXX, *Sapientia Iesu Filii Sirach*.

159. So Dodd, *Interpretation*, 175; Harris, *Prologue and Gospel*, 66.

160. Unless otherwise noted, for translations of Ben Sirach from Greek and Hebrew to English our study uses RSV and Skehan, *Wisdom of Ben Sira*.

161. By God, that is, as the following verses make clear (Skehan, *Wisdom of Ben Sira*, 499).

Ben Sirach most likely echoes the creed not only in Sirach 2:11[162] (as previously argued), but also in Sirach 5:4–6; 16:11–12. Here, *(rb) rḥmîm* is first rendered by *(polus) oiktirmos* (Sir 5:6), but then by *(polu) eleos* (Sir 5:6; 16:11, 12 *(polu)*). The grandson is conscious of the LXX/OG's paradigm for rendering the creed. God's *ʾerek ʾappayim* is translated by *makrothumos* (Sir 5:4), and the *ḥsd* of God is conveyed with *eleos* (Sir 47:22; 50:24), and *rb ḥsd* by *plēthos eleous* (Sir 51:3). The translator does not seem to discern much of a difference between the creedal *raḥûm*, *ḥannûn* and *ḥesed*. Ben Sirach echoes the creed (Sir 5:4–6; 16:11–12) and the grandson at first translates the term *(rb) rḥmîm* with *(polus) oiktirmos* (Sir 5:6) but then with *(polu) eleos* (Sir 5:6; 16:11, 12 *(polu)*). The interpreter also renders the creedal *raḥûm* with *eleēmōn*, "the Merciful One" (Sir 50:19). God is often spoken of as *raḥûm* in the OT. With only one—most likely accidental—exception, the LXX/OG always translates the creedal *raḥûm* with *oiktirmōn*, and *ḥannûn* with *eleēmōn* in reference to God.[163] Since the grandson is aware of the LXX/OG pattern and still renders *raḥûm* with *eleēmōn*, then the creedal attributes *raḥûm* and *ḥannûn* are, perhaps, interchangeable from the point of view of the translator.[164] The terms *charis* and *eleos* may appear synonymous in the eyes of the interpreter as well. The grandson also says of Moses, "the Lord

---

162. No Hebrew text is extant.

163. The creedal *raḥûm* appears by itself in Deut 4:31 and Ps 78:38, both times translated by *oiktirmōn*. The creedal *ḥannûn* is rendered alone in Exod 22:26 and Ps 116:5, and both occurrences are translated with *eleēmōn*. The creedal *raḥûm/oiktirmōn* and *ḥannûn/eleēmōn* occur together in straight order (Exod 34:6; Pss 86:15; 103:8) or reversed sequence (2 Chr 30:9; Neh 9:17, 31; Ps 111:4; 112:4 [arguably of God]; Joel 2:13; Jonah 4:2). If the order is reversed, so is the sequence in the translation. Only once the *ḥannûn wəraḥûm* chain is translated as *oiktirmōn kai eleēmōn* (Ps 145:8). Leslie Allen points out that the priority of *ḥannûn* here is probably due to the exigencies of the acrostic (Allen, *Psalms 101–150*, 368, with the reference to Crüsemann, *Studien zur Formgeschichte*, 186, 298). Perhaps the translator did not notice this change in the order of the creedal terms and automatically rendered the standard sequence of *oiktirmōn . . . eleēmōn*. More likely, however, the interpreter intentionally observed the standard formula in Greek and corrected 1) the order to *oiktirmōn . . . eleēmōn*; and 2) the terminology, translating according to the creed, *ûgədol-ḥāsed*, "great in *ḥesed*," (normally *rab-ḥesed*) with the standard *polueleos*.

164. No objection to translating *raḥûm* with *eleēmōn* is attested in Sir 50:19 (GLXX, *Sapientia Iesu Filii Sirach*, 360). This indicates that other interpreters deemed such a translation appropriate. This distinction had perhaps already been blurred even in Hebrew texts. Manuscripts read "you will find [A: *raḥămîm*; cf. C: *ḥēn*] with God" (Sir 3:18; translated with "you will find *charis* in the sight of the Lord").

brought forth *andra eleous*[165] *heuriskonta charin* [*hēn*] in the sight of all flesh" (Sir 45:1). This evidence from Ben Sirach suggests that by the time of the Evangelist the creedal *raḥûm, ḥannûn,* and *ḥesed* had become virtually identical from the point of view of an interpreter. As such, the terms could have been interchangeably translated by either one of their former strict Greek equivalents, *oiktirmōn, eleēmōn, polueleos* (or *charis,* which became a synonym of *eleos*). One would not have been surprised if the Evangelist rendered *charis* for either *ḥesed* alone or for all three creedal terms—*raḥûm, ḥannûn,* and *ḥesed*—for that matter.

plērēs charitos kai alētheias Probably Alludes to the Whole Creedal Formula

So far we have established that *plērēs charitos kai alētheias* may serve as a legitimate translation for *wərab-ḥesed we'ĕmet*. But *wərab-ḥesed we'ĕmet* is a part of the whole creed *yhwh 'ēl raḥûm wəḥannûn 'erek 'appayim wərab-ḥesed we'ĕmet* (Exod 34:6). The creed contains attributes other than *wərab-ḥesed we'ĕmet*. Various attributes are linked by *w*. Attributes *wərab-ḥesed we'ĕmet* are preceded by *w*. Why and how would the Evangelist "cut" just the two attributes—*wərab-ḥesed we'ĕmet*—out of the whole creed and "paste" them into John 1:14?

Our study proposes that *plērēs charitos kai alētheias* actually alludes to the whole of the creed—*raḥûm wəḥannûn 'erek 'appayim wərab-ḥesed we'ĕmet*—as follows: ~~makrothumos~~ (= ~~'erek 'appayim~~) *plērēs* (= *wə* + *wərab*) *charitos* (= *raḥûm* + *ḥannûn* + *ḥesed*) *kai* (= *we*) *alētheias* (= *'ĕmet*). To begin with, this approach eliminates the matter of the legitimacy of translating *ḥesed* with *charis* and *rab* with *plērēs*. Moreover, this scheme resolves the issue of the otherwise awkward "cut-and-paste" choice of attributes *wərab-ḥesed we'ĕmet* that formerly were envisioned to be behind *plērēs charitos kai alētheias*. Furthermore, this design accounts for all the creedal attributes of the character of God: the absence of the creedal *'erek 'appayim/makrothumos* warns

---

165. There is no equivalent for *eleos* in manuscript B, the only witness to the Hebrew text available for this phrase (Sir 44:23f.). The Syriac has an equivalent of *ḥesed* in it (Beentjes, *Ben Sira*, 60; Barthélemy and Rickenbacher, *Konkordanz zum Hebräischen Sirach*, 19).

that God's longsuffering nature has come to an end.[166] The irregular[167] and excessive *plērēs* hints that all three creedal terms denoting "grace" linked by *w—raḥûm wǝhannûn . . . wǝrab-ḥesed*—are conveyed with the single *charis*.[168] The adjoined distinctive attribute *we'ĕmet* is communicated with *kai alētheias*. Finally, as we will further expound, the resulting *plērēs charitos kai alētheias* bears major theological implications.

plērēs charitos kai alētheias Is Likely to Be the Evangelist's Own Translation of the Creedal Formula

The Evangelist Occasionally Translates from Hebrew if There Is Reason for It

The fact of translation in the case of John 1:14 is, of course, unverifiable.[169] It is possible, however, for the Evangelist does translate from the Hebrew occasionally. The quotations in John 12:40 and 13:18 appear to be independent translations, apparently by the Evangelist, from

---

166. See also 3:36. Two occurrences of the creed—Joel 2:13 and Jonah 4:2—add *nḥm/metanoeō*, "relenting [of evil]," to the standard list of attributes of the character of God originating in Exod 34:6. The fact that neither *makrothumos* nor *metanoeō* is mentioned in 1:14 stresses the notion that the time of judgment has finally come. Further, notice that cognates of *makrothumos* (Exod 34:6, etc.) and *metanoeō* (Joel 2:13, Jonah 4:2)—creedal attributes of the character of God relevant to the trial—never occur in the Gospel.

167. Compare to the lxx/og practice of rendering *rb* with *polu* or *plēthos*.

168. The reason for this "reduction" could have been as simple as a "lack of space precious in the prologue" or "Greek equivalents for three creedal terms—*raḥûm, ḥannûn, ḥesed*—not fitting the poetic metric of the prologue." We will further identify the complex causes.

169. Sanders and Mastin appear to be the first scholars who suggest that *plērēs charitos kai alētheias* was *translated* from *wǝrab-ḥesed we'ĕmet* (Sanders, *John*, 1:14). Lindars later stresses the fact of *structural similarity* of the phrases, as he wrote, "[*wǝrab-ḥesed we'ĕmet* (Exod 34:6)] . . . can be correctly translated 'full of grace and truth.' John has given a more literal translation than the Greek of the lxx, which shows that he is working from the Hebrew scriptures" (Lindars, *John*, 95). It is true that, structurally at least, *plērēs charitos kai alētheias* diverges from the lxx's *polueleos kai alēthinos*, and rather follows *wǝrab-ḥesed we'ĕmet*. Lindars's argument is circular, however, and he does not develop it any further. Hence our study will elaborate and defend the proposal that the Evangelist translates *raḥûm wǝhannûn 'erek 'appayim wǝrab-ḥesed we'ĕmet* with *plērēs charitos kai alētheias*.

the Hebrew.¹⁷⁰ But every time the Evangelist does not quote from the LXX/OG, good reasons can be adduced for him not to have done so. Maarten F. F. Menken states that "in 12:40, the evangelist wished to present determination by God as the cause of unbelief; therefore he could not use the LXX text of Isa. 6:10. In 13:18, the LXX translation of Ps. 40(41):10 would make the quotation suggest that Jesus was beguiled by Judas, a suggestion which was at variance with John's view of Jesus as omniscient. The LXX translation of Zech. 12:10 would not have served John in 19:37, because it lacks the piercing."¹⁷¹

The Evangelist Has Reasons to Translate the Creedal Formula with *plērēs charitos kai alētheias*

Creedal Terms Denoting "Grace" Lost Their Distinctiveness by the Époque of the Evangelist

On the one hand, the difference between *ḥesed* and *ḥēn* (and its cognate *ḥannûn*) had originally been, if anything, vague.¹⁷² This is seen better when *ḥesed* and *ḥēn* are employed together in a phrase and the case recurs in the same book. In the book of Genesis, Lot acknowledges, "Your servant has found *ḥēn* in your sight, and you have magnified your *ḥesed*" (Gen 19:19). The storyteller reports, "the LORD was with Joseph and extended *ḥesed* to him, and gave him *ḥēn* in the sight of the chief jailer" (Gen 39:21). Israel appeals, "Please, if I have found *ḥēn* in your sight . . . deal with me in *ḥesed* and faithfulness" (Gen 47:29). In the book of Esther, the storyteller begins, "the young lady pleased . . . [king Ahasuerus] and found *ḥesed* with him" (Esth 2:9). The writer continues, "Esther found *ḥēn* in the eyes of all who saw her" (Esth 2:15; similarly 5:8; 7:3; 8:5), and concludes, "The king loved Esther more than all the women, and she found *ḥēn* and *ḥesed* with him" (Esth 2:17). Distinctions between *ḥesed* and *ḥēn* are hardly conspicuous.

---

170. Except for the last three words of 12:40, which come from the LXX (Menken, *Quotations*, 99–122, 123–38).

171. Menken, *Quotations*, 205.

172. According to Neubauer, *ḥesed* and *ḥēn* can hardly be distinguished, even in origin (Neubauer, "Stamm *Ch n n*," 26f.). Cf. Goldingay, *Daniel*, 252f.; Kselman, "Grace (OT)," 1086; Reed, "Some Implications of *ḥēn*"; Zimmerli, "*charis* (OT)," n. 64.

The difference in meaning of the three creedal terms—*raḥûm*, *ḥannûn*, *ḥesed*—has also been rather elusive. All these terms (and their cognates) are being used to convey basically the same idea: The storyteller reports, "The Lord gave the people *ḥēn* in the sight of the Egyptians" (Exod 11:3). Israel hopes regarding his sons, "may God Almighty grant you *raḥămîm* in the sight of the man" (Gen 43:14). Ezra prays for the nation, "God has not forsaken us, but has extended *ḥesed* to us in the sight of the kings of Persia" (Ezra 9:9; similarly 7:28). The storyteller reports, "God granted Daniel *ḥesed* and *raḥămîm* in the sight of the commander of the officials" (Dan 1:9). Bultmann concludes that "in the language of later Judaism *ḥesed* and *raḥămîm* can hardly be distinguished."[173] Zimmerli acknowledges that "in the later speech of the OT there is a remarkable merging of *ḥēn* and *ḥesed* in which *ḥesed* loses its earlier distinctiveness in favor of the meaning of *ḥēn*."[174] Conzelmann argues that in the Qumran scrolls the "sense *ḥsd* is hard to distinguish from *rḥmîm* and *ḥnn*,"[175] and gives as an example the following: "Lo, thou hast begun to show *ḥsd* to thy servant, thou art *ḥnn* to me in the spirit of thy *rḥmîm*" (1QH 16:8f.). Later, in rabbinic writings, the distinction (whatever little there may have been) virtually disappears. Conzelmann cites a typical morning prayer in *b. Ber.* 60b.: "Today and every day make me *ḥn* and *ḥsd* and *rḥmîm* in thine eyes and the eyes of all who see me."[176]

On the other hand, even if there had been a distinction between *raḥûm*, *ḥannûn*, and *ḥesed*[177] originally, it was certainly lost in translations into Greek. Whatever the difference between *ḥesed* (mostly translated with *eleos*) and *ḥēn* (mostly translated with *charis*) might have been, it was later lessened with the introduction of the term *rāṣôn*, "pleasure, delight, favor," for this was translated with either *eleos* or *charis*. Consider, "in My *rāṣôn*/*eleos* I [the Lord] have had compassion on you" (Isa 60:10), but "a good man will obtain *rāṣôn*/*charis* from the Lord" (Prov 12:2; cf. 11:27; 18:22).

---

173. Bultmann, "*eleos*," 2:481.
174. Zimmerli, "*charis* (OT)," 9:381.
175. Conzelmann, "*charis*," 9:387; Zimmerli, "*ḥsd* im Schrifttum," 439–49.
176. Conzelmann, "*charis*," 9:387.
177. For the discussion over the distinctiveness of the creedal *raḥûm*, *ḥannûn*, and *ḥesed*, see Bultmann, "*eleos*"; Bultmann, "*oiktirō* "; Kselman, "Grace (OT)"; Sakenfeld, *Faithfulness*; Sakenfeld, *Meaning of ḥesed*; Zimmerli, "*charis* (OT)."

The first creedal adjective *raḥûm* has been translated with *oiktirmōn* (Exod 34:6; Joel 2:13; Jonah 4:2; Pss 86:15; 103:8) and *eleēmōn* (Ps 145:8; Sir 50:19), its verbal cognate *rḥm* with *eleeō* (Deut 13:17; Isa 54:8) and *oikteirō* (Mic 7:19–20), and its noun cognate *raḥămîm* with *eleos* (Deut 13:17; Isa 63:7; Sir 16:11, 12 (*polu*)), *oiktirmos* (Ps 40:12; 51:3; 69:17; 103:4; Hos 2:19; Zech 7:9; Sir 5:6), and *charis* (Gen 43:14; Dan 1:9). The second creedal adjective *ḥannûn* has been rendered with *eleēmōn* (Exod 22:26; 34:6; Ps 86:15; 103:8; 111:4; Joel 2:13; Jonah 4:2) and *oiktirmos* (Ps 109:12; 145:8), its verbal cognate *ḥnn* with *eleeō* (Gen 43:29; Ps 51:3), *eleos* (Judg 21:22), *oikteirō* (Ps 4:2; 37:21; 59:6; 67:2; 102:14, 15; 112:5; 123:2; Isa 30:18), and *oiktirmōn* (Ps 109:12), its noun cognate *taḥănûn* with *oiktirmos* (Zech 12:10), and its noun cognate *ḥēn* with *eleos* (Gen 19:19) and *charis* (Gen 18:3, as well as other multiple examples). The third creedal noun *ḥesed* has been translated with *eleos*[178] as well as with *eleēmosunē* (Gen 47:29; Prov 3:3; 16:6; 19:22; 20:28; 21:21), *eleēmōn* (Prov 11:17; 20:6), *oiktirēma* (Jer 31:3), and *charis* (Sir 7:33; 40:17; Esth 2:9; cf. also 2:17).[179] Remarkably, cognates of every creedal term *raḥûm*, *ḥannûn*, *ḥesed* were translated with *charis*.

Moreover, distinctions between Greek terms, which were used to translate the creedal attributes *raḥûm*, *ḥannûn*, and *ḥesed*, were blurred as well. The terms *oiktirmōn*, *eleēmōn*, and *polueleos* (originally rendered for the creedal *raḥûm*, *ḥannûn*, *rab-ḥesed*) have become virtually interchangeable. Bultmann claims that "there is no palpable distinction between *oiktirein* and *eleein* or *oiktirmoi* and *eleos*; *ḥnn* and *rḥm* are rendered by both *oiktirein* and *eleein* . . . , and in the LXX *oiktirein* and *eleein* are combined or used as par. like the Heb. *rḥm* pi and *ḥnn*."[180] He

---

178. Bultmann's "normally" (Bultmann, "*eleos*," 2:479) and Schnackenburg's "usually" (Schnackenburg, *John*, 1:273) for translating *ḥesed* with *eleos* are somewhat misleading. The scholars list less than half of the occurrences where *ḥesed* is *not* translated with *eleos*. This creates an impression that such occurrences are exceptions to the rule. But this is not really true if one considers the actual range of translations offered for *ḥesed*. Besides those mentioned above, *ḥesed* has also been conveyed with *elpis*, "hope" (2 Chr 35:26); *Esōth* (1 Kgs 4:10; for the proper name Ben-hesed *ben-ḥesed*/*huios Esōth*); *dikaiosunē*, "righteousness" (Gen 19:19; 20:13; 21:23; 24:27; 32:11; Exod 15:13; Isa 63:7; Prov 20:28); *dikaios*, "righteous" (Isa 57:1); *onoma*, "name" (Ps 44:27); *hosios*, "holy" (Isa 55:3; cf. Ps 18:26); *pasa doxa anthrōpou*, "all *the* glory of man" (Isa 40:6); and *timē*, "honor" (Dan 1:9). Sometimes *ḥesed* is not translated at all (Jer 16:5; Hos 10:12).

179. See also multiple translations of *ḥesed* with *charis* in recensions to the LXX/OG.

180. Bultmann, "*oiktirō*," 5:160.

further remarks, "In the language of later Judaism *ḥesed* and *raḥămîm* can hardly be distinguished any more than *eleos* and *oiktirmoi*, which are used interchangeably."[181]

Furthermore, the meaning of the terms *eleos* and *charis* had virtually merged by the time of the Gospel. For example, within the book of Genesis, for the equivalent Hebrew construction *mṣ'* . . . *ḥn* . . . *b* . . . *ʿayin*, under the same narrative circumstances, the term *ḥēn* is translated with either *charis* or *eleos*. Both Abraham and Lot are confused over the identity of their visitors. Abraham says, "My lord, if now I have found *ḥēn/charis* in your sight, please do not pass your servant by" (Gen 18:3). Lot begs, "Now behold, your servant has found *ḥēn/eleos* in your sight . . . Please, let me escape" (Gen 19:19). Moreover, the term *charis* translates either *ḥēn* or *raḥămîm*, both being used for the same purpose. Thus, in Egypt, "the LORD was with Joseph and extended *ḥesed/eleos* to him, and gave him *ḥēn/charis* in the sight of the chief jailer" (Gen 39:21). In the land of Canaan, Joseph's father Israel prays, "may God Almighty grant you *raḥămîm/charis* in the sight of the man" (Gen 43:14). The merging of *eleos* and *charis* is also evident in later Judaism. Consider the phrases "yet our God has not forsaken us in our bondage, but has extended to us his *ḥesed/eleos* before the kings of Persia" (Ezra 9:9 RSV) and "Even in our bondage we were not forsaken by our Lord, but he brought us into *charis* with the kings of the Persians" (1 *Esdr.* 8:80[77 OG] RSV). As it appears, *eleos* and *charis* are used interchangeably to denote God's *ḥesed*. Writers/translators in Greek did not discern much of a difference between *charis* and *eleos* and rendered both at once, perhaps just to be "on the safe side." Thus, Ben Sirach's grandson adds *eleos* while translating from the Hebrew parent text with no equivalent of *eleos* extant in it: "the Lord brought forth a man of *eleos*/—, who found *charis/ḥēn* in the sight of all flesh" (Sir 45:1). An OG writer renders *charis* and *eleos* with no conspicuous distinction between the terms: "Those who trust in him will understand truth, and the faithful will abide with him in love, because *charis* and *eleos* are upon his elect" (Wis 3:9; cf. 4:15 RSV).[182]

181. Bultmann, "*eleos*," 2:481.

182. Cf. Gen 39:21; Ps 84:12. Cf. the NT usage, *charis eleos eirēnē apo Theou patros kai Christou Iēsou tou kuriou hēmōn*, "Grace, mercy *and* peace from God the Father and Christ Jesus our Lord" (1 Tim 1:2; cf. 2 Tim 1:2; 2 John 1:3, especially if one recalls the equation of *ḥesed* and *šālôm*, "peace," in Jer 16:5). Cf. the phrase, "let us draw near with confidence to the throne of *charis*, so that we may receive *eleos* and find *charis* to help in time of need" (Heb 4:16).

A remarkable example comes from the section of the book of Exodus directly relevant to our study. At the theophany at Sinai Moses prays to the Lord, "if I have found *ḥēn/charis* in Your sight, let me know Your ways that I may know You, so that I may find *ḥēn/charis* in Your sight" (Exod 33:13). But for the Masoretic *ḥēn*, the *Targum Neofiti*[183] reads *ḥn wḥsd*![184]

This basic similarity of the creedal terms denoting grace was probably noticed by the époque of the Gospel. This might have caused the Evangelist's predecessors and contemporaries to begin covering a couple of the terms—*raḥûm, ḥannûn, ḥesed* (and cognates)—with a single term. An OG translator renders Esther 2:17 as follows: *ērasthē ho basileus Esthēr kai heuren charin* [MT: *ḥēn wāḥesed*] *para pasas*.[185] The author of the *Prayer of Manasseh* covers both the creedal *ḥannûn/ eleēmōn* and *raḥûm/oiktirmōn* with just one term—*eusplanchnos* (Pr. Man. 7; remarkably, in the latter case the term chosen to convey a couple of creedal terms differs from either one of the terms usually employed for such translation). This practice provides the precedent for the Evangelist to legitimately cover *raḥûm, ḥannûn* and *ḥesed* with a single term.

charis Is Suitable for All Three Creedal Terms Denoting "Grace"

Why would the Evangelist employ *charis* to convey three creedal terms denoting "grace"—*raḥûm/oiktirmōn, ḥannûn/eleēmōn, ḥesed/polueleos*?

---

183. Widely different dates have been proposed for Targum Neofiti. Díez Macho has presented the case for a "pre-Christian" origin for Targum Neofiti (see Díez Macho, "Recently Discovered"). Goshen-Gottstein has argued that certain Targum texts (Esther) may have been edited at the time of the Renaissance (see Goshen-Gottstein, "Third Targum"). Alexander wisely notices that, "In fact, there is no reason why, in principle, Díez Macho *and* Goshen-Gottstein cannot both basically be right" (Alexander, "Targum," 234).

184. See Houtman, *Exodus* 3:697; cf. Levy, *Targum Neophyti*, 1:26.

185. According to NA[27], Luke, in writing, "God was with . . . [Joseph], and rescued him from all his afflictions, and granted him *charis* and wisdom in the sight of Pharaoh, king of Egypt, and he made him governor over Egypt and all his household" (Acts 7:9–10), echoes "the LORD was with Joseph and extended *ḥesed/eleos* to him, and gave him *ḥēn/charis* in the sight of the chief jailer" (Gen 39:21). In this case Luke omits the clause "and extended *ḥesed/eleos*" from the original phrase, perhaps due to its redundancy in the eyes of the writer. This means that *charis* in Acts 7:9–10 covers both terms—*ḥesed/eleos* and *ḥēn/charis*—of Gen 39:21.

To begin with, the writer's intention not to use either *oiktirmōn*, *eleēmōn*, or *eleos* is theologically conditioned. Cognates of *oiktirmōn* "obviously did not become eschatological terms in Greek-speaking Judaism."[186] At first glance, cognates of *eleos* (including *eleēmōn* and *polueleos*) would have fit rather well. As Bultmann notes, the sense of *eleos* tends to predominate in contrast to the wrath and judgment of God: God acts *kata to eleous autou*; his *eleos* applies to Israel, to the *hosioi*, to those who love him and fear him. His *eleos* is gracious action. He reveals it. It is expected, hoped for, prayed for. The age of salvation is the age of *eleos*.[187] But cognates of *eleos* have a strong legalistic ring to them and assume "doing."[188] This strongly prevents the Evangelist from using them. In this respect the Evangelist employs approaches common to NT writers.[189] On the contrary, in Wisdom and apocalyptic literature *charis* was increasingly used for the eschatological reward of the elect (e.g., Wis 3:9; 4:14, 15; 1 *En.* 99:13), as a major term for the blessings of the salvation of the end-time (cf. 1 *En.* 5:4-8), and in association with the revealed wisdom to be found in the Torah.[190] Also, the term *charis* distinctively emphasizes the notion of a free gift.[191] Rudolf Schnackenburg states, "Philo lays much stress on the free, gracious action of God in creating and saving, and his favorite word for it is *charis*; according to his doctrine of the virtues, *charis* is not only God's gracious attitude, but also the communication of the divine gifts and power, so that he can also speak of the *charites* as the streams of God's grace."[192] The

---

186. Bultmann, "*oiktirō*," 5:160.

187. Bultmann, "*eleos*," 2:481.

188. This is expressed in various ways, mostly by linking *eleos* with *poieō*. The term *polueleos* is never used in the NT.

189. As Beker comments, "Paul avoids *eleos* (in favor of *charis*) because in Judaism *eleos* often complements what a person lacks in works, so that God's mercy becomes a supplementary gift" (Beker, *Paul*, 266). So also, Bultmann writes, "It is striking that Paul speaks of God's *eleos* only in the passages in R. 9; 11; 15 which are concerned with the history of salvation (*charis* . . .)" (Bultmann, "*eleos*," 2:484). For discussion see Lincoln, *Ephesians*, 100–113; Dunn, *Romans 9–16*, 570.

190. Lincoln, *Ephesians*, 100–113.

191. On relations between grace and works with reference to *charis* and *eleos*, see Conzelmann, "*charis*"; Bultmann, "*eleos*."

192. Schnackenburg, *John*, 1:272. He further notes that "in Philo, *charis* is far more frequent than *eleos* (cf. Leisegang's index in ed. Cohn and Wendland). In *Immut.*, 104ff., he discusses the frequent OT phrase "to find grace"; see also *Cher.*, 122f. For the plural, cf. *De opif.*, 23; 168; *Leg. all.*, II, 80; III, 163f. etc. The Logos is also *plērēs charitōn*; *De somn.*, II, 223, cf. 183" (Schnackenburg, *John*, 1:273 n. 194).

Evangelist greatly appreciates this stress on the unmerited aspect and employs *charis*.

Moreover, should the Evangelist choose to use either *oiktirmōn*, *eleēmōn* or *(polu)eleos*, the audience may get a wrong impression that the writer alludes to the particular term of the creed. So the usage of *charis* in *plērēs charitos kai alētheias* discourages one from *singling out* either one of the three creedal terms denoting grace. Instead, the chosen *charis* encourages the audience to envision *all three* creedal terms—*raḥûm*, *ḥannûn*, *ḥesed*—because their cognates *were* translated with *charis* elsewhere. The selection of *charis* conveniently allows the Evangelist to allude to LXX/OG passages, which contain either *charis* or *eleos*, because by the time of the Evangelist the two terms virtually merged in meaning.

For these reasons the usage of the standard LXX/OG creedal terminology is completely avoided in the Gospel. Cognates of *oikteirō* and *eleaō* appear in all fourteen known OT occurrences of the creed:[193] *oiktirmōn* (11 occurrences), *oiktirmos* (2), *oikteirō* (1), *eleēmōn* (12), *polueleos* (8), *eleos* (1), *eleaō* (1). In a sharp contrast to other NT authors,[194] the Evangelist never employs cognates of either *oikteirō* or *eleaō*! Instead, *charis* is emphasized in a threefold way: it is introduced in the prologue, positioned densely, and also recurs, which yet increases the intensity (1:14, 16, 16, 17).

kai alētheias Is Proper for we ʾĕmet

The adjoined attribute *ʾĕmet* is communicated with *kai alētheias*. This comes only naturally as *ʾĕmet*, a quality of God's character, obviously differs from the rest of the attributes listed in the creed.

The rendering of *ʾĕmet* with *kai alētheias* provides yet further evidence in support of the proposal that *plērēs charitos kai alētheias* is the Evangelist's own translation from the Hebrew of the creed. The Evangelist has serious reasons to supply a new translation, *plērēs charitos kai alētheiasi*, for *wərab-ḥesed weʾĕmet* instead of using the Septuagint's *polueleos kai alēthinos*. Grammatically, *plērēs charitos kai*

---

193. Exod 34:6; Num 14:18; Ps 77:9–10; 86:15; 103:8; 111:4; 112:4; 116:5; 145:8; Joel 2:13; Jonah 4:2; Neh 9:17; 9:31; 2 Chr 30:9. This count is Kselman's own (Kselman, "Grace (OT)," 1086).

194. Cognates of *oikteirō* or *eleaō* are used ninety times in the NT.

alētheias corresponds better to *wərab-ḥesed we'ĕmet* than *polueleos kai alēthinos*.[195] Semantically, *polueleos kai alēthinos* does not do justice to the meaning of the Hebrew original. In the phrase *wərab-ḥesed we'ĕmet* the term *rab* modifies both *ḥesed* and *'ĕmet*. But in the Septuagint's *polueleos kai alēthinos* the term of extent, *polu*, modifies only *eleos*, not *alēthinos*. The character descriptor *'ĕmet/alēthinos* is also "neglected" in the fourteen OT creedal affirmations of God. The distribution of creedal terms in the MT is *raḥûm* (14 occurrences), *ḥannûn* (13), and *rab-ḥesed* (9), compared to only two occurrences of *'ĕmet*. The distribution of creedal terms in the LXX/OG is *oiktirmōn* (14 occurrences) and *eleēmōn* (22), compared to only three occurrences of *alēthinos*. Thus, most OT allusions to the Exodus 34:6 character description of God do not pick up *'ĕmet/alēthinos*. The Evangelist, with the importance and Christological significance of the notion of *alētheia* in the Gospel, may well have wanted to bring out the sense of the Hebrew *rab-* . . . *'ĕmet* rather than the Septuagint's inadequate *alēthinos*. Hence, the Evangelist translates *'ĕmet* with *kai alētheias*. This accurately reflects the grammar of the parent text and does justice to the value of this quality of the character of God. In the resulting *plērēs charitos kai alētheias* the same significance is assigned to *charis* and *alētheia*.

plērēs charitos kai alētheias Has Major Theological Implications

The phrase *plērēs charitos kai alētheias* applied to Jesus is advantageous for a major goal of the Gospel, even if considered from a solely terminological perspective. *Plērēs* is suitably utilized in the book of Exodus—the frame of reference for the Gospel—as it reports,

> Moses said to Aaron, Take a golden pot, and cast into it one *plērēs* homer of manna; and thou shalt lay it up before God, to be kept for you generations, as the Lord commanded Moses: and Aaron laid it up before *tou marturiou* to be kept.[196]

This passage is a part of the framework for the "bread from heaven" episode of the Gospel.[197] The Evangelist may well echo the *fullness* of the

---

195. So Lindars, *John*, 95.

196. Exod 16:(32)33–34(35) LXE.

197. Borgen, *Bread from Heaven*, 40–42, 47, 65–68, 90. Cf. John 6:31, 51 and Exod 16:15.

manna laid up before the testimony at the Lord's command to Moses (Exod 16:33–34 LXX) by rendering *plērēs* of Jesus the Living Bread in John 1:14. *Charis* is an advantageous term as well. In later antiquity *charis* becomes a fixed term for demonstrations of a ruler's favor, as seen in a number of inscriptions.[198] We should deduce then that the term *charis* suits the Evangelist to emphasize the superiority of Jesus the King over all other rulers of the earth.[199]

The phrase *plērēs charitos kai alētheias* applied to Jesus only increases in significance when considered in its context, *kai ho logos sarx egeneto kai eskēnōsen en hēmin, kai etheasametha tēn doxan autou, doxan hōs monogenous para patros, plērēs charitos kai alētheias*. In the OT terms *ḥesed/eleos* (*charis*), *mlʾ/plērēs* (*empiplēmi*), and *doxa* in reference to the Lord come together in a manner strikingly similar to John 1:14. A chronicler reports regarding those who gathered around the temple that they praised God, saying, "'He indeed is good for His ḥesed is everlasting,' then the house, the house of the Lord, was filled with a cloud [OG: *eneplēsthē nephelēs doxēs kuriou*]" (2 Chr 5:13). The Psalmist exclaims, "The earth is full [OG: *plērēs*] of the ḥesed[200] of the Lord" (Ps 33:5; 119:64). The books of Ezekiel and Isaiah—yet another frame of reference for the Gospel—affiliate *plērēs* with *doxa*. Ezekiel twice reports, *plērēs doxēs kuriou ho oikos* (Ezek 43:5; 44:4). Isaiah "saw the Lord sitting on a high and exalted throne, and *plērēs ho oikos tēs doxēs autou*" (Isa 6:1). Seraphim cried to one another and said, "Holy, holy, holy is the Lord of hosts: *plērēs pasa hē gē tēs doxēs autou*" (Isa 6:3). Such OT usage of *plērēs* with the reference to *doxa* and *kuriou ho oikos* corresponds well with the Gospel's depicting Jesus's *doxa plērēs charitos kai alētheias*, Jesus as God in flesh walking over the earth and replacing the temple.

In our view, however, these valuable features of the phrase *plērēs charitos kai alētheias* merely suitably supplement the major goal of the Gospel, which is to depict Jesus as possessing the exact qualities of the divine character. As we have established, *plērēs charitos kai alētheias* can legitimately serve as a translation for either *wərab-ḥesed weʾĕmet* or

198. Conzelmann, "*charis*," 9:375.

199. 1:49; 6:15; 12:13, 15; 18:33, 37, 37, 39; 19:3, 12, 14, 15, 15, 19, 21, 21. 1:49; 6:15; 12:13, 15; 18:33, 37, 37, 39; 19:3, 12, 14, 15, 15, 19, 21, 21. Cf. Roman soldiers addressing Jesus, *Chaire ho basileus tōn Ioudaiōn*., "Hail, the King of the Jews!" (19:3).

200. OG *eleos*/Quinta *charis*.

raḥûm wəḥannûn ʾerek ʾappayim wərab-ḥesed weʾĕmet. This finally[201] establishes John 1:14 as an allusion to Exodus 34:6. It is in this sense of conveying the creedal attributes of the character of God that the exact phraseology of *plērēs charitos kai alētheias* bears major theological implications. At this point we shall only indicate them: First, *plērēs charitos kai alētheias* echoes a wide range of the OT references derived from the creed. Second, *plērēs* with a following genitive is indeclinable;[202] this allows *plērēs charitos kai alētheias* to modify *doxa*, *logos*, *monogenēs*, or *patēr*, or all of them at once. Third, *plērēs charitos kai alētheias* reminds the reader of the OT covenant of God's presence (*charis*) initiated at Sinai (Exod 33:12–34:10, the broader context of the creed of Exod 34:6 itself). Fourth, the character of the Father and of the Son being *plērēs charitos kai alētheias* (1:14) matches the character of the Spirit being *charitos kai alētheias ek metrou* (3:34; 14:17; 15:26; 16:13; 19:37 + Zech 12:10 LXX).

Conclusion: Retrospective and Prospective of *plērēs charitos kai alētheias* (John 1:14) and *hē charis kai hē alētheia* (John 1:17)

In this section of our study we have established that the phraseology of *plērēs charitos kai alētheias* (John 1:14) and *hē charis kai hē alētheia* (John 1:17) is an allusion to *raḥûm wəḥannûn ʾerek ʾappayim wərab-ḥesed weʾĕmet* (Exod 34:6). Our study has accounted for the discrepancy between *wərab-ḥesed weʾĕmet* (Exod 34:6 MT), *polueleos kai alēthinos* (Exod 34:6 LXX), and *plērēs charitos kai alētheias* (John 1:14). We have demonstrated that previous attempts to explain the discrepancy by arguing from modern comparative linguistics, unfaithfulness of usage of the Septuagint, practices of Hellenistic Judaism, feebleness of the Septuagint translation, and from translations into Syriac Versions or the Christian Palestinian Dialect, have actually failed to make the case for the suitability of rendering *wərab-ḥesed weʾĕmet* with *plērēs charitos kai alētheias*. The discrepancy cannot be plausibly explained by hypothesizing that the Evangelist's Greek version of Exodus 34:6 diverges from the Septuagint. It may not plausibly stem from the Evangelist exercising

---

201. As one of the five factors listed above.
202. BDF, §137.

stylistic terminological variation. Our study has acknowledged that it is possible that the discrepancy reflects the Evangelist's own translation of Exodus 34:6 from the Hebrew.[203] To defend this proposal, we have elucidated a couple of previously unresolved major issues:

First, can the creedal ʾĕmet be translated with *alētheia*?[204] Our study has demonstrated that it should. Cognates of *alētheia* convey the meaning of cognates of ʾĕmet throughout the OT/LXX/OG. The meaning of "being true to the word," and "doing what's right"—ultimately resulting from the utmost integrity of Jesus—is widely attested for cognates of *alētheia* throughout the Gospel.

Second, neither is *rab* translated with *plērēs* nor is the creedal *ḥesed* ever conveyed with *charis* anywhere in the LXX/OG. Can *plērēs charitos kai alētheias* serve as a legitimate translation of *wərab-ḥesed weʾĕmet*? Our study has shown that it certainly can. To begin with, the translation of ʾĕmet with *alētheia* is indisputably justifiable. Moreover, the Evangelist can properly translate *ḥesed* with *charis*. It has become increasingly common by the époque of the writer. The term *ḥesed* is translated with *charis* (and cognates) in Esth 2:9, 17; Sir 7:33; 40:17; Ps 31:22,[205] Ps 109:12 (an unknown translator); Prov 31:26 (Theodotion); Ps 106:7[206] (Aquila); 2 Sam 10:2; Pss 31:8, 40:11, 12[207]; 89:25; Prov 31:26[208]; Lam 3:32 (Symmachus[209]); Ps 33:5 (Quinta); Pss 31:17; 33:18 (Sexta).[210] Remarkably, in depicting a quality of God's character the terms *charis* and *eleos*[211] are utilized interchangeably (Eph 2:4, 7). Furthermore, the Evangelist can appropriately translate *rab* with *plērēs*. The Evangelist is not bound by the LXX/OG's standard *polu* or *plēthos* for *rab*. The extent of the creedal *wərab-ḥesed weʾĕmet*, which origi-

---

203. The suggestion probably originated with Sanders.

204. Contra Bultmann.

205. *charisma*.

206. Likely.

207. Likely.

208. *epicharis*.

209. Symmachus does not translate *ḥesed* with *charis* in 2 Sam 2:6; contra Hanson, "John I. 14–18 and Exodus XXXIV," 93; Schnackenburg, *John*, 272 n. 193.

210. It can be demonstrated that even though Symmachus, Quinta, and Sexta post-date the Gospel they still should be treated as independent and unbiased witnesses to practices of translating *ḥesed* during the époque of the Gospel.

211. Cf. the Septuagintal *polueleos* for *rab-ḥesed* (Exod 34:6).

nated in Exodus 34:6, was already elaborated elsewhere in the book of Exodus,[212] the Evangelist's frame of reference. It was also emphasized in the OT by utilizing terms other than *rab*,[213] the plural form of *ḥesed*, the grandeur of cosmic imagery, an extraordinary degree of success, generous scope of time, vast number of events or/and people. There was no unanimity already in translating *rab-ḥesed* on the part of the LXX/OG interpreters. NT authors, and others preceding and contemporary with the Evangelist, have further diverged from the LXX/OG's *polu/plēthos* pattern. They employ various and excessive expressions—*ametrētos*, "unmeasured, immeasurable, immense, unnumbered, countless"; *megas*, "great"; *mestos*, "full"; *pollō mallon . . . eis tous pollous eperisseusen*, "much more . . . abound to the many"; *pleonazō*, "increase, spread"; *plēthunō*, "increase"; *perisseia*, "abundance, overflow"; *huperperisseuō*, "abound all the more"; *huperpleonazō*, "overflow, be present without measure,"—to convey the extent of the divine *charis*. The Evangelist's own language of the Divine is extremely excessive all throughout the Gospel. Certain features peculiar to the Scriptures and the époque of the Evangelist may well have influenced the writer's choice of *plērēs*[214] *charitos*[215] *kai alētheias*. Finally, this phrase reflects a rather flexible approach, which writers of the époque of the Evangelist took, in alluding to/echoing creedal attributes of God. For this purpose, authors innovatively utilized terminology such as *chrēstos/chrēstotēs* (Rom 2:4, cf. Pr. Man. 11) or even *eusplanchnos* (Pr. Man. 7)/*polusplanchnos* (Jas 5:11), which had never been used in the LXX/OG's renderings of the creed. These factors determine that *plērēs charitos kai alētheias* can serve as a valid translation for *wərab-ḥesed we'ĕmet*.

---

212. *rab-ḥesed/polueleos* (Exod 34:6); cf. *nōṣēr ḥesed lā'ălāpîm/poiōn eleos eis chiliadas*, "keeping *ḥesed/eleos* for thousands" (Exod 34:7; also 20:6).

213. Particularly *gōdel*, "greatness," (Gen 19:19, Num 14:19) and *haggādōl*, "great" (1 Kgs 3:6; 2 Chr 1:8; Pss 57:11; 86:13; 108:5; 145:8).

214. The Evangelist's *doxa . . . plērēs charitos* may well have also been influenced by the OT phraseology of *ḥesed/eleos* (*charis*), *ml'/plērēs* (*empiplēmi*), and the *doxa* of the Lord (2 Chr 5:13; Ps 33:5; 119:64; Isa 6:1, 3; Ezek 43:5; 44:4). The Evangelist may well echo the *fullness* of the manna laid up before the testimony at the Lord's command to Moses (Exod 16:33–34 LXX) by rendering *plērēs* in reference to Jesus the Living Bread in 1:14.

215. Perhaps *charis* suits the Evangelist in emphasizing the superiority of Jesus the king over all other rulers of the earth. Cf. Roman soldiers addressing Jesus, *Chaire ho basileus tōn Ioudaiōn.*, "Hail, the King of the Jews!" (19:3). See Conzelmann, "*charis*."

Third, *wərab-ḥesed we'ĕmet* is a part of the creed *yhwh 'ēl raḥûm wəḥannûn 'erek 'appayim wərab-ḥesed we'ĕmet* (Exod 34:6). Why would the Evangelist "cut" just the two attributes—*wərab-ḥesed we'ĕmet*—out of the whole creed and "paste" it to John 1:14? Our study has demonstrated that this technique is not unusual. Writers from his époque do not feel obligated to list all of the creedal attributes. They extract the attributes and change their order rather freely. Sometimes writers may allude to only one of God's creedal attributes, a cognate of *makrothumeō* (Luke 18:7; Rom 2:4, 9:22), *oiktirō* (Luke 6:35–36; perhaps also 2 Cor 1:3), or *eleeō* (Luke 1:58, 72; 1 Pet 1:3). Occasionally, authors allude to a pair of the attributes—*eleeō* and *oiktirō* (Rom 9:15), or *polusplanchnos* and *oiktirmōn* (Jas 5:11). One cannot help but think of Paul's appeal, *ē tou ploutou tēs chrēstotētos autou kai tēs anochēs kai tēs makrothumias kataphroneis, agnoōn hoti to chrēston tou Theou eis metanoian se agei*, "Or do you think lightly of the riches of His kindness and tolerance and patience, not knowing that the kindness of God leads you to repentance?" (Rom 2:4), as an echo of three, if not four, creedal attributes of God.[216] Moreover, we have suggested that *plērēs charitos kai alētheias* perhaps alludes to the whole creed, *yhwh 'ēl raḥûm wəḥannûn 'erek 'appayim wərab-ḥesed we'ĕmet*. This approach eliminates the question of the legitimacy of translating *ḥesed* with *charis* and *rab* with *plērēs*. This scheme resolves the issue of the otherwise awkward "cut-and-paste" choice of attributes *wərab-ḥesed we'ĕmet* in place of the whole creed. This design accounts for all of the creedal attributes of the character of God in *plērēs charitos kai alētheias*. The absence of the creedal *'erek 'appayim/makrothumos* warns that God's longsuffering nature has come to an end.[217] The irregular[218] and excessive *plērēs* hints that all three creedal terms denoting "grace" linked by *w—raḥûm wəḥannûn . . . wərab-ḥesed*—are conveyed with a single *charis*.[219] The adjoined distinctive attribute *'ĕmet* is communicated with *kai alētheias*. Thus,

---

216. Cf. Joel 2:13; Jonah 4:2; Wis 15:1.

217. Cf. 3:36. Notice the absence of cognates of *metanoeō*, another creedal attribute relevant to God's character (Joel 2:13; Jonah 4:2) in the Gospel. On the Gospel as a legal case of the Lord v. humanity, see Lincoln, *Truth*.

218. Cf. the LXX/OG's standard *polu/plēthos* for *rb*.

219. This technique is practiced during the époque of the Evangelist. For example, both the creedal *ḥannûn/eleēmōn* and *raḥûm/oiktirmōn* are likely to be conveyed with a single *eusplanchnos* (Pr. Man. 7).

plērēs charitos kai alētheias in all likelihood alludes to *yhwh ʾēl raḥûm wəḥannûn ʾerek ʾappayim wərab-ḥesed weʾĕmet*.

Fourth, the Evangelist writes in Greek for an audience that speaks Greek and is familiar with, if anything, the Septuagint. The Evangelist generally uses the Septuagint. But the rendering *plērēs charitos kai alētheias* offers a reading different from the Septuagint's *polueleos kai alēthinos* of Exodus 34:6. This blurs the suggested allusion. Why would the Evangelist make a new translation from Hebrew? It has been observed that the Evangelist does translate from Hebrew if there is a reason for it.[220] Our study has evinced that the Evangelist has serious reasons to translate *wərab-ḥesed weʾĕmet* (Exod 34:6) with *plērēs charitos kai alētheias* (John 1:14) instead of using *polueleos kai alēthinos* (Exod 34:6 LXX). First, the Septuagint's *polueleos kai alēthinos* does not do justice to the meaning of the Hebrew original, as the translation does not convey the extent of *ʾĕmet*.[221] The character descriptor *ʾĕmet/alēthinos* is also "neglected" in the OT creedal affirmations of God. The Evangelist, in light of the importance and Christological significance of the notion of *alētheia* in the Gospel, may well have wanted to bring out the sense of the Hebrew *rab-* . . . *ʾĕmet* rather than the inadequate *alētheias* of the LXX. Second, the Evangelist may well desire to reduce the three creedal terms denoting grace to a single *charis* for a variety of reasons. Space is precious in the prologue. Besides, Greek equivalents for the three creedal terms—*raḥûm, ḥannûn, ḥesed*—may not fit the poetic meter of the prologue. Moreover, creedal terms denoting "grace" have lost their distinctiveness by the époque of the Evangelist. Should the Evangelist choose to use either *oiktirmōn, eleēmōn*, or *(polu)eleos* the audience may get the wrong impression that the writer alludes to the particular term of the creed,[222] so the usage of *charis* in *plērēs charitos kai alētheias* discourages one from singling out either one of the three creedal terms denoting grace. Instead, the chosen term *charis* encourages the audience to envision all three creedal terms—*raḥûm, ḥannûn, ḥesed*—because their cognates have been translated with *charis* elsewhere. Furthermore, the writer's decision not to use either *oiktirmōn, eleēmōn*, or *eleos* may well

---

220. 12:40; 13:18; 19:37. See Menken, *Quotations*, 205.

221. Grammatically, *plērēs charitos kai alētheias* corresponds better to *wərab-ḥesed weʾĕmet* than *polueleos kai alēthinos*.

222. Cognates of *oiktirmōn, eleēmōn*, or *(polu)eleos* are never used in the Gospel.

be theologically conditioned. Cognates of *oiktirmōn* have not become eschatological terms in Greek-speaking Judaism. Cognates of *eleos* (including *eleēmōn* and *polueleos*) have a strong legalistic ring to them and assume "doing."[223] These factors prevent the Evangelist from using them. Instead, the Evangelist stresses the notion of unmeritedness by covering all three terms with a single *charis*. Finally, the selection of *charis* allows the Evangelist to conveniently allude to the LXX/OG passages, which contain either *charis* or *eleos*, as the terms had virtually merged in meaning by this time (Eph 2:4, 7). Third, *plērēs* with a following genitive is indeclinable.[224] This feature allows *plērēs charitos kai alētheias* to modify *patēr, logos, monogenēs, doxa*, or all of them at once. Fourth, *plērēs charitos kai alētheias* calls to mind the OT covenant of God's presence (*charis*) initiated at Sinai (Exod 33:12—34:10 LXX, the broader context of the creed of Exod 34:6 itself). Fifth, the character of the Father and of the Son being *plērēs charitos kai alētheias* (1:14) matches the character of the Spirit being *charitos kai alētheias ek metrou* (3:34; 14:17; 15:26; 16:13; 19:37 + Zech 12:10 LXX).

Our study concludes that in all likelihood the Evangelist has translated *yhwh ʾēl raḥûm wəḥannûn ʾerek ʾappayim wərab-ḥesed weʾĕmet*—creedal attributes of God's character (Exod 34:6)—with *plērēs charitos kai alētheias* (John 1:14) and *hē charis kai hē alētheia* (John 1:17).

---

223. Besides, the LXX's *polueleos* may well have become obsolete as it is never used in the NT.

224. BDF, §137.

2

Terms of John 1:14–18

A number of scholars treat *(hē) charis kai (hē) alētheia* as hendiadys[1] —"the co-ordination[2] of two ideas, one of which is dependent on the other"[3] (hereafter the working definition[4]). As long ago as 1892 a correspondent writing to the *Expository Times* suggested that the phrase might mean "the true grace or power."[5] Beasley-Murray comments, "*charis kai alētheia*, 'grace and truth,' = the common ḥsd w ʾmt (ḥesed weʾĕmet) . . . 'gracious constancy' of God."[6] Brown translates both *charitos kai alētheias* and *hē charis kai hē alētheia* (1:14, 17) with "*enduring love.*"[7] Bultmann believes that "*charis* and *alētheia* [in 1:14] are . . . a hendiadys, since *charis* has the formal meaning of "giving grace" and "gracious gift," while *alētheia* denotes the content of the gift, the divine

---

1. Literally, "one through two" (Greek).
2. By *kai*.
3. BDF, § 442 (16).
4. Definitions of hendiadys vary. Waltke and O'Connor identify hendiadys *widely*, as "a single expression of two apparently separate parts" (*IBHS*, 691). König *moderately* restricts hendiadys, limiting it to nouns and verbs (König, *Stilistik*). Avishur defines hendiadys *narrowly*, as "a linguistic-stylistic figure wherein two nouns are connected by a conjunctive letter or preposition and one noun serves as a modifier of the second . . . a unique one-time combination whose components never again appear in any other form of pairing" (Avishur, *Stylistic Studies*, 99–100, 103). Scholars agree that a clear-cut example of hendiadys is found in the phrase, "You are seeking to destroy ʿîr waʾēm in Israel" (2 Sam 20:19). Here, the word-pair ʿîr waʾēm, "a city and a mother," stands for "metropolis." This variety of definitions does not affect our study. Word-pairs ḥesed weʾĕmet, *charitos kai alētheias*, and *hē charis kai hē alētheia*, as noun-conjunction-noun phrases, comply with any of the above definitions. The matter at stake is whether one of the nouns modifies the other.
5. Gurzon-Siggers, *Grace and Truth*, 480, as referred to in Hanson, *John 1:14–18 and Exodus 34*, 94 n. 1.
6. Beasley-Murray, *John*, 14, emphasis added.
7. R. Brown, *John (I–XII)*, 4, 14, 16, emphasis added.

reality revealing itself."[8] De la Potterie maintains that the Evangelist, instead of rendering *hē charis kai hē alētheia . . . egeneto* in 1:17, might just as well have written *hē alētheia echaristhē*.[9] This scholar states that he is

> certain that *(hē) charis kai (hē) alētheia* in John 1:14,17 form a hendiadys. This has considerable exegetical consequences: *charis* (which thematically corresponds to *edothē* in v.17) can only mean 'gift, grace'. . . . the nature of this 'grace' is indicated by the noun which determines it: it is 'the grace of the truth'. The expression indicates only a single reality: 'the truth' is considered by John as one 'grace', that comes from the Father in Jesus Christ.[10]

Edwards claims that "*charis kai alētheia*,[11] in [1:] v. 17 . . . is the *true charis*."[12] Harris opts for "gracious gift of divine reality" as a translation for *hē charis kai hē alētheia*.[13] Loisy paraphrases *hē charis kai hē alētheia* as "*the reality of the grace*."[14] For Katharine D. Sakenfeld, "The Greek behind the phrase 'grace and truth' [of 1:14] reflects the classic Hebrew combination 'loyalty and faithfulness,' [*ḥesed weʾĕmet*] or *sure loyalty*."[15] Schnackenburg remarks on *plērēs charitos kai alētheias*, "In this grouping, *alētheia* is the subordinate term."[16]

Is treating *(hē) charis kai (hē) alētheia* as hendiadys justified or not? It is crucial to determine whether the phrase *(hē) charis kai (hē) alētheia* depicts one (if hendiadys) or two (if not hendiadys) attributes. We have already demonstrated that *(hē) charis kai (hē) alētheia* alludes to *ḥesed weʾĕmet*. Therefore, to evaluate the likelihood of *(hē) charis kai (hē) alētheia* constituting hendiadys, our study should 1) assess whether

---

8. Bultmann, *John*, 73.

9. La Potterie, "*Charis*," 275.

10. Ibid., 276.

11. *Sic*.

12. Edwards, "*Charin anti charitos*," 11–12, emphasis added.

13. Harris, *Prologue and Gospel*, 71. Cf. her rather enigmatic (with regard to the matter of hendiadys) remark in parentheses: "in v. 14 . . . it is . . . the manifested being . . . of the unique Son of a heavenly Father which is characterized as being full of grace (and truth)" (Harris, *Prologue and Gospel*, 50).

14. "la réalité . . . de la grâce" (Loisy, *Le quatrième Évangile*, 193; emphasis added). See La Potterie, "*Charis*," 266.

15. Sakenfeld, *Faithfulness*, 134; emphasis added.

16. Schnackenburg, *John*, 1:273; similarly, Dumbrell, "Grace and Truth," 115.

the word-pair *ḥesed we'ĕmet* in reference to God functions as hendiadys in the OT, 2) consider whether the LXX/OG translators perceive *ḥesed we'ĕmet* as hendiadys, and 3) evaluate whether *(hē) charis kai (hē) alētheia* constitutes hendiadys in the Gospel.

OT Writers Render *ḥesed we'ĕmet* to Convey Two Subjective Qualities

Discussion over hendiadys in the OT was initiated in 1900 by E. König[17] and carried on by Ezra Z. Melamed,[18] Hendrik A. Brongers,[19] J. P. van der Westhuizen,[20] and Yitzhak Avishur,[21] among other scholars.[22] Discussion over whether *ḥesed we'ĕmet* constitutes hendiadys or not has always been characterized as uncertain.

Nelson Glueck, in a pioneering study on *ḥesed*,[23] suggests that the phrase *rab ḥesed we'ĕmet* constitutes hendiadys. On the one hand, he states that

> God's *ḥesed* corresponds to the demands of loyalty, justice and righteousness and already contains these concepts. God's *ḥesed* and *'ĕmet* are to be considered a hendiadys, in which *'ĕmet* has the value of a descriptive adjective.[24]

He translates the word-pair as hendiadys on numerous occasions.[25] On the other hand, Glueck interprets *rab ḥesed we'ĕmet* as two separate attributes.[26]

17. König, *Stilistik*.
18. Melamed, "Hendiadys."
19. Brongers, *Merismus, Synekdoche und Hendidys*.
20. Westhuizen, "Hendiadys."
21. Avishur, *Stylistic Studies*; "Pairs of Synonymous Words"; *Construct State*.
22. See Moore, "Judith"; Myers, "Interpreting"; Scullion, "Righteousnessn (OT)."
23. Glueck, *Ḥesed*.
24. Ibid., 102.
25. Gen 24:27, 49; 47:29; Pss 40:10–11; 69:14, 17; 85:11. See Glueck, *Ḥesed*, 39, 72, 79, 99, 100, 102. Hanson somehow misses all of Glueck's explicit statements on the matter of hendiadys when he writes, "Glueck in his . . . exposition on the phrase *ḥsd w'mt*, comes very near to claiming it is a hendiadys" (Hanson, *John 1:14–18 and Exodus 34*, 94 n. 1, with a reference to Glueck, *Ḥesed*, 72).
26. Josh 2:14; Prov 16:6; 20:28. See Glueck, *Ḥesed*, 44, 62, 65, 79, 94 n. 196; he does not explain the basis for making a decision regarding which pair of *'ĕmet* and *ḥesed* constitutes hendiadys and which does not.

Sakenfeld also claims, in the most recent study on *ḥesed*, that, "*ḥesed we'ĕmet*, 'loyalty' and 'truth' are not to be regarded as two separate qualities . . . Rather, as has often been suggested,²⁷ the noun "truth" (better, 'faithfulness' or 'trustworthiness') here functions by hendiadys to qualify the basic notion of loyalty."²⁸

For Sakenfeld, *ḥesed we'ĕmet* "exemplifies hendiadys, with a nuance of constancy being added to emphasize the basic sense of loyalty itself."²⁹ But, her translations betray the uncertainty over the matter. On several occasions Sakenfeld interprets the phrase *ḥesed . . . 'ĕmet* as hendiadys where *'ĕmet* modifies *ḥesed*, resulting in one quality—"sure loyalty"—of the Lord.³⁰ In other cases, she conveys similar constructions as denoting two distinctive attributes of God—"loyalty" and "faithfulness."³¹ This indecision over the number of God's attributes reaches its climax when Sakenfeld translates two identical versions of the creed *'ēl raḥûm wəḥannûn 'erek 'appayim wərab-ḥesed we'ĕmet* with "God merciful and gracious, slow to anger and abounding in *loyalty and faithfulness*"³² in Exodus 34:6, but with "God merciful and gracious, slow to anger and abounding in *sure loyalty*"³³ in Psalm 86:15 MT. The uncertainty is finally crystallized in Sakenfeld's comment: "The Greek behind the phrase 'grace and truth' [of 1:14] reflects the classic Hebrew combination 'loyalty and faithfulness,' [*ḥesed we'ĕmet*] *or* sure loyalty."³⁴ This "or" gives the uncertainty away, for it can only be "either/or": *ḥesed we'ĕmet* denotes either *one* or *two* attributes of God!

This indecision is also evident in the rather elusive wording of other scholars' speculations on the matter (italicized in the following examples): "[*ḥesed we'ĕmet*,] the reward for the good *can be understood as hendiadys*: faithful love";³⁵ "*'mt . . . commonly accompanies ḥsd . . .*

---

27. Sakenfeld does not provide references for this claim.

28. Sakenfeld, *Faithfulness*, 31; see also 55, 57–60; translations.

29. Ibid., 55.

30. Gen 24:27; 32:10; Pss 86:15; 138:2. See Sakenfeld, *Faithfulness*, 85, 86, 89, 91, 95, 133.

31. Exod 34:6; Pss 89:25; 98:3. See Sakenfeld, *Faithfulness*, 47, 56, 59; "Love (OT)," 381.

32. Sakenfeld, *Faithfulness*, 47; emphasis added.

33. Ibid., 95; emphasis added.

34. Ibid., 134; emphasis added.

35. Murphy, *Proverbs*, 14:22; emphasis added.

Sometimes the two terms are a hendiadys *suggesting* a commitment that can be relied on; *where they can be distinguished*, the former *may suggest* protective faithfulness, the latter active kindness";[36] "*alētheia* and *eleos* correspond to *ḥesed weʾĕmet* and function *more or less* as a hendiadys";[37] "It *appears* . . . that when *ḥesed* and *ʾĕmet* appear together they become a hendiadys in which the second term intends to confirm and enrich the concept of the first."[38] Moreover, a scholar may render a translation that distinguishes the two attributes and, in the same phrase, suggest that the word-pair is a hendiadys. For example, John S. Kselman writes that "in the confessional formula in Exod 34:6 . . . the expression is *rab-ḥesed weʾĕmet*, 'abundant in *ḥesed* and fidelity' (a hendiadys *more accurately* translated 'abundant in reliable, unfailing *ḥesed*')."[39] Marvin E. Tate interprets *ḥesed weʾĕmet man yinṣəruhû* (Ps 61:8) as "assign Loyal-love and Truth to safeguard him,"[40] but adds at once that "A. R. Johnson[41] . . . *may be* correct to conclude that *ḥsd w ʾmt* is a hendiadys, meaning 'true devotion' or 'true loyal-love.'"[42] Roland E. Murphy translates *wəḥesed weʾĕmet ḥōršê ṭôb* (Prov 14:22) with "But those who plan good, kindness and fidelity,"[43] and immediately remarks that "the reward for the good *can be* understood as a hendiadys: faithful love."[44] Furthermore, a writer may interpret *ḥesed weʾĕmet* as a hendiadys but at once indicate the "literal" meaning of the word-pair. A. A. Anderson gives us "may Yahweh show you lasting loyalty [*ḥesed weʾĕmet*]," followed immediately by the comment, "Lit., 'loyalty and truth' (*ḥsd w ʾmt*) but *perhaps* a hendiadys."[45] He further exercises this approach by characteristically rendering *ḥesed weʾĕmet* as "'True loyalty' (lit. 'loyalty and truth')."[46]

---

36. Goldingay, *Daniel*, 252f.; emphasis added.
37. Dunn, *Romans 9–16*, 848; emphasis added.
38. Kuyper, "Grace and Truth," 6–7; emphasis added.
39. Kselman, "Grace (OT)," 1086; emphasis added.
40. Tate, *Psalms 51–100*, 109.
41. Johnson, *Cultic Prophet*, 357.
42. Tate, *Psalms 51–100*, 109 n. b; emphasis added, or "true/faithful loyal-love" (Tate, *Psalms 51–100*, 376).
43. Murphy, *Proverbs*, 100.
44. Ibid., 106; emphasis added.
45. Anderson, *2 Samuel*, 27.
46. Ibid., 204. Anderson here makes a reference to Sakenfeld, *Faithfulness*, 31–32.

Critique of Arguments that *ḥesed weʾĕmet* Constitutes Hendiadys

Several scholars simply declare *ḥesed weʾĕmet* to be hendiadys with no real evidence to substantiate the claim.[47] For example, Artur Weiser states that "in what is almost a fixed liturgical expression like *ḥesed weʾĕmet* or *ḥesed weʾĕmûnāʰ* the word *ḥesed* (love, grace) provides the *material definition*, while *ʾĕmet* (*ʾĕmûnāʰ*) (the steadfast faithfulness of love and its expression) represents the more *formal element*."[48] With due respect, we ought to acknowledge that the personal opinions of scholars regarding the matter cannot constitute evidence.

Other researchers try defending their position. The first approach is to provide a speculative account or propose a thesis that is immune to criticism. Thus, for Hans J. Zobel, "the context . . . most easily explains the combination of *ḥesed* and *ʾĕmet*, because the close and intimate society of the family requires enduring and reliable kindness as an essential element of its protective function."[49] Sakenfeld argues similarly, "It is quite possible that since the longer phrase [*ḥesed weʾĕmet*] became a fixed expression, it was used simply as a variant for the single word, perhaps for emphasis, but without a clear purpose to say something different."[50] Hence Johnson writes, "As I hope to make clear elsewhere, this twofold expression [*ḥesed weʾĕmet*] is an example of hendiadys meaning 'true (as being an assured) loyalty' . . . , i. e. essentially 'devotion.'"[51] But Johnson's only assertion is the following:

> The fact is that in the Old Testament the quality [*ʾĕmet*] which was recognized from the first as actually necessary for the keeping of a covenant was indicated by means of the expression *ḥesed weʾĕmet* which, as an example of hendiadys, conveys the thought of what we understand by "true devotion"; for basically these two terms *ḥesed weʾĕmet*, taken together in this way ["true devotion"], denote the "loyalty" (*ḥesed*) to which one commits oneself by a sworn undertaking or pledge of "truth" (*ʾĕmet*) as

---

47. Most notably Kuyper, "Grace and Truth," 6–7.
48. Weiser, "*pisteuō*," 6:185; emphasis added.
49. Zobel, "*ḥesed*," 51.
50. Sakenfeld, *Faithfulness*, 37 n. 27.
51. Johnson, *Cultic Prophet*, 56 n. 2.

the basic requirement for carrying out the responsibilities accepted under such a covenant.⁵²

Glueck also states that "wherever *ḥesed* appears together with *ʾĕmet* or *ʾĕmûnāʰ*, the quality of loyalty inherent in the concept *ḥesed* is emphasized."⁵³ Glueck's solution for the opposite case is, "Where *ḥesed* is used alone and not in the combination *ḥsd w ʾmt*, as is frequently the case, one may still picture mentally *ʾmt* next to *ḥsd*."⁵⁴ These suggestions, due to their speculative nature or/and immunity to criticism, cannot be taken into consideration in evaluating the probability of the case.

The second approach is to combine two in one by *associating ḥesed and ʾĕmet*. Sakenfeld, who notes that *rab-ḥesed* is rendered only "of God, never of human beings,"⁵⁵ further asserts, "It is this greatness of God's loyalty that distinguishes it from human loyalty, which is often by contrast characterized as frail or fickle,"⁵⁶ and finally sums up by claiming that

> faithfulness encompasses both the reliability of God as constancy over time and the assurance that divine promises will be kept. For those who know their very existence to be in dependence upon the loyalty of Yahweh, this strengthening of loyalty to "faithful loyalty" or "sure loyalty" gives heightened expression to the trustworthiness of the benevolent and saving God.⁵⁷

Now, in depicting the same God, the attributes *ḥesed* and *ʾĕmet*⁵⁸ are no doubt associated. But from this association, it by no means follows that one attribute necessarily modifies the other.⁵⁹

---

52. Ibid., 65–66. Johnson's suggestion is not only speculative, but also circular and illogical. Moreover, Johnson offers this argument while commenting on Ps 78. But he immediately recognizes that "the term *ḥesed* does not occur in the psalm under discussion," but only *raḥûm* (Ps 78:38)!

53. Glueck, *Ḥesed*, 72. Glueck adds a long list of references in the footnote, but neither one of them contains evidence for the claim.

54. Ibid., 40.

55. Sakenfeld, *Faithfulness*, 49.

56. Ibid.

57. Ibid., 60. Edgar Kellenberger associates this persistent character of divine loyalty with the term "faithfulness" as well (Kellenberger, *Häsäd waʾuämät*, 81); see Sakenfeld, *Faithfulness*, 49 n. 20.

58. As well as other creedal terms *raḥûm, ḥannûn, ʾerek ʾappayim*, for that matter.

59. For methodological reservations over the assumption that association means similarity in the meanings of the words (as related to *ḥesed*), see Stoebe, "Bedeutung des *Häsäd*."

The third approach is to make a reference to an authority in the field. This is what Anderson does: "[ḥesed weʾĕmet] 'True loyalty' (lit. 'loyalty and truth') describes the constancy of Yahweh in maintaining his promises. See also K. D. Sakenfeld, *Faithfulness in Action: Loyalty in Biblical Perspective*. OBT 16. Philadelphia: Fortress Press, 1985, 31–32."[60] But Sakenfeld only claims *ḥesed weʾĕmet* to be hendiadys on the pages referred to and provides no evidence for the claim elsewhere in the book. In fact, Sakenfeld (as it has already been demonstrated) is not quite sure whether *ḥesed weʾĕmet* is hendiadys or not herself. Perhaps this lack of consistency and confidence on the part of the authority to which he refers is reflected in the "double offer" of the referring scholar. Anderson also appeals to an authority when he writes, "may Yahweh show you lasting loyalty [*ḥesed weʾĕmet*]," immediately followed by, "Lit., 'loyalty and truth' (*ḥsd w ʾmt*) but perhaps a hendiadys,"[61] and then adds, "cf. Williams, *Syntax*, § 72."[62] Ronald J. Williams merely asserts that "a single concept may be expressed by two words linked by the conjunction *we*, e. g. . . . *ḥesed weʾĕmet*, 'true loyalty' (Ex 34:6, Jo 2:14, II Sm 2:6, 15:20; it is significant that in Pr 16:6 only one preposition is used)."[63] Of course, Williams's entry as such does not establish *ḥesed weʾĕmet* as a hendiadys; it can only suggest that it is.[64] His note that "it is significant that in Pr 16:6 only one preposition is used" is rather enigmatic.[65] Perhaps Williams's thought is more clearly expressed by Zobel, who argues as follows:

> That we are in fact dealing with a hendiadys [in Prov 3:3; 14:22; 16:6; 20:28] can be seen from [Prov] 16:6; only the first noun is preceded by the prep. *be*, which thus applies to the phrase as a whole, a single concept meaning "lasting, constant *ḥesed*."[66]

But a preposition (particularly *b*) preceding only the first of two nouns joined by *w* simply cannot serve to identify hendiadys, even less to establish the case "in fact"! Proverbs 16:6 reads, "*bəḥesed weʾĕmet*

---

60. Anderson, *2 Samuel*, 204.
61. Ibid., 27.
62. Williams, *Hebrew Syntax*.
63. Ibid., 16 § 72.
64. Cf., for example, *IBHS*, which does not list *ḥesed weʾĕmet* as hendiadys.
65. Williams does not develop this thought any further.
66. Zobel, "*ḥesed*," 51.

iniquity is atoned for." This construction, "preposition-noun-*w*-noun," is used in phraseology, which has long been thought to constitute hendiadys.[67] But such a suspicion does not constitute proof that such phraseology actually constitutes hendiadys. Neither does it determine that this syntax is an indicator of the presence of hendiadys.

On the one hand, this construction appears in a context, which rules out hendiadys, where one noun serves as a modifier for the other. For example, consider the following phrases: *bəkārîm wəʾêlîm wəʿattûdîm*, "for lambs, rams and goats" (Ezek 27:21); *bəṣôm wəśaq wāʾēper*, "with fasting, sackcloth and ashes" (Dan 9:3); *mēʾādām ûbahēmāʰ*, "of man or animal" (Lev 27:28); *ləʿōšer wəhokmāʰ*, "in riches and wisdom" (2 Chr 9:22); *ʾel-mōšeʰ wəʾahărōn*, "to Moses and Aaron" (Exod 12:43); *ʿal-bāḥûr ûbətûlāʰ*, "on young man or virgin[68]" (2 Chr 36:17). In these phrases (matching the "preposition-noun-conjunction-noun" construction of Prov 16:6), nouns cannot conceivably modify each other. This completely invalidates Williams's and Zobel's "indicator of hendiadys."

On the other hand, there are OT examples where *both ḥesed* and *ʾĕmet* are preceded by a preposition. Consider the following: "I will . . . give thanks to Your name for Your *ḥesed* and Your *ʾĕmet* [*ʿal-ḥasdəkā wəʿal-ʾămittekā*]" (Ps 138:2); "I am unworthy of all the *ḥesed* and of all the *ʾĕmet* [*mikkōl haḥăsādîm ûmikkol-hāʾĕmet*] which You have shown to Your servant" (Gen 32:11); and, "Not to us, O LORD, not to us, But to Your name give glory Because of Your *ḥesed*, because of Your *ʾĕmet* [*ʿal-ḥasdəkā ʿal-ʾămittekā*]" (Ps 115:1). Should not then *ḥesed weʾĕmet* be discarded as hendiadys on Zobel's and Williams's terms? Apparently, neither provides evidence for *ḥesed weʾĕmet* being hendiadys. Therefore neither of Anderson's referents—Sakenfeld, Williams (Zobel)—provides any support for his assessment.[69]

The fourth approach is to attempt to establish that *ḥesed weʾĕmet* is a hendiadys for a particular case and then to project the result onto the rest of the occurrences of the word pair. Zobel does this in the case of the book of Hosea, as follows: Hosea 6:6 ("For I delight in *ḥesed* rather

---

67. Most often exemplified by Isa 58:4; 1 Sam 15:22; Prov 22:20; Isa 29:6; 35:10, 1 Kgs 8:51; Pss 31:4; 71:3; Prov 8:14.

68. "Virgin," as is in NASB.

69. Examples to this practice of making an unsubstantiated reference to an authority in the field are numerous. See, Goldingay, *Daniel*, 242; Andersen, "Yahweh," 55, 58, 66, 84 n. 26.

than sacrifice, in the knowledge of God [wədaʿat ʾĕlōhîm] rather than burnt offerings") speaks only of ḥesed and daʿat ʾĕlōhîm as objects of Yahweh's desire. Neither is ʾĕmet mentioned in Hosea 10:12 ("Sow with a view to righteousness, reap in accordance with ḥesed; break up your fallow ground, for it is time to seek the LORD [lidrôš ʾet-yhwh] until he comes to rain righteousness on you") as a third term alongside ḥesed and daʿat ʾĕlōhîm. Therefore, in Hosea 4:1 ("Listen to the word of the LORD, O sons of Israel, for the LORD has a case against the inhabitants of the land, Because there is no ʾĕmet or ḥesed Or knowledge of God [kî ʾên-ʾĕmet wəʾên-ḥesed wəʾên-daʿat ʾĕlōhîm] in the land"), the first noun ʾĕmet must be conceived in combination with both ḥesed and daʿat ʾĕlōhîm,[70] which it dominates through its initial position. Thus the emphasis, he concludes, is on the transitory nature of the ḥesed practiced by the inhabitants of the land, which is derived in turn from the absence of enduring knowledge of God.[71]

But Zobel's argument is fallacious in many ways.[72] First, Hosea 10:12 does not mention daʿat ʾĕlōhîm, "knowledge of God," but urges lidrôš ʾet-yhwh, "to seek the LORD."[73] Hence, his observation that "Hosea 6:6 speaks only of ḥesed and daʿat ʾĕlōhîm as objects of Yahweh's desire" is inaccurate and undermines all the implications made on its basis. Second, daʿat and ḥesed occur in Hosea individually, without referring to each other or to ʾĕmet.[74] Since the terms function independently in Hosea as a whole, they are likely individual requisites in the particular case of Hosea 4:1 ("Because there is no ʾĕmet or ḥesed or knowledge of

---

70. Similarly, Glueck states that "ḥesed comprises ʾĕmet, and both are contained in daʿat ʾĕlōhîm" (Glueck, Ḥesed, 57), but does not support the claim.

71. Zobel, "ḥesed," 51.

72. Particularly incredible are interpretations made on the basis of Zobel's argument. For example, Zobel notes that "Hos. 6:4 says of Ephraim and Judah: 'Your love [ḥesed] is like a morning cloud, like the dew that goes early away.' Both images portray a fleeting ḥesed, in the absence of ʾĕmet" (ibid., 52). There is simply nothing in the context to support this claim.

73. Zobel generally equates terms rather freely. He starts with making no distinction between daʿat ʾĕlōhîm, "knowledge of God," and lidrôš ʾet-yhwh, "to seek the LORD," in the book of Nehemiah. Then he alleges that ḥesed ʿôlām (Isa 54:8) "is equivalent to Jeremiah's 'everlasting love' [ʾahăbat ʿôlām] (Jer. 31:3)" (ibid., 51). Notice that in Jer 31:3 ʾahăbāh is the cause for the effect ḥesed, so that the two simply cannot be equated. Then Zobel claims that "ḥesed can simply be equated with goodness (ṭôb, Ps. 23:6)" (ibid., 56–57).

74. daʿat, "knowledge," in Hos 4:6, 6; ḥesed in Hos 2:21; 6:4; 10:12; 12:7.

God [*kî ʾên-ʾĕmet wəʾên-ḥesed wəʾên-daʿat ʾĕlōhîm*]") as well. Third, Zobel fails to take into consideration Hosea 2:22 ("And I will betroth you to Me in *ʾĕmûnāʰ*. Then you will know the LORD [*beʾĕmûnāʰ wəyādaʿat ʾet-yhwh*]"). In this verse, the terms *ʾĕmûnāʰ*[75] and *yd*[76] are clearly related but in such a way as to exclude the possibility of one term modifying the other. Therefore, it is unlikely that *ʾĕmet* modifies *daʿat* in Hosea 4:1. Fourth, the placement of *ʾĕmet* at the beginning of the chain *kî ʾên-ʾĕmet wəʾên-ḥesed wəʾên-daʿat ʾĕlōhîm*, "Because there is no *ʾĕmet* or *ḥesed* Or knowledge of God," by no means establishes its dominance over the following terms of the chain. Linking nouns by *w* appears to be a feature of the style of Hosea, who renders *ḥodšāʰ wəšabbattāʰ wəkōl môʿădāʰ*, "her new moons, and[77] her sabbaths and all her festal assemblies" (2:13); *ʿim-ḥayyat haśśādeʰ wəʿim-ʿôp haššāmayim wəremeś hāʾădāmāʰ*, "with the beasts of the field, and[78] the birds of the sky, and the creeping things of the ground" (2:20); *wəqešet wəḥereb ûmilḥāmāʰ*, "and[79] the bow, and the sword, and war" (2:20); *zənût wəyayin watîrôš*, "harlotry, and wine, and new wine" (4:11); and *ʾallôn wəlibneʰ wəʾēlāʰ*, "oak, poplar and terebinth" (4:13). This feature of Hosea's style readily refutes Zobel's suggestion of the "dominance" of *ʾĕmet*, the first term of the chain *kî ʾên-ʾĕmet wəʾên-ḥesed wəʾên-daʿat ʾĕlōhîm*, over the rest of the terms linked. If Zobel's proposal reflected reality, then "the beasts of the field" would have likely dominated over "the birds of the sky" and "the creeping things of the ground" as well! Moreover, the terms in Hosea's chains of nouns linked by *w* cannot conceivably modify each other. Therefore, it is likely that in Hosea's other chain *kî ʾên-ʾĕmet wəʾên-ḥesed wəʾên-daʿat ʾĕlōhîm* the terms involved do not modify each other, and therefore do not constitute hendiadys. Furthermore, the OT word pair *ḥesed . . . ʾĕmet* (*ʾĕmûnāʰ*) occurs in both straight and reverse orders, even within the same literary unit of Psalm 89. In Zobel's terms, this would have meant instant switching from something

---

75. Noun cognate of *ʾĕmet*; see *TWOT* 0116.0. On the replacement of *ʾĕmet* with *ʾĕmûnāʰ* and the equivalence of their meaning in conjunction with *ḥesed* and with the reference to God, see Jepsen, "*ʾĕmet*," 319. Notice the parallel usage of *ʾĕmet* with *ʾĕmûnāʰ* in Ps 40:11 and especially in the literary unity of Ps 89:15, 25.

76. Verbal cognate of *daʿat*, "knowledge"; see *TWOT* 0848.0.

77. "and" is added to the NASB translation to reflect *w*.

78. "and" is added to the NASB translation to reflect *w*.

79. "and" is added to the NASB translation to reflect *w*.

like "true grace" to "gracious truth," which is not really a viable option. Finally, Zobel's argument by its very design cannot establish that ʾĕmet constitutes hendiadys in Hosea 4:1. No firm conclusion can be derived from the absence of ʾĕmet[80], as some scholars—Zobel, Glueck—suggest. The fact that ʾĕmet is absent may conceivably signify that ḥesed weʾĕmet is a hendiadys with the emphasis on ḥesed and, therefore, the word-pair should be translated as "true grace." But it may just as well be that only one of two distinctive requisites is reiterated. These observations, being perfectly valid as far as they go, by their very nature cannot either support or undermine the thesis that the creedal phrase ḥesed weʾĕmet is hendiadys. Neither could Zobel's argument, even it was flawless.[81]

Thus, as far as our study has been able to discern, the *suggestion*[82] that ḥesed weʾĕmet constitutes a hendiadys has no support.

Arguments contra ḥesed weʾĕmet Being Hendiadys

Since definitions and the nature of hendiadys allow speculations, usage of this literary device ought not be assumed, but should be verified. Our study will assess whether scholarly findings confirm or undermine the suggestion that ḥesed weʾĕmet is hendiadys and evaluate the *likelihood* of the case.

Avishur, among other scholars, explains the phenomenon of hendiadys by the relatively late date of the construct state development in affinity with syndetic parataxis,[83] and by the paucity of adjectives in Biblical Hebrew.[84] As it appears, these factors did not affect the particular word pair—the creedal ḥesed weʾĕmet. First, the relatively late date of the construct state as a development in affinity with syndetic parataxis does not seem to have influenced the particular case of the

---

80. Our study has identified and evaluated five examples of the so-called "absence of ʾĕmet": 1) Prov 20:28; 2) Gen 24:14, 27; 3) 2 Sam 2:5–6; 4) Exod 34:6; Ps 86:15 cf. Num 14:18; Joel 2:13; Jonah 4:2; Ps 103:8; Neh 9:17; and 5) Isa 16:5 cf. Isa 54:8, 10. See Avishur, *Stylistic Studies*, 130–33.

81. Perhaps, Zobel is not convinced by his own arguments. Or, he is not willing to apply his conclusions to the case of the creed. Quite unexpectedly and with no explanation whatsoever, Zobel translates the creed of Exod 34:6 as, "abounding in kindness and faithfulness," thus preserving the distinction of the two attributes (see Zobel, "ḥesed," 57).

82. With due respect to the personal opinions of the scholars.

83. Avishur, *Stylistic Studies*, 103; "Pairs of Synonymous Words," 75–81.

84. Avishur, *Stylistic Studies*, 103, in agreement with Segal, *Introduction*, 42–43.

creedal *ḥesed weʾĕmet*.⁸⁵ Second, the paucity of adjectives in Biblical Hebrew does not seem to be an issue in the particular case of the creedal phrase *ḥesed weʾĕmet*. The family of the assumed root *ḥsd* does include an adjective *ḥāsîd*. This adjective is used to depict God's attribute,⁸⁶ *kî-ḥāsîd ʾănî nəʾum-yhwh*, "'for I am gracious,' declares the LORD."⁸⁷ If the creed was to depict God's "gracious truth," the writer could have employed the adjective *ḥāsîd* coupled with an appropriate term of the root *ʾmn*.⁸⁸ But the writer does not use the adjective *ḥāsîd* in the creed (and it is not because the narrator for some reason does not want to use an adjective-noun construction, for he does employ it in rendering *ʾerek ʾappayim*, "slow-[to]-anger," in the very same creed). This discourages one from assigning *ḥesed weʾĕmet* with the meaning "gracious truth." The family of the assumed root *ʾmn* does not include an adjective. But if "true grace" was meant then the writer would have had plenty of literary devices to convey this exact meaning. The Hebrew language employs a construct state of two consecutive nouns *not linked by w* to express the idea of a noun modified by an adjective.⁸⁹ This approach was widely used, particularly with terms of the family of *ʾmn* (to which the creedal *ʾĕmet* belongs). Consider: "O Lord, . . . you have worked wonders, plans *formed* long ago, with perfect faithfulness [*ʾĕmûnāʰ ʾōmen*]" (Isa 25:1);⁹⁰ "Thus has the LORD of hosts said, 'Dispense true justice and practice *ḥesed* and compassion [*mišpaṭ ʾĕmet šəpōṭû wəḥesed wəraḥămîm*] each to his brother" (Zech 7:9);⁹¹ and, "O

---

85. Cf. Exod 34:6 and Ps 86:15.

86. The adjective *ḥāsîd* is used "as denoting active practice of *ḥesed*" (BDB, 339 [03298]).

87. Jer 3:12. Similarly, "The Lord is righteous in all His ways *wəḥāsîd* in all His deeds" (Ps 145:17). The noun *ḥesed* is used for the same purpose. See *ʾĕlōhê ḥasdî*, "my gracious God," in Ps 59:11Q, 18; and *ḥasdî* of the Lord in Ps 144:2 (Zobel, "*ḥesed*," 56, 62).

88. Multiple masculine and feminine nouns with a similar range of meanings—truth, faithfulness, firmness, fidelity, steadiness—are derived from the root *ʾmn* (see *TWOT* 0.116; BDB, 52–54).

89. IBHS, 6.4.2. Cf., "*ʾanšê-ḥesed* are taken away, while no one understands" (Isa 57:1).

90. Both feminine noun *ʾĕmûnāʰ* and masculine noun *ʾōmen* are derived from the same root as creedal *ʾĕmet*.

91. Notice the construct state of the feminine noun *ʾĕmet* (from the family of *ʾmn*) to modify the masculine noun *mišpāṭ*, "justice." Notice that other creedal attributes—*ḥesed*, *raḥămîm*—are also present and even joined by *w*, but not with *ʾĕmet*. See also *mišpaṭ ʾĕmet*, "true justice" (Ezek 18:8). These two examples are also listed in Avishur, "Pairs of Synonymous Words," 22, 22 n. 20.

God, in the greatness of Your ḥesed [bərob-ḥasdekā], answer me with Your saving ʾĕmet [beʾĕmet yišʿekā]" (Ps 69:14). In fact, the very book containing the original creed employs ʾĕmet in a construct state of two nouns. Consider: "Furthermore, you shall select out of all the people able men who fear God, men of truth [ʾanšê ʾĕmet], those who hate dishonest gain" (Exod 18:21).[92] Besides, a participle can be employed to express the same idea of a cognate of ʾĕmet modifying ḥesed. So Isaiah speaks of God's ḥasdê dāwīd hanneʾĕmānîm, "faithful mercies shown to David" (Isa 55:3). Thus, had "true grace" or "gracious truth" been meant in the creed, the writer would likely have written ʾĕmet ḥesed / ḥesed ʾĕmet or used a participle form of ʾmn. But the writer renders ḥesed weʾĕmet. Therefore, the conjunction w in the creedal phrase ḥesed weʾĕmet indicates two separate individual attributes.

Avishur[93] and Jepsen[94] observe that ḥesed and ʾĕmet (ʾĕmûnāʰ) often parallel each other.[95] Our study should enhance this observation by noticing that a) ḥesed/ʾĕmet (ʾĕmûnāʰ) employed in parallel colons are often not parallel,[96] and b) the attributes ḥesed and ʾĕmet (ʾĕmûnāʰ) of God are often separated in non-parallel structures.[97] The appearance of the individual terms of a word pair in parallel forms does not necessarily make the case of the word pair constituting hendiadys elsewhere impossible.[98] But it is altogether different in the case of "a word-pair occurring in various modes of pairing in a literary unit."[99] For example, in Psalm 89 the term ʾĕmûnāʰ is rendered twice without any connection to ḥesed.[100] Rendering of the word pair in both direct (ḥesed weʾĕmet,

92. Here ʾĕmet is used in a way that suggests ʾĕmet is playing the role of modifier. Noticeably, the translator realizes this, for he translates ʾanšê ʾĕmet with andras dikaious.

93. Avishur, *Stylistic Studies*, 102, 126, 130, 132–33, 261, 263, 274, 281, 294, 321.

94. Jepsen, "ʾĕmet," 314.

95. Pss 26:3; 36:6; 88:12; 89:2 92:3 100:5 (cf. also Pss 57:11; 89:2; 108:5); Mic 7:20.

96. Pss 89:34; 89:50; 117:2; Isa 16:5.

97. Dan 9:4–19 (see Goldingay, *Daniel*, 231f.); Hos 4:1 (see Stuart, *Hosea-Jonah*, 75).

98. See Avishur's list of "fixed word pairing that occur as hendiadys and other formations [including parallelism]" (Avishur, *Stylistic Studies*, 104–16).

99. Ibid., 274.

100. Ibid., 274 n. 1. Avishur does not specify the reference but Ps 89:6, 9 are obviously in view. Our study would also point to Ps 89:34, 50, where ḥesed and ʾĕmûnāʰ are placed in parallel colons but the attributes seem to be used independently as well.

89:15) and reverse (*weʾemûnātî wəḥasdî*, 89:25) order makes the case of hendiadys even more unlikely (otherwise this should have been an unthinkable momentary switch from "gracious truth" to "true grace"). To these arguments our study should also add that God is often characterized by an *unaccompanied* attribute of either one of the families of *ḥsd* or *ʾmn*.[101]

The decisive argument against viewing *ḥesed weʾĕmet* as hendiadys is syntactical. Whenever the word-pair *ḥesed* . . . *ʾĕmet* is the subject of a verb, the verb is *always* in the third person plural. Consider all the relevant[102] OT examples:

- *ḥesed weʾĕmet ʾal-yaʿazbūkā*, "Do not let *ḥesed weʾĕmet* [them] leave you" (Prov 3:3)[103]

- *ḥesed weʾĕmet yiṣṣərû-melek*, "*ḥesed weʾĕmet* [they] preserve the king" (Prov 20:28)

- *ḥasdəkā waʾămittəkā tāmîd yiṣṣərûnî*, "Your *ḥesed* and Your *ʾĕmet* [they] will continually preserve me" (Ps 40:12)

- *ḥesed weʾĕmet man yinṣəruhû*, "Appoint *ḥesed weʾĕmet* that they may preserve him" (Ps 61:8)

- *ḥesed-weʾĕmet nipgāšû*, "*ḥesed weʾĕmet* [they] have met together" (Ps 85:11)[104]

- *ḥesed weʾĕmet yəqaddəmû pāneykā*, "*ḥesed weʾĕmet* [they] go before you" (Ps 89:15)

The verb, which has the word-pair *ḥesed* . . . *ʾĕmet* as the subject, is *always* in the third person plural throughout the OT. Five of the six examples—Prov 3:3; 20:28; Pss 61:8; 85:11; 89:15—employ the exact creedal phrase *ḥesed weʾĕmet*. At least four of the six instances—Pss

---

101. Deut 7:9; 32:4; Ps 31:6 (cf. Pss 25:5; 43:3; 91:4; Dan 9:13); Isa 49:7; 65:16; Jer 3:12; 31:3; 42:5.

102. It is conceivable that Prov 3:3 does not speak of the *ḥesed weʾĕmet* of God, especially if the saying is related to Prov 6:20–21.

103. Sakenfeld seems to be hesitant to cite *ḥesed weʾĕmet* of Prov 3:3 as a hendiadys (perhaps because this case of the word-pair supplied with a verb in plural obviously contradicts her argument that *ḥesed weʾĕmet* constitutes hendiadys?) but enigmatically labels it as depicting "double quality" (Sakenfeld, *Faithfulness*, 31).

104. Contra Glueck, commenting on Ps 85:11, "*ḥesed* . . . together with *ʾĕmet* is a hendiadys and forms an indissoluble unity" (Glueck, *Ḥesed*, 79).

40:12; 61:8; 85:11; 89:15—have God's *ʾĕmet* and *ḥesed* in view. This evidence firmly establishes that the creedal phrase *ḥesed weʾĕmet* denotes two distinctive attributes of God.

Likely with the above data in mind, in 1984 Avishur did not place *ḥesed weʾĕmet* on the list of cases of hendiadys,[105] but into the category of "a combination of non-synonymous components."[106] So, for Jepsen,

> Frequently God's *ʾĕmet* is connected with his *ḥesed*. It might be asked whether *ʾĕmet* is only a characteristic of *ḥesed*, or whether it stands independent of it. However, the parallelism of these two words in adjoining half-verses and the plural form of verbs used with these two words as subject favor the idea that *ḥesed* and *ʾĕmet* were understood as two separate attributes of God, who manifests himself in active kindness and protective faithfulness respectively.[107]

Brongers is, perhaps, on the right track in his attempt to dismiss *ḥesed weʾĕmet* as hendiadys on literary grounds. He notes that biblical writers strive to provide an exhaustive and all-embracing picture. For example, the earth is depicted as *tōhû wābōhû*, "formless and void" (Gen 1:2). The writer could have described the earth as merely *tōhû*, "formless," as is often the case (Deut 32:10; Ps 107:40; Job 12:24; Isa 45:18; etc.). But this would not have done justice to the object, and the writer renders both *tōhû wābōhû* to portray all of its aspects.[108] Job is characterized as *ʾîš tām wəyāšār yərēʾ ʾĕlōhîm wəsār mērāʿ*, "a blameless and upright man, fearing God and turning away from evil" (Job 1:8). It has taken no less than four qualifications to make a fair description of the man. This

---

105. Avishur, *Stylistic Studies*, 99–116. The reference list includes occurrences of hendiadys in Biblical Hebrew, Ugaritic, Aramaic, and Akkadian. This scholar's earlier work, "Pairs of Synonymous Words," which addresses the matter of hendiadys at length, does not list *ḥesed weʾĕmet* as hendiadys either.

106. Avishur, *Stylistic Studies*, 102 n. 2. Westhuizen, having considered texts of the book of Psalms, Old Poetry, and biblical apocryphic hymns, does not view *ḥesed weʾĕmet* as hendiadys either (Westhuizen, "Hendiadys," 50–57).

107. Jepsen, "*ʾĕmet*," 314.

108. In Isa 34:11, both *tōhû*, "formlessness," and *bōhû*, "emptiness," are used to describe the land and the terms are clearly separated. Cf. Wenham, who simply states, "*tōhû wābōhû* 'Total chaos' an example of hendiadys, literally, 'waste and void'" (Wenham, *Genesis 1–15*, 15).

is also the case with *ḥesed we'ĕmet* rendered to depict two aspects of the object, argues Brongers.[109]

Thus, to the best of our knowledge no scholar has *demonstrated* that in the creedal phrase *ḥesed we'ĕmet* one term modifies the other. But the above provides *evidence* that the creedal *ḥesed we'ĕmet* conveys two individual attributes.[110]

Conclusion

Our study has evaluated arguments for and against the case that *ḥesed we'ĕmet* constitutes hendiadys. On the one hand, the word-pair *ḥesed we'ĕmet* is sometimes declared to be hendiadys with no evidence whatsoever to substantiate the claim.[111] Often scholars' reasoning for the case of hendiadys is speculative or/and immune to criticism,[112] occasionally being circular and illogical as well.[113] Suggestions to combine the two into one by associating *ḥesed* and *'ĕmet*[114] have been dismissed as invalid. Attempts in support of *ḥesed we'ĕmet* as hendiadys[115] have been demonstrated to be fallacious. As far as our study can discern, the suggestion[116] that *ḥesed we'ĕmet* constitutes a hendiadys has not been proven. On the other hand, our study has identified and offered a number of arguments against reading *ḥesed we'ĕmet* as hendiadys. It has been demonstrated that causes which might have constituted hendiadys generally—the

---

109. Brongers, *Merismus, Synekdoche und Hendidys*, 112.

110. It is notable that numerous translations of Exod 34:6—ASV, BBE, DBY, KJV, NAB, NASB, NIV, NJB, NKJV, NLT, NRSV, RSV, RWB, WEB, YLT, and Durham, *Exodus*, 450—unanimously render two distinct attributes for *warab-ḥesed we'ĕmet*. BDB also recognizes the individuality of the attributes by claiming that "*ḥesed* is grouped with other divine attributes: *ḥsd w 'mt* kindness (lovingkindness) and fidelity" (338 [03297.2]). Perhaps these factors preclude modern grammarians from exemplifying *ḥesed we'ĕmet* as hendiadys (see *IBHS*).

111. So Sakenfeld, *Faithfulness*, 31, 55, 57–60, 134; Speiser, *Genesis*, 175, 180 n. 27.

112. Sakenfeld, *Faithfulness*, 37 n. 27; Zobel, "*ḥesed*," 51.

113. Johnson, *Cultic Prophet*, 65–66.

114. Sakenfeld, *Faithfulness*, 60; Kellenberger, *Häsäd wa'uämät*, 81.

115. Cf. the argument from only the first noun of the two being preceded by preposition *b* in Prov 16:6 (Williams, *Hebrew Syntax*, 16 § 72; Zobel, "*ḥesed*," 51). Cf. the contention from Hosea's phraseology projected onto the chain *kî 'ên-'ĕmet wə'ên-ḥesed wə'ên-da'at 'ĕlōhîm*, "Because there is no *'ĕmet* or *ḥesed* Or knowledge of God in the land" in Hos 4:1 (Zobel, "*ḥesed*," 51).

116. With due respect to the personal opinions of the scholars.

relatively late date of the construct state development in affinity with syndetic parataxis[117] and the paucity of adjectives in Biblical Hebrew[118]—hardly affect the particular case of the creedal *ḥesed we'ĕmet*. The terms *ḥesed* and *'ĕmet* (*'ĕmûnāʰ*) are often parallel to each other in adjoining colons (Pss 26:3; 36:6 [similarly 57:11; 89:2; 108:5]; 88:12; 89:2; 92:3; 100:5; Mic 7:20) *and* frequently without paralleling each other in meaning (Pss 69:14; 89:34, 50; 117:2; Isa 16:5). The terms are often separated outside of parallel forms (Dan 9:4, 13; Hos 4:1). These factors—lack of parallelism between *ḥesed* and *'ĕmet* (*'ĕmûnāʰ*) in both parallel colons and outside of parallel forms as well—strongly discourage one from envisioning *ḥesed* and *'ĕmet* (*'ĕmûnāʰ*) as modifying each other. Moreover, the terms *ḥesed* and *'ĕmet* (*'ĕmûnāʰ*) occur in various modes of pairing in a literary unit (Ps 89; cf. Dan 9:4-19; Hos 4:1). Since the terms *ḥesed* and *'ĕmet* (*'ĕmûnāʰ*) occur as a pair (*ḥesed we'ĕmet/we'emûnātî waḥasdî*, Ps 89:15, 25), and *'ĕmûnāʰ*, one of the terms of the pair, occurs independently of *ḥesed* (Ps 89:6, 9)—all occurrences referring to God and in the same literary unit—then it is more than likely that the word pair *ḥesed we'ĕmet/we'emûnātî waḥasdî* denotes two distinct attributes of God. Rendering the word pair in both direct (*ḥesed we'ĕmet*, Ps 89:15) and reverse (*we'emûnātî waḥasdî*, Ps 89:25) order in the same literary unit makes the case for hendiadys even more unlikely (otherwise this must have signified a virtually unthinkable momentary switch from "gracious truth" to "true grace"). Furthermore, God is often characterized by an *unaccompanied* attribute of either one of the families of either *ḥsd* or *'mn* (Deut 7:9; 32:4; Ps 31:6 [cf. also Pss 25:5; 43:3; 91:4; Dan 9:13]; Isa 49:7; 65:16; Jer 3:12 [cf. 31:3]; 42:5). This implies that God's attributes derived from families of *ḥsd* and *'mn* are perceived as distinctive. Finally, whenever the word-pair *ḥesed . . . 'ĕmet* is the subject of a verb, the verb is always in the third person plural (Prov 3:3; 20:28; Pss 40:12; 61:8; 85:11; 89:15).[119] This evidence firmly establishes that the creedal *ḥesed we'ĕmet* denote two distinctive

---

117. Avishur, *Stylistic Studies*, 103; "Pairs of Synonymous Words," 75-81.

118. Avishur, *Stylistic Studies*, 103, agreeing with Segal, *Introduction*, 42-43.

119. Schoneveld wrongly asserts, "the corresponding [to 'the-grace-and-the-truth' (1:14, 17)] Hebrew phrase, *ḥsd w 'mt*, occurs . . . in the Hebrew Bible . . . generally as . . . a *single* concept" (Schoneveld, "Torah in the Flesh," 83).

attributes of God.[120] Our study concludes that OT writers render *ḥesed we'ĕmet* not as hendiadys but to convey two distinct attributes.

LXX/OG Translators Take *ḥesed we'ĕmet* to Denote Two Subjective Qualities

To properly evaluate whether *(hē) charis kai (hē) alētheia* constitutes hendiadys, our study will assess how the LXX/OG translators understood *ḥesed we'ĕmet*.[121]

Arguments contra Hendiadys Behind *ḥesed we'ĕmet* in LXX/OG

In the OT, hendiadys is caused by the paucity of adjectives in Biblical Hebrew.[122] But Greek differs from Hebrew in respect to the relevant terminology. On the one hand, for the Hebrew *ḥesed* and *'ĕmet* (*'ĕmûnāh*, cognates), Greek vocabulary includes not only the nouns *eleos* and *alētheia* but also the corresponding adjectives *eleēmōn* and *alēthinos*.[123] Greek grammar employs noun-adjective[124] and noun-noun-in-genitive[125] constructions, which are suitable to express the modification of one term

---

120. Practices of Rabbinic Judaism, which postdate the Gospel, cannot serve as direct evidence in our discussion. If introduced, however, they only confirm our OT findings. The Rabbis apparently understood *ḥesed* and *'ĕmet* as two distinct attributes of the character of God just as the OT writers did. Kittel points out that when the verb *dîn*, "judge," is used of God, "an exegetical question arises concerning the relationship between *ḥesed* and *'ĕmet*, i.e., concerning the God who is kind but who also judges. The real antithesis is between the words *ḥesed* and *dîn*, but *'ĕmet* can also be involved, and it thus comes to be synonymous with *dîn*. There are different ways in which the divine attributes may then be related. The two may sometimes be set alongside (b.Ber., 46b), but sometimes it may be emphasized that *'ĕmet* comes first and then, and therefore definitively, *ḥesed* (b.RH, 17b)." He concludes that "it is always the concern of the Rabbi who interprets the Old Testament to show that both elements are essential in his view of God" (Kittel, "*alētheia*").

121. *alēthinos* occurs only in the creed in Exod 34:6, Num 14:18 (with no equivalent of *alēthinos* in the parent Hebrew text), and Ps 86:15.

122. Avishur, *Stylistic Studies*, 103.

123. Greek is rich in adjectives. The whole creed—*kurios ho Theos oiktirmōn kai eleēmōn makrothumos kai polueleos kai alēthinos*—is conveyed in adjectives. Besides *eleēmōn*, *polueleos* and *alēthinos* there are also the suitable adjectives *hileōs*, "merciful," and *alēthēs*, "true, truthful."

124. So-called "positive adjective."

125. So-called "attributive genitive" or "genitive of quality."

by the other. That is, the Greek language has the *means* to convey a hendiadys if there is one in the parent Hebrew text. On the other hand, the LXX/OG translators are *capable* of discerning hendiadys and rendering it with an appropriate Greek construction. Leslie Allen notices that an OG translator interprets *bəsûs ûbərekeb ûbəpārāšîm wəqāhāl waʿam-rāb* (lit. "with horses, and chariots, and cavalry and army and many people") as *meth' hippōn kai harmatōn kai hippeōn kai sunagōgēs ethnōn pollōn sphodra* (Ezek 26:7). Apparently, the translator sees *wəqāhāl waʿam-rāb*—lit. "and army and many people"—as a hendiadys[126] and translates the word pair as *sunagōgēs ethnōn pollōn sphodra*, "a concourse of very many nations."

Thus, had the LXX/OG translators understood *ḥesed weʾĕmet* as hendiadys they would have been able to discern it, and they had the means to convey it with something like *alētheia eleous*[127]/*hē alētheia eleēmōn*, "merciful truth," or *eleos alētheias*[128]/*to eleos to alēthinon*, "true mercy." But the translators employ neither of the expected constructions. Instead, they render *wərab-ḥesed weʾĕmet* with the recurrent *kai polueleos kai alēthinos* (Exod 34:6; Ps 86:15).[129] Therefore, the LXX/OG translators most likely identify the creedal *ḥesed weʾĕmet*[130] not as hendiadys but as a pair of distinct attributes. Moreover, *polueleos kai alēthinos*, rendered for *ḥesed weʾĕmet*, are *adjectives*, which do not form a hendiadys.[131] This again signifies that the Greek translators saw *ḥesed weʾĕmet* as two different attributes. Furthermore, the creed[132] *raḥûm wəḥannûn ʾerek ʾappayim wərab-ḥesed weʾĕmet*, a heterogeneous construction of nouns and adjectives, is conveyed by *oiktirmōn kai eleēmōn*

---

126. Allen, *Ezekiel 20–48*, 72. Many modern translators do so as well; consider "a great army" (NASB), "a host of many soldiers" (RSV), "a great and mighty army" (NAB), "an enormous army" (NJB).

127. Cf. *basileis Israēl basileis eleous eisin*, "kings of Israel are merciful kings," lit. "kings of mercy," for *malkê ḥesed* (1 Kgs 21:31 OG).

128. As in *nomos alētheias*, "true law," lit. "law of truth," for *tôrat ʾĕmet* (Mal 2:6 OG); or *misthos alētheias*, "true reward," lit. "reward of truth," for *śeker ʾĕmet* (Prov 11:18 OG).

129. A translator even supplies *alēthinos* in Num 14:18 with no equivalent to it in the parent Hebrew text.

130. *alēthinos* occurs only in the creed in Exod 34:6, Num 14:18 (with no equivalent of *alēthinos* in the parent Hebrew text), and Ps 86:15.

131. According to the strict definition of the term.

132. Notice the similarity of this construction with the one of Ezek 26:7 where hendiadys is discerned and properly conveyed in Greek.

makrothumos kai polueleos kai alēthinos, a homogeneous recurrence of adjectives only. The creedal *ḥesed weʾĕmet*, the only component, which, as a pair of "two nouns connected by a conjunctive letter," might have been potentially suspicious for hendiadys, is now *dissolved* in the translation. The resulting phraseology also discourages one from perceiving hendiadys in the whole creed. Even if adjectives could conceivably form hendiadys, then which pair would that be: *makrothumos kai polueleos*, "longsuffering—multi-merciful," or *polueleos kai alēthinos*, "multi-merciful—true"? This yet again indicates that interpreters had not initially perceived *ḥesed weʾĕmet* as hendiadys. Finally, translators are consistent in conveying the pair *ḥesed* . . . *ʾĕmet* (*ʾĕmûnāʰ*, cognates) as two distinctive attributes. Already in the creeds, different translators show no sign of uncertainty whatsoever, but always and unanimously translate the creedal *wərab-ḥesed weʾĕmet* with *kai polueleos kai alēthinos*. The attribute *alēthinos* is still listed distinctively preceded by *kai* even if *ʾĕmet* is actually absent in the parent Hebrew text of the creed (Num 14:18). But also, throughout the OT, the pair *ḥesed* . . . *ʾĕmet* (*ʾĕmûnāʰ*, cognates) occurs in forty-six verses and is never translated in the LXX/OG with either noun-adjective or noun-noun-in-genitive construction. These factors strongly suggest that the different LXX/OG translators perceive the creedal *ḥesed weʾĕmet* in the same way, namely, as a word pair denoting two distinct attributes.

In the OT, whenever the word pair *ḥesed* . . . *ʾĕmet* is the subject of a verb, the verb is always in the third person plural (Prov 3:3; 20:28; Pss 40:12; 61:8; 85:11; 89:15). This signifies that the OT writers envision several attributes when they render the word-pair *ḥesed* . . . *ʾĕmet*. This is not always the case in the LXX/OG. On four of the six occasions, translators preserve the plural form of the verb of the parent text (Prov 3:3; 20:28 OG; Ps 39:12; 84:11 OG). Once, in the phrase translated from Hebrew to Greek, the word-pair *ḥesed* . . . *ʾĕmet* is not the subject of a verb (Ps 60:8 OG). Once the relevant terms are the subject of a verb in the singular: *eleos kai alētheia proporeusetai pro prosōpou sou*, "*eleos kai alētheia* shall go [sg.] before thy face" (Ps 88:15 OG). But this does not mean that one of the nouns necessarily modifies the other.[133] There are syntactically matching examples where such modification is clearly im-

---

133. Besides, the singular *proporeusetai* may well have been rendered to match the singular *hetoimasia* to follow the poetic rhythm of the stanza. In this respect Ps 88:15 OG is quite similar to John 1:17.

possible: *artos kai oinos huparchei moi*, "bread and wine belong [sg.] to me" (Judg (A) 19:19; cf. Judg 19:19); *genea kai genea epainesei*, "generation after generation shall praise [sg.]" (Ps 144:4 OG); *megistan kai kritēs kai dunastēs doxasthēsetai*, "*the* nobleman, and *the* judge, and *the* ruler will be honored [sg.]" (Sir 10:24); *ara kai pseudos kai phonos kai klopē kai moicheia kechutai epi tēs gēs*, "cursing, and lying, and murder, and theft, and adultery abound [sg.] in the land" (Hos 4:2); *bous kai onos patei*, "*the* ox and ass tread [sg.]" (Isa 32:20); *Elnathan kai Godolias kai Gamarias hupethento tō basilei*, "Elnathan, and Godolias, and Gamarias suggested [sg.] to the king" (Jer 43:25); *sēs kai brōsis aphanizei*, "moth and rust destroy [sg.]" (Matthew 6:19).[134] These examples speak in favor of envisioning two distinctive qualities denoted by the nouns in the phrase *eleos kai alētheia proporeusetai* (Ps 88:15 OG), even though the verb is in singular.

Conclusion

Our study has considered ways in which the LXX/OG translators deal with the pair *ḥesed . . . ʾĕmet* (*ʾĕmûnāʰ*, cognates). The LXX/OG translators were capable of recognizing hendiadys in Hebrew. The Greek language is capable of expressing Hebrew hendiadys by means of adjectival or genitival constructions. But not one of the forty-six constructions of *ḥesed . . . ʾĕmet* (*ʾĕmûnāʰ*, cognates) that occur within one verse is conveyed in Greek by such an adjectival or genitival construction. Particularly, the creed *raḥûm wəḥannûn ʾerek ʾappayim wərab-ḥesed weʾĕmet*, a heterogeneous construction of nouns and adjectives, is conveyed by *oiktirmōn kai eleēmōn makrothumos kai polueleos kai alēthinos*, a homogeneous recurrence of adjectives, which strongly precludes hendiadys in both the Hebrew parent and the Greek resulting text. With only one entirely, grammatically justified exception,[135] whenever the word-pair *ḥesed . . . ʾĕmet* is the subject of a verb, the LXX renders the verb in the third person plural (Prov 3:3; 20:28; Pss 40:12; 85:11), thus differentiating the attributes. Our study concludes that the evidence demonstrates that the LXX/OG translators interpreted the word-pair *ḥesed . . . ʾĕmet* (*ʾĕmûnāʰ*, cognates) as two distinct attributes.

---

134. See the NT section of our discussion of hendiadys.

135. Ps 88:15 OG; cf. Greek grammar of Judg (A) 19:19 (cf. Judg 19:19); Ps 144:4 OG; Sir 10:24; Hos 4:2; Isa 32:20; Jer 43:25. See also Matt 6:19.

The Evangelist Conveys Two Subjective Qualities with *(hē) charis kai (hē) alētheia*

Our study further argues that the Evangelist conveys two subjective qualities with *(hē) charis kai (hē) alētheia*.

CRITIQUE OF ARGUMENTS THAT *(hē) charis kai (hē) alētheia* CONSTITUTES HENDIADYS

Sometimes no evidence is given for the claim that *(hē) charis kai (hē) alētheia* constitute hendiadys.[136] Often a reference to an authority is made to support such a suggestion. Thus Edwards remarks that

> Scholars have long drawn attention to the correspondence between John's phrase here [*hē charis kai hē alētheia*] and the familiar Old Testament concept of *ḥesed weʾĕmet*—in Hebrew a hendiadys meaning 'faithful (or enduring) love'.

She refers to "R. Brown, *op. cit.* (above n 33), p. 16;[137] see further J. A. Montgomery, 'Hebrew *ḥesed* and Greek *charis*', in *NTR* 32 (1939); pp. 97–102; L. J. Kuyper, 'Grace and Truth: an Old Testament Description of God and its Use in the Johannine Gospel', *Interpretation* 18 (1964), pp. 3–19; on the meaning of *ḥesed* in the Old Testament, see further H. J. Stoebe, 'Die Bedeutung des Wortes Häsäd im Alten Testament', *VT* 2 (1952), pp. 244–54, esp. 248; N. Gluech, *Hesed in the Bible* (ET, Cincinnati, 1967), together with H.-J. Zobel, *TDOT* V (1986), pp. 44–64, esp. 53."[138]

Brown, however, does not provide a single piece of evidence that either *ḥesed weʾĕmet* or its Greek counterparts constitute hendiadys, but merely translates both *charitos kai alētheias* and *hē charis kai hē alētheia* with "enduring love."[139] Montgomery does not even suggest either *ḥesed weʾĕmet*, *charitos kai alētheias* or *hē charis kai hē alētheia* as hendiadys. Kuyper offers no evidence on the matter, but only states, "It appears to me that when *ḥesed* and *ʾĕmet* appear together they become a hendiadys in which the second term intends to confirm and enrich the

---

136. Beasley-Murray, *John*, 14, R. Brown, *John (I–XII)*, 4, 14, 16.
137. R. Brown, *John (I–XII)*, 16.
138. Edwards, "*Charin anti charitos*," 11–22, n. 41.
139. R. Brown, *John (I–XII)*, 4, 14, 16.

concept of the first."¹⁴⁰ Glueck's and Zobel's arguments are fallacious, as our study has demonstrated. ¹⁴¹ Thus, Edwards's reference to authorities gains her no support for her claim.

Dunn comments in a similar fashion on the following Pauline passage:

> For I say that Christ has become a servant to the circumcision on behalf of the truth of God [*alētheias theou*] to confirm the promises *given* to the fathers, and for the Gentiles to glorify God for His mercy [*eleous doxasai ton theon*] (Romans 15:8-9).

He remarks, "Relevant also is Michel's¹⁴² observation that *alētheia* and *eleos* correspond to *ḥesed weʾĕmet* (a regular OT combination in reference to God; BDB, *ḥesed* II.2) and function *more or less* as a hendiadys (cf. John 1:14, 17)."¹⁴³

However, Otto Michel provides no evidence for the claim, and only states that "God's revelation consists of 'Wahrheit' and 'Barmherzigkeit'; both notions form an indissoluble whole,"¹⁴⁴ and comments in the footnote, "*alētheia* and *eleos* correspond to *ḥesed weʾĕmet*. Both notions together prove the fullness of the revelation of God after Jewish as well as after Christian observation of God (cf. John 1:14, 17)."¹⁴⁵ Moreover, BDB remarks, "*ḥesed* is grouped with other divine attributes: *ḥesed weʾĕmet kindness (loving-kindness) and fidelity*,"¹⁴⁶ thus apparently distinguishing *ḥesed* and *ʾĕmet*! Furthermore, to suggest that *alētheia* modifies *eleos*¹⁴⁷

---

140. Kuyper, "Grace and Truth," 6-7. At the outset Kuyper acknowledges, "Dr. Nelson Glueck . . . has written a very significant monograph for his doctoral dissertation *Das Word hesed im alttestamentlichen Sprachgebrauche*. This work of Dr. Glueck has profound effect upon present-day understanding of *ḥesed*, and I want to acknowledge my indebtedness to this little book" (ibid., 4). Thus, Kuyper relies on Glueck's results, which are originally unsupported and contradictory on the matter of hendiadys (see elsewhere in our study).

141. See also Stoebe, "Bedeutung des *Häsäd*." Stoebe's work is not available for our study. But being comparatively old, it is included in bibliographies of OT scholars whose views on *ḥesed weʾĕmet* as hendiadys we have already dismissed as invalid. For a summary of Stoebe's views see Larue, "Recent Studies," 14-18.

142. Michel, *Der Brief an die Römer*.

143. Dunn, *Romans 9-16*, 848; emphasis added. Notice the language of uncertainty.

144. Michel, *Der Brief an die Römer*, 359; my translation.

145. Ibid., 359 n. 3; my translation.

146. BDB, "*ḥesed*," 339. A list of such occurrences follows.

147. Or vice versa.

in Romans 15:8–9 seems to be just as valid as to propose that "the Israel" (the circumcised) modifies "the Gentiles" (cf. Rom 11:25). Instead, the differences between Israelites and Gentiles in Romans 15:8–9 definitely emphasize the distinctiveness of God's attributes *alētheia* and *eleos*!

Occasionally, the discussion over the matter displays the arbitrary nature of both the feature of hendiadys and the argumentation regarding its presence. So Bultmann comments,

> *Charis* and *alētheia* are here [in 1:14] a hendiadys, since *charis* has the formal meaning of "giving grace" and "gracious gift," while *alētheia* denotes the content of the gift, the divine reality revealing itself. Moreover, each of these expressions can denote both the content and the form; in the *charis* as the *divine* gift, the *alētheia* is included (v. 16), just as the *alētheia* is the *gift* which one receives from the Revealer (8.32; 14.6).[148]

First, Bultmann's choice of meaning for *charis* is tendentious. His association of *charis* as "giving, gift" with the form rather than the content is nullified if one selects an alternative meaning—particularly "one of the attributes of God"—for *charis*.[149] Second, Bultmann's emphasis that "*alētheia* denotes the *content*[150] of the gift" is arbitrary. There is no obvious distinction between the terms *charis* and *alētheia* in the phrases *charitos kai alētheias* and *hē charis kai hē alētheia*. It is conceivable that the term *charis* denotes content just as well as *alētheia* does. He even recognizes that "each of these expressions [*charis, alētheia*] can denote both the content and the form," and such is the case with *charis* already in the prologue![151] Third, Bultmann's logic is fallacious. The substantive—content, not description—meaning of objects cannot prove that the objects themselves constitute hendiadys. His choice of connotations may result in *charitos kai alētheias* meaning "gracious gift *and* the divine reality," but not necessarily "gracious gift *of* the divine reality." Fourth, Bultmann's declaration that, "in the *charis* as the divine gift, the

---

148. Bultmann, *John*, 73–74.
149. See Conzelmann, "*charis*"; Zimmerli, "*charis* (OT)."
150. Emphasis added.
151. This makes one wonder on what basis Bultmann chooses *charis* as a modifier for *alētheia*, and not vice versa. In fact, Bultmann himself invalidates his own choice by maintaining that immediately in the prologue *charis* in *charin anti charitos* includes *alētheia*. This makes *charis* a better candidate for denoting the content, and *alētheia* the form, in such a "hendiadys."

alētheia is included[152] ([in the phrase *charin anti charitos*,] v. 16)," is unwarranted.[153] Thus, there is no basis for Bultmann's claim that *charitos kai alētheias* constitutes hendiadys. Besides, had the Evangelist wanted to express the idea of a gift he would have likely employed the familiar construction *tēn dōrean tou Theou*, "the gift of God," (4:10; cf. 15:25) already used elsewhere in the Gospel. The Evangelist does not employ the expression *hē dōrea tou Theou* but *hē charis kai hē alētheia*, which indicates that expressing the idea of a gift of God is not the intention of the Evangelist in 1:14–17.

In some instances scholars attempt to actually argue the case. De la Potterie[154] draws on four arguments in favor of hendiadys in regard to the phrase *(hē) charis kai (hē) alētheia*.[155] First, De la Potterie reasons that *(hē) charis kai (hē) alētheia* constitutes hendiadys on the basis of a chiastic structure he finds in 2 John 1–3:

A: *hous egō agapō en alētheia*, "whom I love in truth," (2 John 1a)
. . .
    C: *dia tēn alētheian tēn menousan en hēmin*, "for the sake of the truth which abides in us,"(2 John 2a)
        D: *meth' hēmōn estai eis ton aiōna*, "will be with us forever," (2 John 2b)
            D`: *estai meth' hēmōn*, "will be with us," (2 John 3a)
        C`: *charis eleos eirēnē*, "grace, mercy, peace," (2 John 3b)
. . .
A`: *en alētheia kai agapē*, "in truth and love," (2 John 3d)

From this observation De la Potterie contends that *tēn alētheian* (2 John 2) is the equivalent of *charis* (2 John 3). He further concludes that *alētheia* means "revelation" and *charis* denotes "gift of revelation" or "the gift of truth." He even suggests that *hē alētheia echaristhē*, "the truth has been granted," could have been written instead of *hē charis kai hē alētheia . . . egeneto* in John 1:17, with the same effect.

---

152. Emphasis added.

153. This is a thesis that is immune to criticism. Cf. Glueck: "Where *ḥesed* is used alone and not in the combination *ḥsd w 'mt*, as is frequently the case, one may still picture mentally *'mt* next to *ḥsd*" (Glueck, *Ḥesed*, 40).

154. La Potterie, "*Charis*," 273.

155. La Potterie utilizes earlier findings by Panimolle, *Il dono della legge*, 380–83.

Hanson has rightly criticized De la Potterie's argument.[156] First, it is by no means clear that 2 John 1–3 does afford a real parallel to John 1:14–18. Second, there is no certainty whether there really is a chiastic structure in 2 John 1–3. It is weakened when one includes B *kai ouk egō monos alla kai pantes hoi egnōkotes tēn alētheian*, "and not only I, but also all who know the truth," (2 John 1b) and B` *para Theou patros kai para Iēsou Christou tou huiou tou patros*, "from God the Father and from Jesus Christ, the Son of the Father" (2 John 3c). But even if one excludes B and B`, such a "chiastic structure" breaks down at the point that is crucial for the validity of the argument. *Dia tēn alētheian tēn menousan en hēmin*, "for the sake of the truth, which abides in us," (2 John 2a) is not parallel to *charis eleos eirēnē*, "grace, mercy, peace," (2 John 3b), and De la Potterie's mere assertion that "in spite of the difference of vocabulary, these two members are parallels, too"[157] does not make up for the deficiency in the argument. Third, it is doubtful whether the author of 2 John uses *alētheia* in an entirely uniform manner throughout the three verses; *hous egō agapō en alētheia*, "whom I love in truth," (2 John 1a) does not seem to have exactly the same meaning as *dia tēn alētheian tēn menousan en hēmin*, "for the sake of the truth, which abides in us" (2 John 2a). Finally, the idea that *charis* and *alētheia* forms a hendiadys can hardly be said to be found in the 2 John 1–3 passage, where *charis* is clearly separated from *alētheia* and can only be associated by assuming a chiastic structure.

Second, De la Potterie argues that it is necessary to take the shape of the expression *charis kai* followed by the second noun, into account. Here is the flow of De la Potterie's argument: We find several examples of "*charis kai* . . ." in the NT. With the exception of the stereotypical formula *charis kai eirēnē*[158] (1 Thess 1:1; 2 Thess 1:2; etc.), texts can be divided into two categories: sometimes the second noun is so similar to the first one that it is practically synonymous to it (*hē charis . . . kai hē dōrea*, Rom 5:15, 17), elsewhere it is almost certainly a hendiadys or, at least, an explanatory *kai* (the second noun explains the first one). So, in Romans 1:5, *charin kai apostolēn* means "the grace to be an apostle." In the same way, in 2 Corinthians 8:4, *tēn charin kai tēn*

---

156. Hanson, *John 1:14–18 and Exodus 34*, 94.
157. La Potterie, "*Charis*," 272; my translation.
158. It is actually *charis humin kai eirēnē* (1 Thess 1:1; 2 Thess 1:2).

koinōnian tēs diakonias tēs eis tous hagious has to be translated as "the grace to participate in this service for the benefit of the saints." Further still, *en chariti kai gnōsei tou kuriou hēmōn kai sōtēros Iēsou Christou* (2 Pet 3:18) probably indicates "the grace of the knowledge of Jesus Christ."[159] Thus, in each instance the construction *charis kai* is in regard to two synonyms or a hendiadys, and the second noun, as we see it, far from opposing to the first one, depicts the same reality, but from a more specific point of view.[160] The formula *(hē) charis kai (hē) alētheia* (John 1:14, 17) is, De la Potterie argues, of the same type. Because *(hē) alētheia* is not a simple synonym of *(hē) charis* (as in the texts of the first series), we have good reason for believing that both nouns form a hendiadys—in other words, a construction in which the word "truth" serves for explaining later what "grace" is. Thus, it is necessary to translate it as "the grace of the truth" or "the grace that is the truth."[161]

One can see that De la Potterie's observation is hardly an argument at all. First, none of the examples employing the expression *charis kai* to which De la Potterie refers (Rom 1:5; 5:15, 17; 2 Cor 8:4; 2 Pet 3:18) has been *established* as constituting hendiadys. Therefore, his reference to them is but a speculation. Second, there are constructions employing *charis kai* that are neither "hendiadys" nor "synonimical sequence," even on De la Potterie's terms (1 Thess 1:1; 2 Thess 1:2; etc.). Third, it is perilous to apply findings in Romans, 2 Corintians 8:4, 2 Peter, and 1 & 2 Thessalonians to the Gospel. De la Potterie seems to acknowledge this weakness in his argumentation, as he writes, "Both previous arguments (usage of the formula *charis kai* ... somewhere else in the NT; the parallel text of 2 John 3) still leaned on data outside the context."[162]

Third, De la Potterie attempts to establish that *(hē) charis kai (hē) alētheia* is hendiadys from the "structural parallels" of John 1:14–17. Two parts of John 1:17, he argues, are structural parallels in the form of A || A': (a) *ho nomos* || (a') *hē charis kai hē alētheia*, (b) *dia Mōuseōs* || (b') *dia Iēsou Christou*, and (c) *edothē* || (c') *egeneto*. De la Potterie then remarks that, at first sight, the parallelism limits itself to the first two members (a || a' and b || b'), but then a detail draws one's attention

---

159. La Potterie, "*Charis*," 271.
160. Ibid., 272.
161. Ibid.
162. Ibid., 273; my translation.

at once: it is only the one noun, (a) *ho nomos*, that corresponds to two nouns (a') *hē charis kai hē alētheia*. On the other hand, there are (c) *edothē* and (c') *egeneto*, and we do not readily see what is in common between them. But the regularity of the composition makes one suspect that the *edothē* of A has to correspond to some element of A'. It can only be *charis*: for it is the Law, it is said, that was given (*edothē*), and *charis* mostly means "gift." Doubtless, in each part of the verse, *edothē* and *charis* play different grammatical roles (the first word is a verb, the other one a noun); but as to the semantic structure, their functions are the same. From the thematic point of view, *charis* corresponds to *edothē*. It follows that *(hē) charis kai (hē) alētheia* is a hendiadys, argues De la Potterie, and he concludes that if *charis* corresponds to *edothē*, then it is really not part of a', but c': *hē charis . . . egeneto*. Certainly, *hē charis* points to *hē alētheia* as the grammatical subject of the sentence, but it is *hē alētheia* that acts as the *logical subject*. In this sense, the accent falls on *hē alētheia*; the words *hē charis + egeneto* amount, more or less, to *echaristhē* (with *hē alētheia* as the subject).[163]

De la Potterie continues: If we take into account these different observations, we are invited, for the sake of clarity, to abolish the dislocation, which produces the hendiadys, and to replace *hē charis + egeneto* with *echaristhē*. We then obtain a perfectly regular A ǁ A' structure: (a) *ho nomos* ǁ (a') *hē alētheia*, (b) *dia Mōuseōs* ǁ (b') *dia Iēsou Christou*, and (c) *edothē* ǁ (c') *echaristhē* = *hē charis + egeneto*. He concludes:

> Indeed, the author who did not employ the verb *echaristhē*, but the strange circumlocution *hē charis kai hē alētheia egeneto*, has to have his certain reason for that. But it deprives nothing of the fact that the deep structure of the verse is indeed the one that we indicated.[164]

Our study admits that it is hardly even possible to argue against De la Potterie's stance because of its totally arbitrary nature. It is a relief to note that he apparently realizes this as well when he writes, "We shall say that this classification of the text is no doubt arbitrary."[165] Our study can only agree. We should also ask why the Evangelist would even bother to formulate such a sophisticated construction to express the

---

163. Ibid., 274.
164. Ibid., 275; my translation.
165. Ibid.; my translation.

very simple idea of a gift of God. After all, the Evangelist is well aware of alternative expressions and uses the appropriate terminology elsewhere, as in *tēn dōrean tou Theou*, "the gift of God" (4:10; cf. 15:25)! The very fact that this expression, *tēn dōrean tou Theou*, was apparently known to the Evangelist prevents one from envisioning anything like "a gift of" behind the phraseology of either *plērēs charitos kai alētheias* or *hē charis kai hē alētheia*.[166]

Forth, De la Potterie appeals to a sense of *alētheia* that is very different from *charis* in the Johannine vocabulary and theology. He argues that if the expression of verses 14 and 17 did not form hendiadys, then *charis* would take an autonomous value different from that of "truth." But what then would this "grace" be? And, especially in light of the fact that it serves to characterize the coming of Jesus Christ, how is one to explain that the Evangelist speaks about it nowhere else in the remainder of the Gospel? If, on the contrary, it is all about hendiadys, then the Evangelist considers here only one thing brought by Jesus Christ: the gift of the truth. This is in perfect harmony with the remainder of the Gospel, because *alētheia* appears in it as a key word; it reappears again in the story of the Passion (John 18:37). Only the author accentuates it from the prologue: the mission of Jesus Christ, for the Evangelist, consisted fundamentally in that he communicated to us "the grace of the truth."[167]

This last argument of De la Potterie—"from the further absence of *charis*"—cannot possibly prove that *(hē) charis kai (hē) alētheia* constitutes hendiadys. We have already demonstrated in reference to the phrase *ḥesed weʾĕmet* that the argument "from the absence" is intrinsically fallacious. This fact can only be again confirmed by recalling Schnackenburg's remark on the matter: "In this grouping, *alētheia* is the subordinate term, as may be seen from the fact that only *charis* is taken up again in v. 16."[168] It is indicative of the inappropriateness of the methodology itself to realize that two scholars—De la Potterie and Schnackenburg—essentially use the same "from the absence" argument and come to completely opposite conclusions on the meaning of the phrase! Of course, the same criticism directed at De la Potterie's pro-

---

166. Contra Bultmann, *John*; La Potterie, "*Charis*"; Harris, *Prologue and Gospel*, and others pursing this line of argument.

167. La Potterie, "*Charis*," 275; my translation.

168. Schnackenburg, *John*, 1:273; similarly, Dumbrell, "Grace and Truth," 115.

posal applies to Schnackenburg's observation. True, the phraseology of *plērēs charitos kai alētheias* is linked[169] to the following *ek tou plērōmatos . . . charin anti charitos*. One may 1) point out that the term *alētheia* in the phrase *plērēs charitos kai alētheias* is omitted in *charin anti charitos*, 2) derive from this observation that *alētheia* is a secondary term in *plērēs charitos kai alētheias*, and 3) claim that *alētheia*, as the secondary term, must serve as the modifier in *plērēs charitos kai alētheias*. But no such conclusion can be derived with any certainty from the absence of the term *alētheia* from *plērēs charitos kai alētheias* in the following *charin anti charitos*. This "omission" of *alētheia* does not necessarily mean that *alētheia* is secondary to *charis* in *plērēs charitos kai alētheias*, either. In fact, *alētheia* is hardly secondary to *charis*, because *alētheia* (and cognates) is greatly emphasized in the rest of the Gospel.[170] And, even if *alētheia* were secondary to *charis*, this would not automatically mean that *alētheia* serves as the modifier of *charis* in *plērēs charitos kai alētheias*. After all, the absence of *alētheia* does not necessarily indicate its omission or incorporation with respect to *charis*, but can be an element of the design.[171] So, such attempts to establish that *plērēs charitos kai alētheias* constitutes hendiadys on the basis of the absence of the term *alētheia* from the phrase *plērēs charitos kai alētheias* in *charin anti charitos* are not conclusive. We should recognize, however, that the matter of the absence of the term *charis* beyond the prologue *is* rather fascinating. Our study will further address this issue in detail. At this

---

169. So Nigel Turner observes, "The poetry [of the prologue] has . . . a chain-locking device which links the clauses together, e.g. *in him was LIFE : and the LIFE was the LIGHT of men. And the LIGHT in DARKNESS shined : and the DARKNESS did not comprehend it.* Subsequent links are *world, his own, glory,* and *full*" (N. Turner, "Style of John," 65).

170. The noun *alētheia* occurs twenty-five times in John, seven times in the three Synoptics together; the adjective *alēthēs* is found fourteen times in John, once in Mark and once in Matthew; the adjective *alēthinos* is featured nine times in John, once in Luke; the adverb *alēthōs* occurs seven times in John, three times each in Matthew and Luke and two times in Mark. The Evangelists do no use the verb *alētheuō* (employed in Gal 4:16 and Eph 4:15).

171. For example, as Harris (erroneously) suggests, "The element of communication by God and participation by human beings is emphasized in 'grace' by the fact that, whereas 'grace and truth' are twice conjoined (vv. 14, 17), it is only 'grace' that human beings are said to participate in (v. 16), not 'truth'" (Harris, *Prologue and Gospel*, 66–67). Similarly (and also erroneously) Dumbrell, "Grace and Truth," 119.

point we must conclude that it has not been demonstrated that *(hē) charis kai (hē) alētheia* constitutes hendiadys.

Arguments contra *(hē) charis kai (hē) alētheia* Being Hendiadys

Arguments like William J. Dumbrell's—"The implication of verse 14 is that we are dealing with the content of revelation rather than the fact of revelation,[172] which makes a hendiadys less probable"[173]—will not suffice. Our study offers rather tangible evidence that *(hē) charis kai (hē) alētheia* does not constitute hendiadys.

(hē) charis kai (hē) alētheia Has Never Been Demonstrated to Constitute Hendiadys

Definitions[174] and the nature of hendiadys allow speculation. Hendiadys is also a comparatively rare literary device.[175] Therefore, the presence of hendiadys should not be assumed, but proven. But, as our study has established, *(hē) charis kai (hē) alētheia* has never been demonstrated to constitute hendiadys. Since hendiadys is a rare literary feature then it is more likely that the phrases *plērēs charitos kai alētheias* and *hē charis kai hē alētheia* denote two distinctive attributes.

Hendiadys Is Not a Feature of the Literary Style of the Evangelist

Hendiadys is not a feature of the literary style of the Evangelist. Scholars occasionally suggest that the expressions *ex hudatos kai pneumatos* (3:5),[176] *en pneumati kai alētheia* (4:23, 24),[177] and *pneuma estin kai zōē estin* (6:63) constitute hendiadys. [178] But this proves not to be the case when one considers the evidence.

---

172. Dumbrell here refers to Hanson, *John 1:14–18 and Exodus 34*.

173. Dumbrell, "Grace and Truth," 115–16.

174. See elsewhere in this study. Curiously, Schmidt states that hendiadys occurs when the *synonymous* expressions are introduced by a *kai* (Schmidt, "Section E. The Word Group *basileus*," 1:583).

175. See Westhuizen, "Hendiadys," 56.

176. Dunn, *Baptism*, 191–92; M. Turner, *Holy Spirit*, 68.

177. So Dodd, *Interpretation*, 314, 314 n. 2, 341; similarly Dunn renders, "Spirit-of-truth (*pneuma kai alētheia*) . . . 4.23f" (Dunn, *Baptism*, 192).

178. Discussion over hendiadys in *ex hudatos kai pneumatos, en pneumati kai*

Sometimes scholars attempt to support their argument for the presence of hendiadys in the Gospel by reasoning "from the grammar." Hence, Dodd contends that "the grammatical form, in which a single preposition governs both substantives, indicates that *pneuma kai alētheia* forms a single concept."[179] Dunn makes a similar claim: "The phrase is a hendiadys, and the single preposition governing both words indicates that *hudōr kai pneuma* forms a single concept—water-and-Spirit."[180] Even if this "authentication" of hendiadys were true it would not affect our case, because no preposition governs either *plērēs charitos kai alētheias* or *hē charis kai hē alētheia*. We should observe, though, that such "verification" from the presence of a preposition simply does not stand the test anyway. If a single preposition governing a couple of substantives was an "indicator" of hendiadys, then one should have declared as hendiadys not only *en pneumati kai alētheia* (4:23, 24) and *ex hudatos kai pneumatos* (3:5), but also *meta phanōn kai lampadōn kai hoplōn*, "with lanterns and torches and weapons" (18:3)![181]

Ben Witherington III refutes the alleged case that *ex hudatos kai pneumatos* (3:5) is hendiadys on both syntactical and contextual grounds:

> In the parallel text in 1 John 5:6–8 we have articleless references to water and blood preceded by one preposition (*dia*, through), and it is very clear there that water and blood are metaphors for two different events. . . . the context of John 3:5 does not favor the view that water and Spirit refer to one and the same event. Verse 6 says that flesh is born from (*ek*) flesh, and spirit (i.e., spiritual birth) is born from the Spirit. This is a clear reference to two "births"—physical and spiritual birth.[182]

---

alētheia, and *pneuma estin kai zōē estin* does not actually affect the case of *plērēs charitos kai alētheias* and *hē charis kai hē alētheia* (beyond the discussion over the literary style of the Evangelist). Phrases of the latter group differ from the former structurally and have no preposition governing them.

179. Dodd, *Interpretation*, 314 n. 2.

180. Dunn, *Baptism*, 191–92.

181. See our critique of the alleged argument "from a single preposition" in the OT hendiadys section.

182. Witherington, *John's Wisdom*, 97.

These syntactical (3:5; cf. 4:23, 24; 18:3; 1 John 5:6–8) and grammatical considerations (3:5–6) completely invalidate the proposal that *ex hudatos kai pneumatos* (3:5) constitutes hendiadys.

Sometimes a phrase is labeled "hendiadys" because it allegedly describes a "singular concept" or "unitary event." So, Dodd writes,

> It is the worship of God *en pneumati* and it is *en alētheia*, that is, it operates with that which is ultimately real.[183] ... the new approach to God opened up by Christ is worship *en pneumati kai alētheia*, the two terms, *pneuma* and *alētheia*, forming a virtual [!] hendiadys: the sphere of *pneuma* (*ta anō*) is the sphere of *alētheia*, absolute reality, as distinct from the phenomenal order of *sarx*.[184]

Thus Max Turner declares,

> The explanatory 'birth "of water-and-Spirit"' here [in *ex hudatos kai pneumatos* of John 3:5] is a special construction called a *hendiadys* and must [!] refer to a *unitary* event, a single metaphorical 'birth' accomplished through some sort of combination of water and Spirit.[185]

Similarly Dunn maintains that

> *hudōr kai pneuma* [3:5] cannot be regarded as independent and unrelated elements in the birth *anōthen*; far less can we speak of two births.[186] The phrase is a hendiadys, and the single preposition governing both words indicates that *hudōr kai pneuma* forms a single concept—water-and-Spirit.[187]

To begin with, these observations cannot constitute evidence in favor of hendiadys because of their speculative nature. Judgments on the matter are arbitrary at best.[188] For example, it is sometimes suggested that *hudatos kai* is a later addition to the original text by either the Evangelist or a redactor or copyist. Scholars often distinguish between

---

183. Dodd, *Interpretation*, 314.
184. Ibid., 341.
185. M. Turner, *Holy Spirit*, 68.
186. Dunn, *Baptism*, 191–92.
187. Ibid.
188. If they are not arbitrary, they are fallacious in logic. For example, Max Turner draws conclusions from his suggestion that *ex hudatos kai pneumatos* constitutes hendiadys, but the initial point has not yet been proven.

the births of *hudōr* and of *pneuma* (both in time and in essence).[189] In the Gospel, *hudōr* and *pneuma*, while related, still apparently denote individual elements (1:26–33; 3:23). This makes postulating hendiadys in *ex hudatos kai pneumatos* unwarranted and pointless.

Moreover, scholars cannot satisfactorily explain what such a "unitary event" or "single concept" *hudōr kai pneuma* might conceivably depict. Some suggestions are: "water-and-Sprit," "'water' with 'Spirit,'" "water-of-the-Spirit,"[190] "water-which-is-(also)-Spirit,"[191] or "water made potent by the Spirit."[192] Remarkably, in viewing *hudōr kai pneuma* as hendiadys the role of the modifier is given to *pneuma*. This is yet another example of making unwarranted conclusions, for the choice is illogical. One cannot but observe that the expressions *ex hudatos kai pneumatos* (3:5), *en pneumati kai alētheia* (4:23, 24), and *pneuma estin kai zōē estin* (6:63) have *pneuma* in common. Therefore, if they constituted hendiadys then *pneuma* would have likely been the main substantive, with *hudōr*, *alētheia*, and *zōē* playing the modifying role. This role, particularly for *hudōr*, would have been only confirmed by Jesus's answer: "unless one is born *ex hudatos kai pneumatos* he cannot enter into the kingdom of God. That which is born of the flesh is flesh, and that which is born *ek tou pneumatos pneuma estin*. . . . so is everyone who is born *ek tou pneumatos*" (3:5–8). In the replica, it is *hudōr* that may be said to be "dropped," whereas *pneuma* "remains." This, if one was to argue for hendiadys, would have been yet another indication that *hudōr* plays the modifying role in the phrase *ex hudatos kai pneumatos*. But this should have resulted in *ex hudatos kai pneumatos* meaning something like (born) "from watery spirit," which makes no sense. This incredible implication discourages one from discerning hendiadys in *ex hudatos kai pneumatos*, *en pneumati kai alētheia*, or *pneuma estin kai zōē estin*—as

---

189. One of these scholars—Hoskyns, *Fourth Gospel*, 215—Dunn lists himself (Dunn, *Baptism*, 192 n. 24). One interpretation has it that water represents human birth, whether semen of man or waters in the womb, in contrast to birth from the Spirit. Another explanation of the phrase is "you must be 'born from God' by first submitting to John's (or water) baptism and subsequently receiving the Spirit (or having another baptism of the Spirit)." There are many other interpretations that do not require *ex hudatos kai pneumatos* to be hendiadys; see Beasley-Murray, *John*, 48f.

190. So Dunn, *Baptism*, 192, all three in the same paragraph.

191. Dodd, *Interpretation*, 312.

192. Lee, *Religious Thought*, 189.

does the fact that suggestions regarding hendiadys are apparently made without taking the actual data into consideration.

Furthermore, neither "singular concept" nor "unitary event" essentially requires a blending of its components into a single entity[193] (as would have been the case had it been hendiadys). For example, the resulting phrase *pneuma estin kai zōē estin* stems from the same source—the "words of Jesus"; the phrase *en pneumati kai alētheia* characterizes a single concept of "worship," *ex hudatos kai pneumatos* explains "birth," *en tō nomō kai hoi prophētai* refers to "Scripture," both *plērēs charitos kai alētheias* and *hē charis kai hē alētheia* define "character." But from this observation it does not necessarily follow that one of the terms depicting such single concept *modifies* the other so that two individual elements become one (as would be the case with hendiadys). For example, receiving the Spirit (7:37-39) and the life (5:39-40) are separate benefits of the words of Jesus, the same source.[194] "The Law" and "the Prophets" are explicitly distinctive segments of the Scripture, a single entity. So *charis* and *alētheia* can legitimately be individual facets of the single concept, the "character" of God. Therefore, appeals to a "singular concept" or "unitary event" cannot demonstrate the presence of hendiadys.

Finally, sometimes a reference to authorities is made to support the claim for an alleged hendiadys. Dunn writes, "[Hendiadys is a] fairly typical feature of the Johannine style. See also 4.23f.; 6.63; Dodd 314 n.2, 341f.; Brown, Gospel 130, 297. Schnackenburg 471 n. 3 refers also to 1.14, 17; 14:6; I John 3.18; II John 3." [195] But these references gain no support for the claim. Dunn's own reflections on "4.23f.; 6.63" do not contribute to his claim that *hudōr kai pneuma* (3:5) constitutes hendiadys.[196] Neither do they demonstrate the presence of hendiadys in 4:23-24; 6:63.[197] As our study has demonstrated, Dodd's arguments

---

193. Cf. *Egō eimi hē hodos kai hē alētheia kai hē zōē*, "I am the way, and the truth, and the life," (14:6) or *eis to onoma tou patros kai tou huiou kai tou hagiou pneumatos*, "in the name of the Father and the Son and the Holy Spirit" (Matt 28:19).

194. See Beasley-Murray, *John*, 96.

195. Dunn, *Baptism*, 192 n. 25.

196. In fact, as our study has demonstrated, 3:5; 4:23; 6:3 taken together rather discourage one from maintaining the presence of hendiadys in the Gospel.

197. On 4:23f. see Dunn, *Baptism*, 187, 192; on 6:63 consider ibid., 95, 180, 184, 187, 192, 198, 203, 226.

"from preposition"[198] and "from singular concept"[199] cannot support the claim. Brown comments on 3:5: "*of water and Spirit* . . . The two nouns are anarthrous and are governed by one preposition,"[200] and on 6:63: "*are both Spirit and Life* . . . Literally 'are Spirit and are life.' Dodd, Interpretation, p. 342, is correct, however, in seeing 'Spirit and life' as a virtual hendiadys. See COMMENT." But these authorities do not provide a single evidence toward Dunn's alleged case. Brown only mentions "life-giving Spirit" once.[201] Schnackenburg hardly even argues for hendiadys but only comments on the phrase *pneumati kai alētheia*: "The pair of words, in which the emphasis is on *pneumati*, means the same thing in both of its elements."[202] He then states in the footnote, "The phrases, *charis kai alētheia* 1:14, 17; *alētheia kai zōē* 14:6; *en ergō kai alētheia* 1 Jn 3:18; *en alētheia kai agapē* 2 Jn 3 are comparable. The *pneuma* is also characterized by *zōē* (6:63) as well as by *alētheia* (14:17; 15:26; 16:13; 1 Jn 4:6; 5:6)."[203] Thus Dunn's conclusion that hendiadys is a "fairly typical feature of the Johannine style" is simply unwarranted.

One can only observe that the usage of hendiadys just does not make much sense in regard to the phrases *ex hudatos kai pneumatos, en pneumati kai alētheia*, and *pneuma estin kai zōē estin*. Why would the Evangelist want to obscure *pneuma*-related matters by employing complex hendiadys instead of using a simple adjectival *en pneumati hagiō* (1:33), *to pneuma to hagion* (14:26), *pneuma hagion* (20:22), "*the* Holy Spirit," or genitive constructions *to pneuma tēs alētheias*, "the Spirit of truth," (14:17; 15:26; 16:13), as he does elsewhere in the Gospel? Why would the Evangelist choose to employ the odd hendiadys in the phrases *charitos kai alētheias, hē charis kai hē alētheia*, and *en pneumati kai alētheia* over his favorite "true something" expressions, *to phōs to alēthinon*, "the true Light" (1:9); *hoi alēthinoi proskunētai*, "the true wor-

---

198. Dodd, *Interpretation*, 314 n. 2.

199. Ibid., 314 n. 2, 341f.

200. R. Brown, *John (I-XII)*, 130-31.

201. Ibid., 297, 300.

202. Schnackenburg, *John*, 1:437 (Dunn refers to the German edition, Schnackenburg, *Johannesevangelium 1-4*, in his reference "Schnackenburg at 471 n. 3"). These two clauses contradict each other. The second clause excludes the very possibility of hendiadys where one terms modifies the other.

203. Schnackenburg, *John*, 1:437 n. 52, an equivalent English translation of Schnackenburg, *Johannesevangelium 1-4*, 471 n. 3. References to 1 John appear to be irrelevant in a discussion over the presence of hendiadys in the Gospel.

shipers" (4:23); *ton arton ek tou ouranou ton alēthinon*, "the true bread out of heaven" (6:32); *hē ampelos hē alēthinē*, "the true vine" (15:1); and *ton monon alēthinon Theon*, "the only true God" (17:3)? These stylistic features of the Evangelist make the alleged presence of hendiadys in *pneuma*- and *charis*-related passages unlikely.

Remarkably, scholars who are not driven by the desire to establish a particular theological point do not find hendiadys to be a feature of the style of the Evangelist at all. Johannine grammar and style scholars—Abbott[204] and Turner[205]—do not detect hendiadys in the Gospel. In 1939 Eduard Schweizer identified 33 characteristics of Johannine style.[206] In 1951 Eugen Ruckstuhl increased the number to 50. [207] In 1972 Nicol produced a list containing 82 Johannine literary features.[208] In 1991 Ruckstuhl and Peter Dschulnigg recognized 153 such characteristics.[209] In 1977 Boismard, Lamouille, and Rochais listed 416 characteristics of the Evangelist's literary style.[210] None of the lists identified hendiadys[211] as one of these features. Having considered the evidence, our study concludes that the style and grammar of the Evangelist strongly discourage one from perceiving hendiadys in the phrase *(hē) charis kai (hē) alētheia*; the phraseology rather denotes two individual attributes.

---

204. Abbott, *Johannine Grammar*. Abbott discusses the usage of the conjunction *kai* in the Gospel (including the prologue) in detail and does not suggest it indicates hendiadys (133–50). The grammar's indices on the subject matter do not even have "hendiadys" as an entry (671). Abbot discusses 1:14–18 widely but nowhere even hints that any of its language constitutes hendiadys. To the contrary, this scholar translates "the grace [of God] and the truth [of God] through Jesus Christ came into being" (158, 225, 236; brackets by Abbott). Apparently, the grammarian does not perceive hendiadys in *hē charis kai hē alētheia* (1:17).

205. N. Turner, "Style of John."

206. Schweizer, *Ego Eimi*, 82–112.

207. Ruckstuhl, *Die literarische Einheit des Johannesevangeliums*, 291–303.

208. Nicol, *Semeia*, 16–27, especially 22–24: "Additions to Ruckstuhl's List" (positions 51–82). For Ruckstuhl's response, see Ruckstuhl, "Johannine Language and Style," 127, 141.

209. Ruckstuhl and Dschulnigg, *Stilkritik und Verfasserfrage im Johannesevangelium*, 63–162, 164–68, 269–75.

210. Boismard, Lamouille, and Rochais, *L'Évangile de Jean*, 491–514.

211. A convenient juxtaposition of the lists is available in Belle, *Signs Source*, 405–17.

The Evangelist Uses Neither His Favorite Adjectival or Genitive of Quality Constructions in *(hē) charis kai (hē) alētheia*

Edwards—while arguing for (!) hendiadys—remarks that "we must also allow for John giving a fresh nuance to the familiar phrase [*hē charis kai hē alētheia dia Iēsou Christou egeneto*]: the coming of Jesus Christ is not just God's *charis* (gracious gift); it is the true *charis*, just as Christ is the true vine, the true or real bread from heaven."[212] Our study notes that this observation really proves the opposite of Edwards's conclusion that *hē charis kai hē alētheia* is a hendiadys! The Evangelist is quite capable of using adjectival constructions, particularly those conveying the idea of "true something." The writer employs such phrases as *to phōs to alēthinon*, "the true Light" (1:9); *hoi alēthinoi proskunētai*, "the true worshipers" (4:23); *ton arton ek tou ouranou ton alēthinon*, "the true bread out of heaven" (6:32); *hē ampelos hē alēthinē*, "the true vine" (15:1); and *ton monon alēthinon Theon*, "the only true God" (17:3). The Evangelist uses the genitive 2017 times in the Gospel; he is quite capable of utilizing the genitive of quality.[213] Had the Evangelist meant to convey "true grace" or "gracious[214] truth" by *(hē) charis kai (hē) alētheia*, the writer would have likely used either his favorite adjectival construction (1:9; 4:23; 6:32; 15:1; 17:3) or the genitive of quality. But the Evangelist employs neither, which suggests that by *(hē) charis kai (hē) alētheia* he uses the nouns *charis* and *alētheia* as distinct entities.

hē charis kai hē alētheia Refer to *charitos kai alētheias*, which Allude to *ḥesed weʾĕmet*

Hē charis kai hē alētheia are supplied with articles, hence, they refer to *charitos kai alētheias*. In turn, *charitos kai alētheias* allude to *ḥesed weʾĕmet*. In the OT, whenever the word-pair *ḥesed . . . weʾĕmet* is the subject of a verb, the verb is always in the third person plural (Prov 3:3; 20:28; Pss 40:12; 61:8; 85:11; 89:15). Therefore, both *charitos kai*

---

212. Edwards, "*Charin anti charitos*," 11–12.

213. Cf. *tois logois tēs charitos*, "the gracious words" (Luke 4:22); *eklogēn charitos*, "gracious choice" (Rom 11:5). See BDF, §165.

214. Cf. the usage of the adjectives *charizomai, charitoō, acharis, acharistos, epichaēs, epichartos, eucharistos, perichrēs, huperchares, charieis,* and *charistērios* in the LXX/OG/NT.

alētheias and *hē charis kai hē alētheia*, as alluding to *ḥesed we'ĕmet*, denote two subjective qualities.

LXX/OG/NT Usage of the Construction "*plērēs*-noun-*kai*-noun" against Perceiving Hendiadys in *plērēs charitos kai alētheias*

In the Gospel, the construction "adjective-noun-*kai*-noun" occurs only in constructing the phrase *plērēs charitos kai alētheias*. But the plausibility of *plērēs charitos kai alētheias* being hendiadys can be evaluated on the basis of the practices of the LXX/OG and the NT.

In the LXX/OG, the construction *plērēs*-noun-*kai*-noun always denotes different objects. Samson stands between the pillars of the house *plērēs andrōn kai tōn gunaikōn*, "full of men and women" (Judg A[215] 16:27). The way along which the Syrians flee is *plērēs himatiōn kai skeuōn* (2 Kgs 7:15), that is, "full of garments and vessels," which the Syrians have cast away in their panic. Similar phraseology is employed to depict Balaam, who cannot do anything contrary to the command of the LORD, even if Balak should give Balaam *plērē ton oikon autou arguriou kai chrusiou*, "his house full of silver and gold" (Num 22:18; 24:13). In these phrases, nouns joined by *kai* cannot conceivably modify each other.[216] Thus, practices in the LXX/OG[217] prevent one from envisioning hendiadys in *plērēs charitos kai alētheias*.

In the NT, the construction *plērēs*-noun-*kai*-noun occurs only in Acts.[218] The apostles define the procedure of election and qualifications of deacons as follows:

> Brethren, select from among you seven men of good reputation, *plēreis pneumatos kai sophias*, . . . and they chose Stephen, a man *plērēs pisteōs kai pneumatos hagiou* . . . And Stephen, *plērēs charitos kai dunameōs*, was performing great wonders and signs among the people. (Acts 6:3–8)

---

215. In Judg 16:27, codex Alexandrinus reads *ho de oikos ēn plērēs andrōn kai gunaikōn*; codex Vaticanus renders *ho oikos plērēs tōn andrōn kai tōn gunaikōn*.

216. Cf. 2 Sam 23:7; 2 Kgs 6:17.

217. Judg A 16:27; 2 Sam 23:7; 2 Kgs 7:15; Num 22:18; 24:13; 2 Kgs 6:17.

218. Curiously, for Boismard the construction of the adjective "full" followed by two determinatives is a proof that Luke edited the prologue, for there are five examples of such a construction in Acts. See Boismard, *St. John's Prologue*; Boismard, "Dans le sein du Père"; R. Brown, *John (I–XII)*, 14.

In this passage, nouns modified by *plērēs*—*pneuma*, "the Spirit"; *sophia*, "wisdom"; *pistis*, "faith"; *pneuma hagios*, "the Holy Spirit"; *charis*, "grace"; *dunamis*, "power,"—do not overlap, and this emphasizes the *distinctiveness* of the nouns. Each quality in the list is mentioned elsewhere in Acts on its own. These considerations make the option of the writer's intention to merge the qualities by the means of hendiadys unlikely. This paradigm of listing individual nouns modified by *plērēs* is further confirmed throughout the book of Acts in both positive and negative descriptions. Tabitha, a female disciple, is depicted as *plērēs ergōn agathōn kai eleēmosunōn hōn epoiei*, "abounding with deeds of kindness and charity which she continually did" (Acts 9:36). Since mentioning the same deed twice would be redundant, the writer evidently perceives Tabitha's two activities—*erga agatha* and *eleēmosunai*—as distinct from each other.[219] Barnabas becomes known as *anēr agathos kai plērēs pneumatos hagiou kai pisteōs*, "a good man, full of the Holy Spirit and of faith" (Acts 11:24).[220] Paul accuses Elymas the magician of being *plērēs pantos dolou kai pasēs rhadiourgias*, "full of every kind of deceit and every sort of fraud" (Acts 13:10). Mentioning the same characteristic of Elymas twice in Paul's address would not make sense. Therefore the reporter probably differentiates Elymas's *dolos* and *rhadiourgia*.[221]

Thus, the usage of *plērēs*-noun-*kai*-noun phraseology in the LXX/OG/NT emphasizes the distinctiveness of attributes modified by *plērēs* and discourages one from perceiving hendiadys in *plērēs charitos kai alētheias*.

The Evangelist Always Uses "article-noun in singular-*kai*-article-noun in singular" Phraseology to Convey Two Subjective Qualities

Schnackenburg reviews Panimolle's study[222] and mentions in passing, "I am not sure if [*hē charis kai hē alētheia*] can be translated as 'grace of

---

219. Tabitha's *erga agatha* particularly were sowing tunics and garments for widows (Acts 9:39). Her *eleēmosunai* might have been generous almsgiving (see Bultmann, "eleos"; Dunn, *Romans 9–16*, 730; Hagner, *Matthew 1–13*, 132; Witherington, *Women*, 149–51; Witherington, "Dorcas," 226).

220. See the list of qualities characteristic of a deacon (Acts 6:3–8).

221. Gerhard Delling notices this plurality of powers filling Elymas (Delling, "*plērēs*," 6:286).

222. Panimolle, *Il dono della legge*.

truth', especially since both words are supplied with an article."[223] De la Potterie evaluates this factor as follows: "this real autonomy seems to be the case only at the first glance. But the [Schnackenburg's] argument is not valid: in the NT we can find several examples of hendiadys with two articles; let us recall, in particular, the text of 2 Cor 8:4 ... *tēn charin kai tēn koinōnian tēs diakonias*, 'la grâce de participer à ce service.'"[224] De la Potterie also refers to "Blass-Debrunner, § 442,16; among the examples of hendiadys which he quotes, let us mention the following passages, where both nouns have the article: Luke 2:47 (*existanto... epi tē sunesei kai tais apokrisesin autou*); 2 Tim 4:1; Jas 5:10; 1 Pet 4:14)."[225]

De la Potterie's argumentation is invalid. First, references provided by him and BDF have not yet been *established* as exemplifying hendiadys. Therefore, one cannot draw any conclusion regarding hendiadys on such basis. Second, all these references—whether they constitute hendiadys or not—come from some literature other than the Gospel of John. As such, they are useless in evaluating features of the Evangelist's literary style.

In fact, our research demonstrates that the two definite articles employed in *hē charis kai hē alētheia* specify that the Evangelist has two subjective qualities in view. The construction "article-noun in singular-*kai*-article-noun in singular" (as in *hē charis kai hē alētheia*) often occurs in the Gospel. Consider the relevant phrases:[226] *hē charis kai hē alētheia* (1:17); *tē graphē kai tō logō*, "the Scripture and the word" (2:22); *ton patera kai tēn mētera*, "the father and the mother" (6:42); *tēn Marthan kai tēn adelphēn autēs kai ton Lazaron*, "Martha and her sister and Lazarus" (11:5); *hē anastasis kai hē zōē*, "the resurrection and the life" (11:25); *ton topon kai to ethnos*, "the place and the nation" (11:48); *ho didaskalos, kai: ho kurios*, "the Teacher and the Lord" (13:13); *ho kurios kai ho didaskalos*, "the Lord and the Teacher" (13:14); *hē hodos kai hē alētheia kai hē zōē*, "the way, and the truth, and the life" (14:6); *hē mētēr autou kai hē adelphē tēs mētros autou, Maria hē tou Klōpa kai Maria hē Magdalēnē*, "His mother, and His mother's sister, Mary the *wife* of Clopas, and Mary Magdalene" (19:25); *tēn mētera kai ton*

223. Schnackenburg, "Zur johanneischen Forschung," 284; my translation.
224. La Potterie, "*Charis*," 276; my translation.
225. Ibid., 276 n. 47; my translation.
226. Cf. 1:1; 6:51; 8:32; 10:15; 13:31; 14:10; 14:11; 16:22, and also *hoi grammateis kai hoi Pharisaioi*, "the scribes and the Pharisees" (8:3).

mathētēn, "the mother and the disciple" (19:26); *ho kurios mou kai ho Theos mou*, "My Lord and my God" (20:28). None of the eleven "article-noun in singular-*kai*-article-noun in singular" constructions[227] of the Gospel provides a case where one of the nouns can conceivably modify the other. Therefore, hendiadys is not likely occurring in *hē charis kai hē alētheia* either. In all likelihood the phrase is but the twelfth example of the "article-noun in singular-*kai*-article-noun in singular" construction. Consistent with the style of the Evangelist, *hē charis kai hē alētheia* delineates two distinct attributes.

LXX/OG/NT Usage of the Construction "article-noun-*kai*-article-noun-verb in singular" against Perceiving Hendiadys in *hē charis kai hē alētheia . . . egeneto*

There is yet another attempt to argue that the phrase *hē charis kai hē alētheia . . . egeneto* (1:17) constitutes hendiadys. Harris observes, "the verb in singular in v. 17, *egeneto*, would seem to indicate that the phrase [*hē charis kai hē alētheia*] is intended to be taken as a compound one."[228] So also Schoneveld deduces, "the verb following 'the-grace-and-the-truth' is in the singular, not in the plural, which means that grace-and-truth is seen as hendiadys, as one single concept denoted by a pair of terms."[229] Our study reasons that these conclusions are fallacious, as they fail to take peculiarities of the Greek syntax into consideration.

Generally, one should be rather cautious in deducing evidence from the syntax. Consider the witness's testimony to Jesus's death, *heis tōn stratiōtōn lonchē autou tēn pleuran enuxen*, "one of the soldiers pierced His side with a spear" (19:34). The Evangelist further quotes from the Scripture, *opsontai eis hon exekentēsan*, "THEY SHALL LOOK ON HIM WHOM THEY PIERCED" (19:37). Contrary to what it may

---

227. Not yet counting *hē charis kai hē alētheia* under discussion. Notice also examples similar to *hē charis kai hē alētheia* that discourage one from perceiving hendiadys, such as *kai autos ex autou epien kai hoi huioi autou kai ta thremmata autou*, "and drank of it himself and his sons and his cattle" (4:12).

228. Harris, *Prologue and Gospel*, 66.

229. Schoneveld, "Torah in the Flesh," 83. Schoneveld further (wrongly) asserts that, "the corresponding Hebrew phrase . . . , occurs . . . in the Hebrew Bible . . . generally as such a *single* concept" (ibid.; emphasis added). As our study demonstrated, whenever the word-pair *hesed . . . ʾĕmet* is the subject of a verb, the verb is always in the third person *plural* (Prov 3:3; 20:28; Pss 40:12; 61:8; 85:11; 89:15).

suggest at first glance, there is really no discrepancy in number between "one of the soldiers pierced" and "they pierced." The plural *exekentēsan* may actually refer to one of the soldiers who pierced Jesus's side with a spear.[230] The Evangelist's syntax may well be governed by the sense of the sentence[231] and/or disclose the inner thoughts of the writer. Consider the passage *Hoi oun Ioudaioi, epei paraskeuē ēn, hina mē meinē epi tou staurou ta sōmata en tō sabbatō*, "Then the Jews, because it was the day of preparation, so that the bodies would not remain on the cross on the Sabbath" (19:31). It may well be that the singular *epi tou staurou*, "on the cross," hints that the Evangelist actually keeps the very particular cross with the body of Jesus in mind even though the writer refers to *ta sōmata*, "the bodies," of the crucified on the three crosses.[232] The same may well be the case with *hē charis kai hē alētheia . . . egeneto*. The Evangelist employs the singular verb, for it is the character of God as Jesus that is on the writer's mind. But at the same time, the Evangelist is well aware that there are two subjective qualities—*(hē) charis kai (hē) alētheia*—in the character. We argue that this is confirmed by the practice attested in the LXX/OG/NT.

The BDF rule on "agreement with two or more co-ordinate words connected by *kai (hē)*"[233] reads,

> (1) When the subject consists of sing. + sing. or sing. + plur. the verb agrees (a) with the first subject if the verb stands before it,

---

230. The so-called "indefinite subject." For other various options see Bultmann, *John*, 677; Calvin, *John 11–21*, 187, Westcott, *John*, 2:321, Abbott, *Johannine Grammar*, 247.

231. The Evangelist habitually employs the so-called *"constructio ad sensum*, without following any fixed rules" style (BDF, §134). This approach was very widespread in Greek from early times and is found in the NT. The principal instance is that in which a collective, embracing a plurality of persons in a singular noun, is construed as if the subject were plural. The plural that conforms to this sense may then actually appear in the following clauses: cf. *ēkolouthei* [sg.] *de autō ochlos polus, hoti etheōroun* [pl.] *ta sēmeia*, "a large crowd followed [sg.] Him, because they saw [pl.] the signs" (6:2, cf. 6:22–24; 7:20; 11:42; 12:12–13; 12:34); *ta probata tēs phōnēs autou akouei* [sg.], "the sheep hear [sg.] his voice," (10:3), but *ta probata autō akolouthei* [sg.], *hoti oidasin* [pl.] *tēn phōnēn autou*, "the sheep follow [sg.] him because they know [pl.] his voice," (10:4) and *all' ouk ēkousan* [pl.] *autōn ta probata*, "but the sheep did not hear [pl.] them" (10:8); *emnēsthēsan hoti tauta ēn* [sg.] *ep' autō gegrammena* [pl.], "they remembered that these things were [sg.] written [pl.]" (12:16).

232. It may also be a case of the grammatically normal singular with neuter plural subject or a "distributive singular" (see BDF, §140).

233. BDF, §135.

except when the subject-group is basically conceived as a whole; (b) with both subjects taken together if the verb stands after the second subject; (c) with the first if the verb stands between; (d) rules (a) and (b) can be combined when a finite verb stands before and a participle after the group, or the reverse.

According to section 1b, the subject *hē charis kai hē alētheia* should have been followed by the plural *egenonto*, not *egeneto* in the singular! Using the singular *egeneto* is not a mistake on the part of the Evangelist. The writer follows the "agreement with two or more co-ordinate words connected by *kai (hē)*" rule elsewhere.[234] This is not an oversight on the part of the Evangelist either. Scribes did not "correct" the rendering.[235] We argue that the Evangelist *intentionally* renders *hē charis kai hē alētheia . . . egeneto* to simultaneously 1) emphasize the distinctiveness of the two subjective qualities, and 2) to accentuate their affiliation under the single objective reality of the character.

Our study identified *all* of the LXX/OG/NT examples syntactically matching the construction *hē charis kai hē alētheia . . . egeneto*. Consider: *ho tromos humōn kai ho phobos estai*, "the dread of you and the fear will be [sg.]" (Gen 9:2); *ho Chettaios kai ho Euaios kai ho Iebousaios kai ho Amorraios katoikei*, "the Chettite, and the Evite, and the Jebusite, and the Amorite dwell [sg.]" (Num 13:29); *to argurion sou kai to chrusion sou emon estin*, "your silver and your gold are [sg.] mine" (1 Kgs 21:3a. Similarly, 1 Esd 8:61; Zeph 1:18)[236]; *to argurion kai to chrusion paredothē*, "the silver and the gold were delivered [sg.]" (1 Esd 8:61); *hē kallonē hēmōn kai hē doxa hēmōn erēmōthē*, "our beauty, and our glory have been laid waste [sg.]" (1 Macc 2:12); *ho de kosmos kai ho tōn anthrōpōn bios etheōrei*, "the world and the human race observed [sg.]" (4 Macc 17:14); *hē de machē sou kai hē echthra ouk apestai all' estai soi isē thanatō*, "your quarrel and enmity will not depart [sg.], but will be [sg.] to you like death" (Prov 25:10); *to argurion autōn kai to chrusion autōn ou mē dunētai*, "their silver and their gold will in nowise be able [sg.]" (Zeph

---

234. See 1:35, 45; 2:2, 12; 3:22; 4:12; 6:24; 12:22; 18:1, 15; 19:34; 20:3; 21:2 for 1a); 4:36 for 1c); 12:22 for 1d).

235. NA[27].

236. This may remind one of the regular "singular verb with a neuter plural subject" construction (BDF, § 133), but cf. masculine *ho chrusos humōn kai ho arguros katiōtai* [sg.] *kai ho ios autōn* [pl.], "your gold and your silver have rusted [sg.]; and their rust [pl.]" (Jas 5:3).

1:18. Cf. Jas 5:3); *apo te tēs porphuras kai tēs marmarou tēs ep' autois sēpomenēs*, "by the purple and the marble that rot [sg.] upon them" (Ep Jer 1:71); *ho karpos autēs kai ho blastos autēs egeneto*, "her fruit and her shoot appeared [sg.]" (Ezek 19:10); *hē sophia kai hē megalōsunē autou esti*, "the wisdom and the majesty are [sg.] his" (Dan 2:20); *hē sophia kai hē sunesis autou estin*, "the wisdom and the understanding are [sg.] his" (Dan (TH) 2:20); *hē basileia kai hē exousia kai hē megalōsunē tōn basileōn tōn hupokatō pantos tou ouranou edothē*, "the kingdom and the power and the greatness of the kings that are under the whole heaven were given [sg.]" (Dan (TH) 7:27, cf. 7:27 OG); *hē merimna tou aiōnos kai hē apatē tou ploutou sumpnigei ton logon*, "the worry of the world and the deceitfulness of wealth choke [sg.] the word" (Matt 13:22); *hē cheir sou kai hē boulē sou proōrisen genesthai*, "Your hand and Your purpose predestined [sg.] to occur" (Acts 4:28); *holē hē Asia kai hē oikoumenē sebetai*, "all of Asia and the world worship [sg.]" (Acts 19:27); *hē charis tou Theou kai hē dōrea en chariti tē tou henos anthrōpou Iēsou Christou eis tous pollous eperisseusen*, "the grace of God and the gift by the grace of the one Man, Jesus Christ, abound [sg.] to the many" (Rom 5:15); *hē perisseia tēs charas autōn kai hē kata bathous ptōcheia autōn eperisseusen*, "their abundance of joy and their deep poverty overflowed [sg.]" (2 Cor 8:2); *Autos de ho Theos kai patēr hēmōn kai ho kurios hēmōn Iēsous kateuthunai tēn hodon hēmōn pros humas*, "may our God and Father Himself and Jesus our Lord direct [sg.] our way to you" (1 Thess 3:11); *Autos de ho kurios hēmōn Iēsous Christos kai [ho] Theos ho patēr hēmōn ho agapēsas hēmas kai dous paraklēsin aiōnian kai elpida agathēn en chariti, 17 parakalesai humōn tas kardias kai stērixai*, "may our Lord Jesus Christ Himself and God our Father, who has loved us and given us eternal comfort and good hope by grace, comfort [sg.] and strengthen [sg.] your hearts" (2 Thess 2:16–17); *ho chrusos humōn kai ho arguros katiōtai*, "your gold and your silver have rusted [sg.]" (Jas 5:3).

None of the LXX/OG/NT constructions matching *hē charis kai hē alētheia . . . egeneto* can conceivably constitute hendiadys.[237] Neither

---

237. In the phrase *ho tromos humōn kai ho phobos estai* (Gen 9:2), the terms *tromos*, "trembling," and *phobos*, "fear," may constitute hendiadys, meaning "dreadful fear." They are synonyms, though, which makes their usage hardly applicable to the case of *hē charis kai hē alētheia*. They also occur in parallel colons, such as *douleusate tō kuriō en phobō kai agalliasthe autō en tromō*, "serve the Lord with fear, and rejoice in Him with trembling" (Ps 2:11 OG, cf. Deut 1:21, 31:8).

should the phrase *hē charis kai hē alētheia . . . egeneto* be perceived as hendiadys. Therefore, the conclusions of Harris and Schoneveld are fallacious. The articles balance the singular form of the verb by reminding one not to blend the two terms into one *grammatically*. The *singular* of *egeneto* preserves *hē charis kai hē alētheia* from being torn apart. This resulting coherency discourages one from envisioning an antithesis *ho nomos/hē charis* and from either opposing or equating *ho nomos/hē alētheia*. The singular of *egeneto* matches the singular of *edothē* to indicate that *hē charis kai hē alētheia*, considered as a whole, denotes an objective singular reality, just as *ho nomos* does. This encourages one to envision *doxa* behind *hē charis kai hē alētheia*. The passage implicitly reads, *ho nomos dia Mōuseōs edothē, hē charis kai hē alētheia* [= *hē doxa hōs monogenous para patros, plērēs charitos kai alētheias*] *dia Iēsou Christou egeneto*.[238] Hence, *hē charis kai hē alētheia* does not constitute hendiadys but denotes two individual attributes under the one aspect of the character.

What if *(hē) charis kai (hē) alētheia* Constitutes Hendiadys "No Matter What"?

Douglas Stuart rightly notes that in the exegesis of a text any special semantic features must be identified and analyzed as to their meaning for the interpretation of the passage. Such features could include hendiadys and etymological oddities. He correctly states, "in all lexical study, it is imperative that the meaning in the present context be given precedence over all other considerations." Stuart points out that it is essentially irrelevant if a word found in ancient writings is used 99 percent of the time to mean one thing, if in the biblical passage under study it is used to mean something else. Any author may choose to use even a common word in an unusual way. Thus, the final question—Stuart wisely advises—must always be "How is it used here?" rather than "How does its use elsewhere tell us what it means here?"[239]

Our study has already demonstrated that in all likelihood *(hē) charis kai (hē) alētheia* denotes two distinct attributes. Significantly, we have established this by providing evidence derived from the Gospel itself.

---

238. Cf. *panta* [pl.] *di' autou egeneto* [sg.], "all things [pl.] came into being [sg.] through Him" (1:3).

239. Stuart, "Exegesis," 686.

But, what if the Evangelist for whatever mysterious reason still renders *(hē) charis kai (hē) alētheia* as hendiadys in the particular case of 1:14, 17? Let us suppose, for the sake of the argument, that *plērēs charitos kai alētheias* (1:14) and *hē charis kai hē alētheia* (1:17) constitute hendiadys. Would its meaning likely be "gracious truth" or "true grace"?

OT scholars who view *ḥesed weʾĕmet* as hendiadys commonly suggest it is *ʾĕmet* that modifies *ḥesed* with the word-pair resulting in something like "true grace." Remarkably, NT scholars largely advocate just the opposite, namely, that it is *ḥesed* that modifies *ʾĕmet* in the word pair, with the expression meaning "gracious truth." One cannot help but wonder if there is a reason for such a sudden shift. Perhaps some Johannine scholars are biased towards translating *ḥesed weʾĕmet* as "gracious truth" because of the absence of the very term *charis* beyond the prologue. In all likelihood, *ḥesed weʾĕmet* serves as the background for *(hē) charis kai (hē) alētheia*. If one assigns the meaning "gracious truth" to *ḥesed weʾĕmet*, then both *plērēs charitos kai alētheias* and *hē charis kai hē alētheia* gain the meaning "gracious truth" as well. This emphasizes *alētheia* (already prevalent in the Gospel) and makes explaining the absence of the word *charis* beyond the prologue unnecessary.

If one is to *choose* between the meanings "gracious truth" and "true grace" for *(hē) charis kai (hē) alētheia*, "true grace" is far more preferable (of course, as we have already evinced elsewhere, the following considerations *cannot* prove that the phraseology of *ḥesed weʾĕmet/(hē) charis kai (hē) alētheia actually* constitutes hendiadys). First, the writer of the creed is familiar with the adjective-noun construction as it is employed in *ʾerek ʾappayim*, "slow-(to)-anger." The adjective *ḥāsîd* is from the root *ḥsd*. If the creed was to depict God's "gracious truth," the writer would likely use the adjective *ḥāsîd*, coupled with the appropriate term from the root *ʾmn*. But the writer does not use the adjective *ḥāsîd* in the creed. This discourages one from perceiving *ḥesed weʾĕmet* to mean "gracious truth." Second, the family of *ʾĕmet* does not include an adjective. This may potentially cause the writer to employ the nouns *ḥesed weʾĕmet* as hendiadys where *ʾĕmet* serves as a modifier, the phrase meaning "true grace." Third, it is *ʾĕmet* that is seemingly "dropped" when *ḥesed weʾĕmet* is "reiterated" (Gen 24:14; cf. 24:27; 2 Sam 2:5–6; 2 Sam 7:15; cf. Ps 89:24; Prov 20:28; Isa 16:5; cf. 54:8, 10). Fourth, after *ḥesed weʾĕmet* appears in Exodus 34:6, *ḥesed* is reiterated in Exodus 34:7 but *ʾĕmet* is not. Fifth, the book of Exodus—the frame of reference for the Gospel—contains several references to God's *ḥesed* alone (Exod 15:13; 20:6; 34:7). Sixth, in the book of Exodus *'ĕmet* is used as a modifier in *'anšē 'ĕmet*, "men of truth" (Exod 18:21). Seventh, each of the fourteen occurrences of the creed mention *ḥesed*, but *'ĕmet* appears in only two of them (Exod 34:6; Ps 86:15). Eighth, *charitos kai alētheias* is followed by *charin anti charitos*. Since *alētheia* is seemingly "dropped" in *charin anti charitos*, it is more likely that it is *alētheia* that serves as the modifier to *charis* in *charitos kai alētheias*. Finally, the phraseology of the *alēthē charin*, "true grace," of God is attested in the NT (1 Pet 5:12).

These observations determine that even if the Evangelist for whatever mysterious reason intends *(hē) charis kai (hē) alētheia* as hendiadys, the meaning is by far more likely "true grace." This means that it is *charis*—just as other key terms in the prologue[240]—that introduces a concept developed further in the Gospel. Since such concepts will use cognates of the term first introduced in the prologue, the question "Where is *charis* in the Gospel?" remains.

Conclusion: *(hē) charis kai (hē) alētheia* Denote Two Subjective Qualities

The phraseology *(hē) charis kai (hē) alētheia* has not been demonstrated to constitute hendiadys. Hence, the very fact that hendiadys is a rare literary feature makes it more likely that *(hē) charis kai (hē) alētheia* denotes two distinct attributes. This is further confirmed by the evidence. First, *(hē) charis kai (hē) alētheia* alludes to *wərab-ḥesed we'ĕmet*. As our study has demonstrated, *wərab-ḥesed we'ĕmet* does not constitute hendiadys. Therefore *(hē) charis kai (hē) alētheia* is not likely to constitute hendiadys either. Second, hendiadys is not a feature of the literary style of the Evangelist. Third, the writer is well aware of the usage of adjectival and genitival constructions to express the idea of modification, but does not use them in 1:14, 17. Fourth, the usage of the construction "*plērēs*-noun-*kai*-noun" in the LXX/OG/NT discourages one from perceiving hendiadys in *plērēs charitos kai alētheias*. Fifth, throughout the Gospel the Evangelist always uses the phraseology "article-noun in singular-*kai*-article-noun in singular" to convey

---

240. *Logos, Christos, zōē, phōs, skotia, teknon, marturia, kosmos, sarx, doxa, alētheia, monogenēs, patēr, nomos, Mōusēs.*

two distinct attributes. Sixth, the practices of the LXX/OG/NT in utilizing the construction "article-noun-*kai*-article-noun-verb in singular" prevent one from perceiving hendiadys in *hē charis kai hē alētheia* . . . *egeneto*. Hence, these two terms do not modify each other, and the expression does not mean anything like either "true grace" or "gracious truth." Neither do they collapse into anything akin to either "gracious gift of divine reality" or "the reality of the grace." The phrase *hē charis kai hē alētheia* denotes *two subjective qualities* of the *single objective reality* of the divine character (*doxa*).[241]

---

241. Our study has also established that even if the Evangelist for whatever mysterious reason still intends *(hē) charis kai (hē) alētheia* as hendiadys then the meaning of the phrase is by far more likely to be "true grace." Therefore, the absence of the word *charis* beyond the prologue cannot be explained by taking *(hē) charis kai (hē) alētheia* as hendiadys meaning "gracious truth." Since *charis* is introduced in the prologue then it must be conceptually developed further in the Gospel. Hence, the question "Where is *charis* in the Gospel?" remains.

3

Allusions to Exodus 33:12—34:10 LXX

We have demonstrated that *(hē) charis kai (hē) alētheia* in John 1:14, 17 alludes to *ḥesed weʾĕmet* in Exodus 34:6. We further propose that the Evangelist intentionally translates *ḥesed* from Exodus 34:6 not with the corresponding LXX's *eleos* but with *charis*[1] in John 1:14, 17, to draw the attention of the audience to the context of Exodus 34:6, specifically to the *charis* cluster of Exodus 33:12—34:10 LXX.[2] As a result, John 1:14-18, in alluding to Exodus 33:12—34:10 LXX, defines: 1) the connotations of *(hē) charis kai (hē) alētheia* (John 1:14, 17) as subjective qualities of the character of God, 2) the meaning of each occurrence of the term *charis* in *charin anti charitos* (John 1:16) as the objective reality of God's presence (*charis*),[3] and 3) the fourfold Sinaitic aspect of

---

1. A perfectly legitimate translation from the philological point of view, as we have demonstrated.

2. The Evangelist generally utilizes the LXX. But it is unfeasible to assess which particular Greek variant(s)/recension(s) of Exod 33:12—34:10 he employs. The Evangelist occasionally translates from Hebrew (12:40; 13:18; see Menken, *Quotations*, 99–122, 123–38, 205). It is unrealistic, however, to evaluate the extent to which the Evangelist considers the Hebrew text of Exod 33:12—34:10. In our view, since the Evangelist *translates wərab-ḥesed weʾĕmet* of Exod 34:6 with *(hē) charis kai (hē) alētheia* it is likely that the writer is *acquainted* with the Hebrew text of Exod 33:12—34:10, the context of the creed. The relevant terminology of the Gospel suggests that the Evangelist may well have considered both the Hebrew parent text and several Greek translations in echoing/alluding to Exod 33:12—34:10. In our study we follow the critical texts of Exod 33:12—34:10 for both Hebrew and Greek. See the *BHS* and GLXX *Exodus*. We will remark on Hebrew/Greek peculiarities of the segment relevant to our case. See Wevers, *Notes*, 547–60.

3. It has been suggested that the meaning of *charis* in 1:14, 17 and in 1:16, may differ. For example, Schnackenburg maintains that the term *charis* in 1:14 is to be taken in the subjective sense of "der Gnadenreimtum, die Spendergüte" of Logos, but in 1:16 it would have the objective meaning of "das Gnadengesmenk selbst" (Schnackenburg, *Johannesevangelium*, 1:248). Sometimes, *charis* would be understood in the subjective sense of *agapē* in 1:14, but in the objective sense of the grace of the redemption in 1:17.

divine *doxa*[4]—visible appearance (*doxa*), inner character (*doxa*), miraculous splendor (*endoxa*), divine honor (*endoxasthēsomai*)—evident to believers.

Covenant of the Presence (*charis*) Formalized by the *charis* Cluster in Exodus 33:12—34:10 LXX

The term *ḥēn* is utilized in Exodus 3:21; 11:3; 12:36, 33:12, 13, 16, 17; and 34:9. These two groups differ in terminology, phraseology, and conceptuality. In the first group, the expression *nḥn ḥēn bʿênê* is used. God *nḥn*, "gives," *ḥēn*, i.e., causes *human(s)* to exercise *ḥēn* towards human(s): the Egyptians are favorably disposed toward the people of Israel. In the second group, the expression *māṣāʾ ḥēn bʿênê*, "find favor in the sight of," is utilized. Here, it is not that of a human, but *God's ḥēn* that one seeks.[5]

The term *ḥēn* is always translated with *charis* in the book of Exodus LXX. What we have discussed above with respect to the Hebrew text holds true when it comes to the Septuagint. Occurrences of *charis* are distributed into two distinctive groups. One cluster speaks of the people obtaining *charis* in the sight of the Egyptians (Exod 3:21; 11:13; 12:36). Another cluster depicts Moses seeking *charis* before God (Exod 33:12, 13, 16, 17; 34:9). It is the second cluster framed by Exod 33:12—34:9 that inevitably draws the attention of the reader of John 1:14-18. At first, the reader grasps that *(hē) charis kai (hē) alētheia* (John 1:14, 17) alludes to *ḥesed weʾĕmet/polueleos kai alēthinos* (Exod 34:6). Then, the

---

To this De la Potterie reacts, "Why this difference?" (La Potterie, "*Charis*," 270). In our view, since *(hē) charis kai (hē) alētheia* and *charin anti charitos* obviously differ both terminologically and phraseologically, it is rather natural to envision *different* connotations to various occurrences of *charis* in *(hē) charis kai (hē) alētheia* and *charin anti charitos*; the burden of proof lays on those who argue that *charis* possesses the *same* meaning in both phrases. We maintain, though, that *charin anti charitos*—incessant presence of God—*results* from *(hē) charis kai (hē) alētheia*—the character of God.

4. See elsewhere in our study.

5. We also find that this distinction was not only observed but also *emphasized* in Targum Neofiti 1. Both the Masoretic and the Targumic texts of the book of Exodus qualify *only* God as exercising/having *ḥesed*. In all the episodes depicting a human's *ḥēn* towards another human, for the Masoretic *ḥēn* the Targum renders a cognate of *ḥēn*. But when it comes to God's *ḥēn*, the Masoretic *ḥēn* is always conveyed in the Targum with *ḥēn wḥsd*! In this way the Targum makes sure the audience realizes it is God's *ḥēn* that is in view in Exod 33:12—34:10. For the critical text see Díez Macho, *Éxodo*.

reader realizes that Exod 34:6 is an indispensable part of the natural context of Exod 33:12—34:10. Soon he notices that Exod 33:12—34:9 and John 1:14-18 resemble each other in many respects. Both narratives have God and Moses as principle actors. Moreover, the two texts correlate God and Moses with the same factor—*charis*. Furthermore, both episodes strikingly emphasize the issue by employing the term *charis* intensively: *six* times in Exod 33:12—34:10 and *four* times in John 1:14-18 in a row! The reader realizes that John 1:14-18 and Exod 33:12—34:10 must be related.

The *charis* cluster of Exod 33:12—34:10 deals with the aftermath of a crisis. The crisis is set up in the narrative of the golden calf (Exod 32:1-6). Israel is disobedient to Yahweh and rejects Moses. The devastating consequences of the crisis are depicted in the account of Moses's anger and Yahweh's judgment (Exod 32:7-34). The people are commanded to leave under the prospect of Yahweh's *absence*, which makes Israel's fate unbearable (Exod 33:1-11). The Lord is both displeased with and concerned about the nation, saying, "I will not go up in your midst, because you are an obstinate people, and I might destroy you on the way" (Exod 33:3). Will the justified anger or undeserved mercy prevail? Moses realizes the vital importance of God's presence as he pleads, "O Lord, I pray, let the Lord go along in our midst, even though the people are so obstinate, and pardon our iniquity and our sin, and take us as Your own possession" (Exod 34:9). He hopes to resolve the situation by appealing for God's *charis*.

The pericope of Exod 33:12—34:10 depicts the process of renewing the relationships and establishing *the covenant of God's presence (charis)* among the people. Moses appeals to God: "Lo! thou sayest to me, Lead on this people; but thou hast not shewed me whom thou wilt send with me, but thou hast said to me, I know thee above all,[6] and thou hast *charis* with me" (Exod 33:12 LXE). Moses complains that Yahweh only claims that God's *charis* is granted without actually supporting the declaration since the Lord has not shown Moses the one capable of leading. This is not really a request for guidance; guidance has already been promised in Exod 33:2.[7] This is but a "bargaining ploy."[8] Moses

---

6. *oida se para pantas* for *yədaʿtīkā bəšēm*, "I have known you by name."
7. Durham, *Exodus*, 446.
8. This is Wevers's expression (Wevers, *Notes*, 547).

recognizes that a human is unable to manage the people and wants God to take the lead. Moses is pleading for *God's presence* among the people (cf. Exod 32:7–10, 31–35; 33:3–5). Moreover, the man wishes to have some rather immediate evidence of God's presence. It is Yahweh himself that Moses longs to see as an evidence of God's *charis*. "If then I have found *charis* in thy sight, reveal thyself to me, that I may evidently know/see[9] thee; that I may find *charis* in thy sight and that I may know that this great nation *is* thy people" (Exod 33:13 LXE). Neither part of this latest request is yet granted.

There is progress, however, as the Lord promises to be Moses's *personal* guide; "I myself will go before thee, and give thee rest" (Exod 33:14 LXE). But Moses refuses to divorce himself from the people's fate (Exod 33:15). Moses's greatest concern is the presence of God with the *people*,[10] so he presses on, "how shall it be surely known, that both I and this people have found *charis* with thee, except only if thou go with us? So both I and thy people shall be glorified beyond all the nations, as many as are upon the earth" (Exod 33:13, 16 LXE). Yahweh promises to grant this request: "I will also do for thee this thing, which thou hast spoken; for thou hast found *charis* before me, and I know thee above all" (Exod 33:17 LXE). God's presence (*charis*) is now promised to Moses *and* to the people, as the Lord will go with them. What Moses "achieves" is the extension of God's presence (*charis*) from himself to the whole people.

But, Moses wonders, will these relationships last? Will Yahweh be present for long? Is it in the character of God to change his mind? To assess this, the man pleads of God, "Manifest thy glory[11] to me!"[12] Yahweh pledges to pass by Moses with all his glory[13] and to declare his name

---

9. Cf. our discussion regarding variants of the reading of Exod 33:13 LXX elsewhere in our study.

10. As God had earlier said to Moses, "Now then let Me alone, that My anger may burn against them and that I may destroy them; and I will make of you a great nation" (Exod 32:10).

11. The divine presence unfolds itself in the divine visible appearance (*doxa*), the divine character (*doxa*), the miraculous splendor (*endoxa*), and the divine honor (*endoxasthēsomai*). See elsewhere in our study.

12. *Deixon moi tēn seautou doxan* (Exod 33:18 GLXX). Several texts—including uncial B—have *emphanison moi seauton* instead (a direct borrowing from Exod 33:13, according to Wevers, *Notes*, 551). See our discussion over textual variants elsewhere in our study.

13. Notice, that the LXX renders *doxa* for the Masoretic *ṭôb*, "goodness," in Exod

before him. He explains that Moses will not be able to see the face of the Lord, "for no man shall see My face, and live." Instead, Moses should stand upon a rock nearby. When the glory passes by, then the Lord will put Moses into a hole of the rock and cover him over with his hand. When he has passed by, the Lord will remove the hand, and then Moses will see his "back parts." The Lord also charges Moses to hew two tables of stone and promises, "I will write upon the tables the words, which were on the first tables, which thou brokest" (Exod 34:1 LXE).

The revelation takes place at Mount Sinai. Moses arises early, takes the two tables of stone, and goes up to the top of the mountain. Yahweh descends in a cloud, and stands near him there, and declares the name of the Lord. And the Lord passes by before Moses's face and proclaims *yhwh yhwh ʾēl raḥûm wəḥannûn ʾerek ʾappayim wərab-ḥesed weʾĕmet* (Exod 34:6). The revelation at Sinai makes Moses bow to the earth and worship. Then he makes his final request to ensure the reality of God's *charis*: "If I have found *charis* before thee, let my Lord go with us[14]; for the people is stiff-necked: and thou shalt take away our sins and our iniquities, and we will be thine" (Exod 34:9 LXE). Moses's conditional statement, *ei . . . heurēka charin*, "if I have found *charis*," contains a new element[15] designed to verify the actuality of God's *charis*. Moses wants God to express his *charis* in forgiving; presumably he asks this because of the nature of God's character just revealed (Exod 34:6–7). Yahweh agrees to meet this condition as well, saying, "Behold, I establish a covenant for thee in the presence of all thy people; I will do glorious things [*endoxa*], which have not been done in all the earth, or in any nation; and all the people among whom thou art shall see the works of the Lord, that they are marvellous[16], which I will do for thee" (Exod 34:10 LXE).

33:19. The LXX's rendering may reflect a variant Hebrew reading *bikəbôdî*, or, perhaps, shows influence of Exod 33:18 or 33:22. But, most probably, the interpreter correctly perceives that the Hebrew text speaks of qualities of the character here and appropriately translates *ṭôb*, "goodness," with *doxa*, "character." Wevers, having observed the *doxa/ṭôb* rendering (!) incongruously concludes, "Showing his glory [Exod 33:18] then means 'passing by with his glory'; it thus refers to his appearance" (Wevers, *Notes*, 551).

14. *Meth' hēmōn*; cf. *in mdeio nostrum/en mesō hēmōn* (Theodotion/Symmachus), *in interiore nostrum/entos hēmōn* (Aquila) for *bəqirbēnû*, "in our midst" (MT). See Wevers, *Notes*, 559 n. 5.

15. Moses's request to "let my Lord go with us . . . and we will be thine" has already been secured (Exod 33:12–17).

16. Throughout this study, for cognates of *thaumastos* we render "marvelous" (as

The Lord announces the articles of the covenant (Exod 34:11–26) and commands Moses to "write these words for thyself, for on these words I have established a covenant with thee and with Israel" (Exod 34:27 LXE). Moses spends forty days and forty nights before the Lord and writes on the tables the "words of the covenant, the ten sayings" (Exod 34:28 LXE). As Moses goes down from the mountain with the two tables in his hands, he does not know that "the appearance of the skin of his face was glorified, when God spoke to him" (Exod 34:29 LXE).

The message of Exod 33:12—34:10 LXX—the OT covenant of *charis*—is clear: God's *charis* is the very presence of the Divine.[17] It unfolds itself in multiple ways. The divine presence (*charis*) is attested when God reveals himself so that he may be evidently seen/known (Exod 33:13 (cf. variant readings); cf. Exod 33:18—34:7), when the Lord lets people know his ways that people may know him (Exod 33:13). It becomes comprehensible when God manifests his *doxa* (Exod 33:18—34:7). God's presence (*charis*) is experienced when he leads the people (Exod 33:12; cf. 33:15) and gives rest (Exod 33:14), goes before (Exod 33:14; cf. 34:15) and with (Exod 33:16) the people. The Lord's presence (*charis*) is at work when his people are glorified beyond all the nations, as many as are upon the earth (Exod 33:16)[18]; this great nation remains God's people (Exod 33:13; cf. 34:9). God's presence (*charis*) is encountered when the Lord takes away the sins and iniquities of the people (Exod 34:9). The Lord evinces the establishment of the covenant of his *charis* in the presence of all people by doing glorious things that have not been done in all the earth, or in any nation; all the people see the works of the Lord, that they are marvelous (Exod 34:10).

---

in NASB) instead of "wonderful" (as in the LXE) to reflect the continuity in the usage of cognates of *thaumastos* in the Sinaitic paradigmatic covenant (Exod 34:10 LXX) and the Gospel (3:7; 4:27; 5:20, 28; 7:15, 21; 9:30) in English.

17. Notice the full extent of this *charis*; cf. the *charis* of God (Exod 33:12—34:10) with the reference to the wrath of God (Exod 33:3).

18. Cf. Isa 45:25 LXX.

charis, (hē) charis kai (hē) alētheia, and *doxa* in John 1:14–18 Allude to Exodus 33:12—34:10 LXX

In *charin anti charitos, charis* Denotes the Objective Reality of the Divine Presence

The pericope of Exod 33:12—34:10 LXX, the frame of reference for John 1:14–18, speaks of *charis* as the very presence of God. John 1:14–18 speaks of the presence of God as Jesus Christ. It is, therefore, likely that each occurrence of the term *charis* in the phrase *charin anti charitos* (John 1:16 as alluding to Exod 33:12—34:10 LXX) denotes the single objective reality of the presence (*charis*) of God, first granted at Sinai and then as Jesus.[19]

Viewing John 1:14–18 as alluding to Exodus 33:12—34:10 allows us to reduce the scope of possible meanings for *doxa* in John 1:14, 17: Generally, the term *kābôd* means "abundance," "honor," "glory." Various lexica and dictionaries[20] discern up to seven connotations for *kābôd*, as follows[21]: 1) "abundance, riches"; 2) "honor, splendor, glory" of external condition and circumstances (of things, humans, and God); 3) "honor, dignity" of position; 4) "honor, reputation" of character, of man; 5) "my honor," poetically of the seat of honor in the inner man, the noblest part of man; 6) "honor, reverence, glory," as due to one or ascribed to one (of men, due to a father, "do honor to"; of God, "the honor due to me"); 7) "glory as the object" of honor, reverence and glorifying.

Since *kābôd/doxa* is only used with reference to God in Exod 33:12—34:10, it follows that *doxa*[22] in John 1:14, 17 may not bear the human but only the divine connotations of the term. This variety of divine connotations should be further reduced as conditioned by the Exodus 33:12—34:10 usage of the divine *kābôd/doxa* in the twofold sense of *doxa*: "the visible appearance of God" (cf. Exod 33:20-23; 34:3, 29-30 LXX) and "the intrinsic character of God" (cf. Exod 33:18-19; 34:6-7 LXX), both with the facet of *endoxa*, "glorious things verifying the presence of God" (Exod 34:10 LXX), in mind. In all likelihood,

---

19. For the role of the Spirit in sustaining the presence (*charis*) of God, see elsewhere in the study.

20. See BDB, 04364.2; *TWOT*, 0943; Von Rad, "*kābôd*."

21. Following the categories of BDB, 04364.

22. For the whole range of meanings for *doxa* see elsewhere in our study; also *BDAG*, 203–4.

the Evangelist implies both connotations of *doxa* in John 1:14-18; he intends the reader/audience, being experienced in the Scriptures and acquainted with the Gospel, to grasp them distinctively.[23]

The first clause, *ho logos sarx egeneto kai eskēnōsen en hēmin, kai etheasametha tēn doxan autou*, emphasizes the visible appearance of God. It does not refer to a luminescent glow.[24] First, attempts to argue for the meaning of "luminosity" for *doxa* in John 1:14 are based on events either preceding[25] or following[26] the revelation at Sinai proper. But the phraseology of John 1:14-18 definitely points to the *immediate* theophany at Sinai, which particularly addresses the matter of the visible appearance of God. Second, the Gospel never attests to the literal luminosity of Jesus.[27] Third, *theaomai*—the verb related to *doxa* at John 1:14a—is never used elsewhere in the Gospel in a way suggesting the observance of any kind of luminosity.[28] Fourth, in regard to observing the luminosity of the *doxa*, the Evangelist reserves a *parenthetical* comment, "These things Isaiah said because he saw His glory, and he spoke

---

23. Contra Cook, who attempts to *bind* the facets of "luminosity" and "character" by arguing that *doxa* with reference to the Deity (similarly to *phōs*) may have nuances of "dazzling clarity" *metaphorically*, denoting not the "luminescent glow" but illuminating the "lucid qualities." Along these lines Cook comments, "Christ's glory (John 1:14) . . . was to some degree *dimmed* by his being in flesh (17:5), and while it was not perceived as glory at all by some . . . because of *the cloud of moral darkness* that surrounded them . . . John and others understood that what they beheld was a kind of glory that could only have *emanated* from the One and Only, who came from the Father . . . . It was not merely marked by *flashes* of grace and truth but was filled with these qualities" (Cook, "'Glory' Motif," 295; emphasis added). Contra Bratcher, who overgeneralizes the matter by suggesting that the meaning "divine nature/status" applies to 1:14; 2:11; 7:39; 11:4, 40; 12:16, 23, 28, 41; 13:31-32; 14:13; 15:8; 16:4; 17:1, 4, 5, 10, 22, 24 (Bratcher, "What Does 'Glory' Mean" 407).

24. Contra Norman Petersen who seems to be overly driven by the desire to link *doxa* with *phōs* throughout the Gospel (see N. Petersen, *John*).

25. Exod 33:10. Contra Morris, *John*, 103 n. 87; Mowley, "John 1:14-18"; cf. Hafemann, "Ministry of Moses," 189-254.

26. Exod 34:29 LXX. Contra N. Petersen, *John*, 17-18, 74, 96, 139 n. 2. Besides, he attempts to build the case on the wrong assumption that *plērēs charitos kai alētheias* constitutes hendiadys.

27. Contra Boismard who argues for a link between 1:14 and the transfiguration (Boismard, *St. John's Prologue*, 96f.). This attempt is but a speculation, as the scene of the transfiguration is not depicted in the Gospel.

28. Contra Petersen, who argues that "'beholding' is not 'observing', because only *some* people 'beheld' the 'glory' of 'the Word' in Jesus. Jesus did not have something like a halo that *all* could observe" (N. Petersen, *John*, 17-18; emphasis added).

of Him" (12:41). The style of making this remark—almost "in passing"—is indicative: observing the Lord's *doxa* in some sense other than "the character" is well attested outside of the Gospel (cf. Exod 16:6–10 LXX; Num 12:8 LXX; 2 Chr 5:13; Isa 6:1; Ezek 43:5; 44:4; Sir 45:1–3). The very *grandeur* of the Evangelist's declaration *ho logos sarx egeneto kai eskēnōsen en hēmin, kai etheasametha tēn doxan autou* implies something greater than just "observing luminosity"—fairly common in the OT—hence, the unique event of observing the visible appearance of God (*doxa*).

The second clause, *doxan hōs monogenous para patros, plērēs charitos kai alētheias*, emphasizes the intrinsic character of God. Here, *doxa* is depicted as *plērēs charitos kai alētheias*, which are qualities of God's character. The character of God is the main issue at Sinai. True, the *appearance* of the *doxa* of the Lord is encountered on the mountain (Exod 33:20–23; cf. Num 12:8 LXX). But it has also been previously observed by Moses, Aaron, Nadab, Abihu, seventy of the elders of Israel, and all the nation in various forms (Exod 16:6–10; 24:9–11). Yes, the *name* of the Lord is called upon at the event of the theophany, but Moses (Exod 3:15–16, etc.), Aaron, the elders of the sons of Israel, and all the people knew the name of God long before the Sinaitic event (Exod 4:28–31; 5:21, etc.). The radically new element of the knowledge of God gained at the Sinaitic theophany is an insight into the qualities of the Lord's character. Now these qualities of the divine character (*doxa*) *plērēs charitos kai alētheias*, are evident in the Word became flesh.

According to the Sinaitic covenant of *charis*, the fact of the presence of God among humans—beholding the visible appearance (*doxa*) and intrinsic character (*doxa*) of God—must be witnessed to by incomparable glorious things (*endoxa*) of God. Hence, incomparable miracles depicted in the Gospel testify to the twofold connotations of *doxa*.

IN *charitos kai alētheias* AND *hē charis kai hē alētheia*, *charis* AND *alētheia* DENOTE TWO SUBJECTIVE QUALITIES

Our study has demonstrated that the terms *charis* and *alētheia* in the phrases *charitos kai alētheias* and *hē charis kai hē alētheia* derive their meaning from the creedal *ḥesed weʾĕmet* and denote two subjective qualities of the divine character. We will define the meaning of *charis* and *alētheia* in John 1:14, 17 with this in mind.

ḥesed

The root *ḥsd* occurs in the OT 251 times. The first detailed and systematic treatment of the term was done by Glueck[29] in 1927. Since that time, many other studies on the subject have appeared. Gerald A. Larue[30] produced a convenient survey of opinions on the matter of the meaning of *ḥesed* for the period of 1927–62, but did not take Bible translations into consideration. Our survey will not only consider Bible translations but also trace the development of thought on *ḥesed* from 1962 until now.

The term *ḥesed* used of God in the OT has been translated into English as "aid" ("mutual aid"[31]), "constancy,"[32] "commitment,"[33] "compassion,"[34] "devotion,"[35] "faith,"[36] "faithfulness"[37] ("active faithfulness"[38]), "favor" ("the continuing divine favor"[39]), "fidelity,"[40] "forgiveness,"[41]

---

29. Glueck, *Ḥesed*.

30. Larue, "Recent Studies."

31. Glueck, *Ḥesed*, 102.

32. Milgrom, *Numbers*, 1152 ("God's constancy, his fidelity to his covenant with Israel").

33. Goldingay, *Daniel*, 252f.; so applicable to Exod 34:6.

34. Andersen, "Yahweh," 44, 82.

35. Jepsen, *ḥesed and ḥāsîd*, 108 (see Larue, "Recent Studies," 26–27); Johnson, *Cultic Prophet*, 56 n. 2; Watts, *Isaiah 34–66*, 237.

36. Williamson, *Ezra, Nehemiah*, 166; Wenham, *Genesis 16–50*, 143.

37. *HALOT*, 3053.2 (at Exod 34:6); Quell, "*alētheia*," 243; Martin-Achard, "Resurrection (OT)," 684; Schlier, "*aleiphō*," 1:232; Wenham, *Genesis 16–50*, 143.

38. Nolland, while dealing with the echo of Ps 102(103 LXX):17 in Luke 1:50 contends that term *ḥesed/eleos* means God's "active faithfulness to his covenant commitment to Israel" (Nolland, *Luke 1:1—9:20*, 71).

39. McCarter, *II Samuel*, 208; see 2 Sam 2:15.

40. DeVries, *1 Kings*, 47; Milgrom, *Numbers*, 1152 ("God's constancy, his fidelity to his covenant with Israel").

41. Kselman translates *ḥesed* as "steadfast love" but immediately comments that it has the sense of deliverance or forgiveness in the creedal confession in Exod 34:6–7 and the texts dependent upon it, such as Num 14:18–19; Pss 86:15; 103:8; 145:8; Joel 2:13; Jonah 2:4; Neh 9:17 (Kselman, "Forgiveness (OT)," 833; cf. Sakenfeld, "Love (OT)," 381).

"goodness,"[42] "goodwill,"[43] "grace"[44] ("loyal grace,"[45] "pardoning grace"[46]), "graciousness,"[47] "help" ("faithful and merciful help,"[48] "the bond of helpfulness uniting God to man"[49]), "kindness"[50] ("active kindness,"[51] "gracious lovingkindness,"[52] "lovingkindness,"[53] "merciful kindness,"[54] "steadfast kindness"[55]), "love"[56] ("constant love,"[57] "covenant love,"[58]

---

42. Exod 34:6 DBY; *HALOT*, 3053.2; Exod 34:6 KJV; Exod 34:6 RWB; Exod 34:6 WEB; Exod 34:6 NKJV.

43. Eerdmans, "The Chasidim"; in the substantive form in Exod 34:7 (see Larue, "Recent Studies," 7).

44. Andersen, "Yahweh," 44, 55, 82; Beasley-Murray, *John*, 14 (translating *ḥesed we'ĕmet* of Exod 34:6 as "gracious constancy"); Bultmann, "*eleos*," 2:483 n. 96 (of Exod 34:6); Hanson, *Prophetic Gospel*, 335; Kselman, "Grace (OT)," 1086; Speiser, *Genesis*, 175, 180 n. 27; Stauffer, "*agapaō*," 1:38; Weiser, "*pisteuō*," 6:185.

45. Stuart, *Hosea–Jonah*, 75.

46. Bultmann, "*eleos*," 2:480.

47. *HALOT*, 3053.2.

48. Bultmann, "*eleos*," 2:480.

49. H. Robinson, *Inspiration* (see Larue, "Recent Studies," 9).

50. Bultmann, "*eleos*," 2:479; Kselman, "Grace (OT)," 1086; Mafico, "Ethics (OT)," 652; Exod 34:6 NAB; Exod 34:6 YLT; *TWOT*, 698a; Urbrock, "Blessings and Curses," 759; Wenham, *Genesis 16–50*, 148–49; Zobel, "*ḥesed*," 51.

51. Jepsen, "*'ĕmet*," 314.

52. Hafemann, "Ministry of Moses," 234 (in Exod 32–34).

53. Exod 34:6 ASV; Keown, *Jeremiah 26–52*, 106–8; Craigie, *Psalms 1–50*; Murphy, "Grace in the OT," 67 (in Pss, of God); Exod 34:6 NASB; Exod 34:6 NASB; *TWOT*, 698a; Wenham, *Genesis 16–50*, 143.

54. Zimmerli, "*pais theou*," 5:661.

55. Speiser, *Genesis*, 175, 180 n. 27.

56. Bernard, *John*, 1:26 (according to Bernard, for the Evangelist *charis* is an equivalent to *agapē*); Kselman, "Grace (OT)," 1086; Exod 34:6 NIV; Quell, "*agapaō*," 27 n. 38; Weiser, "*pisteuō*," 6:185.

57. Bratcher, "What Does 'Glory' Mean," 407.

58. Boadt, "Ezekiel," 718 (the term *ḥesed* never occurs in the book of Ezekiel, though); Craigie, *Psalms 1–50*, 87, 93, 143; Kselman, "Grace (OT)," 1086; Martin, "Gifts, Spiritual," 1018 (in Ps 30:22); Reed, "Some Implications of *ḥēn*"; Snaith, *Distinctive Ideas*, 95.

"faithful love,"[59] "loyal love,"[60] "reciprocal love,"[61] "steadfast love,"[62] "unchanging love,"[63] "unfailing love"[64]), "loyalty"[65] ("covenant loyalty,"[66] "loving loyalty"[67]), "mercy,"[68] "magnanimity,"[69] and "solidarity."[70]

Several scholars have attempted to unfold the meaning of *ḥesed* by dealing with the etymology of the term. But, as Sakenfeld rightly concluded in 1996, the cognate languages have not provided any significant help in interpreting the Hebrew term.[71] Some researchers have declared that *ḥesed* has no equivalent in modern languages.[72] Others have claimed that the content of *ḥesed* is complex, so that uniform

---

59. Craigie, *Psalms 1–50*, 80; Hartley, *Leviticus*, 340; Exod 34:6 NJB.

60. Allen, *Psalms 101–150*, 157–58 (Ps 117 with the reference to Exod 34:6); Hartley, *Leviticus*, 340; Tate, *Psalms 51–100*, 3, 92, 109, 406 (Exod 34:6 and Ps 85:11).

61. Glueck, *Ḥesed*, 102.

62. Christensen, *Deuteronomy 1–11*, 114 (within the context of the covenant relationship); Keown, *Jeremiah 26–52*, 106–8; Dunn, *Romans 9–16*, 850, with reference to Ps 117(116 OG):1–2; Hanson, *Prophetic Gospel*, 335; Kselman, "Forgiveness (OT)," 833; Kselman, "Grace (OT)," 1086; Kuyper, "Grace and Truth," 3; Murphy, "Grace in the OT," 63; Exod 34:6 NRSV; Exod 34:6 RSV. The RSV translators decided on four categories for translation: "kindness" in references to a particular act of one person toward another; "(deal) loyally" in reference to continuing behavior of one person toward another; "steadfast love" or "love" in reference to God's consistent behavior toward individuals or Israel; and "love," "devotion," "faithfulness," or "loyalty" (according to context) in reference to Israel or individuals in relation to God (see Hyatt, "God of Love," 20–21); Reumann, "Righteousness (NT)," 749; Sakenfeld, *Faithfulness*, 134; Scullion, "God," 1047–49; Scullion, "Righteousness (OT)," 728–34; R. Smith, *Micah–Malachi*, 59; Wenham, *Genesis 16–50*, 143.

63. Durham, *Exodus*, 276–77, 450, 454–55.

64. Exod 34:6 NLT.

65. Clines, *Job 1–20*, 248; Glueck, *Ḥesed*, 102; Johnson, *Cultic Prophet*, 56 n. 2; Martin-Achard, "Resurrection (OT)," 684; Speiser, *Genesis*, 175, 180 n. 27; Sakenfeld, *Faithfulness*, 134; Scullion, "Righteousness (OT)," 728; Urbrock, "Blessings and Curses," 756; Wenham, *Genesis 16–50*, 381; Williams, *Hebrew Syntax*, 16 § 72; Williamson, *Ezra and Nehemiah*, 166.

66. Keown, *Jeremiah 26–52*, 14; Watts, *Isaiah 34–66*, 324, 329, 331.

67. Williamson, *Ezra and Nehemiah*, 303, 317.

68. Exod 34:6 BBE; D. Smith, "Grace upon Grace," 33–55; *TWOT*, 698a; Wenham, *Genesis 16–50*, 143.

69. Urbrock, "Blessings and Curses," 756.

70. Martin-Achard, "Resurrection (OT)," 684.

71. Sakenfeld, "Love (OT)," 378. For a survey of issues related to the cognate languages see Sakenfeld, *Meaning of ḥesed*, 16–21.

72. So Jacob, *Theology*, 103f.

rendering is almost impossible.[73] A couple of scholars—in both the Old and New Testaments—have come up with rather eclectic definitions. So Sakenfeld states, "From an OT point of view any human loyalty, kindness, love, or mercy (to refer again to the translation options for *ḥesed*), is rooted ultimately in the loyalty, kindness, love, and mercy of God."[74] In this manner Lincoln remarks, "the term *ḥsd, ḥesed*, . . . frequently denotes *Yahweh's* steadfast covenant loyalty and love, including the mercy of forgiveness."[75]

However, despite this difficulty there has been progress in understanding the meaning of *ḥesed*. Initially, the contractual nature of *ḥesed* was alleged. Eventually, scholars attempted to discover a development in the meaning of *ḥesed* from "obligation/duty" in the earlier strata to "unmerited/unconditional love" in the later stages of the OT. Finally, the voluntary or gratuitous love involved in *ḥesed* has become widely recognized as the original meaning of the term. To this we now turn.

In 1927, Glueck innovatively proposed that *ḥesed* had a contractual nature. According to Glueck, "God's *ḥesed* corresponds to the demands of loyalty, justice and righteousness and already contains these concepts."[76] Glueck emphasized the mutual or reciprocal and the *obligatory* character of the term in its religious usage for persons in relation to each other and to God. Glueck viewed God's *ḥesed* as a gift, rather than as a right, yet the mutuality of the relationship between God and the recipient of *ḥesed* remained central to his analysis.[77] Glueck's study quickly became a classic. Several scholars—E. M. Good,[78] Jaques Guillet,[79] Johnson,[80] Kuyper,[81]

---

73. Jepsen, "Gnade und Barmherzigkeit," 266. Along these lines Bultmann evaluates that "the meaning of *ḥesed* fluctuates between (covenant) faithfulness, obligation and love or grace" (Bultmann, "*eleos*," 2:479). So also Sakenfeld remarks that when it comes to conveying the meaning of *ḥesed*, "each of the English translational options—love, loyalty, kindness, and even the less viable mercy—highlights some of these characteristics of *ḥesed* while severely underplaying others of them" (Sakenfeld, "Love (OT)," 381).

74. Sakenfeld, "Love (OT)," 381.

75. Lincoln, *Ephesians*, 100.

76. Glueck, *Ḥesed*, 102.

77. See Sakenfeld, "Love (OT)," 378.

78. Good, "Love."

79. Guillet, *Themes*, 36–40.

80. Johnson, *Cultic Prophet*, 65–66.

81. Kuyper, "Grace and Truth"; see Larue, "Recent Studies," 29–30.

Gottfried Quell,[82] H. Wheeler Robinson,[83] Sakenfeld,[84] Heinrich Schlier,[85] and Stuart[86]—had accepted Glueck's conclusion (largely with no discussion over the matter).

Simultaneously, however, there had been a strong case built against Glueck's proposal on the obligatory nature of ḥesed. Already by 1967, Larue recognized that "key studies of ḥesed may exercise a softening influence on Glueck's interpretation, and perhaps suggest that we are approaching a time when a new investigation of this important term and its relationship to words with which it is often associated including ḥēn, ʾĕmet, bərît, raḥămîm, ʾahăbāʰ, ṣedeq, and ṣədāqāʰ, etc., will have to be made."[87] And such investigations have been conducted.

Since Glueck's thesis was published in 1927, a number of scholars —Boone A. Bowen,[88] Bultmann,[89] Walther Eichrodt,[90] Goldingay,[91] Edmond Jacob,[92] Sakenfeld,[93] Norman H. Snaith,[94] and Hans J. Stoebe[95]— argued for a developmental or evolutionary trend in the interpretation of ḥesed. Their thesis was that even though the connotation of ḥesed might have conceivably been "obligation" in the earlier writings, it eventually

---

82. Quell, "dikē," 175 n. 3; "alētheia," 235–37.

83. H. Robinson, Inspiration, 57, 85.

84. Sakenfeld, Meaning of ḥesed. This study produced in 1978 was perhaps the last attempt to argue for the obligatory nature of ḥesed. Already in this study Sakenfeld recognizes that ḥesed is extralegal and cannot be coerced; the situationally superior party cannot be compelled to act and remains free not to perform the needed act of ḥesed. In Sakenfeld's later studies she becomes quite willing to allow a variety meanings for ḥesed, including the meaning "grace." See also Sakenfeld, Faithfulness, 134; Sakenfeld, "Love (OT)," 378.

85. Schlier, "aleiphō."

86. Stuart, Hosea-Jonah, 75, 109, 498–99.

87. Larue, "Recent Studies," 32.

88. See Sakenfeld, "Love (OT)," 378.

89. Bultmann, "eleos," particularly 2:479 n. 35.

90. Eichrodt, Theology of the OT, 1:238f.

91. Goldingay, Daniel, 252f.

92. Jacob, Theology, 104–7.

93. Sakenfeld, Faithfulness, 134.

94. Guillet, Themes, 36–40.

95. Stoebe, "Bedeutung des Häsäd."

came to mean "grace" and "loving-kindness," and approached "love" in the later writings[96] of the OT.

Not only did scholars allegedly discover a developmental or evolutionary trend in the meaning of *ḥesed*, but Glueck's thesis that *ḥesed* is a mode of conduct corresponding to a relation of right and duty has also been debated and doubted.[97] Recently, scholars have questioned and largely abandoned Glueck's emphasis on rights and duties as quasi-legal or traditional-cultural categories within which *ḥesed* should be interpreted. They have greatly modified Glueck's understanding of mutuality by de-emphasizing reciprocity.[98]

Glueck's approach has been heavily criticized as failing to achieve clear distinctions between *ḥesed* and the terminology of *ṣedeq/ṣədāqāʰ*,[99] "justice, righteousness"; *bərît*,[100] "covenant"; *rḥm*, "have mercy, compassion"; and *slḥ*,[101] "forgive." Félix Asensio[102] has demonstrated the absence of a prior contract or obligation in showing *ḥesed*. Jacob,[103] Jepsen,[104] and Uku Masing[105] have rejected the idea that a pattern of mutual reciprocity is involved in *ḥesed* (Masing particularly emphasized that the aid or favor given by an inferior to a superior was not designated as *ḥesed*). Several

---

96. Particularly in Hos 2:21; Jer 3:12; 31:3; Isa 54:7f.

97. Often quite emphatically so. In 1954 Masing rejected Glueck's analysis as "a talmudizing theory" (eine talmudisierende Theorie), failing to achieve clear distinctions between *ḥesed* and *ṣedeq* and *ṣədāqāʰ*, for these terms also imply a society and a rule of conduct (Masing, "Begriff *ḥesed*," 45; see Larue, "Recent Studies," 22). In 1986 Andersen states, "Glueck's study of *ḥesed* [with its covenantal and obligatory emphasis] set modern research on the wrong track," and heavily criticizes Sakenfeld's choice of "loyalty" for *ḥesed* (Andersen, "Yahweh," 44).

98. See, for example, Sakenfeld, "Love (OT)," 378–81.

99. Masing, "Begriff *ḥesed*," 45.

100. Asensio, *Misericordia et Veritas*, 109; Zimmerli, "*charis* (OT)," 9:381–82.

101. Kselman, "Forgiveness (OT)," 833.

102. Asensio, *Misericordia et Veritas*, 89.

103. Jacob, *Theology*, 106; see Larue, "Recent Studies," 28.

104. Jepsen, "Gnade und Barmherzigkeit," 265.

105. Masing, "Begriff *ḥesed*," 46–54. Masing also argued that the paralleling of *ḥesed* and *bərît*, "covenant," in Deut 7:12 does not make them almost equivalent, for he who has entered into a covenant with a weaker party has already demonstrated *ḥesed* and thus *ḥesed* is already a factor in the covenant. The covenant with God provides assurance of the consistency of relationships. See Larue, "Recent Studies," 22–25.

scholars—Asensio,[106] Jacob,[107] and Stoebe[108]—have pointed to the unexpected, undeserved, or miraculous nature of *hesed*.[109] As Zimmerli has noticed, "How little *hesed* is a mere, self-evident obligation of the covenant Lord may be seen from its connection with references to miracles (Ps 107:8, 15, 21, 31) or the request for the miracle of *hesed* (17:7; 31:21), or the fact that joy (31:7; 90:14; 101:1) and praise (138:2) arise at *hesed* and can be spoken of as a crown (103:4)."[110] He has also correctly observed that a person "must also—and here again we see the freedom with which Yahweh shows His *hesed* as no mere duty—wait for it (33:18, 22; 147:11)."[111]

Recent scholarship has become increasingly dissatisfied with the little weight Glueck et. al. allowed for the evidence from early translations of *hesed*. One can understand this if one considers the quite astonishing claims made by some of proponents of Glueck's proposal. For example, Gottlob Schrenk acknowledges that "*eleos* is the more usual rendering" for *hesed*, but further comments, "*The use of eleos for hesed is customary but it is not the most apt rendering. Like ṣadāqāʰ, hesed is an attitude corresponding to a duty or legal obligation.*"[112] Along these lines Quell complains that a "word not to receive its deserts is *hesed*, for which *dikaiosunē* is a particularly good rendering. Instead, the LXX prefers *eleos* (172), which introduces an emotional element that *hardly does justice to the Heb.*"[113] Accordingly, Jacques Guillet states that *despite the illusion that may be created by the LXX translation of* hesed *as eleos*, hesed *is not a sentiment or feeling for someone, but involves a real*

---

106. Asensio, *Misericordia et Veritas*, 137.
107. Jacob, *Theology*, 106.
108. Stoebe, "Bedeutung des *Häsäd*."
109. See especially Pss 4:4; 17:7; 31:22; 107:8, 15, 21, 31.
110. Zimmerli, "*charis* (OT)," 9:384.
111. Ibid., 9:385.
112. Schrenk, "*dikē, dikaios, dikaiosunē*," 2:195 n. 5; emphasis added, with a reference to the original German edition of Glueck's *Hesed*.
113. Quell, "*dikē*," 275; emphasis added. More fascinating is Quell's evaluation made elsewhere that "there can be no doubt that the thought of the covenant (*diathēkē*) is itself an expression in juridical terms of the experience of the love of God. Hence the concept of love is the ultimate foundation of the whole covenant theory." He comments in the footnote, "The same is to be noted in respect of the related concept of election and also the religious use of the legal term *hesed* (*charis*), which affords the widest possible scope for the thought of love" (Quell, "*agapaō*," 27, 27 n. 38).

sense of obligation or duty, which imposes a requirement of specific action.[114] Thus, Bultmann remarks, "In religious usage God's ḥesed always means His faithful and merciful help, *and this one-sided understanding is expressed in the use of eleos*. We must always remember, however, that it is ḥesed which God has promised, so that, although one cannot claim it, one may certainly expect it."[115] This flaw was particularly noticed and elaborated by Asensio. He has also taken the relationships existing between ḥesed, raḥûm and ḥēn into proper consideration. As a result, Asensio appropriately moved away from the legalistic or duty-obligation interpretation of Glueck to stress the *eleos* connotation of ḥesed as mercy-feeling *(misericordia-sentimento)* and mercy-work *(misericordia-obras)*.[116]

Perhaps the way ḥesed is translated in the Vulgate should not be given as much weight as Asensio advocates. This translation of the OT into Latin post-dates the NT and, therefore, might have been influenced by the NT terminology.[117] But the evidence from translations of the OT that pre-date the NT—the LXX/OG/Theodotion/Aquila—should be given the most serious consideration. In the LXX/OG, translators render ḥesed with *dikaiosunē* in 8 instances and by *eleos* on 172[118] occasions.[119] Apparently, the sense of *eleos* in the range of meanings for ḥesed overwhelmingly prevails. Since *eleos* does not carry the sense of either obligation or duty, ḥesed probably did not have it either. Moreover, translations of ḥesed with *eleos* are spread evenly throughout the LXX/OG. This consistency in translation suggests that 1) different translators in 2) various times and 3) in diverse literary strata/styles confirmed the appropriateness of rendering ḥesed with *eleos*. Furthermore, ḥesed was translated with

114. Guillet, *Themes*, 36–40; see Larue, "Recent Studies," 21.

115. Bultmann, "*eleos*," 2:480; emphasis added.

116. Asensio, *Misericordia et Veritas*; see Larue, "Recent Studies," 10–14.

117. It does confirm the approach taken by translations pre-dating the NT, though. The usual translation of ḥesed in Latin is *misericordia*, but on occasion *gratia, miseror, misereor, miserationes, clemens,* and *clementia* may be used (Asensio, *Misericordia et Veritas*, 57). Particularly, in the New Latin Version of the Psalms, ḥesed is translated by *misericordia*, "mercy" or "pity," eighty-three times; by *gratia*, "grace" or "graciousness," thirty-two times; by *bonitas*, "goodness," seven times; by *clementia*, "clemency," *pietas*, "piety," and *benignitas*, "kindness," once (see Sorg, *Hesed*). Thus *miserationes* follows the pattern of the Greek *eleos*.

118. According to Quell's count (Quell, "*dikē*," 175).

119. For the full scope of translations see elsewhere in our study.

eleos in the key passage of the creedal confession of Exod 34:6, and *all* of the LXX/OG texts dependent upon it. Thus, translation of *ḥesed* predominantly with *eleos* prevents one from envisioning a sense of duty or obligation in *ḥesed*. Theodotion and Aquila confirmed the appropriateness of rendering *ḥesed* with *eleos* (Exod 34:6 and dependant texts). These revisionists also advanced translating *ḥesed* of God with *charis* (cognates). The Peshitta translates *ḥesed* with *taibūthā*,[120] which has the radical meaning of "goodness."[121] In the NT, references to God's *ḥesed* are conveyed by *eleos* (Luke 1:50[122]; Rom 15:9[123]; Eph 2:4[124]; Jude 2[125]) and *charis* (John 1:14; Eph 2:7[126]). The terms *eleos, taibūthā, charis,* and *miserationes* used to convey *ḥesed* in regard to God do not carry the sense of obligation or duty. Therefore, it is likely that the underlying term *ḥesed* did not have the sense of obligation or duty either.

In 1986, Andersen finally evaluates, "Glueck's study of *ḥesed* [with its covenantal and obligatory emphasis] set modern research on the wrong track," and heavily criticizes Sakenfeld's consequent choice of "loyalty" for *ḥesed*. Andersen concludes that "the LXX was still close to the mark when it used *eleos* (mercy) as its preferred translation of *ḥesed*. The modern preference for words like 'duty,' 'obligation,' 'loyalty,' 'solidarity,' has the picture completely out of focus" and correctly determines that *ḥesed* "is associated rather with such words as 'compassion' and 'grace.'"[127] Today's scholarship recognizes the total undeservedness of God's *ḥesed* on the part of humanity. Scholars have demonstrated that *ḥesed* bears the sense of divine compassion, forgiving, forgetting, and following with beneficent love. It is telling that the two major modern

---

120. The Targum translates *ḥesed* with the kindred *tūbā* or *tēbūthā* (Montgomery, "Hebrew *Hesed*," 99).

121. Borbone, *Pentateuch*, 328.

122. Nolland, *Luke 1:1—9:20*, 1:50.

123. Dunn, *Romans 1-8*, 847; Michel, *Der Brief an die Römer*, 359 n. 3.

124. Lincoln, *Ephesians*, 100.

125. Bauckham, *Jude, 2 Peter*, 20.

126. Perhaps, also, *chrēstotēs*; cf. *to huperballon ploutos tēs charitos autou en chrēstotēti*, "the surpassing riches of His grace in kindness" (Eph 2:7).

127. Andersen, "Yahweh," 44, 82.

treatments of *ḥesed* are presented under the rubrics of "Grace"[128] and "Love."[129]

The Exodus experience that virtually equates our key terms *ḥēn*, *ʾahăbāʰ*, and *ḥesed* is aptly summarized by the prophet: "Thus says the LORD, 'The people who survived the sword found *ḥēn* in the wilderness—Israel, when it went to find its rest.' The LORD appeared to him from afar, *saying*, 'I have loved you with an everlasting *ʾahăbāʰ*; therefore I have drawn you with *ḥesed*'" (Jer 31:2–3). It is likely that the Evangelist understood *ḥesed* (in the creed depicting the character of God in Exod 34:6) as denoting "mercy, grace."

charis

What is the meaning of *charis* employed in John 1:14, 17? Scholars unanimously reject options[130] 1 and 4–6 as apparently unsuitable for the case. Options 2—"grace" as a quality—and 3—"gift" as a benefit—remain. The findings of our study determine that *charis*, as employed in John 1:14, 17, is unlikely to mean "gift." First, *charis* in John 1:14, 17 alludes to *ḥesed* in Exodus 34:6, where the latter term does not denote "gift." Therefore, *charis* in John 1:14, 17 may not denote gift either. Second, had *(hē) charis kai (hē) alētheia* constituted hendiadys it would have been possible to argue for the meaning "gift of truth" or "true gift." But as the phrase *(hē) charis kai (hē) alētheia* does not constitute hendiadys, the resulting "gift and *alētheia*" just does not make sense. Third, the Evangelist is aware of the term *dōrea*, "gift," and of the concept of "gift of . . . ," as the writer employs the expression *tēn dōrean tou Theou*, "the gift of God" (4:10).[131] Had the Evangelist meant to convey the idea of "gift" in John 1:14 he would have used the familiar term *dōrea*. But the Evangelist does not, which makes the meaning of "gift" for *charis* in John 1:14, 17 unlikely. Finally, *charis* in John 1:14, 17 alludes to *ḥesed* in Exodus 34:6, where the latter term denotes "quality," an attribute of

---

128. Kselman, "Grace (OT)."

129. Sakenfeld, "Love (OT)."

130. Hereafter we are referring to the options listed in the subsection "John 1:14–18: The Range of Meanings for *doxa*, *charis*, *alētheia*, and *nomos*" of the introduction's heading "Views of Their Relationship from the Perspective of John 1:14–18."

131. Cf. also the cognate adverb *dōrean*, "without cost, as a free gift, without cause" (15:25).

the character of God. In turn, *charis* in John 1:14, 17 is likely to denote a quality as well. Therefore, our study concludes that *charis* as employed in John 1:14, 17 denotes "graciousness" as an attribute of the character of God.

ʾĕmet

The family of the root *ʾmn* includes not only *ʾĕmet* but also *ʾĕmûnāʰ*. Our study on *wərab-ḥesed weʾĕmet* has considered passages where *ḥesed* is employed with *ʾĕmet* and/or *ʾĕmûnāʰ*. When *ʾĕmet* and/or *ʾĕmûnāʰ* are used of God, the difference between the terms is nonexistent. Even when *ḥesed*, *ʾĕmûnāʰ*, and *ʾĕmet* appear in a verse, both *ʾĕmet* and *ʾĕmûnāʰ* are translated with *alētheia*. Readers of the Gospel skilled only in Greek would not have been able to differentiate between *ʾĕmet* and *ʾĕmûnāʰ* at all.

A wide range of meanings is available for the term *ʾĕmet*.[132] It was translated as "assurance,"[133] "constancy,"[134] "endurance,"[135] "faith,"[136] "faithfulness"[137] ("protective faithfulness,"[138] "steadfast faithfulness"[139]), "fidelity,"[140] "firmness,"[141] "loyalty,"[142] "permanence,"[143] "reliability,"[144]

---

132. See Jepsen, "'ĕmet"; Quell, "alētheia,"; *TWOT*, 0116.

133. Johnson, *Cultic Prophet*, 56 n. 2: *ḥesed weʾĕmet* meaning "true (as being an assured) loyalty . . . i. e. essentially 'devotion'"; Sakenfeld, *Faithfulness*, 134.

134. Beasley-Murray, *John*, 14; NJB; Goldingay, *Daniel*, 252f.; Jepsen, "'ĕmet," 323–24.

135. Edwards, "*Charin anti charitos*," 11–12; Zobel, "ḥesed," 51.

136. BBE.

137. Allen, *Psalms 101–150*, 157–58 (Ps 117 with the reference to Exod 34:6); Goldingay, *Daniel*, 252f.; Edwards, "*Charin anti charitos*," 11–12; Hanson, *Prophetic Gospel*, 335; Kuyper, "Grace and Truth," 9, NRSV; NIV; NLT; RSV; Sakenfeld, *Faithfulness*, 134; Seow, "Hosea," 297; Tate, *Psalms 51–100*.

138. Jepsen, "'ĕmet," 314.

139. Weiser, "*pisteuō*," 6:185.

140. BDB, "ḥesed," 339; NAB; Scullion, "Righteousness (OT)," 734.

141. Speiser, *Genesis*, 175, 180 n. 27; *TWOT* 116k.

142. Scullion, "Righteousness (OT), 728.

143. Speiser, *Genesis*, 175, 180 n. 27.

144. Goldingay, *Daniel*, 252f.; Jepsen, "'ĕmet," 323–24; Healey, "Faith (OT)," 747; Zobel, "ḥesed," 51; Wenham, *Genesis 16–50*, 148.

"steadfastness,"[145] "truth,"[146] and cognates of *alētheia*.[147] Scholars recognize the interrelatedness of the terms employed to translate *ʾĕmet* (*ʾĕmûnāh*).[148] Several scholars—Jepsen,[149] Tate,[150] and Lincoln[151]—find that "reliability" is the most comprehensive expression of the idea of *ʾĕmet*. The concept involves relationship, pertains to speech and actions, and represents characteristics that have to be demonstrated.[152] Thus, "truth" is the essential quality of reliability, which is necessary for a proper relationship with God.[153]

alētheia

What is the meaning of *alētheia* in John 1:14, 17? We have established that *(hē) charis kai (hē) alētheia* denote qualities of the divine character. Therefore, of all the options,[154] it is only *alētheia* as "what is characterized by love of truth: 'truthfulness, uprightness'"[155] that applies. If one also takes the meaning of *ʾĕmet*[156] into consideration, then *alētheia* in *(hē) charis kai (hē) alētheia* denotes "being true to the word," and "doing what's right." In our view, the best description of *alētheia*—a quality of the divine character—is the fundamental "integrity."

---

145. Kuyper, "Grace and Truth," 9.

146. ASV; DBY; Hanson, *Prophetic Gospel*, 335; Johnson, *Cultic Prophet*, 357; Quell, "alētheia," 235–36; KJV; NASB; NKJV; RWB; Sakenfeld, *Faithfulness*, 59; R. Smith, *Micah-Malachi*, 59; Tate, *Psalms 51–100*; TWOT 116k; Williams, *Hebrew Syntax*, 16 § 72; WEB; YLT.

147. LXX/OG.

148. For example, Sakenfeld acknowledges that the "connotation of truth remains also a part of the term 'faithfulness'" (Sakenfeld, *Faithfulness*, 59).

149. Jepsen, "ʾĕmet."

150. Tate, *Psalms 51–100*, 6, 20, 201, 420, 494.

151. Lincoln, *Truth*.

152. Cf. Gen 42:16; Exod 18:4; Deut 1:13.

153. Tate, *Psalms 51–100*, 20. Cf. 1 Kgs 2:4; Hos 4:1–2; Jer 4:2; Pss 15:2; 86:11; Isa 38:3; Zech 7:9; Ezek 18:8.

154. See elsewhere in our study.

155. As the opposite of *adikia*, "wrongdoing, unrighteousness" (1 Cor 13:6; cf. 5:8).

156. Of character, referring to Exod 34:6.

Conclusion

Our study concludes that in the phrases *charitos kai alētheias* and *hē charis kai hē alētheia*, the terms *charis* and *alētheia* accordingly denote "graciousness" and "integrity," two subjective qualities of the divine character (*doxa*).

4

Exegesis of John 1:14–18

To sum up our previous findings and to outline our following argument we now will briefly exegete John 1:14–18.[1]

1:14

Our study has established that *plērēs charitos kai alētheias* (1:14) can serve as a legitimate translation for *wərab-ḥesed weʾĕmet* (Exod 34:6). To begin with, this finalizes the argument that John 1:14–18 alludes to Exodus 33–34.[2] Moreover, this invalidates those interpretations of John 1:14–18 that are not keyed to Exodus 34:6.[3] Furthermore, this result has a couple of major implications to it.

First, just as *kābôd*/*doxa* in the narrative of the theophany at Sinai, so do occurrences of *doxa* in John 1:14a, 14b accordingly denote the visible appearance and the intrinsic character of God in the revelation as Jesus. The *appearance* connotation is accentuated with "the Word became flesh, and dwelt among us, and we saw His glory [*doxan*]." What precedes the first occurrence of *doxa* is correlated with physical appearance. The *character* association is emphasized by "glory [*doxan*] as of the only begotten from the Father, *plērēs charitos kai alētheias*." What

---

[1]. Due to limitations on the volume of this study we cannot consider every detail of the text of 1:14–18.

[2]. Contra quasi-Platonic and/or gnostic explanations; particularly contra Bultmann, *John*; Harris, *Prologue and Gospel*; et al.

[3]. Contra Carson and Mowley who envision *kai pōs gnōston estai alēthōs hoti heurēka charin para soi egō te kai ho laos sou*, "how shall it be surely known, that both I and thy people have found favor with thee," (Exod 33:16) behind *(hē) charis kai (hē) alētheia* of 1:14, 17 (Carson, *John*, 130–31; Mowley, "John 1:14–18"). Contra Morris, who parallels "all the people saw the pillar of cloud" (Exod 33:10) with "we saw His glory" (John 1:14). See Morris, *John*, 103 n. 87; similarly Mowley, "John 1:14–18."

follows the second occurrence of *doxa*[4] is linked with qualities of the character. The two prologue occurrences of *doxa* introduce the concept of the immediate divine presence further unfolded in the Gospel. The divine presence, in its fourfold Sinaitic paradigmatic covenantal facets—*doxa*, "the visible appearance of God" (Exod 33:19 LXX); *doxa*, "the intrinsic character of God" (Exod 33:19, 22 LXX); *endoxa*, "the miraculous splendor verifying the presence of God" (Exod 34:10 LXX); and *endoxasthēsomai*, "the divine honor confirming the presence of God," (Exod 33:16 LXX)—is evident to believers in Jesus Christ throughout the incarnation,[5] and further sustained in the Holy Spirit.

Second, just as *ḥesed weʾĕmet* in the account of the revelation of God at Sinai, so does *charitos kai alētheias* denote *two*[6] *subjective*[7] qualities of the divine character.[8] The Evangelist *intentionally* deviates from the Septuagintal *poluleos kai alēthinos* while translating *wərab-ḥesed weʾĕmet* with *plērēs charitos kai alētheias*.

To begin with, even though *plērēs* never translates the creedal *rab* in the LXX/OG (and their recensions), *plērēs* is still a legitimate translation for *rab*.[9] Advantageously, *plērēs* with a following genitive is also indeclinable.[10] This feature allows the writer to 1) account for both the "appearance" and the "character" connotations of *doxa* and 2) specify that both *patēr* and *logos* (*monogenēs*) possess the very same qualities of the character (*charitos kai alētheias*).

---

4. *plērēs charitos kai alētheias* may modify *doxan* as *plērēs* with a following genitive is indeclinable (BDF, §137).

5. Contra Boismard, who states that "St. John . . . had in mind the divine manifestation of the Transfiguration when he wrote these words: 'And we saw his glory, the glory as it were of the only begotten of the Father'" (Boismard, *St. John's Prologue*, 139).

6. In the OT whenever the word-pair *ḥesed* . . . *ʾĕmet* is the subject of a verb, the verb is always in the third person plural (Prov 3:3; 20:28; Pss 40:12; 61:8; 85:11; 89:15). See John 1:17.

7. The allusion of John 1:14, 17 to Exod 34:6, which is now established, invalidates viewing *charitos kai alētheias* (*hē charis kai hē alētheia*) as depicting an *objective reality/realities*. Hence, *charis* does not depict an object ("gift") and *alētheia* does not denote a benefit (neither the Platonic/gnostic "divine truth," "the truth in itself, substantially," nor "the revelation brought by Christ"). Contra Bultmann, *John*, 74–79; La Potterie, "Charis," 258; Harris, *Prologue and Gospel*, 51; Panimolle, *Il dono della legge*, 314.

8. *Doxa* (1:14b, 17; 17:22).

9. To convey *rb* the LXX/OG employs either *polu* or *plēthos*. We have evinced a variety of factors that justify the translation of *rab* with *plērēs*.

10. BDF, §137.

Moreover, even though *charis* never translates the creedal *ḥesed* in the LXX/OG, *charis* does become a legitimate option for rendering *ḥesed* by the time of the Evangelist.[11] In *charitos kai alētheias* the Evangelist *intentionally* translates *ḥesed* exactly with *charis*.

On the one hand, the selection of *charis*[12] draws attention[13] to the six-fold[14] cluster of *charis* in the book of Exodus—the OT covenant of *charis* initiated at Sinai (Exod 33:12—34:10 LXX, the broader context of the creed of Exod 34:6 itself). The message of Exodus 33:12—34:10 LXX—the Sinaitic covenant of *charis*—is clear: God's *charis is* the divine presence. In this way the Evangelist's choice of *charis* in John 1:14 defines Exodus 33:12—34:10 LXX as the background for John 1:14-18. Conveniently, the choice of *charis* also provides a bridge[15] from the subjective qualities of the character (*charitos kai alētheias* in John 1:14) to the objective reality of the presence of God (*charin anti charitos* in John 1:16), just as the two subjects were linked in the narrative of the revelation of God at Sinai (Exod 33:12—34:10 LXX).

On the other hand, the selection of *charis* in John 1:14 reminds the audience that the Spirit is not the Spirit of *alētheia* only but also the Spirit of *charis*. There is no reference to *to pneuma tēs alētheias* in the OT Scripture,[16] but throughout the Gospel the Evangelist records Jesus thrice referring to the Spirit as *to pneuma tēs alētheias* (14:17; 15:26; 16:13). It is Jesus who is uniquely qualified to illumine the people about

11. As our study has demonstrated.

12. There are a number of less significant reasons; see elsewhere in our study.

13. Contra Dumbrell, who suggests that "grace and truth . . . could refer to the communication of the divine revelation to Moses, grace found by Moses in God's sight in Exodus 33:12, 13, 16, and 17, and to Moses as the receptor of grace and mercy in Exodus 33:19" (Dumbrell, "Grace and Truth," 115; as an option, and with a reference to Hooker, "Johannine Prologue," 53-55).

14. Contra Carson and Mowley, who address only one—Exod 33:16 (Carson, *John*, 130-31; Mowley, "John 1:14-18"). Contra Hooker and Hodges, who deal with only two—Exod 33:13, 13 (Hooker, "Johannine Prologue," 53; Hodges, "Grace after Grace," especially 41-42). Contra Dumbrell, who notices only five—Exod 33:12, 13 (2), 16, 17 (Dumbrell, "Grace and Truth," 115). These scholars also misinterpreted their findings.

15. As a result of God being gracious (*charis*) in character (1:14) God is present (*charis*) among the people (1:16).

16. According to Eduard Schweizer, "the phrase 'spirit of truth' occurs in the surrounding world only in Test. Jud. 20:5, where the Spirit is He who 'bears witness to all things and accuses all' (cf. already Wis. 1:5f. of the Spirit), then in Herm.m., 3, 4 and finally in 1 QS" (Schweizer, "*pneuma*," 6:443).

this quality of the Spirit. The Son and the Father are one (10:30), so the Scripture is not broken (10:35). On the other hand, already in the prologue the Evangelist chooses *charis* to depict one of the qualities of the divine character to remind the reader that the Spirit is the Spirit of *charis*. Further along in the Gospel, the Evangelist makes an explicit reference to the *pneuma charitos* (John 19:36, quoting from Zech 12:10). The audience realizes that the Holy Spirit is not just the *pneuma charitos* but also *to pneuma tēs alētheias*. The reader also knows that the Spirit is given "without measure [*ek metrou*]" (3:34). Summarily, this naturally defines the Holy Spirit as the Spirit full of *(hē) charis kai (hē) alētheia*. Hence, the very same qualities of the character—*(hē) charis kai (hē) alētheia*—are fully inherent in all three: *patēr*, *logos* (*monogenēs*), and *pneuma*. This divine character is shared with believers (1:14, 17; 1:32–33; 3:34; 20:22).

Hence, of all the options available to translate *ḥesed*, the Evangelist chooses *charis*[17] to bridge *charitos kai alētheias* with the following *elabomen kai charin anti charitos* and *hē charis kai hē alētheia . . . egeneto*; he does this with the Sinaitic covenant of *charis* and the Spirit of *charis* in mind.

1:15

The very name John (*Yôḥānān*) means "Yahweh is gracious." Hence, by mentioning the name "John" in 1:15 the Evangelist points out the revelation of God at Sinai as the background to 1:14–18 (where, in the exact terminology of Exod 33:12, 13; 13; 16; 17; and 34:9–10, Moses is represented as the one who found grace with Yahweh).

The unbiased eyewitness testimony *Iōannēs marturei peri autou* is an external evidence establishing the fact that the presence of God (*charis*) and qualities of the divine character (*hē charis kai hē alētheia*) are available to both eyewitnesses and *non*-eyewitnesses of Jesus. The Evangelist calls out to the audience of non-eyewitnesses that "John *marturei* about Him and cried out, saying, 'This was He of whom I said, "He who comes after me *emprosthen mou gegonen, hoti prōtos mou ēn*."'" The audience realizes that John the Baptist testified to numerous matters on various occasions. But the phraseology of 1:15 singles out a *particular* testimony given on a *certain* day. In 1:15 the Evangelist renders

---

17. *Charis*, as we have demonstrated, is a perfectly legitimate translation for *ḥesed*.

emprosthen mou gegonen, hoti prōtos mou ēn, which is elsewhere characteristic *only* of 1:30. This singles out John the Baptist's speech delivered on a *certain* day (1:29–34[18]). In 1:15 the writer also employs *martureō* to label John the Baptist's witness. The same term *martureō* twice specifies a *particular* observation John the Baptist makes on this *certain* day (1:32–34). And the threefold observation is: the Spirit descends as a dove from heaven, the Spirit remains on Jesus; and the Son of God is the One who baptizes in the Holy Spirit![19] Hence, *Iōannēs marturei peri autou* is an affidavit made to the role of God the Father, the Son, and the Holy Spirit in sustaining the presence of God (*charis*) and conveying qualities of the divine character (*hē charis kai hē alētheia*).

Since the Spirit is available to both eyewitnesses and non-eyewitnesses to Jesus, there must be no tension (cf. 17:20; 20:29) between these groups over the benefits of *charis* and *(hē) charis kai (hē) alētheia* gained. To make this clear, John the Baptist's affidavit is placed between 1:14 and 16–17: true, it is only among the "we"—eyewitnesses—that *ho logos sarx egeneto kai eskēnōsen*; yes, it is only the "we"—eyewitnesses—*etheasametha tēn doxan autou, doxan hōs monogenous para patros, plērēs charitos kai alētheias*. But it is the "we all"—both eyewitnesses *and* non-eyewitnesses—that have access to *charis*, hence *ek tou plērōmatos autou hēmeis pantes elabomen kai charin anti charitos*;[20] and it is to the "we all" that *hē charis kai hē alētheia dia Iēsou Christou egeneto* equally applies via the Holy Spirit.

1:16

The statement *ek tou plērōmatos*[21] *autou hēmeis pantes elabomen kai charin anti charitos* asserts the incessant presence (*charis*) of God. In

---

18. Days are clearly divided by the marker *tē epaurion*, "the next day" (1:29, 35, 43).

19. The *martureō* link of 1:15, 32–34 in turn constitutes a link between John the Baptist's recognition of Jesus as *ho huios tou Theou*, "the Son of God," (1:34) and the Evangelist's *monogenous para patros*, "*the* only begotten from the Father," (1:14) and *monogenēs Theos [huios]*, "*the* only begotten God [Son]," (1:18) of Jesus. This draws the attention of the audience to the link between the Son of God and the Spirit (1:14–18, 32–34).

20. Emphasis added.

21. The descriptive *plērōma* sums up attributes of the character of God. These attributes—*raḥûm wəḥannûn ʾerek ʾappayim wərab-ḥesed weʾĕmet*—were previously summed up by *kol-ṭûbî*, "all My goodness," (Exod 33:19), afterwards by cognates of *ḥesed weʾĕmet* (throughout the OT), and finally by *plērēs charitos kai alētheias*. Cf. *en*

it, *charis* is being used in reference to the presence of God as Jesus, and *anti charitos* to the presence of God at Sinai.²²

Already the very first occurrence of *charis* in the prologue (*plērēs charitos*) draws attention to the OT covenant of *charis* initiated at Sinai (Exod 33:12—34:10 LXX). The message of the OT covenant of *charis* is clear: God's *charis* is the divine presence.²³ The covenant unfolds itself in multiple facets. God's *charis* is attested when God reveals himself so

---

autō eudokēsen pan to plērōma katoikēsai, "it was [the Father's] good pleasure for all the fullness to dwell in Him [the Son]" (Col 1:19).

22. D'Alès suggests that the phrase *charin anti charitos* refers to the "replacement of grace received through Christ by the grace received, after his physical departure from this earth, by the Holy Spirit" (D'Alès, "*Charin anti charitos*," 386). Turner remarks that *charin anti charitos* may refer to the gift of grace of the Spirit, which has stepped into the place of the grace of Jesus (Turner and Moulton, *Syntax*, 258; as one of the options). Regrettably, these scholars neither argue the case nor define what "grace" means. Also, they have not realized that with regard to *charin anti charitos* the Gospel is modeled after Sinai. To make sense within the intended Sinaitic frame of reference for the Gospel, the phrase *charin anti charitos* must have originally been intended to mean "the presence of God as Jesus over the presence of God at Sinai." Non-eyewitnesses who had first grasped this original meaning of *charin anti charitos* could then apply the typological meaning "the presence of God as the Spirit over the presence of God as Jesus" to the phrase. Both eyewitnesses and non-eyewitnesses would interpret *hēmeis pantes elabomen kai charin anti charitos* as "all believers, eyewitnesses and non-eyewitnesses bestowed with the Spirit, gained the grace of the presence of God over the grace of the presence of God the Israelites encountered at Sinai." We should observe that, first, the Spirit is *pneuma charitos*; the Spirit is given to believers by/through Jesus and sustains God's presence (19:30; 20:22; Zech 12:10). Second, the Spirit is full of *(hē) charis kai (hē) alētheia*, just as are *patēr* and *monogenēs* (cf. 1:14; 3:34; 19:36, Zech 12:10; etc.). Third, the Evangelist is addressing the post-resurrection audience to which the matter of the continuous presence of God must have been at stake. The sameness of the grant—the presence (*charis*) of God—to both the eyewitnesses and non-eyewitnesses may well be hinted at by 1) the language of the *hēmin* (1:14) v. *hēmeis pantes* (1:16), and 2) the usage of *autou* in *ek tou plērōmatos autou* (1:16), which is spelled the same way in the genitive of both the masculine *autos* (cf. *patēr*, *monogenēs*) and the neuter *auto* (cf. *pneuma*). Fourth, the phraseology of 1:15 may well have been intended as a pointer to the narrative where all three—*patēr*, *monogenēs*, and *pneuma*—are depicted in a context, which depicts the presence/grant (1:32–34; cf. 3:34). We should also observe that in the NT when *pneuma* and *charis* appear together within the proximity of one verse, the Lord/God/Jesus Christ (Son of God) is *always* mentioned as well (2 Cor 13:13–14; Gal 6:18; Phil 4:23; 2 Tim 4:22; Phlm 1:25; 1 Pet 1:2; Rev 1:4; Heb 10:29). This rather increases the likelihood of the presence of a similar association in 1:14–18. See elsewhere in our study.

23. Gracious presence, indeed, as the Lord had previously said, "I will not go up in your midst, because you are an obstinate people, and I might destroy you on the way" (Exod 33:3–5; cf. 34:9).

he may be evidently known/seen (Exod 33:13 variant readings; cf. Exod 33:18—34:10 LXX), when the Lord lets people know his ways that people may know him (Exod 33:13 MT). It becomes comprehensible when God manifests his *doxa* (Exod 33:18—34:10 LXX). The Lord's *charis* is experienced when he leads his people (Exod 33:12; cf. 33:15 LXX) and gives rest (Exod 33:14 LXX), goes before and with his people (Exod 33:14-16 LXX). Yahweh's *charis* is at work when his people are glorified beyond all the nations, as many as are upon the earth (Exod 33:16 LXX); this great nation remains God's people (Exod 33:13; cf. 34:9 LXX). God's *charis* is encountered when the Lord takes away sins and iniquities of people (Exod 34:9 LXX). The Lord evinces the establishment of the covenant of *charis* in the presence of all people by doing glorious things that have not been done in all the earth, or in any nation; all the people see the works of the Lord, that they are marvelous (Exod 34:10 LXX). The Gospel echoes and alludes to these facets of the Sinaitic covenant of *charis* in the covenant of the presence (*charis*) of God now offered as Jesus.

Connotations of *charis* in *charitos kai alētheias* (*hē charis kai hē alētheia*) and *charin anti charitos* are related but not the same. In *charitos kai alētheias* and *hē charis kai hē alētheia*, the term *charis* denotes one of the two subjective qualities of the divine character. In *charin anti charitos* each of the occurrences of *charis* depicts a single objective reality of *charis*, used to speak of the presence of God.[24]

The Evangelist intentionally selects the multifaceted *anti* to emphasize the *sameness* of the source (God) and of the grant (*charis* being the presence of God). The verb *lambanō* in *elabomen kai charin anti charitos* excludes the possibility of *anti* meaning "instead of," "in place

---

24. Contra Hooker, who states that "those who have received the grace of being God's own people receive also the grace of his presence among them (*v.* 14)" (Hooker, "Johannine Prologue," 53). Contra Dumbrell, who argues, "To have received of the fullness of his deity as the community of faith had, and grace for grace (*charin anti charitos*), was, in view of the use of *lambanō* ('receive' in v. 12), to have received sonship" (Dumbrell, "Grace and Truth," 116). Of course, *charis* of the presence of God (*charin anti charitos*) results from God's character being *charis kai alētheia* (*hē charis kai hē alētheia*). In this sense all the occurrences of *charis* throughout 1:14-18 are related. This interrelatedness is highlighted by the association of *plērēs/plērōmatos* and *etheasametha/elabomen/egeneto*.

of,"²⁵ "in front of," or "opposite."²⁶ The rest of the scope of meanings²⁷ for *anti*—"corresponding to," "in addition to," and "upon,"—avoids the comparison and accentuates the sameness of *charis* instead.

The presence (*charis*) of God as Jesus *corresponds* to the presence (*charis*) of God at Sinai²⁸ as effect corresponds to cause, because *charis* as Jesus is *modeled* after *charis* at Sinai. Edwards attempts to argue that the interpretation of *anti* meaning "corresponding to" as effect corresponds to cause runs into the major difficulty that *anti* "never actually

---

25. Another objection against the meanings "instead of" or "in place of" for *anti* is that no apparent contrast between "the Law" and "grace and truth" can be postulated for 1:17. Characteristically, a word to express the contrast is sometimes being illegitimately added. So, Abbott, "from his fulness we all received and grace *in the place of* (*anti*) grace: because [whereas] the Law through Moses was given [by God,] the grace [of God] and the truth [of God] through Jesus Christ came into being" (Abbott, *Johannine Grammar*, 225 [2284]; brackets by Abbott). So Pancaro writes, "grace and truth came to be through Jesus, *only* the Law was given through Moses" (Pancaro, *Law*, 541; emphasis added).

26. Blumenthal has recently demonstrated that where both *anti* and *lambanō* (or *didōmi*) are employed, the term *anti* means "instead of" or "in place of," only when objects relevant to *anti* are obviously contrasted (Blumenthal, "Charis anti charitos," 294). But no differentiation is apparently made between the objects placed prior and after the preposition *anti* in *charin anti charitos*. Besides, *anti*, with the meaning of "in front of" or "opposite," is never found in either the LXX or NT (Edwards, "Charin anti charitos," 3). Most modern scholars have rejected the view that *charin anti charitos* refers to the replacement of the Mosaic Law by the Gospel on the grounds that grace in the NT is generally opposed to the Law—cf. Paul, "you are not under law but under grace" (Rom 6:14)—and that no NT writer would ever have referred to the Mosaic Law as *charis*. Edwards rightly warns against the danger of "reading John with Pauline spectacles" (Edwards, "Charin anti charitos," 7). Of course, as we have demonstrated, neither of the terms *charis* in *charin anti charitos* means either the Gospel or the Mosaic Law.

27. *anti* may also mean "in return for." This meaning is sometimes found in the LXX (Exod 21:23–24) and several times in the NT (Matt 5:38; Rom 12:17, cf. 1 Thess 5:15, 1 Pet 3:9). But the meaning of a gift or favor in return for one already given by the recipient "hardly seems consistent with the Christian understanding of God's grace, which is universally seen in the NT as something freely given by God to those who do not merit it" (Edwards, "Charin anti charitos," 4). Blumenthal agrees that taking formula *charin anti charitos* as reflecting a compensation or exchange of favors would only make harmonizing the context difficult (Blumenthal, "Charis anti charitos," 294).

28. Contra Aquinas, Bernard, Bover, Joüon, and Robinson, who suggest that *charin anti charitos* denotes that the grace, which Christians receive corresponds to the grace of Christ. Contra Lacan, who maintains that the phrase depicts "the love which corresponds to God's love, filial love which corresponds with His paternal love" (Lacan, "Prologue," 109 n. 4). These scholars erroneously evaluate the meaning of both uses of the term *charis* in the phrase.

means 'corresponding to', except possibly in certain compounds" such as *antitupos*, literally "counterblow," hence "antitype," or *antiphorton*, "a load balancing another one." She emphasizes that in most of the examples cited by commentators in support of this view, *anti* does not in fact mean "corresponding to" but "in exchange" (e.g., *antichairein*, "to rejoice in response to someone else," and *antiphōnos*, "sounding in answer"). Edwards believes this meaning of *anti* in *charin anti charitos* falls on linguistic grounds, and concludes, "There is nothing in the context to support this obscure meaning."[29] Instead, these examples of Edwards only confirm the accuracy of our conclusion, as they support the case that *charin anti charitos* means "the presence (*charis*) of God as Jesus corresponding to the presence (*charis*) of God at Sinai."

The presence (*charis*) of God as Jesus comes *in addition to* and *upon* the presence (*charis*) of God at Sinai, as the subsequent revelation *builds on* the preceding one. Both reveal the *same*[30] presence of God, but the latter *surpasses* the former in quality. To begin with, in the course of the former revelation only *one* man saw the visible appearance of God (*doxa*), and only *from behind*; in the latter revelation *all* believers have seen the visible appearance of God (*doxa*) *face to face* (1:14a, passim). Moreover, at Sinai only *one* man merely *heard* God's word proclaiming that the divine character (*kābôd*) was *wərab-ḥesed weʾĕmet*. In Jesus, *all* believers in the Word have themselves *become charis kai alētheia* in the divine character (*doxa*) (1:17; 17:22, 20:22). This conformity with the divine character allows believers to be one with God (14:22; 15:4–5; 17:11, 21–23). It also illumines believers in interpreting, and enables them to comply with, the divine Law (13:34; 14:15; 15:10; 20:23). Furthermore, as a result of the former revelation only *one* nation, the Israelites, gained the presence (*charis*) of God. As the result of the latter revelation, *hēmeis pantes*, "we all, i.e., all believers," (1:16)—not only *hēmin*, "we, i.e., those with whom the Word dwelt," (1:14) but also those who believe through the testimony of the Gospel—have received the presence (*charis*) of God through the Holy Spirit.

---

29. Edwards, "*Charin anti charitos*," 5.

30. To this end the Evangelist does not use the common *epi* for "upon, in addition to" (as La Potterie, "*Charis*," 263, argues the Evangelist should have, had he wanted to convey this meaning).

1:17

The descriptor *hē charis kai hē alētheia* denotes the *two qualities* of the divine character (*doxa*), which Jesus Christ possesses himself and bestows on believers.

On the one hand, the descriptor *hē charis kai hē alētheia* denotes the two qualities of the divine character. The *distinctiveness* of the two qualities is emphasized by the *definite articles* supplied. To begin with, the articles in *hē charis kai hē alētheia* ensure that it is the *same two* qualities as in *charitos kai alētheias* that are in view *referentially*: the descriptor *hē charis kai hē alētheia* (1:17) refers to *charitos kai alētheias* (1:14), which alludes to *ḥesed weʾĕmet* (Exod 34:6), which definitely denotes two[31] qualities of the character of God. Moreover, the articles prohibit one from perceiving the two terms of *hē charis kai hē alētheia* as modifying each other *syntactically*:[32] none of the eleven "article-noun in singular-*kai*-article-noun in singular" constructions of the Gospel provides a single case where one of the nouns can conceivably modify the other (2:22; 6:42; 11:5, 25, 48; 13:13, 14; 14:6; 19:25, 26; 20:28. Therefore, it is not likely to take place in *hē charis kai hē alētheia* of 1:17 either). Furthermore, the articles balance the singular form of the verb in *hē charis kai hē alētheia . . . egeneto* by reminding one not to blend the two terms into one *grammatically*:[33] the singular of *egeneto* does not indicate the compound nature of *hē charis kai hē alētheia*.[34] In the LXX/OG/NT, constructions like *hē charis kai hē alētheia . . . egeneto* commonly depict two obviously distinct subjects, which often denote a whole.[35] Hence, the two terms of *hē charis kai hē alētheia* do not constitute hendiadys. They

---

31. In the OT whenever the word-pair *ḥesed . . . ʾĕmet* is the subject of a verb, the verb is always in the third person plural (Prov 3:3; 20:28; Pss 40:12; 61:8; 85:11; 89:15).

32. Contra La Potterie, "Charis," 276, also n. 47.

33. We should observe that the *singular egeneto* in 1:17 may well have been chosen simply to match the poetic structure of the prologue. All forms of *ginomai* are in the singular throughout the prologue (1:3, 3, 3, 6, 10, 12 [infinitive] 14, 15, 17).

34. Contra Harris, *Prologue and Gospel*, 66; Schoneveld, "Torah in the Flesh," 83.

35. Gen 9:2; 21:22; Num 13:29; 1 Kgs 21:3; 1 Esd 8:61; 1 Macc 2:12; 2 Macc 13:26; 4 Macc 17:14; Prov 25:10; Zeph 1:18; Ep Jer 1:71; Ezek 19:10; Dan 2:20 (OG/TH); Dan (TH) 7:27; Matt 13:22; Acts 4:28; 19:27; 2 Cor 8:2; 1 Thess 3:11; 2 Thess 2:16–17; Jas 5:3. Similar examples (no article, adjective/participle instead of noun, participle instead of verb, etc.) are plentiful. Besides, the writer routinely (and perfectly legitimately; see BDF, §133) uses a singular verb with a neuter plural subject, particularly so with *egeneto* (1:3 [!], 28; 10:22; 19:36).

do not modify each other, with the expression resulting in anything like either "true grace"[36] or "gracious truth."[37] Neither do they collapse into anything akin to either "gracious gift of divine reality"[38] or "the reality of the grace."[39] The terms *hē charis kai hē alētheia* denote two distinctive subjective qualities of the divine character (*doxa*).

On the other hand, Jesus Christ possesses *hē charis kai hē alētheia*—qualities of the divine character (*doxa*)—himself and bestows this character on believers.[40] To begin with, the *coordination* of two qualities, *hē charis kai hē alētheia*, with the singular term *doxa* denoting the divine character (*doxan hōs monogenous para patros, plērēs charitos kai alētheias*), is indicated by the *singular egeneto*. The passage implicitly reads, *ho nomos dia Mōuseōs edothē, hē charis kai hē alētheia* [= *hē doxa hōs monogenous para patros, plērēs charitos kai alētheias*] *dia Iēsou Christou egeneto*.[41] Moreover, these qualities are not only inherent in the Word became flesh; Jesus Christ also bestows the divine character on believers. The *reality* of this bestowal is emphasized by the *root* of *egeneto*. Everything described with a form of *ginomai* in the prologue—all things (1:3, 3, 3), a man sent from God (1:6), the world (1:10), children of God (1:12), the Word became flesh (1:14), Jesus Christ (1:15) and the divine character (*hē charis kai hē alētheia dia Iēsou Christou egeneto*)—is tangible.

The two divine entities—the qualities of the character of God (*hē charis kai hē alētheia*) and the Law of God (*ho nomos*)—belong

---

36. Contra "enduring love" (R. Brown, *John (I-XII)*, 4, 14, 16); "true grace or power" (Gurzon-Siggers, "Grace and Truth," 480); "the true *charis*" (Edwards, "Charin anti charitos," 11–12); "sure loyalty" (Sakenfeld, *Faithfulness*, 134); "In this grouping, *alētheia* is the subordinate term" (Schnackenburg, *John*, 1:273).

37. Contra "gracious constancy" (Beasley-Murray, *John*, 14); *hē alētheia echaristhē* (La Potterie, "*Charis*").

38. Contra Bultmann, *John*, 73–74; contra "gracious gift of divine reality," or "divine reality (*alētheia*) as far as it is revealed and communicated to us (*charis*)" (Harris, *Prologue and Gospel*, 71; cf. 50); or "the grace (= the gift) of the truth" (Panimolle, *Il dono della legge*). Besides, this approach introduces an alien Greek notion of the truth (*alētheia* = reality) to the text where the other terms—law, Moses, grace—are biblical and Jewish (see La Potterie, "*Charis*," 266).

39. Contra Loisy, *Le quatrième Évangile*, 193; La Potterie, "*Charis*," 266.

40. Only the divine graciousness and integrity of the character (*doxa* of 1:14b; cf. *doxa* of 17:22). Believers do not gain the visible appearance of God (*doxa* of 1:14a); they do not become God (cf. 10:34–35).

41. Cf. *panta di' autou egeneto*, "all things came into being through Him" (1:3).

to different dimensions. As such, they cannot be either contrasted[42] or compared; neither can they replace or fulfill one another conceivably. The two divine entities of *ho nomos* and *hē charis kai hē alētheia complement* each other.

On the one hand, both the divine character (*hē charis kai hē alētheia*) and the divine Law (*ho nomos*) belong to God. To begin with, the *root* of *egeneto* accentuates the sameness of the source and the mediator of the divine character, as the term recurs throughout the prologue (1:3, 3, 3, 12, 15, 17; cf. 1:6). Moreover, the *middle* of *egeneto* links and also contrasts the middle *egeneto* with the passive *edothē* in the statement *ho nomos dia Mōuseōs edothē, hē charis kai hē alētheia dia Iēsou Christou egeneto*. Moses is only a mediator (as the passive *edothē* entails). Jesus Christ, however, not only mediates but also possesses *hē charis kai hē alētheia* (as the middle of *egeneto* implies). Yet both *ho nomos* and *hē charis kai hē alētheia* come from the same divine source (as both the passive *edothē* and the middle *egeneto* indicate).

On the other hand, there is no contrast or comparison between the divine character (*hē charis kai hē alētheia*) and the divine Law (*ho nomos*). To begin with, there are no relationships between *ho nomos* and any *particular* term of *hē charis kai hē alētheia*. The *singular* of *egeneto* preserves *hē charis kai hē alētheia* from being torn apart. This resulting coherence of *hē charis kai hē alētheia* prohibits one both from envisioning an antithesis *ho nomos/hē charis*[43] and from either opposing[44] or equating *ho nomos/hē alētheia*[45]. Moreover, there is no antithesis between *ho nomos* and *hē charis kai hē alētheia* taken as a *whole*. The

---

42. Neither as "shadow and substance" (Dodd, *Interpretation*, 84; Lindars, *John*, 97), nor in "the significance of one revelation and another" (Dumbrell, "Grace and Truth," 118), nor in the sense of "grace instead of shame" (Black, "Aramaic Tradition," 64, 69–70, with the reference to 1:16), nor in the sense of "Christ being seen as the true Source of grace and truth as Moses was the source of the law" (Hodges, "Grace after Grace," 35).

43. Contra Beasley-Murray, *John*, 15; Conzelmann, "*charis*"; D'Alès, "*Charin anti charitos*," 385; Evans, *Word and Glory*, 80 n. 2; Gnilka, *Johannesevangelium*, 16; Haenchen, *John*, 1:120; Lindars, *John*, 97–98; Pancaro, *Law*, 541; N. Petersen, *John*, 5–6, 21, 43, 111–19; Richardson, *Introduction*, 283f.; Zimmerli, "*charis* (OT)," who, with the reference to 1:16–17, assume that the Evangelist is here referring to a contrast or even opposition between the gospel and the Law or Jesus and Moses. Applying a Pauline antithesis between grace and the Law to this Johannine text is unwarranted anyway.

44. Contra La Potterie, "*Charis*," 266–67; Pancaro, *Law*, 541–42, cf. n. 150.

45. Contra La Potterie, "*Charis*," 266–67.

singular of *egeneto* matches the singular of *edothē* to indicate that *hē charis kai hē alētheia*, considered as a whole, denotes an objective *singular* reality of the character of God (*doxa*) just as *ho nomos* does. There is no adversative—neither *alla* nor *de*[46]—in the critical Greek text of the verse.[47] Furthermore, the statement compares and contrasts Moses and Jesus, but not the divine Law (*ho nomos*) and qualities of the divine character (*hē charis kai hē alētheia*). Grammatically and structurally, the two halves of the statement *ho nomos dia Mōuseōs edothē, hē charis kai hē alētheia dia Iēsou Christou egeneto* are balanced, but not exactly so.[48] The difference is indicated by verbs,[49] both by their root and voice: the passive *edothē* signifies that Moses serves as only a channel, the middle *egeneto* specifies that Jesus Christ not only mediates but also possesses *hē charis kai hē alētheia*.[50] Finally, the Gospel holds the Law in high regard; Jesus engages with the Decalogue. There are allusions to each of the Ten Commandments (Exod 20:1–17): you shall have no other gods before me (10:30), you shall not make for yourself an idol (10:33), you shall not take the name of the Lord your God in vain (10:25), remember the Sabbath day (7:23; cf. 5:18), honor your father (8:49; cf. 5:23), you shall not murder (7:19, 8:40, 44; cf. 5:18), you shall not commit adultery (8:41), you shall not steal (10:1, 8, 10), you shall not bear false witness (8:14[51]), you shall not covet (8:44). There is an allusion to the Shema (8:41b–42a).[52] By challenging, "Which one of you convicts Me of sin?" (8:46), Jesus makes himself a subject to the Law.[53] Jesus approves the fact that believers have kept the Father's word (= the Law, 17:6). Jesus's saying "do not sin anymore" only makes sense in the framework of the

---

46. Reading *hē charis de* in 1:17 is attested by P⁶⁶ (ˢ W ˢ) it syʰ** bo.

47. Edwards, "*Charin anti charitos*," 8.

48. Contra La Potterie, "*Charis*," 273; Edwards, "*Charin anti charitos*," 8; Lindars, *John*, 98; Jeremias, "*Mōusēs*," 4:872. So the phrase may not be translated "Just as the law was given through Moses, so grace and truth came through Jesus Christ," as these scholars suggest.

49. So also Hooker, "Johannine Prologue," 55.

50. This is already clear from *ho logos . . . plērēs charitos kai alētheias* (1:14). This constitutes a contrast between Moses and Jesus but not between *ho nomos* and *hē charis kai hē alētheia*.

51. Motyer here adds also 8:44 (Motyer, *Your Father the Devil?* 130).

52. On the Decalogue and Shema in the Gospel see Brooke, "Christ and the Law," 103–8; Motyer, *Your Father the Devil?* 30, 42, 129–30, 193.

53. To say the opposite is to deny that Jesus was fully human.

Law (5:14, cf. 8:11; 20:23). Furthermore, the Law is a revelation of the Divine.[54] Jesus acknowledges, "the Scripture cannot be broken" (10:35). Christ's new commandment provides the proper insight into the Law (13:34, cf. Lev 19:18). The risen Lord grants, "If you forgive the sins of any, *their sins* have been forgiven them; if you retain the *sins* of any, they have been retained" (20:23). These factors imply that observance of the relevant articles of the Law is expected even after Jesus's departure to the Father.

The two realities of the legal corpus for humanity (*ho nomos*) and the qualities of the character of God (*hē charis kai hē alētheia*) belong to different dimensions. As such, they cannot be either contrasted or compared; neither can they replace or fulfill one another conceivably.[55] The two entities of *ho nomos* and *hē charis kai hē alētheia* complement each other. The divine character of *hē charis kai hē alētheia* is bestowed (*egeneto*) on believers.[56] This possession of the divine *hē charis kai hē alētheia* not only illumines in interpretation but also enables the faithful to comply with the divine *ho nomos* (10:35; 13:34; 20:23).[57]

---

54. As is indicated by the divine passive *edothē*; see Pancaro, *Law*, 470 n. 50. Pancaro's position on references to the Law as depreciatory in the Gospel (Pancaro, *Law*) cannot be sustained for the contexts such as "your Law" (8:17; 10:34), which are simply an indication by Jesus in the contexts of the sharing of common ground (see Carson, *John*, 332).

55. Perhaps, Boismard and Petersen intuitively feel this discrepancy as they attempt to deal with the matter in terms other than "contrast," "comparison," "replacement," or "fulfillment." Boismard concludes on what the scholar labels as "the antithetic parallelism" of 1:17, "Jesus *is* at the same time Law, and Love which forgives rebellions against the Law" (Boismard, *Moses or Jesus*, 70, 98). Petersen comments on 1:17-18, "the assertions made about Jesus in the two statements are also related in such a way as to *qualify* the traditional value of the Law. . . . What Jesus saw is contrasted with the Law given through Moses in such a way as to *require that the Law be evaluated from the perspective of what came through Jesus, rather than have what came through Jesus be evaluated from the perspective of the Law*" (N. Petersen, *John*, 98–99). These attempts do not suffice, though.

56. The reality of bestowing *hē charis kai hē alētheia* is further confirmed under the circumlocutive rubrics of *doxa* and *onoma*, especially the prayer (17: 6–8, 11, 13–17, 22–24, 26); it comes through as disciples observe Jesus's *doxa* (1:14, etc.) and by means of Jesus breathing the Holy Spirit of *hē charis kai hē alētheia* onto believers (20:22; cf. 19:30).

57. The Law of God is now comprehended through the "lenses" of the divine character/presence: God's "commandment is eternal life" (12:50); God's children "love one another" (13:34); the Lord's "If you forgive the sins of any, *their sins* have been forgiven them; if you retain the *sins* of any, they have been retained" (20:23). The concept of

1:18

By *Theon oudeis heōraken pōpote*[58] the Evangelist explains that prior, without this conformity of humans with the Divine, "no one had been capable of dwelling in the presence of God."

The visible *appearance* of God (described in various circumlocutive terms, particularly *doxa*) had been earlier encountered by Moses, Aaron, Nadab, Abihu, seventy of the elders of Israel, and the entire nation in Exodus (Exod 16:6–10; 24:9–11). An appearance of God was further seen by Ezekiel (Ezek 10:4) and, notably, by Isaiah (Isa 6:1f., this the Evangelist even acknowledges in 12:41). The Septuagint confirms explicitly that Moses *tēn doxan kuriou eiden*, "saw the glory of the Lord" (Num 12:8 LXX). Sirach—definitely of the Sinaitic experience—certifies that *edeixen autō tēs doxēs autou*, "[the Lord] manifested him [Moses] His glory" (Sir 45:1–3).[59]

Compared with the theophany at Sinai, there are two radically new elements in the revelation as Jesus with regard to *doxa* (both in the sense of the visible appearance and the intrinsic character). First, in the course of the theophany at Sinai, Moses alone could see the appearance of God (*doxa*), but only "from the back" (Exod 33:20–23) because, as God put it, "no man shall see My face, and live."[60] With Jesus, the notion of theophany was changed radically, in a threefold manner: 1) not just a single individual but all the people could see the visible appearance of God (*doxa*) as Jesus, as eyewitnesses to Christ gained this ability

---

religious obligation is linked directly to the *character* of God elsewhere in the NT (1 John 4:11; Matt 5:48; 19:3–9, Luke 6:36, etc.). See Mendenhall and Herion, "Covenant."

58. The phrase stresses the *uniqueness* of the Revealer. This may indicate a contemporary polemic against "heavenly journey" traditions and other sources of apocalyptic revelation (claimed for the patriarchs and, especially, for Moses). See Dunn, *John*, 322–25; Manns, *John and Jamnia*, 41 n. 41; Meeks, *Prophet-King*, 295–301; Motyer, *Your Father the Devil?* 45 n. 40, 46; Odeberg, *Fourth Gospel*, especially 94.

59. Contra Dumbrell, who suggests that by *etheasametha tēn doxan autou* of 1:14 "the reader is invited to compare the experience of those who received Jesus and saw his glory with the experience of the greatest Israelite of the Old Testament, Moses, whose request to see the glory of God was denied" (Dumbrell, "Grace and Truth," 114). Contra Petersen, who evaluates, "Moses did not see God's glory, and neither did the people who only saw the effect of God's glory on Moses' face [shining]" (N. Petersen, *John*, 96, cf. 17–18). The Evangelist, being well acquainted with the OT, is unlikely to miss all these LXX/OG references to seeing the (*doxa* of) God.

60. As in the LXX.

(*ho logos sarx egeneto kai eskēnōsen*[61] *en hēmin, kai etheasametha tēn doxan autou, doxan hōs monogenous para patros, plērēs charitos kai alētheias,*[62] Exod 40:34[-36]; 44:38); 2) people saw God not "from the back" but "face to face"[63]; and 3) people who had seen God's face not only did not die (cf. Exod 33:20; Isa 6:5), but instead gained everlasting life. Second, in the course of the theophany at Sinai Moses gained an insight into the qualities of the character of God (*doxa*). Moses, though, could only *hear* God's word proclaiming *that* God is *wərab-ḥesed weʾĕmet*, but in the Word made flesh, God's *hē charis kai hē alētheia* . . . *egeneto*.[64]

The radically new element in the revelation as Jesus was that the *monogenēs Theos actually bestowed* (*egeneto*) qualities of the divine character (*doxa*) on *all* believers.[65] With reference to *hē charis kai hē alētheia* . . . *egeneto only*,[66] *exēgēsato* corresponds to eyewitnesses observing the *doxa* (1:14f.), Jesus bestowing God's *hē charis kai hē alētheia* (1:17), giving God's *doxa* (= the character of *hē charis kai hē alētheia*, 17:22), manifesting/making God's name (= the character of *hē charis kai hē alētheia*) known (17:6, 26), and pouring/breathing God's Holy Spirit (of *hē charis kai hē alētheia*) onto believers (20:22; 19:37 + Zech 12:10 LXX). This resulting conformity of the divine character (*doxa*) bestowed on believers allows the divine presence to dwell among people and enables them to be one with God (17:22-24).[67] In this sense the statement *monogenēs Theos ho ōn eis ton kolpon tou patros ekeinos exēgēsato*

---

61. There may be an implicit contrast between Moses and eyewitnesses to Jesus with regard to their capability to observe the glory of God in *hē skēnē*, as "Moses was not able to enter into the tabernacle [*eis tēn skēnēn*] . . . because . . . the tabernacle was filled with the glory of the Lord [*doxēs kuriou eplēsthē hē skēnē*]" (Exod 40:35).

62. Of course, the Logos's *doxa* not only fills the *skēnē*, but Jesus also replaces the temple (1:14; 2:19-22).

63. Cf. *monogenēs Theos ho ōn eis ton kolpon tou patros*, "the only begotten God who is in the bosom of the Father" (1:18).

64. Bauckham, *God Crucified*, 74.

65. Boismard earlier suggested that "grâce et fidélité" are attributes of Logos (1:14), the qualities deposited in the heart of the man (1:17); see Boismard, *St. John's Prologue*, 78-79, 86-87. Boismard has never pursued the argument.

66. The revelation—*exēgēsato*—encompasses more than bestowing the qualities of the divine character onto humans. Other various aspects of *exēgēsato* are beyond the scope of our study.

67. Particularly with regard to considerations of the divine Law while in the world (20:23).

emphatically affirms, "God has now made the immediate incessant presence of God among humans a reality."

1:14–18 Paraphrased

In our view, 1:14–18, if paraphrased, means:

> 14 God became flesh; we, the eyewitnesses, perceived the visible appearance of God as God the Son who retained the intrinsic character of God the Father being full of graciousness and integrity. 15 As was attested by John the Baptist, this divine character was to be shared by the Father through the Son via the Spirit with all believers to allow the divine presence among humanity. 16 The Divine is inexhaustible; hence all believers, eyewitnesses and non-eyewitnesses bestowed with the Spirit, gained the grace of the presence of God over the grace of the presence of God the Israelites encountered at Sinai. 17 The divine Law was given by God to believers through Moses; the divine character—the graciousness and the integrity—God bestowed onto believers through Jesus Christ. 18 Prior, without this conformity of humans with the Divine, no one had been capable of dwelling in the presence of God; the Son abiding in the Father himself has now made dwelling in the presence of God a reality for humans as well.

5

The Covenant of the Presence of God

In the present chapter my intention is to present a proposal for how the Johannine gospel at large may be understood on the assumption that my interpretation of John 1:14–18 is correct. As I am maintaining this argument for the first time (to the best of my knowledge), I have not discovered other scholars presenting the view I am about to present. For this reason my engagement with other scholarship will be slight. In addition, since the overall purpose of this chapter is to present a reading of the Fourth Gospel in the light of my interpretation of 1:14–18, the engagement with alternative particular views of *doxa* and *alētheia* will also be only slight.

There are major challenges with tracing concepts of *(hē) charis kai (hē) alētheia*, *charis*, and *doxa* of the prologue throughout the Gospel. First, the absence of the term *charis* in the Gospel beyond the prologue (1:14, 16, 16, 17) is remarkable. This is puzzling because key terms in the prologue—*logos*,[1] *Christos*, *zōē*, *phōs*, *skotia*, *teknon*, *marturia*, *kosmos*, *sarx*, *doxa*, *monogenēs*, *patēr*, *alētheia*, *nomos*, *Mōusēs*—introduce a concept that is being developed further in the Gospel; the concept utilizes the respective cognates. Does *charis* (of *plērēs charitos kai alētheias*, *hē charis kai hē alētheia*, and *charin anti charitos* in the prologue) introduce a concept(s) of the Gospel? Second, the usage of *doxa* throughout the Gospel is perplexing. Not only are various meanings of *doxa* set alongside one another without restraint (e.g., 12:41–43), but also, whereas the vast majority of NT authors' statements concern the glorification of the risen Lord after Easter,[2] the picture is rather different

---

1. *Logos* of Jesus does not appear beyond the prologue but nevertheless conveys an important aspect of the Gospel's message.

2. Rom 6:4; 1 Tim 3:16; Acts 7:55; 1 Pet 1:11, 21. Cf. Luke 2:14; 19:38; Rev 4:9 with

in John, to the degree that we here find far more references to the *doxa* of the earthly Jesus (e.g., 2:11; 13:31–32; 11:40).³ Besides, Jesus's report to the Father, "The glory which You have given Me I have given to them, that they may be one, just as We are one" (17:22), remains a riddle.

Attempts to Trace *(hē) charis kai (hē) alētheia, charis,* and *doxa* throughout the Gospel

Dwight M. Smith seems to be the only scholar who has attempted to trace the term *charis* in the Gospel.⁴ He observes that it does not appear beyond 1:17, and remarks, "one might . . . ask whether grace, *charis,* is significantly related to . . . the eschatological joy (*chara*), which Jesus promises and brings. There is an obvious linguistic relationship. Is there not also within this linguistic relation a theological one?"⁵ In reference to 15:9–12 Smith comments, "what they receive is a free gift (*charisma*) and a mark of grace (*charis*), although those terms are not used here. In his final prayer Jesus says that his very speaking in the world is "so that they may have My joy made complete in themselves [17:13]."⁶ Having made a comparison of 1 John 1:1–4 over against John 1:1–18, he concludes that "the *charis* of God given in Jesus Christ finds its fruition or realization in the believer as *chara,* joy as the eschatological substance of salvation, . . . In John the first promise of eschatological joy is set in the context of exhortations or commands to love one another [15:11] . . . . Otherwise, grace is negated and joy cannot be realized." Smith is understandably hesitant to pursue the argument, as he remarks,

> Commentators generally do not, however, observe or make much of the similarity of *chara, charis,* and *chairō* . . . . Obviously, etymology can lead exegesis astray, whether in antiquity or modern times. So I do not want to make too much of the relationship of *charis* to *chara.* Words acquire meaning through use

---

Heb 13:21; 1 Pet 4:11; Rev 5:12f. See also Acts 7:2; 1 Cor 2:8; Titus 2:13; 1 Pet 4:13; 5:1; Mark 13:26; etc. The application of the word to the incarnate Jesus is strictly limited. See Matt 19:28; 25:31; Luke 2:9.

3. See Kittel, "*doxa,*" 2:249.

4. D. Smith, "Grace upon Grace." He also misinterpreted the meaning of *charis* in *kai charin anti charitos* and erroneously isolated *charis* from *alētheia* in *(hē) charis kai (hē) alētheia.*

5. Ibid., 27.

6. Ibid., 30.

rather than merely through morphological and phonetic relationships, grace is one thing and joy is another.[7]

Pancaro sets research on a false track by envisioning objective realities behind *(hē) charis kai (hē) alētheia*. Pancaro's explanation is that

> Jesus was full of grace and truth—Jn now says that grace and truth came to be through Jesus, only the Law was given through Moses. But, for Jn, it is "truth" which bears the weight of the contrast he establishes between Moses and Jesus, as is illustrated by the rest of the Gospel.[8]

From this Pancaro deduces that the Evangelist "concludes that 'truth' (like 'life') is to be found in Jesus and not in the Law"[9] and "wishes to give to *charis* the meaning of 'Jesus as the manifestation of God's love for the world.'"[10] Pancaro's vision for tracing *(hē) charis kai (hē) alētheia* throughout the Gospel is unwarranted[11] and misleading.[12] The terms *(hē) charis kai (hē) alētheia* are not objective realities but subjective qualities.

Kuyper treats *(hē) charis kai (hē) alētheia* as a hendiadys where the former term modifies the latter, the meaning of the expression resulting in "redemptive faithfulness."[13] His explanation is,

> The Evangelist abandons the word [*charis* = grace] because he intends to let the word "truth" carry the full import of the concept within the expression, grace and truth. This is to say, John would let "truth" become the word to declare that God's faithfulness to his covenant of redemption has become manifest in Jesus.[14]

---

7. Ibid., 30–31. Cf. *BDAG*, 877.

8. Pancaro, *Law*, 541.

9. Ibid., 542.

10. Ibid., 542 n. 150, with a reference to 3:16f.

11. Pancaro presumes that "Jn was using a pre-existent hymn which spoke of the Word becoming flesh and being full of *charitos kai alētheias*.... *Charis* was mentioned in both vv. 14 and 16. In adding v. 17 Jn did not see fit to omit *charis*; he takes up the same expression used at v. 14" (ibid., 541).

12. Pancaro's claim that it is *alētheia* that constitutes the difference in 1:17 is fundamentally mistaken on grammatical grounds. We have demonstrated that there is no antithesis between either *ho nomos* and *hē charis kai hē alētheia* or *ho nomos* and any particular subject of *hē charis kai hē alētheia*. The singular of *egeneto* preserves *hē charis kai hē alētheia* from being torn apart.

13. Kuyper, "Grace and Truth," 18.

14. Ibid., 15.

Kuyper's argument is fallacious[15] and contradictory[16]. But, it partially[17] recognizes at least *alētheia* as a subjective quality of the character inherent in Jesus.

Sakenfeld treats *(hē) charis kai (hē) alētheia* as hendiadys[18] where the latter term modifies the former, the meaning of the expression resulting in "sure loyalty."[19] She assesses that "Jonah's witness that God's loyalty [*ḥesed*] extended even to forgiving the hated Ninevites opens the way for a new covenant in which forgiveness is proclaimed through Israel to all the world." She further remarks, "The psalmist anticipated the theme in a different way in praising the loyalty of God made manifest in the very act of creating the world (Ps 136:5–9)." Now, continues Sakenfeld,

> The Creator of all extends loyalty [*ḥesed*] to all peoples of the world through Jesus of Nazareth, thus establishing in a new key the Abrahamic promise of blessing to the nations. The New Testament bears witness to Jesus as expression of God's continuing but transformed loyalty to the Davidic line. At the same time, it testifies to the ongoing role of Israel as a light to the nations, another way for the outpouring of divine loyalty in the world.[20]

---

15. Kuyper operates on the wrong assumption that *ḥesed weʾĕmet* constitutes a hendiadys, which invalidates the implications he makes on this basis. He completely relies on Glueck's resume on the matter (ibid., 4), which we have demonstrated to be erroneous.

16. Kuyper's suggestion contradicts his own earlier proposal, "It appears to me that when *ḥesed* and *ʾĕmet* appear together they become a hendiadys in which the second term intends to confirm and enrich the concept of the first" (ibid., 6–7). If that was the case, then *ḥesed weʾĕmet* would denote "true grace" and so would *charitos kai alētheias* and *hē charis kai hē alētheia*. Then Kuyper's suggestion that "the Evangelist abandons the word ['grace'] because he intends to let the word truth carry the full import of the concept within the expression, grace and truth" makes no sense because the emphasis, according to this scholar himself, must rest on "grace."

17. Kuyper freely shuffles objective and subjective meanings of *alētheia*; he instantly switches from the phraseology of "faithful and redemptive act" to "faithfulness to . . . covenant of redemption" to "redemptive faithfulness."

18. Curiously, Sakenfeld is not quite sure whether *(hē) charis kai (hē) alētheia* constitutes hendiadys or not herself as she comments, "The Greek behind the phrase 'grace and truth' [1:14] reflects the classic Hebrew combination 'loyalty and faithfulness,' [*ḥesed weʾĕmet*] *or* sure loyalty" (Sakenfeld, *Faithfulness*, 134; emphasis added).

19. Kuyper, "Grace and Truth," 18.

20. Sakenfeld, *Faithfulness*, 133, 150 n. 1.

Thus, "In Christ, the world experiences in a unique way the abounding, sure loyalty[21] of God." Sakenfeld at least seems to recognize that *ḥesed* = *charis* = "loyalty" is inherent in Jesus Christ. She evaluates, "All the acts of Jesus' earthly life can be viewed as embodying what loyalty is really all about. Choose any pericope, and one finds Jesus portrayed as a person freely living out commitment to others, a person especially concerned for the downtrodden and outcast, those overlooked or ignored."[22]

Zane C. Hodges advances the argument by attempting to differentiate qualities listed by *(hē) charis kai (hē) alētheia*. He remarks, "It is certainly true that neither of the shared concepts of verses 14 and 16 [*plērēs*, *plērōma*, and *charis*] reappear elsewhere in the Gospel."[23] He quite rightly assesses that "though the term *grace* does not reappear explicitly in the remainder of the Gospel, it is implicitly present throughout wherever emphasis falls on the freeness of the offer of eternal life through the Lord Jesus." According to him,

> when Jesus offered the "gift of God" to a sin-stained Samaritan woman (4:10–14), John's readers might be expected to perceive that He was "full of grace." Equally, when he exposed to that same woman His knowledge of her guilty life—a life He in no sense condones—and then revealed to her the sublime character of *real* worship (John 4:16–24), it is manifest that He is likewise "full of truth."[24]

Attempts to link *charis* in 1:14–18 with *charis* in either Exodus 33:13–14[25] or Exodus 33:12–19[26] have been inadequate. Morna D. Hooker examined Moses's request, "If I have found favor in thy sight, show me now thy ways, that I may know thee and find favor in thy sight" (Exod 33:13 LXX), and concluded that "this request is apparently granted in the promise: 'My presence will go with you'; through God's presence

---

21. Sakenfeld erroneously claims *ḥesed weʾĕmet* to be hendiadys meaning "sure loyalty" (ibid., 31, 57–60).

22. Ibid., 134. Sakenfeld manages to draw right conclusions from erroneous assumptions. In Jonah and Ps 136:5–9 it is only *ḥesed*, not *ḥesed weʾĕmet* corresponding to *(hē) charis kai (hē) alētheia* that is utilized. Neither *ḥesed weʾĕmet* nor *(hē) charis kai (hē) alētheia* constitutes hendiadys. Neither *(hē) charis kai (hē) alētheia* nor *charis* denote "sure loyalty" in the Gospel.

23. Hodges, "Grace after Grace," 37.

24. Ibid., 39.

25. Hooker, "Johannine Prologue."

26. Dumbrell, "Grace and Truth."

with them, God's people will be distinct from all other people."[27] Then she observed that the noun *ḥēn*, used twice here, was translated with *charis*, and asked,

> Is it this idea of favor given to one who has already received favor, which lies behind the notoriously difficult phrase in John i. 16, *charin anti charitos*? Those who have received the grace of being God's own people receive also the grace of his presence among them (v. 14).[28]

Hooker was on the right track but missed the mark. To begin with, she did not notice that in the Sinaitic conversation between God and Moses the matter of *charis* was at stake not just twice (Exod 33:13, 13 LXX), but six times (Exod 33:12, 13, 13, 16, 17; 34:9 LXX). She therefore drew a hasty conclusion from a mere third of the available evidence. Moreover, Hooker did not realize that at this point of the conversation God offers his presence not to all the people but to Moses only (Exod 33:14 LXX). Neither did she take the larger context of the revelation at Sinai into consideration (cf. Exod 33:3 LXX). As a result, Hooker also failed to recognize that the Sinaitic conversation between God and Moses was about the presence of God with the whole nation of Israel, and not in some remote future but immediately at Sinai and further on.[29] Furthermore, she improperly equated the presence of God as such with only a benefit of the distinctiveness—"being God's own people"—caused by his presence with Israel.[30] Finally, Hooker did not examine the Greek text of Exodus 33–34 beyond noticing *charis* in Exodus 33:13 and *skēnē* in Exodus 33:7–11.

Hodges later approved Hooker's observations on the two occurrences of *charis* in Exodus 33:3, but also failed to take the rest of the

---

27. Hooker, "Johannine Prologue," 53, for Exod 33:16. This translation "distinct" hints the reader that Hooker works with the Hebrew text; so she misses the point. Crucially, the LXX has here *endoxasthēsomai*, "I will be glorified."

28. Hooker, "Johannine Prologue," 53.

29. This shifts Hooker's attention to God dwelling in the *skēnē* outside of the camp due to Israel's failure at Sinai (Exod 33:7–11), i.e., to the *cause* of the intercession of Moses before God. This scholar misses the *effect* of the revelation of God at Sinai—God's glory filling the *skēnē* and dwelling among the people of Israel (Exod 44:34–38).

30. This causes Hooker to inadequately associate dwelling of (the *doxa* of) God in the *skēnē outside* of the camp due to Israel's failure at Sinai (Exod 33:7–11) with *eis ta idia ēlthen*, "He came to His own," (1:11) and further—as a benefit—with *ho logos . . . eskēnōsen en hēmin*, "the Word . . . dwelt among us" (1:14).

cluster's four occurrences of *charis* into consideration. In addition, his superficial evaluation of what *charis* stood for in Exodus 32:7—34:10 caused him to inadequately conclude that *charin anti charitos* would refer to two examples of "the forgiving grace of God," consequently expressed in sparing life at Sinai and offering life in Jesus.[31]

Dumbrell noticed the first five occurrences of *charis*, and yet missed the sixth and crucial one (Exod 34:9 LXX). He attempted to build on Hooker and Hodges's observations[32] but ended up with a rather eclectic attempt to combine the incompatible: "Grace and truth may refer to the *ḥesed weʾĕmet* of Exodus 34:6 . . . But, on the other hand, it could refer to the communication of the divine revelation to Moses, grace found by Moses in God's sight in Exodus 33:12, 13, 16, and 17, and to Moses as the receptor of grace and mercy in Exodus 33:19."[33]

Scholars exercise a couple of approaches in dealing with the peculiarities of the usage of the term *doxa* in the Gospel. First, there are studies where matters of *doxa* in the Gospel are evaluated from a particular perspective, concepts of Wisdom[34] and Light[35] being the most prominent. Second, there is a tendency to define the meaning of *doxa* and cognates so broadly that almost anything fits under them. These researchers would argue by the following steps: a) the NT authors without exception use *doxa* as a biblical[36] term to express the "divine mode of being"; b) in the NT, as in the LXX, the meanings "divine honor," "divine splendor," "divine power," and "visible divine radiance" are fluid, and can only be distinguished artificially; and c) in content, however, there is always expressed the divine mode of being, though with varying emphasis on the element of visibility.[37] Along these lines Robert G. Bratcher evaluates that in the Gospel, "in many passages . . . *doxa* means more than power, or majesty, or splendor, or honor, or greatness. It means

---

31. Hodges, "Grace after Grace," especially 41–42. In our view, there is a profound truth to Hodges's observation; it is just that the life of humanity is only an effect of the cause of *charis*—the presence of God.

32. Dumbrell refers to Hooker, "Johannine Prologue," 53–55, and Hodges, "Grace after Grace," 40.

33. Dumbrell, "Grace and Truth," 115.

34. Witherington, *John's Wisdom*.

35. N. Petersen, *John*, 74; see also Cook, "'Glory' Motif," 295.

36. As used in the LXX rather than in Hellenistic Greek.

37. Kittel, "*doxa*," 2:247 (cf. Luke 2:9; 9:31f.; 2 Pet 1:17; Acts 22:11; Rev 15:8; 21:23).

'the divine being,' 'the divine nature,' 'divinity,' 'the divine One.'"[38] Kerry S. Robichaux suggests yet another overarching connotation: "the core of meaning common to all the various senses of glory in the Gospel of John is the expression of some excellent virtue or virtues."[39] This approach can neither satisfactorily explain the variety of connotations of *doxa* in the Gospel[40] nor adequately solve the peculiarities listed above. Third, there are attempts to define the meaning of *doxa* and cognates against some background alleged for the Gospel. Such scholars would a) argue for a certain background for the Gospel, b) consider the general scope of meanings inherent in *doxa* and cognates in the alleged background, and c) try to apply the connotations of *doxa* found in the alleged background to occurrences of *doxa* and cognates in the Gospel. There are two dangers in the approach. On the one hand, a wrong background—Gnostic, Hellenistic, etc.—may be suggested for the Gospel. On the other hand, the correct, Jewish background can be utilized in such a generic sense—"The Old Testament," "Early Jewish Literature," etc.—that it cannot really help to narrow down the possible scope of meanings of *doxa* and cognates in the Gospel. So Beasley-Murray views *doxa* and cognates in the Gospel mainly with reference to the book of Isaiah—already with a rather broad brush. He maintains that the change signified by the miracle of changing water into wine is the coming of the kingdom of God in and through Jesus. The picture of the kingdom of God as a feast is prominent in Judaism and in the synoptic teaching,[41] and abundance of wine is a feature of the feast, as attested in Isa 25:6. As in the OT, the coming of God for his kingdom results in the gathering of the Gentiles to see his glory, and their proclamation

---

38. Bratcher, "What Does 'Glory' Mean," 407. This scholar finds the meaning "divine nature" applicable to both occurrences of *doxa* in 1:14, and further remarks that the meaning "divine nature/status" applies to 2:11; 7:39; 11:4, 40; 12:16, 23, 28, 41; 13:31–32; 14:13; 15:8; 16:4; 17:1, 4, 5, 10, 22, 24.

39. Robichaux, "Christ, the Spirit, and Glory," 10.

40. Adherents of this approach realize this eventually. So Robichaux further deals with seven (!) categories: "glory in the sense of simple praise, be it glory bestowed on humanity by God . . . glory bestowed on humans by humans, or vain self-glory . . . the divine glory that is expressed in Christ . . . : His divine, eternal glory, which He had with the Father in eternity past; His glorification of the Father, which He, as both the Son of God and the Son of Man, accomplished on the earth; and His won glorification by the Father, by the Spirit, and by believers." (ibid.).

41. This scholar gives as examples Matt 5:6; 8:11–12; Mark 2:19; Luke 22:15–18, 29–30a.

of it to nations that have not seen it, as in Isa 66:19.[42] Beasley-Murray further observes that the term "lift up" is closely associated with "glorify" (*doxazō*),[43] and concludes that the lifting up of Jesus on the cross is one with his exaltation in heaven, and the *whole* event reveals his glory. As this scholar asserts, this event reflects Isa 52:13: "My servant *hupsōthēsetai kai doxasthēsetai sphodra*," i.e., will be exalted and greatly glorified.[44] Beasley-Murray concludes that "the glory of God that Isaiah saw in his vision (Isa 6:1–4) is identified with the glory of the Logos-Son, in accordance with 1:18 and 17:5."[45] The book of Isaiah as the frame of reference obviously cannot explain all of the occurrences of cognates of *doxa* in the Gospel in a conceptually coherent way, so this scholar also brings in the book of Exodus as yet another background, again in a noticeably generic way:

> The language [of *skēnoō/doxa*] is evocative of the revelation of God's glory in the Exodus—by the Red Sea, on Mount Sinai, and at the tent of meeting by Israel's camp (especially the last; see Exod 33:7–11; for the glory in and upon the Tabernacle cf. Exod 40:34–38). The Exodus associations are intentional, and are part of the theme of the revelation and redemption of the Logos-Christ as fulfilling the hope of a *second* Exodus.[46]

To this already rather broad background of Isaiah and Exodus, Beasley-Murray still adds the Wisdom concept, as

> . . . a coalescence of Semitic and Greek thought, wherein the principle of creation becomes the expression of the glory of the Almighty, pervading the whole creation and the souls of men. This concept plays a major part in the formulation of the hymn within the prologue, but it also is a major constituent in the Christology of the Gospel as a whole.[47]

As a result, the alleged frame of reference turns out to be so generic that the whole approach of interpreting cognates of *doxa* in the Gospel against such a background becomes unreliable. These views are so broad they are immune to critique and cannot be verified or falsified.

42. Beasley-Murray, *John*, 33.
43. This scholar invites to compare 12:23 with 13:31–32; 17:1.
44. Beasley-Murray, *John*, 131.
45. Ibid., 217.
46. Ibid., 14.
47. Ibid., lx.

Evaluation of the Attempts

Attempts to trace the terminology of *doxa*, *alētheia*, and *charis* throughout the Gospel are numerous, but there are six fundamental errors that have been commonly made in the process. First, researchers simply ignore the issue of tracing the terms (especially *charis*, as it does not appear beyond the prologue),[48] whereas *doxa*, *alētheia*, and *charis*—just as other terms of the prologue[49]—do introduce concepts that will be developed further in the Gospel, and in cognate terms (particularly *charis*; see 19:37 + Zech 12:10 LXX). Second, scholars attempt to avoid tracing *charis* by assigning a *figurative*—"gospel,"[50] "prophecy,"[51] "riches of divine life,"[52] "salvation,"[53] etc.—connotation to the term, whereas the meaning of *charis* is actually *literal*: *charis* in *charitos kai alētheias* and *hē charis kai hē alētheia* denotes the graciousness of the character of God, and *charis* in *charin anti charitos* depicts the presence of God. Third, scholars attempt to avoid tracing *charis* by declaring *(hē) charis kai (hē) alētheia* as hendiadys with the single objective meaning

---

48. For example, Lincoln first recognizes that, "In the prologue, ... the grace and truth previously associated with the glory of Yahweh in the covenant with Moses (cf. Exod 34:6) [are] now associated with the glory of the incarnate Logos (1:14)" (Lincoln, *Truth*, 232). But he then drops *charis* and abandons the original connotation of *alētheia* maintaining that the latter term embraces the entire issue at stake in the cosmic lawsuit. *Alētheia* in the Gospel, then, becomes a term denoting a rather controversial variety of "the true judgment about God's acting in Jesus in a salvific trial that intends life for the world," "the reality of God's existence," God's "self-expression ... embodied in Jesus," "the establishment of the divine verdict of life" through the death of Jesus, "love between the Father and the Son," "the reliability of the divine word," "the oneness between Jesus and God" (Lincoln, *Truth*, 188, 230–31, 246). Not only do these definitions widely deviate from the original meaning of *alētheia*—a quality of the divine character—initially declared in the prologue to indicate the way the word should be perceived further in the Gospel, but they also do not allow for *charis*, the other quality of the divine character denoted by the pair!

49. *Logos, Christos, zōē, phōs, skotia, teknon, marturia, kosmos, sarx, monogenēs, patēr, nomos, Mōusēs*.

50. Westcott, *John*, 1:24–26.

51. Origen *Commentary on the Gospel of John* 6:3, ANF 10:352.

52. Schnackenburg, *John*, 1:275. Schnackenburg evaluates that the Evangelist, in rendering *charin anti charitos*, "is not just thinking of the superabundant mercy of God. He also means the riches of divine life which the Logos receives from the Father (5:26) and from which he enriches his own (10:10)."

53. Beasley-Murray is exemplary: "the salvation brought by the Word thus is defined in terms of inexhaustible grace, a significant feature in view of the absence of further mention of *charis* in the Gospel" (Beasley-Murray, *John*, 15).

"gracious truth" or "gift of truth,"⁵⁴ whereas *(hē) charis kai (hē) alētheia* actually denote two subjective qualities of the divine character. Fourth, scholars attempt to trace *charis* throughout the Gospel as if *charis* in the prologue stood for just *one* concept, whereas there are actually *two*: *charis* in *charitos kai alētheias* and *hē charis kai hē alētheia* is a subjective quality of the character of God, and *charis* in *charin anti charitos* is an objective reality of the presence of God. Fifth, scholars attempt to trace *charis* throughout the Gospel as if *hē charis kai hē alētheia dia Iēsou Christou egeneto* meant that graciousness and integrity were only *inherent in* Jesus Christ's character, whereas they were not only inherent in but also actually *bestowed through* Jesus Christ *onto* believers. Sixth, scholars attempt to trace the concepts of *doxa* and *charis* throughout the Gospel as if these were *unrelated* categories, whereas they are actually *interrelated*. One of the subjective qualities of the character of God (*charis*, 1:14, 17) is one of the attributes of the character of God (*doxa*). The objective reality of the presence of God (*charis*, 1:16) is evident in four Sinaitic covenantal aspects of God's *doxa*: the visible appearance of God (*doxa*), the intrinsic character of God (*doxa*), the miraculous splendor verifying the presence of God (*endoxa*), and the divine honor confirming the presence of God (*endoxasthēsomai*).

(hē) charis kai (hē) alētheia, charis, and *doxa* in John with Reference to the Covenant of the Presence (*charis*)

We have established that John 1:14 alludes to Exodus 34:6. We have also demonstrated that John 1:14–18 alludes to Exodus 33:12—34:10 LXX. This makes it only natural to propose that it is the usage of terms *doxa*, *charis*, and *alētheia* in Exodus 33:12—34:10 LXX that defines the connotations of terms *doxa*, *charis*, and *alētheia* in the prologue and throughout the Gospel. Our study argues that the Gospel's concepts of *(hē) charis kai (hē) alētheia, charis,* and *doxa* are developed with reference to the covenant of the presence (*charis*) of God initiated at Sinai (Exod 33:12—34:10 LXX), reinforced in Jesus, and retained through the Spirit. We advocate that the Gospel follows the Sinaitic paradigm of the covenant of *charis* in the following aspects: 1) the character of God—qualities *(hē) charis kai (hē) alētheia*—is bestowed on believers, 2) the presence of God is incessant—*charin anti charitos*—to believers, and 3) the four

---

54. Or any other meaning behind the wrongly alleged hendiadys, for that matter.

aspects of the presence of God—visible appearance (*doxa*), intrinsic character (*doxa*), miraculous splendor verifying his presence (*endoxa*), and divine honor confirming his presence (*endoxasthēsomai*)—are evident to believers in the course of the revelation and ratification[55] of the covenant of *charis*.

The Character of God Bestowed onto Believers

We have demonstrated that the phraseology of *plērēs charitos kai alētheias* (1:14) and *hē charis kai hē alētheia* (1:17) alludes to *wərab-ḥesed we'ĕmet* (Exod 34:6). At Sinai, the expression *wərab-ḥesed we'ĕmet* clearly depicts the *character* of God. Therefore, the prologue's phraseology of *plērēs charitos kai alētheias* and *hē charis kai hē alētheia* introduces Jesus as possessing the intrinsic—full of graciousness and integrity—character of God. The Gospel no doubt unfolds this concept. Our major concern, though, is that rare attempts to trace *hē charis kai hē alētheia* throughout the Gospel are confined[56] to demonstrating that Jesus *himself* is depicted as a gracious person and/or a man of integrity, as if *hē charis kai hē alētheia* were inherent only *in* Christ. We argue that Jesus not only possesses *hē charis kai hē alētheia* but also grants these qualities of the character of God to believers.[57] This concept of bestowing the divine character onto humans is introduced in the prologue and further developed throughout the rest of the Gospel.

The Divine Character Depicted in Terms of Qualities, Glory, and Name

At Sinai, the Lord addresses Moses from the midst of a burning bush. God sends the man to deliver the people. Moses expresses a concern, "Now they may say to me, 'What is His name?' What shall I say to

---

55. We use cognates of "to ratify" in the sense of "to confirm or make valid," "to guarantee or ensure the fulfillment of," "to declare or confirm the truth or correctness of," "to consummate, carry out, bring to fulfillment or completion" (*OED* 13:215).

56. With the exception of D. Smith, "Grace upon Grace."

57. Origen suggested, "God . . . made grace and truth through Jesus Christ, that grace and truth which came to man" (Origin *Commentary on the Gospel of John* 6:3, *ANF* 10:353). Boismard maintained that "grace and fidelity come from God to us, they have been 'made' in us by Jesus Christ, they have become our own possession, qualities of our heart" (Boismard, *St. John's Prologue*, 64, similarly 62, 70). But these scholars have not gone beyond this mere assertion.

them?" God answers, *'ehye^h 'ăšer 'ehye^h*.⁵⁸ The larger significance of the Hebrew term *šēm*, "name," is a "designation of God, specifically of Yahweh . . . ; = his reputation, fame . . . ; especially as embodying the (revealed) character of Yahweh."⁵⁹ With this in mind John I. Durham correctly asserts, "What Moses asks, then, has to do with whether God can accomplish what he is promising. What is there in his reputation . . . that lends credibility to the claim in his call?"⁶⁰

Moses's second encounter with God at Sinai is remarkably similar to the first one. Only now Moses's concern is whether Yahweh will be *present* and go up from Sinai with the people, in spite of the sin of idolatry the people have committed. Again, it is the matter of the character that defines the outcome. At the outset Moses appeals to the Lord's former appraisal, "I know you by name, and you have indeed found favor in my estimation."⁶¹ It is hardly the proper name "Moses" that is in view here. One does not find favor just on the basis of the given name. Besides, the Lord has known the birth name of the man long before this conversation occurs (Exod 3:4). No narrative earlier in Exodus (cf. Exod 33:17) reports of Yahweh making this statement about Moses, though Exodus 32:9–10 reflects a similar theme.⁶² The Lord says to Moses, "I have seen this people, and behold, they are an obstinate people. Now then let Me alone, that My anger may burn against them and that I may destroy them; and I will make of you a great nation" (Exod 32:9–10). Apparently, God favors Moses because of his character. Hence, the expression "I know you by name," among other connotations,⁶³ carries the meaning "I know your character."⁶⁴

Their following dialogue only confirms this pattern. The Lord acknowledges the quality of Moses's character: "you have found favor in My sight and I have known you by name." (Exod 33:17 LXX). Now—almost "in return"—Moses wants to know the character of God, asking,

58. As Durham puts it, "To the question *ma^h-ššəmô*, 'What is His name?' or, better, 'What is He *really* like?' Yahweh replied, 'I really AM'" (Durham, *Exodus*, 452).

59. BDB, 10356.

60. Durham, *Exodus*, 38. This scholar points out similar cases depicted in Num 6:27; Deut 12:5, 11; 16:2–6; Pss 8:1; 74:7; Amos 5:8; 9:5–6; Jer 33:2.

61. Translation as in Durham, *Exodus*, 44.

62. Ibid., 446.

63. Such as "singling out," etc.

64. The LXX translates *bəšēm*, "by name," with *para pantas*, "beyond, above all" (Exod 33:12).

"how then can it be known that I have found favor in Your sight, I and Your people? Is it not by Your going with us . . . ?" (Exod 33:16 LXX). Actually, it is in God's character to favor people, as he agrees, "I will also do this thing of which you have spoken" (Exod 33:17 LXX). So Yahweh has promised, but is it in his character to fulfill what he has promised? Hence, Moses seeks for a vivid confirmation of God's character, as he replies, "I pray You, show me Your glory!" (Exod 33:18 LXX). The Lord makes no mistake. To Moses's request presented in terms of *glory* God responds with categories of the *character* apparently expressed in terms of qualities/name. Yahweh promises, "I Myself will make all My *goodness*[65] pass before you, and will proclaim the *name* of the Lord before you; and I will be *gracious* to whom I will be *gracious*, and will show *compassion* on whom I will show *compassion*." (Exod 33:19; emphasis added). The Lord is willing to give "a description not of how he *looks* but of how he *is*,"[66] to demonstrate his character.

This pattern is further crystallized in the very event of the theophany. Moses calls upon the *name* (Exod 34:6 LXX) of the Lord, God's *glory*[67] passes before Moses, and the Lord proclaims the *qualities*, "The Lord, the Lord God, *compassionate and gracious, slow to anger, and abounding in lovingkindness and truth*" (Exod 34:6; emphasis added). Hence, as Durham puts it, "As the first request became the question that led to the revelation of Yahweh's name, so the second request becomes the plea that leads to the revelation of Yahweh's character . . . the exegesis of the revelation of his name."[68]

Three categories—the qualities, the glory, and the name—are utilized to denote the character of God in the course of the theophany at Sinai.[69] We have established that the revelation as Jesus is modeled after the theophany at Sinai. We further argue that the same three Sinaitic categories are utilized to depict the character of God in the Gospel:

---

65. The LXX translator realizes this well: *ṭôb*, "goodness," is interpreted with *doxa*, "glory." Modern translators agree. Durham evaluates, "*ṭôb* refers not to an appearance of beauty but to a recital of character" (Durham, *Exodus*, 452). Notice "all my attributes" for *kol-ṭûbî* of Exod 33:19 in Houtman, *Exodus* 3:701.

66. Durham, *Exodus*, 452.

67. Cf. the Lord's "while My glory is passing by" (Exod 33:22).

68. Durham, *Exodus*, 455. Similarly, Dumbrell, "Grace and Truth," 114.

69. The original Sinaitic association of the three categories had been perhaps noticed and further echoed. Cf. Pss 44:27/43:27 OG; 84:12/83:11 OG; 89:25; 138:2; 115:1.

in terms of *qualities* in the prologue (1:14, 17) and pouring/breathing God's Holy Spirit of *(hē) charis kai (hē) alētheia* onto believers (3:34; 19:30; 19:37 + Zech 12:10; 20:22); in terms of *glory* in the prologue (1:14, 17) and Jesus giving God's *doxa* to believers (17:22); and in terms of *name* in Jesus manifesting/making known God's name (17:6, 26). Remarkably, all three categories depict the character being bestowed onto believers.

Jesus Bestows God's Character (*charis* and *alethēia*) by Pouring/Breathing God's Holy Spirit onto Believers

We advocate that the prologue's statement *hē charis kai hē alētheia dia Iēsou Christou egeneto* introduces the concept of the qualities of the character of God bestowed onto believers by Jesus Christ. The Son possesses the Father's character *plērēs charitos kai alētheias*. But the Evangelist also reports *ho nomos dia Mōuseōs edothē, hē charis kai hē alētheia dia Iēsou Christou egeneto*. First, the preposition *dia* assumes a recipient. There must be someone beyond Moses and Jesus to whom *ho nomos*/*hē charis kai hē alētheia* are conveyed. Second, structurally the two halves of this statement are balanced. This balance defines the recipient; since the Law was given through Moses (to the people) then *hē charis kai hē alētheia* must have been granted through Jesus Christ (to the people) as well. Third, the verb *egeneto* indicates that *hē charis kai hē alētheia*—qualities of the character of God—were conveyed to the people in a way just as real as in every act of *ginomai* depicted in the prologue: "All things came into being [*egeneto*] through Him, and apart from Him nothing came into being [*egeneto*] that has come into being [*gegonen*]" (1:3, 3, 3); "there came [*egeneto*] a man sent from God, whose name was John" (1:6); "the world was made [*egeneto*]" (1:10); "as many as received Him, to them He gave the right to become [*genesthai*] children of God" (1:12); "the Word became [*egeneto*] flesh" (1:14); "He [Jesus Christ] who comes after me [John the Baptist] has a higher rank [*gegonen*] than I [John the Baptist]" (1:15). Hence, the qualities *hē charis kai hē alētheia* must be tangible and remain in the world just as well. Fourth, since the statement's components *ho nomos* (the legal corpus) and *hē charis kai hē alētheia* (the qualities of the character) belong to different dimensions, they cannot be either contrasted or compared; neither can they replace or fulfill one another. Therefore, the phrase *hē charis kai hē alētheia dia Iēsou Christou egeneto* introduces a progression (in both quantity and quality) from the Sinaitic "Moses *alone* only *heard* of God's character being *ḥesed we'ĕmet*" to the Gospel's "Jesus *bestowed*[70] *hē charis kai hē alētheia*—qualities of the character of God—onto *all* believers."[71]

We propose that the Spirit plays the key role in the bestowal of the character of God—qualities *(hē) charis kai (hē) alētheia*—onto believers. Jesus thrice refers to the Spirit as *to pneuma tēs alētheias* (14:17; 15:26; 16:13).[72] Eventually, though, the audience of the Gospel realizes that the Spirit is not only *to pneuma tēs alētheias* but actually the Spirit of *hē charis kai hē alētheia*. The Evangelist renders, "Scripture says, 'THEY SHALL LOOK ON HIM WHOM THEY PIERCED'" (19:37). This is a *quotation* from Zechariah 12:10.[73] His explicit reference, "Scripture says," invites the audience to consider the OT passage as evidence (cf. 5:39). So the audience follows the hint only to find that there is more to the prophecy than meets the eye. Zechariah reports of the Lord's promise,

> I [the Lord] will pour out on the house of David and on the inhabitants of Jerusalem, the Spirit of grace [*pneuma charitos*] and of supplication, so that they will look on Me whom they have pierced ...[74]

The audience recalls that Jesus breathes on the disciples (who are Jews of the house of David, gathered in Jerusalem and looking at Jesus pierced) and says to them, "Receive the Holy Spirit" (20:22). The audience realizes that the Holy Spirit is not only *to pneuma tēs alētheias* (14:17; 15:26; 16:13) but also *pneuma charitos* (19:37; Zech 12:10). Summarily, this makes the Holy Spirit the Spirit of *(hē) charis kai (hē) alētheia*. The audience further grasps that the Spirit is *full [ek metrou]* of *(hē) charis*

---

70. The middle of *egeneto* indicates that Jesus possesses *hē charis kai hē alētheia* himself. Of course, Jesus is *plērēs charitos kai alētheias* (1:14).

71. The conformity to the divine character restored to humans allows believers to dwell in the presence of God. Believers do not gain the visible appearance of God (*doxa* of 1:14a); they do not become God (cf. 10:34–35).

72. There is no reference to *to pneuma tēs alētheias* in the OT Scripture (cf. Schweizer, "pneuma," 6:443). It is exactly Jesus, though, who is perfectly qualified to illumine this matter of the Spirit, for the Son and the Father are one (10:30 et al.), so the Scripture is not broken (10:35).

73. Menken, *Zechariah 12:10*, 167–86.

74. Zech 12:10 (NASB, to simplify); for the Hebrew/Greek discrepancy see ibid.

kai (hē) alētheia (3:34). Hence, *hē charis kai hē alētheia*—qualities of the character of God—are conveyed to believers (1:17; 1:32–33; 3:34; 20:22; notice also 15:11; 16:13; 17:13) by the means of the Spirit (3:34; 14:17; 15:26; 16:13; 19:37 cf. Zech 12:10; (19:30); 20:22).

Now the time when "the Spirit was not yet *given*, because Jesus was not yet glorified" (7:39) is over. Jesus is glorified on the cross; believers receive the Spirit. The post-resurrection audience naturally envisions both qualities *hē charis kai hē alētheia* in various references to the Spirit in the Gospel: "an hour is coming, and now is, when the true worshipers will worship the Father in spirit [i.e. in grace] and truth; for such people the Father seeks to be His worshipers" (4:23); "God is spirit [of grace and truth], and those who worship Him must worship in spirit [i.e., in grace] and truth" (4:24); "the Spirit of [grace and] truth, whom the world cannot receive, because it does not see Him or know Him, *but you know Him because He abides with you and will be in you*" (14:17); "When the Helper comes, whom I will send to you from the Father, *that is* the Spirit of [grace and] truth who proceeds from the Father, He will testify about Me" (15:26); "when He, the Spirit of [grace and] truth, comes, He will guide you into all the truth; for He will not speak on His own initiative, but whatever He hears, He will speak; and He will disclose to you what is to come" (16:13).

Jesus Gives God's Character (*doxa*) to Believers

Jesus reports to the Father, "The glory which You have given Me I have given to them, that they may be one, just as We are one" (17:22). There are many suggestions as to what the nature of this "glory" is. C. K. Barrett proposes that it is the unity with the death and resurrection of Jesus from which that life flows.[75] Beasley-Murray evaluates, "the glory of the Christ is the glory of God's love, beheld by his people, and transforming them into bearers of Christly love."[76] Bultmann views it as the *name* of God and the *words* of God given to Jesus, by which Jesus is known and confessed as Revealer and Redeemer (cf. vv. 8, 11, 14).[77] Marie J.

---

75. Barrett, *John*, 513.
76. Beasley-Murray, *John*, 305.
77. Bultmann, *John*, 513.

Lagrange understands it as the incarnate glory, which is Jesus's divine glory, at once veiled and revealed in his ministry.[78] Pancaro evaluates,

> The *doxa* which Jesus has received from the Father and given to the disciples [John 17:22] is neither grace,[79] nor faith,[80] nor the glory of the resurrection,[81] but a share in the very unity he has with the Father,[82] or, better yet, it is the radiance of his communion of love with the Father as revealed to the disciples and as creatively drawing them into this communion of love.[83] This "Liebesgemeinschaft" has become a reality (in Christ) for the disciples and shines forth in them just as it shines forth in Christ. His *doxa* has become their *doxa*.[84]

Schnackenburg suggests that glory is the divine life, which is the eternal life brought by Jesus, anticipating its fullness in the world to come.[85] Beasley-Murray, though, having listed the views above[86] summarizes, "Unfortunately the precise nature of that 'glory' given to believers is uncertain."[87]

As we have evidenced, at the theophany at Sinai the concept of character is expressed in terms of glory.[88] The revelation as Jesus is modeled after the theophany at Sinai. The concept of glory denoting the character (1:14) and conveyed to believers (1:17[89]) is introduced in the prologue. It is only natural to recognize that in his conversation with the Father, the Son by "glory" means the divine "character." This makes

---

78. Lagrange, *Évangile selon Saint Jean*, 427–28.

79. Chrysostom *Homilies on St. John*; Lagrange, *Évangile selon Saint Jean*.

80. Bultmann, *John*, 395.

81. Pancaro makes a reference "Thomas Aq., ad loc." in the footnote at Pancaro, *Law*, 236.

82. Schlatter, *Evangelium nach Johannes*; *Evangelist*.

83. Thüsing, *Erhöhung*, 182–85.

84. Pancaro, *Law*, 236. To Pancaro this explains the nature of "that *doxa* which comes from God and which men are asked to 'seek' (5,44), to 'love' (12,43)."

85. Schnackenburg, *John*, 3:192.

86. With the exception of Pancaro's view in his *Law*, which is neither listed in the bibliography nor referred to in Beasley-Murray, *John*.

87. Beasley-Murray, *John*, 302.

88. Notice interpretation of *ḥesed* with *pasa doxa anthrōpou*, "all the glory of man," (Isa 40:6) and *endoxos*, "glorious, famous/honored (of men)" (Sir 44:1).

89. The singular of *egeneto* correlates *hē charis kai hē alētheia* (1:17) with the intrinsic character (*doxa*) of God (1:14b).

much sense of Jesus's report. Consider, "The glory [cf. *ḥesed we'ĕmet*] which You have given Me [cf. *doxan hōs monogenous para patros, plērēs charitos kai alētheias*] I have given to them [cf. *hē charis kai hē alētheian hōs monogenous para patrosdia Iēsou Christou egeneto*], that they may be one, just as We are one" (17:22, cf. 1:14; 17:24). It is the *character* of God that Jesus conveys to believers. The Lord restores the image of God in people so that they may become one.

Jesus Manifests/Makes Known God's Character (*onoma*) to Believers

Jesus makes a puzzling[90] petition with reference to the name: "Holy Father, keep them in Your name, *the name* which You have given Me [*tērēson autous en tō onomati sou hō dedōkas moi*], that they may be one even as We *are.*" (17:11). It is most natural[91] to translate *en* as "in," and to interpret the prayer as "Keep them *in* Your name" or, more fully, "*in adherence to* what Jesus has revealed to the disciples of the character of God."[92] Researchers essentially agree that Jesus's petition, "Father, keep them in Your name," has God's character in view.[93] The difficulty arises when scholars attempt to *coherently* explain 1) the matter of "giving" the Father's name to the Son, and 2) just how exactly this commonality of the "name" enables believers to be one even as the Divine persons are. What scholars fail to realize is that the concept of the character is readily applicable not only to the rest of this petition (17:11) but also to all of the interrelated *onoma* sayings preserved in the prayer (17:6, 11, 26).

The Sinaitic paradigm of the character expressed in terms of name (see especially Exod 33:19; 34:5–6) allows one to interpret the whole

---

90. As Beasley-Murray gently puts it, "the precise meaning of the petition is variously construed" (Beasley-Murray, *John*, 299).

91. It is possible to translate *en tō onomati sou* as "*by* Your name," and to interpret as "protect *by the power* of your name." So suggest Bruce, *John*, 332; Bultmann, *John*, 503; Heitmüller, *Evangelium des Johannes*, 132–34; Hoskyns, *Fourth Gospel*, 500; NIB; Schlatter, *Evangelist*, 321. Such an approach seems to be lacking in argumentation, though. Bruce appeals to the alleged parallelism of "Save me, O God, by Your *name*, and vindicate me by Your *might*" (Ps 54:1), but this may or may not be a case of parallelism.

92. Beasley-Murray, *John*, 299; also Barrett, *John*, 507; Lagrange, *Évangile selon Saint Jean*, 445; Lindars, *John*, 524; Schnackenburg, *John*, 3:180.

93. Beasley-Murray, *John*, 299. Notice interpretation of *ḥesed* with *onoma* (both of God) in Ps 44:27/43:27 OG.

phrase coherently: Jesus prays, "Holy Father, keep them in Your name [wərab-ḥesed weʾĕmet, cf. Exod 34:5–6], *the name* which You have given Me [hōs monogenous para patros, plērēs charitos kai alētheias], that they may be one even as We are" (17:11). The petition addresses the matter of bestowing of the divine character (described in terms of the name identical to the Father and the Son) to believers. In turn, the conformity of the divine character restored to humans allows believers to be one with the Divine just as the Son and the Father who possess the same character are one.

This interpretation of 17:6 is only confirmed if one takes the interrelated verses 17:6, 11, and 26 into consideration. Further in the prayer Jesus accounts to God, "I have manifested Your name [hē charis kai hē alētheia dia Iēsou Christou egeneto . . . exēgēsato] to the men whom You gave Me out of the world" (17:6). He even reinforces, "I have made Your name known to them [hē charis kai hē alētheia dia Iēsou Christou . . . exēgēsato], and will make it known, so that the love with which You loved Me may be in them, and I in them" (17:26). It is not the proper name *yhwh* that is being manifested and made known to believers; there can be no doubt they are perfectly aware of it. Surely, it is the character of God that is in view, as *hē charis kai hē alētheia dia Iēsou Christou egeneto*. And again, this conformity of the character allows the unity now expressed by Jesus's request, "so that the love with which You loved Me may be in them, and I in them."

Hence, the three Sinaitic categories are utilized in the Gospel to depict the bestowal of the character of God onto believers, in terms of *qualities* (1:14, 17; 3:34; 19:30; 19:37; 20:22), *glory* (1:14, 17; 17:22), and *name* (17:6, 26). This conformity of the divine character inherent in God and now granted to people allows their oneness.

Echoes of the Notion of the Character of God in the Gospel

The Sinaitic covenant has influenced biblical theology enormously. Quotes from, allusions to, and echoes of the Sinaitic covenant are dispersed throughout the OT/LXX/OG/NT. This seems to be true particularly with the Gospel. The Evangelist, while *alluding* to the Sinaitic covenant proper (Exod 33:12—34:10 LXX), may have also *echoed* the notion of the Sinaitic covenant evident elsewhere in the OT. Scholars have recently become increasingly alert to just how intensively the Evangelist employs the OT.[94] The writer often draws from a cluster of sources rather than a single identifiable one.[95] In our view, this OT notion of the qualities of the character of God (*ḥesed we'ĕmet/charis kai hē alētheia*) may well be not only alluded to but also *echoed* throughout the Gospel.[96]

To begin with, some of the OT materials may well have been perceived as prophecies fulfilled by Jesus. First, Micah[97] hoped, "You will give *'ĕmet* to Jacob And *ḥesed* to Abraham, Which You swore to our forefathers From the days of old" (Mic 7:20).[98] This prophecy[99] may well have been echoed in the Evangelist's *ho nomos dia Mōuseōs edothē, hē charis kai hē alētheia dia Iēsou Christou egeneto*, "the Law was given through Moses; grace and truth came through Jesus Christ." (1:17). Second, Hosea warned, "Listen [OG: *akousate*] to the word [OG: *logon*] of the LORD, O sons of Israel, For the LORD has a case [OG: *krisis*] against the inhabitants of the land, Because there is no *'ĕmet* or *ḥesed* or knowledge of God in the land" (Hos 4:1). The Evangelist may well

---

94. See Hanson, *Prophetic Gospel*; Menken, *Quotations*.

95. Lincoln, *Truth*, 62. The Evangelist may have hesitated to quote/allude to *ḥesed we'ĕmet* passages because they occasionally utilize *ḥesed* with other creedal *raḥûm, ḥannûn*. Besides, the LXX/OG translates creedal qualities inconsistently. The Evangelist is well aware of both Hebrew and Greek versions and intentionally operates with the single *charis* as utilized in the Sinaitic covenant. For these reasons the Evangelist may have preferred to only echo *ḥesed we'ĕmet* accounts other than the Sinaitic one he alludes to.

96. Due to the time and volume constraints of this study we did not intend to formally establish cases of this list (for the proper methodology regarding the establishment of echoes see Bauckham, "Study of Gospel Traditions"; Davila, "Perils of Parallels"; Hays, *Echoes*; Michael Thompson, *Clothed with Christ*). Hence, in this section we list our observations as mere suggestions for future research.

97. The Evangelist may have been acquainted with Micah's writings (cf. John/Mic 4:37/6:15; 7:42/5:1). See NA[27], *Appendix IV: Loci citati vel allegati*, 770–806. Notice also echoes of themes prominent to the Gospel in materials immediately leading to the prophecy (Mic 7:7–20).

98. Ralph Smith remarks, "Jesus is the fulfillment of God's covenant promise to Abraham and Jacob" (R. Smith, *Micah–Malachi*, Mic 7:20, without arguing the case).

99. There are a couple of factors one may want to consider in evaluating the relevance of Micah's "You will give *'ĕmet* to Jacob And *ḥesed* to Abraham" to the Gospel. First, it is the last phrase in the whole book of Micah; this makes the statement recognizable. Second, as a prophecy put in the future tense it naturally makes one seek for its fulfillment. Third, the phrase is symbolic, as Micah cannot refer to the actual characters of Jacob and Abraham due to historic timeline considerations. Fifth, it is exactly Jacob (4:1–42) and Abraham (8:31–59) who, of all the patriarchs, are peculiarly emphasized in the Gospel. Sixth, the mentioning of *ḥesed* . . . *'ĕmet* echoes the Sinaitic revelation the Gospel is modeled after.

have also echoed Hosea's prophecy.[100] The Gospel states, *Theos ēn ho logos... ho logos sarx egeneto*, "the Word was God... the Word became flesh" (1:1, 14) to have a case (*krisis*, cf. 3:19; 5:22, 24, 27, 29f; 7:24; 8:16; 12:31; 16:8, 11) against Israel, the inhabitants of the land. The Word incarnate urges, "he who hears [*akouōn*] My word [*logon*] ... does not come into judgment [*krisin*]" (5:24). The Word restores ḥesed and ʾĕmet of God in the land: *hē charis kai hē alētheia dia Iēsou Christou egeneto*, "grace and truth were realized through Jesus Christ" (1:17). The Word restores the knowledge of God in the land: *monogenēs Theos ho ōn eis ton kolpon tou patros ekeinos exēgēsato*, "the only begotten God who is in the bosom of the Father, He has explained *Him*." (1:18). Third, David[101] prayed, "O God, in the greatness of Your ḥesed, Answer me with Your saving ʾĕmet" (Ps 69:14). The Psalmist[102] showed his trust by writing, "He will send from heaven and save [OG: *esōsen*] me; He reproaches him who tramples upon me. God will send forth His ḥesed and His ʾĕmet" (Ps 57:4). The Lord declared, "I have found David My servant ... My ʾĕmûnāʰ and My ḥesed will be with him" (Ps 89:25).[103] This appeal for salvation through sending ḥesed and ʾĕmet had further been viewed as an accomplished act: *exapesteilen ex ouranou kai esōsen me ... exapesteilen ho Theos to eleos autou kai tēn alētheian autou*, "He sent from heaven and saved me; ... God has sent forth his mercy and his truth" (Ps 56:4 OG). This concept may have been echoed in the Gospel, with its emphasis on Jesus the Savior[104] being *plērēs charitos*

---

100. The Evangelist may well have been aware of Hosea's writings (cf. John 5:21 and Hos 6:2). See NA²⁷, *Appendix IV: Loci citati vel allegati*, 770–806.

101. David is remarkably associated with God's ḥesed weʾĕmet elsewhere. Daly-Denton has argued from the Jewish tendency to draw comparisons between Moses and David, and concluded, "If Jesus was to replace Moses, he would do so as 'David'" (Daly-Denton, *David*, 101).

102. Ps 57:4. The Evangelist is certainly familiar with the Psalms; see NA²⁷, *Appendix IV: Loci citati vel allegati*, 770–806.

103. Notably, this OT covenant is perceived as messianic at the time of the Evangelist; cf. Luke 1:68–69. See Nolland, *Luke* 1:1—9:20, 91–93.

104. Jesus is *alēthōs ho sōtēr tou kosmou*, "indeed the Savior of the world" (4:42). Cf. the very meaning of the name *Iēsous*, "Jesus," being "YHWH is salvation" or "YHWH saves/has saved" (Meyer, "Jesus"). Notice the terminology and phraseology of *anistēmi*, "raise up"; *apothnēskō*, "die"; *zaō*, "live"; *egeirō*, "raise up"; *zōopoieō*, "give life"; *sōzō*, "save"; *hē aiōnios zōē*, "the eternal life"; *en tē eschatē hēmera*, "in the last day"; *ek nekrōn*, "from the dead"; and similar examples widely utilized in the Gospel.

kai alētheias, "full of grace and truth" sent[105] from heaven[106] by God.[107] Fourth, Heman the Ezrahite enquired of the Lord, "Will Your *ḥesed* be declared in the grave, Your *'ĕmûnāʰ* in Abaddon?" (Ps 88:12) or "Shall anyone declare thy mercy in the tomb? and thy truth in destruction?"[108] (Ps 87:12 OG/LXE). The Gospel may have echoed this motif by answering the question affirmatively: Yes, there is One; God's (*hē*) *charis kai* (*hē*) *alētheia* have been declared by Jesus, so exactly in the tomb! Jesus is risen[109] and ascends to the heavens,[110] going to the Father.[111] This might have echoed numerous OT references linking *ḥesed weʾĕmet* with the heavenly realm, particularly those that report of establishing *ḥesed weʾĕmet* in the heavens/skies/clouds.[112] Ultimately, the prophecy "By *ḥesed* and *'ĕmet* iniquity is atoned for" (Prov 16:6) comes true in Jesus, "the Lamb of God who takes away the sin of the world" (1:29).

Moreover, there may be echoes of *ḥesed* and *'ĕmet*, qualities of the divine character, perfectly revealed in Jesus in the Gospel. First, the wise contemplated, "Will they not go astray [OG: *planōmenoi*] who devise evil? But *ḥesed* and *'ĕmet will be to* those who devise good [OG: *agathois*]."[113] The Evangelist reports, "There was much grumbling

---

105. Cf. cognates of *apostellō*, "send"; *pempō*, "send"; etc. Notice the comment in the charge, "*hupage nipsai eis tēn kolumbēthran tou Silōam*" [*ho hermēneuetai apestalmenos*], "'Go, wash in the pool of Siloam' (which is translated, Sent)" (9:7). Cf. the phraseology *ho ōn para tou Theou*, "the One who is from God," (6:46 and alike); *ho christos ho huios tou Theou ho eis ton kosmon erchomenos*, "the Christ, the Son of God, even He who comes into the world," (11:27 and alike).

106. Cf. the terminology of *ouranos*, "heaven"; *katabainō*, "go down"; *anō*, "above"; etc.

107. Consider for example 6:38–39.

108. The OG translates *'ăbaddôn* with *apōleia*. The Evangelist is aware of the term *apōleia* (17:12).

109. Notice the appeal "Rise up, be our help, And redeem us for the sake of Your *ḥesed*" (Ps 44:27) translated as "Arise [*anasta*], O Lord, help us, and redeem us for thy name's [*onomatos*] sake" (Ps 43:27 OG). Jesus is risen (*anistēmi*, 20:9) from the dead and, being the resurrection (*anastasis*, 11:25, cf. 5:29, 11:24) himself, is to raise up (*anistēmi*, 6:39, 40, 44, 54; 11:23, 24) others from the dead.

110. 6:62; 20:17. Of course, Jesus comes from the heavens and speaks of the heavenly realm much in terms of *anabainō/katabainō*, "go down/go up"; *anō*, "above"; *anōthen*, "from above"; *ouranos*, "heaven."

111. 14:12, 28; 16:5, 10, 17, 28; 17:11, 13.

112. Ps 36:6; 57:4, 11; 89:3. Cf. 1 Kgs 8:23; Neh 1:5; 2 Chr 6:14; Pss 103:11; 136:5, 26.

113. Prov 14:22. The Evangelist may well have been aware of the book of Proverbs (cf. John/Prov 1:2/8:22f.; 3:13/30:4; 7:34/1:28; 7:38/18:4; 9:31/15:8, 29; 14:23/8:17;

among the crowds concerning Him; some were saying, 'He is a good [*agathos*] man,' others said, 'No, he is leading the people astray [*plana*]'" (7:12). Thus, those who say Jesus is a good man may have implicitly echoed the Divine qualities of *ḥesed* and *ʾĕmet* as inherent in Christ's character.[114] Second, David responded to God, "Your *ḥesed* is before my eyes, And I have walked in Your *ʾĕmet*" (Ps 26:3, etc.). God's *ḥesed* and *ʾĕmet* bestowed upon David, the paradigmatic king, may well have been discerned as naturally inherent to Jesus, the ultimate king.

Furthermore, the concept of *ḥesed weʾĕmet/hē charis kai hē alētheia* may have been echoed in the settings of Jesus's teaching. On the one hand, there are public settings for teaching. David testified, "I have not hidden [OG: *ekrupsa*] Your righteousness[115] within my heart; I have spoken of Your *ʾĕmûnāh* and Your salvation[116]; I have not concealed [OG: *ekrupsa*] Your *ḥesed*[117] and Your *ʾĕmet* from the great congregation [OG: *sunagōgēs*]"[118] (Ps 40:11). Jesus, when being questioned by the high priest with regard to his disciples and teaching, replies, "I have spoken openly to the world; I always taught in synagogues[119] [*sunagōgē*[120]] and in the temple,[121] where all the Jews come together;[122] and I spoke nothing in secret [*kruptō*]" (18:20). Noticeably, the terms *kruptos* and *kruptō*[123] are employed where Jesus has either just spoken

---

17:12/24:22a); see NA[27], *Appendix IV: Loci citati vel allegati*, 770–806.

114. Cf. also Ps 44:3 OG; Prov 10:32 OG.

115. *ṣədāqāh*/*dikaiosunē*. Notice Jesus's appeal *pater dikaie*, "righteous Father," (17:25).

116. *tašûʿāh*/*sōtērion*. Notice the usage of terms *sōtēria*, "salvation," (4:22) and *sōtēr*, "Savior," (4:42).

117. OG *eleos*/Symmachus *charis* (as attested by Nobil.; see Field, *Jobus–Malachias*, 151). Cambridge LXX, *1 Chronicle – Tobit*, and GLXX, *Psalmi cum Odis*, do not mention the case.

118. Ps 40:11. Notice also the immediately following "You, O Lord, will not withhold Your compassion from me; Your *ḥesed* [OG *eleos*/Symmachus *charis*] and Your truth *ʾĕmet* will continually preserve me" (Ps 40:12).

119. NASB has "synagogues."

120. A true statement, see 6:59.

121. A true statement, see 2:14, 15f.; 5:14, especially 7:14, 28; 8:2, 20, 59; 10:23f., etc.

122. A true statement, see such designations as *ochlos polus ek tōn Ioudaiōn*, "large crowd of the Jews" (12:9, etc.).

123. The terminology of *kruptos*, "secret," such as in the phrase *en kruptō*, "in secret," (7:4, 10; 18:20) is a characteristic feature of the Evangelist's literary style. See position 201/416 of Boismard, Lamouille, and Rochais, *L'évangile de Jean*, in alphabetical rear-

The Covenant of the Presence of God 203

or is about to speak to a large group. The Evangelist generally relates these terms to Jesus's teaching.[124] On the other hand, there are private settings for teaching. David recognized, "All the paths of the Lord are *ḥesed* and *ʾĕmet* To those who keep His covenant and His testimonies" (Ps 25:10, etc.). Jesus exhorts, "If you love Me, you will keep My commandments" (14:15), and continues, "He who has My commandments and keeps them is the one who loves Me; and he who loves Me will be loved by My Father, and I will love him and will disclose[125] Myself to him" (14:21; 15:10, 12, 14, 17).[126]

Whatever the case may be with the echoes listed above, they are merely suggestive observations. They do stem from the Sinaitic covenant, though. And, as we have established, the Evangelist does *allude* to the Sinaitic covenant with *plērēs charitos kai alētheias . . . hē charis kai hē alētheia* (qualities of the character of God), and further *throughout* the Gospel.

The Presence of God is Incessant—*charin anti charitos*—to Believers

We argue[127] that the presence of God is conceptually attested in the Gospel with reference to the covenant of *charis*. The *subject* of the covenant of *charis* is the very presence of God (Exod 33:12—34:10 LXX).

---

rangement of 416 characteristics by Neirynck, *Jean et les Synoptiques*, 45–66; position B52 in Ruckstuhl and Dschulnigg, *Stilkritik und Verfasserfrage*. For a correlation of the lists see Belle, *Signs Source*, 411, 418–20.

124. The world/feast (7:4, 10); the temple (8:59); the world/crowd (12:19, 29, 34, 36); cf. 19:38.

125. *emphanizō*; cf. the Sinaitic covenant's *emphanison moi seauton*, "reveal Yourself to me" (Exod 33:13 LXX).

126. Also, on the relevance of the Wisdom literature, see Witherington, *John's Wisdom*.

127. The Gospel attests to the presence of God in other numerous ways. The Evangelist declares *Theos ēn ho logos . . . kai ho logos sarx egeneto*, "the Word was God . . . and the Word became flesh," (1:1, 14) and depicts Jesus as *monogenēs Theos*, "the only begotten God" (1:18). Jesus's *egō eimi*, "I am" (cf. 8:58 and Exod 3:14; Isa 43:10); *egō kai ho patēr hen esmen*, "I and the Father are one" (10:30); *ho heōrakōs eme heōraken ton patera*, "he who has seen Me has seen the Father," (14:9) sayings (cf. 5:18; 10:33) and Thomas's recognition of Jesus as *ho kurios mou kai ho Theos mou*, "my Lord and my God," (20:28) serve the same purpose. The Spirit (4:24), the Wisdom, the Revealer (1:18; 6:46; 14:9), and the Son of Man (1:47–51; 3:12–13; 6:60–62) aspects of the Gospel contribute to the case.

The *ratification* of the covenant of *charis* is prescribed by the articles of the covenant preserved in its *charis* cluster (Exod 33:12, 13, 13, 16, 17; 34:9-10 LXX). The prologue introduces the *subject*: the presence of God is incessant—*charin anti charitos*.

Subject of the Covenant of *charis*—the Presence of God among People

According to the covenant of *charis*,[128] God's *charis* is his gracious presence. Prior to the covenant of *charis*, the people observed the presence of God on Mount Sinai but could not approach it safely (Exod 19:12-23; 24:1-2, 17). Later the people failed God (Exod 32:1f.). Moses tried to make an appeal on behalf of the people, but the Lord objected, "let Me alone, that My anger may burn against them and that I may destroy them; and I will make of you a great nation" (Exod 32:10). At Moses's plea, the Lord changed his mind about doing harm to his people (Exod 32:14), but did withdraw his presence (Exod 32:34—33:3) and notified the nation, "I will not go up in your midst, because you are an obstinate people, and I might destroy you on the way" (Exod 33:3, 5). The glory of the Lord moved outside of the camp (Exod 33:7-11). Moses interceded on behalf of the people, asking for the presence of God to return (Exod 33:12—33:9). This request was granted; the Lord made his presence dwell among the people. As the Lord ratified the covenant of *charis* with the nation (Exod 34:10f.), the cloud covered the tent of meeting, and the glory of the Lord filled the tabernacle (Exod 40:34-35). Later on, God became flesh and *eskēnōsen*, "tabernacled," among believers (1:1, 14). The prologue introduces the subject of the covenant of *charis*. The presence of God is incessant—*charin anti charitos*.

Ratification of the Covenant of *charis*

The ratification of the covenant of *charis* is prescribed by the articles of the paradigmatic Sinaitic covenant as preserved by its *charis* cluster (Exod 33:12, 13, 13, 16, 17; 34:9-10). The whole Gospel attests to the *ratification* of the covenant of *charis* conducted in full accord with the articles of the covenant. To demonstrate this we will compare articles of the Sinaitic paradigmatic covenant of *charis* with the account of the Gospel.

---

128. Originated at Sinai, see Exod 33:12—34:10.

God's *charis* Experienced

According to the Sinaitic covenant, God's *charis* is experienced when God leads his people (Exod 33:12 LXX; cf. 33:15), gives them rest (Exod 33:14 LXX), and goes before (Exod 33:14 LXX; cf. 34:15) and with (Exod 33:16 LXX) them; God is present in grace, not in wrath (cf. Exod 33:3 LXX). So Moses pleads with the Lord,

> Lo! thou sayest to me, Lead on [*anagage*] this people; but thou hast not shewed me whom thou wilt send with me, but thou hast said to me, . . . thou hast grace [*charin*] with me (Exod 33:12 LXE).

This is not actually a request for guidance. Guidance had already been promised (Exod 33:2 LXX). The real question is whether God will lead the people himself.[129] Crucially, Moses seeks God to be present in *grace*, rather than in wrath—which is the reason God had said he would not go up with the people (Exod 33:3 LXX). Hence, the Lord's leading of the people is a feature characteristic of his *charis*. This becomes clearer as Moses further persuades Yahweh. God promises to give relief to Moses personally: "I myself will go before [*proporeusomai*] thee, and give thee rest." Moses, though, identifies himself with the nation: "If thou go not up [*poreuē*] with us thyself, bring me not up [*anagagēs*] hence" (Exod 33:15 LXX). His major concern is the presence of God among all the people, as he presses on, "how shall it be surely known, that both I and this people have found grace [*charin*] with thee, except only if thou go [*sumporeuomenou*] with us?" (Exod 33:16 LXX). The Lord agrees, "I will also do for thee this thing, which thou hast spoken; for thou hast found grace [*charin*] before me" (Exod 33:17 LXX). Moses again seeks to confirm this later: "If I have found grace [*charin*] before thee, let my Lord go [*sumporeuthētō*] with us" (Exod 34:9 LXX). This dialogue's emphasis on *anagō*, *proporeuomai*, *poreuomai*, *sumporeuomai* (Exod 33:14–16;

---

129. Durham (who comments on the Hebrew text) evaluates, "Moses is represented raising the question by asking who is to go with him and with Israel . . . . The real question, of course, is the continuation of Yahweh's Presence with Israel, . . . when Yahweh . . . promises after all that he *will* go, Moses blurts out in a flood of relief, this real concern" (Durham, *Exodus*, 448). Wevers (who interprets the Greek text) agrees: "This was merely a bargaining ploy, since Moses was not really interested in having God's messenger pointed out to him; he wanted God himself to accompany the people" (Wevers, *Notes*, 547).

34:9 LXX) makes clear that God's *charis* is at work when he graciously goes before and with the people himself.

This notion of God leading people, going before and with them, is echoed in the Gospel. The Son goes [*poreuomai*] to the Father before the disciples (14:2-4). Jesus is the Good Shepherd, who calls his "own sheep by name and leads them out [*exagei*].... goes ahead [*poreuetai*] of them," and who discloses, "I have other sheep . . . I must bring [*agagein*] them also" (10:1-16). Hence, the Gospel attests to the presence (*charis*) of God among the people.

God's *charis* Attested

According to the Sinaitic covenant, God's *charis* is attested when he reveals himself so that he may be evidently known/seen (Exod 33:13; cf. Exod 33:18—34:7 LXX), when he lets people know his ways so that they may know him (Exod 33:13 LXX), and when God manifests his *doxa* (Exod 33:18—34:10 LXX).

The Sinaitic stipulation "If then I have found grace [*charin*] in Your sight, reveal Yourself to me [*emphanison moi seauton*]" (Exod 33:13 LXX) is met in the Gospel precisely. The Sinaitic covenant of *charis* interrelates the revelation of various facets of the presence of God—the visible appearance (*doxa*), intrinsic character (*doxa*), and miraculous splendor (*endoxa . . . ta erga kuriou . . . thaumasta*) (Exod 33:12—34:10 LXX). These connotations of the revelation are interrelated in the covenant of *charis* reinforced in Jesus. The Gospel reserves cognates of *phaneroō*, "reveal," exclusively for this purpose of depicting the revelation of the visible appearance, the intrinsic character (1:31; 2:11; 14:21-22; 17:6; 21:1-14; 17:6) and the miraculous splendor (1:5 and 3:21; 2:11; 7:3-4; 9:3) of the Divine.[130]

According to the covenant of *charis*, this revelation should be of a certain kind. There are three major variants—one in Hebrew and two in Greek—for this article of the Sinaitic covenant of *charis*:[131] 1) the Hebrew variant reads, *hôdīʿēnî nāʾ ʾet-dərākekā wəʾēdāʿăkā*, "let me

---

130. Remarkably, in the book of Exodus cognates of *phaneroō*, "reveal," are utilized only twice (with the reference to the divine cf. Exod 33:13 and John 1:5, 31; 2:11; 3:21; 7:4; 9:3; 14:21, 22; 17:6; 21:1, 14; with the reference to the lamp cf. Exod 25:37 with John 5:35).

131. Exod 33:13. See GLXX, *Exodus*, 370-71.

know Your ways that I may know You"; 2) a majority variant reads, *emphanison moi seauton gnōstōs idō se*, "reveal Yourself to me so that I may evidently see you";[132] and 3) the Göttingen LXX constructs[133] the critical[134] reading *emphanison moi seauton gnōstōs eidō se*, "reveal Yourself to me so that I may evidently know you."[135] The Gospel attests to God's *charis* according to all the three readings of the article. To reflect the Göttingen LXX variant's *gnōstōs eidō*, the Gospel greatly

132. Rahlfs's LXX follows this variant.

133. Basically, on the basis of the reading preserved in the MT. Wevers—the editor of GLXX, Exodus— recognizes that "a majority itacistic variant reads *idō*, but only *eidō* can be Exod in view of MT's *ʾdʿ*" with the reference "as convincingly argued by Walters, *Text of the Septuagint*, 199f. See the discussion in THGE VII.O" (Wevers, *Notes*, 548 n. 12). In the THGE (*Text History of the Greek Exodus*) Wevers reasons, "Walters (199f) is certainly correct in insisting that *eidō* is the correct spelling of the original text, since the Hebrew has *wʾdʿkā*, and not the verb *rʾeʰ*, which the itacistic variant *idō* would presuppose. When the variant *id*— v. *eid*— is at stake the Hebrew is usually decisive. It is, however, not automatic since in some contexts "to see" and "to know" are both possible interpretations. Here *eidō* can only represent the subjunctive of *oida*, whereas *idō* can only be the aorist subjunctive of *horaō*, and the former alone can correctly render *ʾdʿ*" (Wevers, *Text History*, 269). Peter Walters only observes, "Exod. 33:13, *wəʾēdāʿăkā*, *that I may know thee* (AV), reads *gnōstōs idō se* in our editions; but Fo (*eidōs*) pra2 *eidō*, confirmed by *ut noscam* Arm. and the conflation *et noscam et vidam*, Eth., is the correct reading, which moreover is supported by Gen. 2:9 . . . Mal. 3:18 . . . Isa. 26:11" (Walters [Katz], *Text of the Septuagint*, 199f.).

134. In our view, Wevers's decision over this matter is misleading from the standpoint of reconstructing the critical text. A majority variant does read *idō*; hence the *idō* reading is textually attested no less, if not more, than *eidō*. Under the circumstance, while reconstructing the critical text the governing issue must be not "how the interpreter should have correctly translated the parent text" but "how one chooses among extant variants of the text." When it comes to choosing between *idō* and *eidō* for *wəʾēdāʿăkā*, the criteria of "the more difficult reading" should prevail and *idō* should be chosen.

135. Arguing the case for a particular variant, which the Evangelist utilized, is not a viable option. In our view, the Evangelist may well have been acquainted with all the three readings: First, since the Evangelist *translates wərab-ḥesed weʾĕmet* of Exod 34:6 with *(hē) charis kai (hē) alētheia*, it is likely that the writer is *acquainted* with the Hebrew text of Exod 33:12—34:10, the context of the creed. Second, since both *idō* and *eidō* variants are widely attested then both may have been available to the Evangelist. Third, the *et noscam et videam Aeth* conflated reading suggests that the presence of both *idō* and *eidō* variants had been recognized; perhaps, a similar conflated reading was available to the Evangelist. Fourth, the three readings may well be conflated in the Gospel itself: 14:5-9 remarkably mixes these Sinaitic variants of reading while linking them with the disciples' request *deixon hēmin ton patera*, "manifest us the Father," yet another allusion to the Sinaitic covenantal appeal made by Moses, *Deixon moi tēn seautou doxan*, "Manifest Your glory to me" (Exod 33:18 GLXX). Cf. 14:5-17; 19-31.

emphasizes the matter of *knowing* the Divine (cf. 1:10, 1:26; 3:2; 4:22, 32; 5:13; 6:42, 69; 7:17, 26–27, 28; 7:51; 8: 14, 19, 28–32, 55; 9:24, 29, 30; 10:4–5, 14–15, 38; 11:42; 12:35, 50; 15:15, 21; 16:3, 30; 17:3–26; notice also the progression from "not knowing" to "knowing" in 1:31–33; 5:13; 9:12, 21, 25, 31; 11:49–51; 20:9, 14; 21:4, 12). To account for the majority variant's *gnōstōs idō*, the prominence of *seeing* Jesus in the Gospel is enormous (1:14, 18, 46; 6:36; 9:37; 12:21; 19:37; 16:16, 17–19; 19:35; 20:18; 20:20, 25, 27–29). To correspond the Hebrew text's *hôdīʿēnî nā' ʾet-dərākekā wəʾēdāʿăkā*, "the way" is a major concept of the Gospel (1:23; 14:4–6; cf. 10:1).

The request "reveal Yourself to me so that I may evidently *know/see* you," designed to attest to God's *charis*, actually deals with two facets of the presence of God: *knowing* the intrinsic character (*doxa*) of God and *seeing* the visible appearance (*doxa*) of God. So, as soon as God agrees (Exod 33:13–17) to fulfill Moses's appeal to evidently know/see him, the man wishes to have an immediate demonstration of both of these components. Moses requests, *Deixon moi tēn seautou doxan*, "Manifest Your glory to me" (Exod 33:18). Yahweh allows Moses to access both dimensions of his presence, but with reservations: he may observe the appearance (*doxa*) of God only from the back, and only hear of his intrinsic character (*doxa*). The Lord promises, "I will pass by before thee my glory [*tē doxē mou*],[136] and I will call by my name, the Lord, before thee; and I will have mercy on whom I will have mercy, and will have pity on whom I will have pity" (Exod 33:19 LXE). Precautions are taken not to overexpose Moses to the presence of God. He *sees* the visible appearance (*doxa*) of God from behind and gets to *know* the intrinsic character (*doxa*) of God *rab-ḥesed weʾĕmet* (Exod 34:6). Immediately after, God promises that Moses will *see* his miraculous splendor (*endoxa = ta erga kuriou hoti thaumasta estin*, Exod 34:10 LXX).

The Sinaitic stipulation "If then I have found grace [*charin*] in Your sight, ... Manifest Your glory to me [*Deixon moi tēn seautou doxan*]" (Exod 33:13–18 LXX) is met in the Gospel precisely. As the Sinaitic covenant of *charis* interrelates the manifestation of various facets of the presence of God—his visible appearance, intrinsic character, and

---

136. This shift from visible appearance to qualities of the character is even more evident in the Hebrew text; to Moses's "I pray You, show me Your glory [*kābôd*]!" Yahweh responds, "I Myself will make all My goodness [*ṭôb/doxa*] pass before you" (Exod 33:19).

miraculous splendor (*endoxa . . . ta erga kuriou . . . thaumasta*, Exod 33:12—34:10 LXX)—so the Gospel utilizes cognates of *deiknumi*,[137] "manifest," exclusively for the purpose of depicting the manifestation of the visible appearance (14:8–9; 20:20), intrinsic character (13:15; 14:8–9) and miraculous splendor (2:18 cf. 20:20; 5:20; 10:32)[138] of the Divine.

Moses's requests made at Sinai to attest to the presence (*charis*) of God—*emphanison moi seauton gnōstōs (e)idō se*, "reveal Yourself to me so that I may evidently know/see you," and *Deixon moi tēn seautou doxan*, "Manifest Your glory to me"—blend naturally. This blend of seeing God and knowing God's character is concisely introduced in the prologue (1:14).[139]

These Sinaitic attestations to the presence (*charis*) of God—*hôdīʿēnî nāʾ ʾet-dərākekā wəʾēdāʿăkā, gnōstōs eidō, gnōstōs idō, Deixon moi tēn seautou doxan*—are evident in the Gospel's blend of the terms *hodos*, "way"; *ginōskō*, "know"; *oida*, "know"; *horaō*, "see"; and *deiknumi*, "manifest." Consider, particularly,[140] the "Way to the Father" narrative (14:5–9): Jesus exhorts, "you know the way [*oidate tēn hodon*] where I am going." Thomas doubts, "Lord, we do not know [*ouk oidamen*] where You are going, how do we know the way [*tēn hodon eidenai*]?" Jesus answers, "I am the way [*egō eimi hē hodos*], . . . no one comes to the Father but through Me." He further explains, "If you had known [*egnōkate*] Me, you would have known [*gnōsesthe*] My Father also; from now on you know [*ginōskete*] Him, and have seen [*heōrakate*] Him" (14:7). To Philip's immediate request, "Lord, manifest [*deixon*] us the Father,"[141] Jesus replies, "Have I been so long with you, and *yet* you have not come to know [*egnōkas*] Me, Philip? He who has seen Me has seen the Father [*heōrakōs eme heōraken ton patera*]; how can you say, 'Manifest [*deixon*][142] us the Father'?" (14:5–9).

---

137. In the book of Exodus the verb *deiknumi* is used only to depict the divine activity of Yahweh (Exod 13:21; 15:25; 25:9, 40; 26:30; 33:5, 18). Similarly, in the Gospel the verb is employed exclusively of either God the Father or Jesus the Son.

138. Notice the language of the Gospel matching the Sinaitic *endoxa . . . ta erga kuriou . . . thaumasta* (Exod 34:10).

139. See our discussion over the usage of the term *doxa* in the Gospel.

140. See also 3:11; 14:17; 14:19–31.

141. Cf. *Deixon moi tēn seautou doxan* (Exod 33:18 GLXX).

142. NASB renders "show" for "*deixon*."

Hence the Gospel, read against the Sinaitic *emphanison moi seauton gnōstōs (e)idō se (hôdīʿēnî nāʾ ʾet-dərākekā wəʾēdāʿăkā) . . . Deixon moi tēn seautou doxan*, makes it clear that whoever has seen and known Jesus the Way has experienced the presence (*charis*) of God.

God's *charis* at Work

According to the Sinaitic covenant, God's *charis* is at work when his people are glorified beyond all the nations, as many as are upon the earth (Exod 33:16 LXX); this great nation remains God's people (Exod 33:13, cf. 34:9 LXX). Moses defines his request to God: "that I may find grace [*charin*] in thy sight, and that I may know that this great nation *is* thy people [*laos sou to ethnos to mega touto*] (Exod 33:13 LXX). In the Gospel, the terms *laos* (11:50; 18:14) and *ethnos* (11:48, 50, 51, 52; 18:35) are used only of Jews. Christ, by teaching Jews and dying for Jews (11:45–50; 18:14)—his own nation—evinces God's *charis*.

Moses wishes to have yet another indication of the presence (*charis*) of God when he asks, "how shall it be surely known, that both I and this people have grace [*charin*] with thee . . . So both I and thy people shall be glorified beyond all the nations, as many as are upon the earth [*endoxasthēsomai*[143] *egō te kai ho laos sou para panta ta ethnē hosa epi tēs gēs estin*]?" (Exod 33:16 LXE). Moses (Exod 34:29–35 LXX; Sir 45:1–3) and the people of God were honored at Sinai and in the course of the conquest of Canaan. This sign of God's *charis* is evident in the Gospel. Moses *is* depicted in exalted terms. God spoke to Moses (9:29), the Law was given through Moses (1:17; 7:19, 22, 23, cf. 8:5), and he is given the position of accusing violators of the Law before the Father (5:45). In the Scripture, Moses wrote of Jesus (1:45; 5:46). In "the serpent in the wilderness" (3:14f.) and "the bread out of heaven" (6:30–35) episodes, Moses is narrated as the predecessor of the saving activity of God in Jesus.

Jews *are* glorified in the Gospel. Isaiah, an Israelite, has been privileged to see God's glory (12:41). It is likely Jews among whom the Word become flesh dwells, who see his glory, glory as of the only begotten from the Father (1:14). It is to Jews that Jesus manifests his glory when he performs the sign of turning the water into wine at a *Jewish* wedding in the *Jewish* city of Cana of Galilee (2:11). It is Jews who see the glory

---

143. MT reads *wəniplênû*, "may be distinguished."

of God when Jesus raises Lazarus from the dead in the vicinity of the *Jewish* village of Bethany nearby Jerusalem (11:40). It is likely Jews that Jesus has been glorified in (17:10), and to whom the glory of the Father has been given (17:22). It is Jews who first see Jesus glorified after the resurrection and who first receive the Spirit. It is Jews who by receiving the Holy Spirit of *(hē) charis kai (hē) alētheia* gain the intrinsic character (*doxa*) of God, which makes them ultimately glorified. It is the Jews on whom Jesus bestows the privilege of hearing his interpretation of the Law (20:23). The Jews *are* narrated as the legitimate mediator of blessing for all the nations, which the Samaritan woman represents[144] (4:22). The Greeks, representing all the nations,[145] are among those who were going up to worship at the Jewish feast of the Passover (12:20). Hence, by depicting Moses and the Jews as glorified beyond all the nations,[146] the Gospel testifies to the vivid reality of God's *charis*.

Moses seeks yet another confirmation of the Lord's *charis* when he enquires, "If I have found grace [*charin*] before thee . . . we will be thine [*esometha soi*]" (Exod 34:9 LXX). The Gospel meets this expectation as well. The true Light comes to his own (1:11). Jesus acknowledges that Galilee is his own country (4:44). The Good Shepherd refers to the Jews as *ta idia* (10:3, 4, 12; 13:1; cf. 15:9) or *ta ema* (10:14; 27). Hence, God's presence (*charis*) is evident in the fact that the Jews remain God's people.

God's *charis* Encountered and Evinced

According to the Sinaitic covenant, God's *charis* is encountered when he takes away the sins and iniquities of the people (Exod 34:9 LXX). Moses makes his final request to ensure the reality of God's *charis*: "If I have found grace [*charin*] before thee . . . thou shalt take away our sins and our iniquities [*apheleis su tas hamartias hēmōn kai tas anomias hēmōn*]" (Exod 34:9 LXX). To this Yahweh agrees:

> Behold, I establish a covenant for thee in the presence of all thy people; I will do glorious things [*endoxa*], which have not been

---

144. Jews perceived Samaritans as a mixed race settled in the northern kingdom by the king of Assyria (2 Kgs 17:24–41).

145. See Windisch, "*Hellēn*," 2:509–10.

146. For a contemporary interpretation of the Gospel as favorable toward Jews see Motyer, *Your Father the Devil?*

done in all the earth, or in any nation; and all the people among whom thou art shall see the works of the Lord, that they are marvelous [*ta erga kuriou hoti thaumasta estin*] which I will do for thee.[147]

The Gospel evinces this indication of the presence (*charis*) of God. Jesus takes away "the sin [*hamartian*] of the world" (1:29). The disciples are clean (13:10–11; 15:3) and granted the right to take away the sins of others (20:23). Since the sins and iniquities of believers are taken away, they experience the presence (*charis*) of God.

We further argue that the Gospel's signs (*sēmeia*), works (*erga*),[148] wonders (*terata*),[149] and marvels (*thaumasta*)[150] serve the purpose of certifying the ratification of the covenant of *charis* in Jesus and in the Spirit.[151]

First, the ratification of the Sinaitic covenant of *charis* serves the purpose of ensuring the presence—visible appearance (*doxa*) and in-

---

147. Exod 34:10 LXE (modified, as *thaumasta* is translated "marvelous").

148. In the whole book of Exodus marvelous *erga* are mentioned only once, exactly under the rubrics of the Sinaitic covenant of *charis* (*ta erga kuriou hoti thaumasta estin*). The *erga* of the Lord clearly play a key role in the Gospel. This peculiar positioning of *erga* would draw the attention of the audience exactly to the Sinaitic covenant of *charis*.

149. The terms *sēmeion* and *teras* are not employed immediately in Exod 33:12—34:10, but, when utilized to denote wondrous deeds of *God*, the terms *sēmeia* and *terata* are virtually indistinguishable from each other. They are often paired and frequently stand as a pair for a single parent Hebrew term (cf. Exod 7:3; 9; 11:9, 10; etc.). The terms *doxa* and *sēmeia* of God also come together (Num 14:22). The covenantal *endoxa* renders *niplāʾōt* at Exod 34:10. But elsewhere, *plʾ*, "be surpassing, extraordinary," is translated with cognates of *thaumastoō* (Exod 3:20; 15:20; etc.), *doxazō* (Exod 34:10; 2 Chr 2:8; Job 9:10; Deut 28:59), and *teras* (Isa 28:29). Likely, the writer of the book of Exodus covers such wondrous deeds of the Lord—*sēmeia, erga, terata, endoxa, thaumasta*—with the overarching *endoxa . . . ta erga kuriou . . . thaumasta* in Exod 34:10. The major point in ratification of the covenant of *charis* is that these *endoxa . . . ta erga kuriou . . . thaumasta* are to be incomparable, and this requirement is certainly met in Jesus performing *sēmeia, erga, terata, thaumasta* in the Gospel.

150. God's *thaumasta* have often been related to God's *ḥesed* (Pss 17:7; 31:22; 106:7; 107:8, 15, 21, 31; Mic 7:15). The *endoxa* have been recalled since the Sinaitic covenant (Deut 10:21; Isa 12:4; 48:9; 64:3; cf. Jdt 16:13, Job 5:9; 9:10; notice Luke 13:17). This may have reminded the Gospel's audience of the Sinaitic covenant link between *ta erga kuriou hoti thaumasta estin* and *charis*.

151. The Sinaitic article on ratification of the covenant of *charis* was put into the future tense. The article was originally ratified in the conquest of Canaan. But the future tense of the article would also allow one to apply it to ratification of the covenant of *charis* in Jesus.

trinsic character (*doxa*)—of God among the people. Likewise, Jesus's first miracle sets the paradigm for the whole Gospel: signs/works/wonders/marvels serve the purpose of certifying the presence of God as Jesus among the people. Jesus "manifested His glory [*doxan*] and His disciples believed in Him" (2:11).

Second, as prescribed by the Exod 34:10 article of the paradigmatic Sinaitic covenant, the incomparable signs/works/wonders/marvels are performed in the Gospel in the presence of the Jews—Jesus's own people.

Third, in the course of setting the paradigm for the covenant of *charis* at Sinai,[152] the Lord declares, "I will do glorious things [*endoxa*], which have not been done in all the earth, or in any nation" (Exod 34:10 LXX). The very *incomparability* of the signs/works/wonders/marvels depicted in the Gospel attests to ratification of the covenant of *charis*.

Fourth, with reference to the incomparable *endoxa . . . ta erga kuriou hoti thaumasta* of Exod 34:10, the ratification of the covenant of *charis* in Jesus is evident in the Gospel's peculiar usage of cognates of *thaumazō*,[153] "marvel." Jesus speaks of things previously unheard and does things that no one has ever done before; this causes participants to marvel (3:7; 4:27; 5:28; 7:15). Other covenantal themes and the relevant terminology often blend in with the usage of cognates of *thaumazō*. Jesus challenges a crowd of the Jews[154] in the temple using the very terms of the covenant of *charis*: "I did one deed [*ergon*], and you all marvel [*thaumazete*]" (7:21). He points out, "the Father loves the Son, and manifests [*deiknusin*] Him all things that He Himself is doing; and *the Father* will manifest [*deixei*][155] Him greater works [*erga*] than these, so that you will marvel [*thaumazēte*]" (5:20). The man who received his sight amply summarizes it all when he challenges the Jews, "here is

---

152. Remarkably, when Moses was performing miracles in Egypt—turning staff into serpent, turning water into blood; covering up the land with frogs—the magicians, or the wise men and the sorcerers, still did the same with their secret arts (Exod 7:12, 22; 8:7).

153. Cognates of plʾ/*thaumastoō* occur with the reference to creedal qualities of God's character ʾĕmûnāʰ ʾōmen, "perfect integrity" (Isa 25:1); rōb ḥăsādeʸkā, "Your abundant grace" (Ps 106:7); hasdô, "His grace" (Ps 136:4); hannûn wəraḥûm, "gracious and compassionate" (Ps 111:4).

154. Over the healing of a cripple on a Sabbath, an unheard of thing to do (5:1–9, 10–18).

155. NASB has "shows."

a marvelous[156] thing [*thaumaston*], that you do not know where He is from, and *yet* He opened my eyes.... Since the beginning of time it has never been heard that anyone opened the eyes of a person born blind" (9:30–32). This marvelous thing (*thaumastos*),[157] within the framework of such incomparable manifestations, attests to Jesus's ratifying of the covenant of *charis*.

Fifth, the ratification of the covenant of *charis* in Jesus is evident in the Gospel's link between "taking away sins and iniquities" and "incomparable signs/works/wonders/marvels" (Exod 34:9, 10 LXX). To begin with, Jesus deals with sins and iniquities conclusively (1:29; 8:21–46; 9:34–41; 15:22–24; 16:8–9; 19:11; 20:23) and the Gospel's incomparable *sēmeia, terata, erga* testify to this (20:30–31).[158] Moreover, Jesus explains the cause for the man who was born blind: "*It was* neither *that* this man sinned [*hēmarten*], nor his parents; but *it was* so that the works of God [*ta erga tou Theou*] might be revealed [*phanerōthē*][159] in him" (9:3). It is the discernment of the Pharisees that is actually at stake, though. They did see/hear of an incomparable work of God (9:3, 16, 30–32, 40) but failed to recognize the ratification of the covenant of *charis* behind the event. Jesus, therefore, is not obligated to keep his part of the covenant—to take sins and iniquities away—either. Hence, Jesus says to the Pharisees, "If you were blind, you would have no sin [*hamartian*]; but since you say, 'We see,' your sin [*hamartia*] remains" (9:41). Of all those who remain in their sins due to their failure to recognize ratification of the covenant of *charis* in the incomparable works of God, Jesus concludes, "If I had not come and spoken to them, they would not have sin [*hamartian*], but now they have no excuse for their sin [*hamartias*] ... If I had not done among them the works [*erga*] which no one else did [!], they would not have sin [*hamartian*]; but now they have both seen and hated Me and My Father as well" (15:22–24). Furthermore, both the writer and the participants in the events are aware of the concept that sins and iniquities can cause sicknesses that lead to death

---

156. NASB has "amazing."

157. Sometimes, even though no cognate of *thaumastos* is utilized, the sense of the marvelous is still rather obvious (2:10; 11:37).

158. Life in Jesus who takes away the sin v. death of illnesses caused by sins (Deut 28:20, 22, 27, 35, 45).

159. NASB has "displayed."

(Deut 28:15–46).[160] The sickness (*astheneia*) of a man who had been ill for thirty-eight years is clearly caused by sin (5:14). By implication, an underlying sin might well have been the cause of the sickness (*astheneia*) of the son of a royal official (4:46) and the sickness (*astheneia*) of Lazarus (11:1–6); more so since the boy's fever (*puretos*) is listed as a sickness caused by sin and leading to death (4:52; cf. Deut 28:22), and since both sicknesses are described as deadly (4:47–49; 11:13–14; cf. Deut 28:20, 22, 27, 35, 45). Of course, the healing of a man who had been ill for thirty-eight (!) years, the healing of a boy at a distance (!) by a word (!), and the raising of a dead man who had been in a tomb for four (!) days are miracles, which—by their very virtue of *incomparability*—witness to ratification of the covenant of *charis* (article Exod 34:10). But they may also demonstrate yet another dimension of the ratification[161]—taking away sins and iniquities, as listed by the Exod 34:9 article. The content and the language of the paradigmatic covenant of *charis* are clearly evident in each and every one of the seven signs of the Gospel.[162]

The presence of God is incessant, and so are the signs/works/wonders/marvels certifying the ratification of the covenant of *charis*. With regard to this the Son accounts to the Father for his time on earth (17:4). Beyond this point, it is the responsibility of believers enabled by the possession of the character of God (1:17; 3:34; 17:6, 22, 26; 19:30; 19:37; 20:22) and empowered by the Spirit (14:12 cf. 5:19–20; 16:13–15)

---

160. First, Jesus, the disciples, the Pharisees, and the Jews apparently refer to this concept in the episode of the man born blind who receives his sight. Notice, "Cursed *shall be* the offspring of your body" (Deut 28:18) and the fact that blindness is listed among such illnesses (Deut 28:28). Second, the list of illnesses mentioned in the Gospel closely resemble the Deuteronomic list of curses. Notice the blindness, fever, and sickness of those gathered around the pool of Bethesda (cf. Deut 28:22, 28, etc.). Third, the cause-effect notion of sin–illness–death (Deut 28:20, 22, 27, 35, 45) is attested in the Gospel (4:49–52; 11:14). Fourth, the sins and illnesses are associated with *sēmeia kai terata*, "signs and wonders," in the concept of curses (Deut 28:46). Fifth, the Evangelist is well aware of the book of Deuteronomy (NA^{27}, 776–78 lists John/Deut 7:51/1:16f.; 6:49/1:35; 5:5/2:14; 5:37/2:12; 4:20/11:29; 12:5; 8:7/17:7; 1:21; 5:46/18:15; 8:17/19:15; 7:51/19:18; 19:31/21:23; 8:5/22:22–24; 8:21/24:16; 4:20/27:12; 7:49/27:26; 3:13/30:12; 5:45f./31:26; 5:21/32:39). For a further correlation between *astheneia*, "sickness"; *adikia*, "iniquity"; and *hamartia*, "sin," see Jer 18:23; John 5:1–15; etc.

161. Certainly so in the case of a man who had been ill for thirty-eight years (5:14).

162. See elsewhere in our study.

to perform signs and works that witness to the ongoing ratification of the covenant of *charis*. Jesus encourages this continuity (10:25; 14:1–11; 14: 12–13; 15:8). The Evangelist comments on both Jesus's and Peter's death in terms of *signs* (12:33; 18:32; 21:19). As Jesus does these works, so believers will do even greater *works* (14:12, cf. 3:21) to ratify the covenant of *charis*, to witness to the presence of God in the Spirit. Hence, the principal purpose of the Gospel's signs/works/wonders/marvels is to provide the incomparable *endoxa* . . . *erga* . . . and *thaumasta* required by the paradigmatic Sinaitic covenant of *charis* to signal its ratification in Jesus and the Spirit.

Echoes of the Notion of the Incessant Presence (*ḥesed/charis*) of God in the Gospel

Just as we have argued that the OT notion of the qualities of the character of God are not only alluded to but echoed throughout the Gospel, we now seek to demonstrate how this is also true of the OT notion of God's presence (*ḥesed/charis*).

Initially, the Lord established the covenant of the presence of God (*charis*) with the Jews at Sinai.[163] The people failed to keep the covenant and the presence of God was withdrawn from the nation. As Jeremiah[164] conveyed, "thus says the LORD, ' . . . I have withdrawn My peace [*eirēnē*] from this people,' declares the LORD, "*My ḥesed*."[165] With this in mind, the earlier message of Isaiah,[166] "'My *ḥesed*[167] will not be removed from you, And My covenant of peace [*eirēnē*] will not be shaken,' Says the

---

163. Exod 33:12—34:10.

164. The Evangelist is likely to be aware of Jeremiah's writings (cf. John/Jer 4:10/2:13; 6:45/31:33ff.; 7:42/23:5; 15:1/2:21). See NA[27], *Appendix IV: Loci citati vel allegati*, 770–806.

165. Jer 16:5. Keown rightly translates, "'for I have taken away my peace from this people,' says the LORD, 'even my steadfast love and mercy'" and notes on "'even my,'" "The possessive is carried from 'my peace'" (Keown, *Jeremiah 26–52*, translation of 16:5, n. 5b). OG does not have equivalents for *ḥesed* and *raḥămîm* as its phrase stops at "Thus saith the Lord, . . . 'I have removed my peace [*eirēnē*] from this people'" (Jer 16:5). But Theodotion conveys the parent text exactly: . . . *hoti aphestaka tēn eirēnēn mou apo tou laou toutou*. Theodotion's *phēsin kurios* continues *ton eleon kai tous oikt[e]irmos* (as attested by reliable Q and 86; see GLXX, *Jeremias (Threni)*.

166. The Evangelist is well aware of Isaiah's writings. See NA[27], *Appendix IV: Loci citati vel allegati*, 770–806.

167. *eleos* = *charis*.

Lord,"[168] may well have been perceived as a prophecy of the coming re-establishment of the Sinaitic covenant of the presence. The Gospel may well be depicting restoration of this presence of God (*ḥesed/charis = eirēnē*)[169] to the people. The disciples are concerned that Jesus, the presence of God, is going away (13:33, 36; 14:4-5). Jesus promises, "'I will not leave you as orphans; I will come to you. . . . Peace [*Eirēnēn*] I leave with you; My peace [*eirēnēn*] I give to you; not as the world gives do I give to you. Do not let your heart be troubled, nor let it be fearful. You heard that I said to you, 'I go away, and I will come to you'" (14:18, 27-28). Later on, Jesus again reminds the troubled disciples of this *eirēnē*, the presence of God, that dwells in him and will remain with them: "These things I have spoken to you, so that in Me you may have peace [*eirēnēn*]. In the world you have tribulation, but take courage; I have overcome the world" (16:33). So, when the resurrected Jesus does come to the disciples, they comprehend that, by his statement "Peace [*eirēnē*] *be* with you" (20:21, 26), Jesus does not merely offer them some kind of a "shalom" greeting, but actually restores the *eirēnē* = *ḥesed/charis* = presence of God, in accordance with the prophecies (Jer 16:5; Isa 54:10).[170]

The covenant of the presence (*charis*) of God remains valid in the Spirit.[171] The disciples are scared;[172] the martyrdom of Peter is even predicted.[173] But neither despair nor death can nullify God's presence (*charis*). On the contrary, these poignant accounts of the Gospel may have echoed Isaiah's: "The righteous man perishes, and no man takes it to heart; And *ḥesed* men [i.e. those who adhere to *ḥesed*, the presence of God] are taken away, while no one understands. For the righteous man

168. Isa 54:10. Notice also, "Incline your ear and come to Me. Listen, that you may live; And I will make an everlasting covenant with you, *According to* the faithful mercies [*ḥesed* pl.] shown to David" (Isa 55:3); MT has *ḥesed* pl., GLXX has *hosios* pl., Theodotion has *eleos* pl. (as attested by 86, Chr., Pr.), Symmachus *eleos* pl. (as attested by sec. Pr.); *hoi l' eleos* (as attested by sec. Chr.), see GLXX, *Isaiah*.

169. 14:27; 16:33; 20:19, 21, 26.

170. Of course, even without this "*eirēnē* = *ḥesed/charis* = the presence of God" element, this whole episode (20:19-28) already exactly reflects the ratification of articles of the Sinaitic covenant of the presence of God (Exod 33:12—34:10 LXX), as we have demonstrated elsewhere in this study.

171. 1:32f; 3:5f, 8; 4:23f; 6:63; 7:39; 14:17, 26; 15:26; 16:13; 19:30; 20:22.

172. 19:38; 20:19.

173. 21:18-19, 22-23.

is taken away from evil" (Isa 57:1). The disciples would also be encouraged by the word of Wisdom:

> There was one who pleased God and was loved by him, and while living among sinners he was taken up.... Being perfected in a short time, he fulfilled long years; for his soul was pleasing to the Lord, therefore he took him quickly from the midst of wickedness. Yet the peoples saw and did not understand, nor take such a thing to heart, that God's *charis* [i.e. the presence of God] and mercy are upon his elect, and he watches over his holy ones. (Wis 4:10–15 RSV; cf. Wis 3:14)

Thus, even in despair and death, God's presence (*charis*) abides with the disciples.

These echoes of God's presence (*ḥesed*/*charis*), like those of the qualities of the character of God (*ḥesed we'ĕmet*/*charis kai hē alētheia*) previously discussed, are intended as merely suggestive observations. But they too stem from the Sinaitic covenant, to which, as we have established earlier, the Evangelist alludes with his use of *charin anti charitos* (the incessant presence of God).

Four Sinaitic *doxa* Aspects of the Presence Evident in the Ratification of the Covenant in Jesus

We argue that the notion of *doxa* and the usage of cognates of *doxa* in the Gospel ought to be interpreted with reference to the covenant of the presence (*charis*) of God regained at Sinai (Exod 33:12—34:10 LXX), reinforced in Jesus, and retained through the Spirit. It is the four covenantal Sinaitic connotations of the presence of God—1) the visible appearance of God (*doxa*), 2) the intrinsic character of God (*doxa*), 3) the miraculous splendor verifying the presence of God (*endoxa*), and 4) the divine honor confirming the presence of God (*endoxasthēsomai*)—to which the Gospel alludes. These connotations of *doxa* naturally blend in the Sinaitic paradigmatic covenant of *charis*, as they all frame the very same entity—the presence of God. This is also the case in the Gospel's account of the covenant of *charis*. On the one hand, a single occurrence of a cognate of *doxa* in the Gospel may simultaneously carry a couple of the Sinaitic connotations. On the other hand, when cognates of *doxa* are set alongside one another in the Gospel, they may denote different Sinaitic dimensions.

Echoes and Allusions to the Covenant of *charis* in Cognates of *doxa* in the Gospel

The Gospel's textual indications allow one to discern Sinaitic covenantal counterparts of the Gospel's occurrences of cognates of *doxa*. We will consider these in turn.

To begin with, the Sinaitic covenant counterparts of several of the Gospel's occurrences of cognates of *doxa* are made clear by their immediate context. First, in the Evangelist's reports "the Word became flesh, and dwelt among us, and we saw His appearance [*doxan*]" and "Isaiah ... saw His appearance [*doxan*]," (12:41) and in Jesus's prayer "Father, I desire that ... they [believers] may see My appearance [*doxan*][174] which You have given Me" (17: 24), the term *doxan* alludes to the visible appearance (*doxa*) connotation of the covenant.[175] This is clearly indicated by the usage of the term "saw." Second, in the writer's assertion "character [*doxan*] as of the only begotten from the Father, *plērēs charitos kai alētheias*" (1:14), the term *doxan* alludes to the intrinsic character (*doxa*) connotation of the covenant since the clause deals with qualities of the character. Third, in the conversation in 12:23–28—"'Father, honor [*doxazō*][176] Your name.' ... 'I have both honored [*edoxasa*] it, and will honor [*doxasō*][177] it again'"[178]—it is honoring (with) the intrinsic

---

174. The visible appearance of God (*doxa*). Notice this explicit "see." It is this conformity of the intrinsic character (*doxa*) inherent in God and now granted to believers (17:22) that allows believers to see the visible appearance of God (*doxa*).

175. The Evangelist's report "the Word became flesh, and dwelt among us, and we saw His glory [*doxan*]" may also *echo* covenantal articles of the miraculous splendor verifying the presence of God (*endoxa*) and the divine honor confirming the presence of God (*endoxasthēsomai*), since 1) events certifying to ratification of these articles are also rather visible (the incomparable signs and the cross, accordingly) and 2) the reference is made to the earthly period of Jesus.

176. See our comments on 12:28 (cf. 17:6, 26; Exod 33:19; 34:5-6).

177. In 12:23-28, NASB for cognates of *doxa* renders cognates of "glory."

178. Remarkably, it is exactly the Sinaitic matters of the name—the character of God—that come together in this the only preserved verbal conversation between the Son and the Father. When has God glorified his name? At Sinai (Exod 33:19; 34:6). When will God glorify his name again? In Jesus, as the Son prays for (12:28) and reports of to the Father (17:6, 26). What is common to the revelations at Sinai and in Jesus? The character of God described in terms of the name. In the sense of this "name"—the character of God, which causes Holy God to be *present* among sinful people—the Father's *edoxasa kai palin doxasō* (12:28) may well correspond to the Evangelist's *charin anti charitos* (1:16).

character (*doxa*) of God that is in view. This is signified by the usage of the term "name," which at Sinai nominated the intrinsic character of God.[179] Fourth, Jesus's exhortation to the disciples concerning the Holy Spirit, "He will honor [*doxasei*] Me, for He will take of Mine and will disclose *it* to you" (16:14), echoes[180] the bestowal of the intrinsic character (*doxa*) of God. This echo is indicated by Jesus's immediately following explanation, "for He will take of Mine and will disclose *it* to you" (16:14). The Holy Spirit "takes" of (i.e., possesses) Jesus's divine character and "discloses" (i.e., grants[181]) it to his disciples.[182] The possession of the qualities of the divine character allows the incessant presence of God among the disciples.

Moreover, Sinaitic covenant counterparts of several of the Gospel's occurrences of cognates of *doxa* are made known by the *form* and the *referent* of those terms. According to the Sinaitic covenant, the ratification of the article *endoxasthēsomai egō te kai ho laos sou*, "I and thy people shall be glorified," (Exod 33:16 LXX) evinces the presence of God. The key to understanding the application of the divine honor (*endoxasthēsomai*) article of the covenant to the matters of *doxa* in the Gospel's account is the *form* of the Sinaitic verb *endoxasthēsomai*. On the one hand, the verb *endoxasthēsomai* is *singular* in number. At Sinai, the singular *endoxasthēsomai* legitimately[183] covers both "I (Moses)" and "thy (God's) people." In the Gospel, this singular *endoxasthēsomai* is legitimately projected on both Jesus (the prophet like Moses) and God's people. *Jesus* (the Son of Man, the Son of God) is the *object* of the divine honor (*endoxasthēsomai*) article of the covenant. On the other hand, the verb *endoxasthēsomai* is *(divine) passive* in voice. At Sinai

---

179. Since the intrinsic character of God is revealed by and in the *persona* of Jesus, this conversation may well echo the divine honor (*endoxasthēsomai*) article of the covenant (see our comments on the form and the object of the Sinaitic *endoxasthēsomai*).

180. It *alludes* to the divine honor (*endoxasthēsomai*) article of the covenant (see our comments elsewhere).

181. Notice the effect caused by actions described with the term *anangellō* (4:25; 5:15; 16:13; 16:14; 16:15; cf. 20:18).

182. Jesus bestows God's character onto believers by the means of the Holy Spirit (1:17; 1:33; 7:39; 20:22, cf. 19:30): the Holy Spirit is not the Spirit of *alētheia* only (14:17; 15:26; 16:13) but also the Spirit of *charis* (John 19:37, cf. Zech 12:10). Both these qualities of the divine character are inherent in the Holy Spirit without measure (*ek metrou*, 3:34).

183. Cf. BDF, §135:1a.

The Covenant of the Presence of God 221

it is God who glorifies by his very presence. In the Gospel, the *divine passive* voice of cognates of *doxa* specifies that such glorification—the *divine* honor—must come from *God*, not people. (Of course, by the very nature of the case such divine honor can also be alluded to by a direct *doxa* related reference to the Divine.) This projection of the divine passive singular verb *endoxasthēsomai* from the Sinaitic covenant onto the Gospel explains numerous sayings of Jesus and comments of the Evangelist.

According to the covenant, honoring oneself or seeking such honor from humans is of no avail, because only the divine honor evinces the presence of God (cf. 7:18; 8:50–54, 12:43). The Gospel emphasizes this point: the matter of the honor "from below" or "self-honor" is always and immediately being contrasted with the honor "from above." Consider Jesus's statements, "I do not receive honor [*doxan*] from men; . . . How can you believe, when you receive honor [*doxan*] from one another and you do not seek the honor [*doxan*] that is from the *one and* only God?" (5:41–44); "He who speaks from himself seeks his own honor [*doxan*]; but He who is seeking the honor [*doxan*] of the One who sent Him, He is true, and there is no unrighteousness in Him" (7:18); "But I do not seek My honor [*doxan*]; there is One who seeks [to honor Me][184]" (8:50); and "If I honor [*doxasō*] Myself, My honor [*doxa*] is nothing; it is My Father who glorifies [*doxazōn*] Me, of whom you say, 'He is our God'" (8:54). So also consider the Evangelist's statement "they loved the honor [*doxan*] of men rather than the honor [*doxan*] of God" (12:43).

According to the covenant, it is only the divine honor required for ratification of the covenant of the presence of God that evinces the presence of God. The Gospel employs two approaches to make the latter point. On the one hand, the Gospel indicates an allusion to the divine honor (*endoxasthēsomai*) article of the Sinaitic covenant by the usage of the divine passive form of cognates of *doxa*, e.g.:[185] "Jesus was not yet honored [*edoxasthē*]" (7:39); "the Son of God may be honored [*doxasthē*] by it" (11:4); "when Jesus was honored [*edoxasthē*]" (12:16); "The hour has come for the Son of Man to be honored [*doxasthē*] (12:23); "Now

---

184. Even though no cognate of *doxa* is being used here in 8:50b, the term is nevertheless implied by the immediate preceding context.

185. In the following examples cognates of the terms "glory"/"approval" utilized in NASB are substituted with cognates of "honor."

is the Son of Man honored [*edoxasthē*]" (13:31); and "I have been honored [*dedoxasmai*][186] in them" (17:10). On the other hand, the Gospel specifies such an allusion to the divine honor (*endoxasthēsomai*) article of the Sinaitic covenant by making a direct reference to the Divine with regard to *doxa*, e.g.: "glory [*doxan*] that is from the *one and* only God" (5:44); "the honor [*doxan*] of the One who sent Him" (7:18); "there is One who seeks [to honor Jesus][187] (8:50); "it is My Father who honors [*doxazōn*] Me" (8:54); "the honor [*doxan*] of God" (12:43); "God will also honor Him [*doxasei*] in Himself, and will honor [*doxasei*] Him immediately" (13:32); "He [the Holy Spirit] will honor [*doxasei*][188] Me [Jesus]" (16:14); and "Father... honor [*doxason*] Your Son" (17:1). Such divine honor confirms the presence of God: "He is true" (7:18) and "His is our God" (8:54). In this way the Gospel attests to God's ratification of the divine honor (*endoxasthēsomai*) article of the covenant in Jesus.

Furthermore, several *doxa* related statements of the Gospel allude to the miraculous splendor (*endoxa*) article of the covenant. According to the covenant, "glorious things [*endoxa*], which have not been done in all the earth, or in any nation" (Exod 34:10 LXE) verify the presence of God. This *endoxa* requirement of the covenant is met by the incomparable signs (*sēmeia*), works (*erga*), wonders (*terata*), and marvels (*thaumasta*) in the Gospel. To make an allusion to the miraculous splendor (*endoxa*) article of the covenant, the Gospel refers to *God (the Father)* as the *object* of such glorification. God is glorified by glorious things (*endoxa*) that verify God's presence as Jesus (and, further, in believers). From this covenantal perspective Jesus perceives the crucifixion: "Now is the Son of Man honored [*edoxasthē*],[189] and God is glorified

---

186. The divine honor (*endoxasthēsomai*) article. Disciples enabled by their possession of the divine character (conveyed by Jesus through the Holy Spirit) perform divine glorious things (*endoxa*) continuously verifying the incessant presence of God. Significantly, Jesus is not honored *by* believers but *in* them, i.e., divinely by God just as required by the covenant (notice the divine passive of *dedoxasmai*).

187. Even though no cognate of *doxa* is being utilized here in the text of 8:50b, such term is nevertheless implied by the immediate preceding context.

188. This saying may well also *echo* the matters of the intrinsic character (*doxa*) of God (see our comments elsewhere).

189. The crucifixion, besides being one of the incomparable glorious things (*endoxa*), is also the moment and the place where Jesus receives the divine honor (*endoxasthēsomai*). Hence, the crucifixion serves the purpose of certifying the ratification of both articles of the covenant of the presence of God.

[*edoxasthē*] in Him; if God is glorified [*edoxasthē*[190]]" (13:31–32). The crucifixion/resurrection—the ultimate of the glorious things (*endoxa*), an incomparable miracle that glorifies God—attests to the ultimate revelation of both the visible appearance (*doxa*) and the intrinsic character (*doxa*) of God. The presence of God is incessant,[191] as are the signs/works/wonders/marvels certifying the ratification of the covenant. The incomparable glorious things (*endoxa*) continue attesting to the presence of God even after Jesus's resurrection, in believers. The disciples have been granted the intrinsic character (*doxa*) of God (1:17; 17:6, 22, 26; 20:22). The "all things" the Spirit takes of Jesus and discloses to disciples include marvelous works (16:13–15; 14:12; cf. 5:19–20). This enables believers to do works greater than Jesus (14:12) to attest to the ongoing presence of God in accord with the miraculous splendor (*endoxa*) article of the covenant. It is about this ability of believers that the Evangelist comments, "this He [Jesus] said, signifying[192] by what kind of death he [Peter] would glorify [*doxasei*] God" (21:19). The martyrdom of Peter is one of the glorious things (*endoxa*) verifying the incessant presence of God. But Peter is not alone in this respect. Having been granted the divine character, all believers become capable of verifying the incessant presence of God by demonstrating the incomparable. To this end Jesus encourages and empowers believers, "he who believes in Me, the works that I do, he will do also; and greater *works* than these he will do . . . Whatever you ask in My name, that will I do, so that the Father may be glorified [*doxasthē*] in the Son" (14:13). Jesus approves this continuity: "My Father is glorified [*edoxasthē*] by this, that you bear much fruit, and *so* prove to be My disciples" (15:8). Hence, as believers perform greater works [*erga*] than Jesus (14:12) they attest to the ongoing presence of God according to the miraculous splendor (*endoxa*) article of the covenant (cf. 15:8; 16:14).

---

190. These two occurrences of *edoxasthē* (13:31b; 32a) may well also echo the miraculous splendor (*endoxa*) article of the covenant. Incomparable *endoxa*—Jesus's *sēmeia, erga, terata, thaumasta*—are required by the covenant to verify the presence of God. The crucifixion/resurrection of Christ is such *endoxon*—the ultimate incomparable glorious deed—which glorifies God.

191. *charin anti charitos*.

192. Notice this *sēmainōn*, "signifying," (21:19) of Peter paralleled with *sēmainōn* of Jesus's death—the ultimate sign of God's presence (12:33; 18:32).

Finally, covenantal connotations of *doxa* naturally—just as was the case at Sinai—blend together. This is exemplarily the case in the conversation in the Gospel between God the Son and God the Father:

> Jesus . . . said, "Father, the hour has come; honor [*doxason*][193] Your Son, that the Son may glorify [*doxasē*][194] You, . . . I glorified [*edoxasa*[195]] You on the earth, having accomplished the work which You have given Me to do. Now, Father, honor [*doxason*] [196] Me together with Yourself, with the honor [*doxē*][197] which I had with You before the world was. . . . all things that are Mine are Yours, and Yours are Mine; and I have been honored [*dedoxasmai*][198] in them. . . . The character [*doxan*][199] which You have

193. The divine honor (*endoxasthēsomai*) article. Jesus (the Son) is the object of the divine honor coming from the Father.

194. The miraculous splendor (*endoxa*) article. God (the Father) is the object. Jesus's crucifixion/resurrection is the ultimate one of the glorious things (*endoxa*) required to evince the presence of God.

195. The miraculous splendor (*endoxa*) article. Notice Jesus's remark, "on the earth [*gēs*]," pointing to the Sinaitic covenant's "I will do glorious things (*endoxa*), which have not been done in all the earth [*gē*]" (Exod 34:10 LXE). The clarification "having accomplished the work which You have given Me to do" refers to incomparable works—glorious things (*endoxa*)—verifying the presence of God, specifically on the earth.

196. The divine honor (*endoxasthēsomai*) article. Jesus (the Son) is the object of the divine honor coming from the Father. In terms of the miraculous splendor (*endoxa*) article, the Son's crucifixion and resurrection is the ultimate glorious thing (*endoxa*) that glorifies the Father. Hence, Jesus's plea, "*doxason* Me together with Yourself."

197. The divine honor (*endoxasthēsomai*) article. Jesus (the Son) is the object of the divine honor coming from the Father. This occurrence of *doxa* may also have connotations of both the visible appearance (*doxa*) and the intrinsic character (*doxa*) of God to which the explanatory "*tē doxē* which I had with You before the world was" points. But it may not mean that Jesus gains this *doxa* because Jesus has never given up the *doxa* inherent in him (1:14; 17:22), contra Haenchen, who suggests that this prayer assumes that the incarnation entailed a *forfeiture* of the glory that the Son once possessed (Haenchen, *John*, 2:502), and contra Beasley-Murray, who evaluates, "The prayer for glory, accordingly, is for a restoration of that which the Son enjoyed with the Father prior to creation (cf. 1:1–5)" (Beasley-Murray, *John*, 297).

198. The divine honor (*endoxasthēsomai*) article. Jesus (the Son) is the object of the divine honor coming from the Father. Disciples enabled by their possession of the divine character (conveyed by Jesus through the Holy Spirit) perform divine glorious things (*endoxa*) continuously verifying the incessant presence of God. Significantly, Jesus is not honored by believers but *in* them, i.e., divinely by God just as required by the covenant (notice the divine passive of *dedoxasmai*).

199. The intrinsic character (*doxa*) of God conveyed by Jesus to believers through the Holy Spirit. Notice the explanatory "which You have given Me" stating that both the Father and the Son share the very same divine character. This "giving," signifying

given Me I have given to them, that they may be one, just as We are one; . . . Father, I desire that they also, whom You have given Me, be with Me where I am, so that they may see My appearance [*doxan*][200] which You have given Me, for You loved Me before the foundation of the world" (17:1–24).

Thus, all four Sinaitic *doxa* aspects of the presence of God—1) visible appearance (*doxa*), 2) intrinsic character (*doxa*), 3) miraculous splendor (*endoxa*), and 4) divine (*endoxasthēsomai*)—become evident in the course of the ratification of the covenant of the presence (*charis*) of God as Jesus.

Each of the Seven Signs in the Gospel Ratifies the Covenant of the Presence

The covenant of the presence (*charis*) of God originated at Sinai[201] requires a ratification. The whole Gospel attests to the ratification of the covenant of *charis*; in particular, its seven signs. To demonstrate this we will compare articles of the Sinaitic covenant of the presence (*charis*) of God with the Gospel's accounts of the miraculous.

According to one of the articles of the covenant, the "glorious things (*endoxa*), which have not been done in all the earth, or in any nation" (Exod 34:10 LXE) verify the presence of God. This presence of God is revealed by the visible appearance (*doxa*) and the intrinsic character of God (*doxa*) as Jesus; it is also confirmed by the divine honor coming from God (*endoxasthēsomai*). Therefore, the Gospel's incomparable miracles—glorious things (*endoxa*)—testify to all the four covenantal connotations of *doxa*. These connotations are evident in all the seven signs of the Gospel. Let us consider them in turn.

---

the bestowal of the divine character (*doxa*) onto believers, conforms the character of humans to that of the Divine; this conformity enables humans to "be one" with the Divine, just as the Son and the Father are one.

200. The visible appearance of God (*doxa*). Notice this explicit "see." It is this conformity of the intrinsic character (*doxa*) inherent in God and now granted to believers (17:22) that allows believers to see the visible appearance of God (*doxa*).

201. As preserved by its *charis* cluster (Exod 33:12, 13, 13, 16, 17; 34:9–10).

Covenantal Connotations of *doxa* in the Sign of Turning Water into Wine

According to the covenant the presence (*charis*) of God is evinced when the Lord does glorious things (*endoxa*) that have not been done in all the earth or in any nation (Exod 34:10 LXX). According to the Scriptures, turning water into wine has never been done in all the earth, or in any nation; hence such sign is *incomparable*. This incomparability alone qualifies the sign as being one of the covenantal glorious things (*endoxa*) evincing the presence (*charis*) of God.

According to the covenant, such incomparable glorious things (*endoxa*) are to be attested by the Israelites. The term *laos* utilized in the Sinaitic paradigmatic covenant makes this clear by relating *ho laos*, "the people," to Moses: "the Lord said to Moses, Behold, I establish a covenant for thee in the presence of all thy people [*tou laou sou*]; I will do glorious things, . . . and all the people among whom thou art [*ho laos en hois ei su*] shall see the works of the Lord" (Exod 34:10). And so, the incomparable sign of turning water into wine is seen precisely by Jews, the covenantal people:[202] the mother of Jesus, his disciples, and the witnessing servants.[203] The sign of turning water into wine again qualifies as being one of the covenantal glorious things (*endoxa*).

According to the covenant, the presence (*charis*) of God is experienced when God leads people (Exod 33:12; cf. 33:15 LXX) and gives them rest (Exod 33:14 LXX), goes before (Exod 33:14; cf. 34:15 LXX) and with (Exod 33:16 LXX) them; God is present in grace, not in wrath (cf. Exod 33:3 LXX). And so does Jesus direct Jewish servants in the midst of Jewish guests and disciples at a Jewish wedding in Cana of Galilee, a Jewish town. By saving the people from the trouble of being short of wine, Jesus gives the people rest at the wedding. The *doxa* of God as Jesus is manifested by an incomparable miracle, precisely in *marriage* settings to remind the participants that it is the *covenant*[204] of *charis* that

---

202. Remarkably, in the Gospel the term *laos* designates Jews only.

203. Ironically, even those who did not see the miracle still recognize the incomparability of the event. So the headwaiter says to the bridegroom, "Every man serves the good wine first, and when *the people* have drunk freely, *then he serves* the poorer *wine*; *but* you have kept the good wine until now" (2:10). This is something that "has not been done in all the earth, or in any nation." The headwaiter's comment may also echo the required covenantal marvelousness (*thaumastos*) of the event.

204. Cf. God's "I establish a covenant [*diathēkēn*]" (Exod 34:10).

is being ratified, in full accord with the Sinaitic paradigm. According to the covenant, the presence (*charis*) of God is at work when this great nation remains God's people (Exod 33:13, cf. 34:9 LXX). This certainly is the case with Jesus attending the wedding.

According to the miraculous splendor (*endoxa*) article of the covenant, such an incomparable sign witnessed by the people verifies the presence of God as Jesus. And so the Evangelist comments, "This beginning of *His* signs Jesus did in Cana of Galilee, and manifested His miraculous splendor [*doxan*], and His disciples believed in Him" (2:11). The Evangelist hints that it is exactly the miraculous splendor (*endoxa*) that is in view here. According to the covenant, the presence (*charis*) of God is also attested when God reveals (*emphanizō*) himself so that he may be evidently known/seen (Exod 33:13; cf. Exod 33:18–34:7 LXX) and when he manifests (*deiknumi*) his *doxa* (Exod 33:18—34:10 LXX). The writer appropriately—according to their covenantal usage—utilizes cognates of both *emphanizō* (14:21, 22) and *deiknumi* (2:18; 5:20ab; 10:32; 14:8, 9; 20:20) elsewhere in the Gospel. But in commenting over the meaning of the sign of turning water into wine, the Evangelist avoids using either *emphanizō* or *deiknumi* and renders "manifested [*ephanerōsen*] His glory [*tēn doxan autou*]" instead. This communicates to the reader that the term *doxa* here is to be understood not as the Lord's appearance or character but as a manifestation of his covenantal miraculous splendor (*endoxa*).

According to the covenant, the miraculous splendor (*endoxa*) verifies the presence of God. As an exposure to God's *doxa* at Sinai makes one worship (Exod 34:8 LXX), so does its manifestation in the Gospel cause the disciples to believe in Jesus (2:11). Both the visible appearance (*doxa*) and the intrinsic character (*doxa*) of God are evident at the wedding. Jesus—the visible appearance (*doxa*) of God—is clearly *seen* by those around. This fulfills one of the requirements of the covenant according to which the presence (*charis*) of God is attested when God reveals himself so that he may be evidently seen (Exod 33:13; cf. Exod 33:18–34:7 LXX). Jesus also exhibits the utmost graciousness and integrity of the *character* (*doxa*) of God. On the one hand, Christ does not have to provide the wine; moreover, has a reason not to: to his mother's remark, "They have no wine," Jesus replies with *integrity*, "Woman, what does that have to do with us? My hour has not yet come." On the other hand, Jesus *graciously* provides the wine, and in *abundance*.

Hence the sign depicts Jesus as being *plērēs charitos kai alētheias* in character (*doxa*).

The sign of turning water into wine sets the paradigm expressed by the Evangelist's comment, "This beginning of *His* signs Jesus did in Cana of Galilee, and manifested His glory, and His disciples believed in Him" (2:11). Conceptually, this and all of the following incomparable signs of the Gospel are the Lord's covenantal glorious things (*endoxa*), which serve the purpose of verifying the presence of God as Jesus.

Covenantal Connotations of *doxa* in the Sign of Healing the Royal Official's Son

At the outset, Jesus reminds the gathered of the miraculous splendor (*endoxa*) article of the covenant: "Unless you *people* see signs and wonders [*sēmeia kai terata*], you *simply* will not believe" (4:48).

According to the covenant, the presence (*charis*) of God is evinced when the he does glorious things (*endoxa*) that have not been done in all the earth or in any nation, and all the people see the works (*erga*) of the Lord, such incomparable *endoxa*, "glorious things," are to be attested by the Israelites (Exod 34:10 LXX). Jesus performs an *incomparable* miracle—healing at a distance by a word (!), and this sign is witnessed by Jewish people[205] and a Jewish royal official[206] altogether with his whole Jewish household. Hence, the sign of healing the son of a royal official attests to the presence of God as Jesus.

According to the covenant, the presence (*charis*) of God is attested when God reveals himself so that he may be evidently seen (Exod 33:13; cf. Exod 33:18–34:7 LXX) and he manifests his *doxa* (Exod 33:18—34:10 LXX). Both the visible appearance (*doxa*) and the intrinsic character (*doxa*) of God are evident in the miracle. Jesus—the visible appearance (*doxa*) of God—is clearly *seen* by those around him. Jesus also exhibits the utmost graciousness and integrity of the *character* (*doxa*) of God.

---

205. Cf. the plural of *pisteusēte*, "you *people* . . . believe" (4:48). Perhaps even slaves (*douloi*) of the royal official were Jews (4:51).

206. Beasley-Murray rightly comments, "*basilikos* as an adjective = royal, as a noun = a relative or official of a king" (Bauer, *Lexicon*, 136). Schlatter points out that Josephus uses the term to describe all the relatives and officials of the Herods, and their troops (Schlatter, *Evangelium nach Johannes*, 137). "If the narrative records the same incident as that in Matt 8:5–13/Luke 7:1–10 we may view him as an officer in the army of Herod Agrippa" (Beasley-Murray, *John*, 69).

On the one hand, Christ does not have to heal the boy; moreover, has a reason not to as the people are stubborn, refusing to believe without signs and wonders (5:48). But Jesus graciously heals the child. On the other hand, Jesus's promise "your son lives" proves to be true (4:50–53). This attests to the integrity of Jesus. Hence the sign depicts Jesus as being *plērēs charitos kai alētheias* in character (*doxa*).

According to the covenant, the presence (*charis*) of God is encountered when the Lord takes away the sins and iniquities of people (Exod 34:9 LXX). In all likelihood the deadly fever of the boy is caused by sin.[207] Jesus takes away the sin causing the sickness and the deadly fever—a curse of God[208]—leaves the son of the royal official. Hence, the presence of God is encountered in Jesus.

According to the covenant, the presence (*charis*) of God is experienced when God leads his people (Exod 33:12; cf. 33:15 LXX) and gives them rest (Exod 33:14 LXX); God is present in grace, not in wrath (cf. Exod 33:3 LXX). Similarly, by saying, "Go; your son lives" (4:50), Jesus directs the royal official and graciously gives rest to one of his own flock. As an exposure to God's *doxa* at Sinai makes one worship (Exod 34:8 LXX), so its manifestation as Jesus causes the royal official and the household to believe (4:53).

Clear pointers of the episode—"Cana of Galilee where He had made the water wine" (4:46) and "This is again a second sign that Jesus performed when He had come out of Judea into Galilee" (4:54)—ensure that the audience recalls the preceding statement, "This beginning of *His* signs Jesus did in Cana of Galilee, and manifested His glory [*doxan*], and His disciples believed in Him" (2:11). Having drawn the parallel to the miracle at Cana, the audience realizes that, like the disciples earlier, the father of the child and his whole household believe because Jesus manifests the miraculous splendor (*endoxa*) and the presence—the visible appearance (*doxa*) and the intrinsic character (*doxa*)—of God.

---

207. Deut 28:15–46. Notice the deadliness (4:47–49; cf. Deut 28:20, 22, 27, 35, 45) of the *puretos*, "fever" (4:52; cf. Deut 28:22). The Evangelist is well acquainted with the book of Deuteronomy; see NA^{27}, 770–806.

208. Deut 15–46, especially 28:22.

Covenantal Connotations of *doxa* in the Sign of Healing the Cripple at the Pool of Bethesda

According to the covenant, the presence (*charis*) of God is evinced when he does glorious things (*endoxa*) that have not been done in all the earth or in any nation, and all the people see the marvelous (*thaumasta*) works (*erga*) of the Lord (Exod 34:10 LXX). In accordance with this covenant, Jesus performs an *incomparable* miracle—the healing of a man who has been ill for thirty-eight (!) years, and even on the Sabbath (!). According to the covenant, the incomparable *endoxa*, "glorious things," are to be attested by the Israelites. This is manifested in the incomparable sign of the healing of the cripple, seen exactly by the covenantal people: the Jews (5:10f.) and a crowd at the pool of Bethesda in Jerusalem, those who came for a feast of the Jews (5:1, 13). Remarkably, Jesus invites the audience to realize the covenantal meaning of this miracle by challenging the gathered exactly in terms of the Sinaitic covenant of *charis*: "I did one deed [*ergon*], and you all marvel [*thaumazete*[209]]" (5:20, 7:21[210]).

According to the covenant, the presence (*charis*) of God is experienced when he leads his people (Exod 33:12; cf. 33:15 LXX) and gives them rest (Exod 33:14 LXX), and goes before (Exod 33:14; cf. 34:15 LXX) and with (Exod 33:16 LXX) them; God is present in grace, not in wrath (cf. Exod 33:3 LXX). Jesus shows this as he directs the cripple, "Get up, pick up your pallet and walk" (5:8), and encounters the healed at the temple (5:14). According to the covenant, the presence (*charis*) of God is encountered when the Lord takes away the sins and iniquities of the people (Exod 34:9 LXX). The man at the pool of Bethesda is crippled due to a sin (5:14). Jesus heals the man by taking the sin away (5:8–9, 14). In covenantal terms this act attests to an encounter with the presence of God. As an exposure to God's *doxa* at Sinai makes one worship (Exod 34:8 LXX), so does its manifestation as Jesus cause the former cripple to attend the temple (5:14).

According to the covenant, the presence (*charis*) of God is attested when God reveals (*emphanizō*) himself so that he may be known/seen

---

209. Cf. the covenantal "all the people among whom thou art shall see the works [*erga*] of the Lord, that they are marvelous [*thaumasta*], which I will do [*poiēsō*] for thee" (Exod 34:10).

210. This makes at least some of the people of Jerusalem to finally realize that Jesus is Christ of God (7:26); further, "many of the crowd believed in Him" (7:31).

(Exod 33:13; cf. Exod 33:18—34:7 LXX), lets people know his ways so that they may know him (Exod 33:13 LXX), and manifests (*deiknumi*) his *doxa* (Exod 33:18—34:10 LXX). By telling the Jews that it was Jesus who had made him well (5:15), the man acknowledges the presence—the visible appearance (*doxa*) and the intrinsic character (*doxa*)—of God as Jesus. Jesus—the visible appearance (*doxa*) of God—is clearly *seen* by those around him. This fulfills one of the requirements of the covenant, according to which the presence (*charis*) of God is attested when God reveals himself so that he may be evidently seen (Exod 33:13; cf. Exod 33:18—34:7 LXX). Noticeably, it is Jesus who initiates the revelation—makes himself seen/known to the healed (5:13–15). Jesus also exhibits the utmost graciousness and integrity of the *character* (*doxa*) of God. On the one hand, Christ does not have to heal the cripple; even less so on a Sabbath. After all, the sickness of the man is caused by sin on his part! Yet Jesus graciously heals the crippled sinner. On the other hand, with utmost integrity Jesus pursues the will of the Father with regard to making humankind well: "My Father is working until now, and I Myself am working" (5:17). Hence the sign depicts Jesus as being *plērēs charitos kai alētheias* in character (*doxa*). The Jews themselves become remarkably aware that Jesus *is* making the point of being God himself; they seek all the more to kill him, because he is not only breaking the Sabbath, but also calling God his own Father, making himself equal with God (5:16–18).

Covenantal Connotations of *doxa* in the Sign of Feeding the Multitude

According to the covenant, the presence (*charis*) of God is evinced when the Lord does glorious things (*endoxa*) that have not been done in all the earth or in any nation, and all the people see the works (*erga*) of the Lord (Exod 34:10 LXX). The covenantal frame of reference of the sign of feeding the multitude is hinted to the audience by the people's question to Jesus "What then do You do for a sign, so that we may see, and believe You? What work do You perform? Our fathers ate the manna in the wilderness" (6:30–31). The expression "What work do You perform? [*ti ergazē;*]" refers the attentive audience back to the Sinaitic covenant's paradigmatic miraculous splendor (*endoxa*) article (Exod 34:10). In all the book of Exodus, it is only in this covenantal article that cognates of *ergon*, "work," are used with reference to the miraculous. Jesus performs the required work, the *incomparable* sign of feeding a multitude of about five thousand people with five barley loaves and two fish (6:7–13). According to the covenant, the incomparable *endoxa*, "glorious things," are to be attested by the Israelites (Exod 34:10 LXX). This incomparable sign of the feeding the multitude is witnessed precisely by the covenantal nation of Jews: a large crowd (6:1),[211] Jesus's disciples (6:3), and the people who saw the sign that he had performed (6:14). This incomparable sign witnessed by the people of God evinces the ratification of the covenant of *charis*—the presence of God as Jesus.

According to the covenant, the presence (*charis*) of God is attested when God reveals himself so that he may be evidently known/seen (Exod 33:13; cf. Exod 33:18—34:7 LXX), and when he manifests his *doxa* (Exod 33:18—34:10 LXX). Again, the covenantal frame of reference of the sign of feeding the multitude is hinted to the audience by the people's challenge to Jesus, "Our fathers ate the manna in the wilderness" (6:31). Remarkably, the experience of the fathers with the manna in the wilderness was depicted exactly as an appearance of the *doxa* of God! To the people murmuring against God, Moses and Aaron explained, "in the morning ye shall see the glory [*doxan*] of the LORD ... when the LORD gives ... bread in the morning to satiety" (Exod 16:7–8). And so it happened in the wilderness, as "the glory [*doxa*] of the LORD appeared in a cloud" (Exod 16:10). Thus, according to the Gospel's counterpart, when Jesus provides the bread (being the bread from heaven himself) the people actually see the *doxa* of God! Jesus is aware of this as he mourns, "you have seen Me, and yet do not believe" (6:36). Both the visible appearance (*doxa*) and the intrinsic character (*doxa*) of God are evident in the miracle. Jesus—the visible appearance (*doxa*) of God—is clearly *seen* by those around him. This fulfills one of the requirements of the covenant according to which the presence (*charis*) of God is attested when God reveals himself so that he may be evidently seen (Exod 33:13; cf. Exod 33:18—34:7 LXX). Jesus also exhibits the utmost graciousness and integrity of the *character* (*doxa*) of God. On the one hand, Christ does not have to feed the multitude.

---

211. In all likelihood it is a Jewish crowd. A large crowd followed Jesus because they saw the signs, which he was performing on those who were sick (6:2). Prior to this point in the Gospel, Jesus heals in areas populated by Jews.

Moreover, Jesus has a reason not to feed the large crowd: the people are following him because "they saw the signs which He was performing on those who were sick" (6:2), and he disapproves of this reason for following him (2:23–24; 5:48). Yet Jesus graciously feeds the people. On the other hand, Jesus "Himself knew what He was intending to do" (6:6). This attests to the integrity of Jesus. Of course, the multitude is fed in abundance (6:12–13, 26). Hence, the sign depicts Jesus as being *plērēs charitos kai alētheias* in character (*doxa*).

According to the covenant, the presence (*charis*) of God is experienced when God leads his people (Exod 33:12; cf. 33:15 LXX), gives them rest (Exod 33:14 LXX), and goes before (Exod 33:14; cf. 34:15 LXX) and with (Exod 33:16 LXX) them; God is present in grace, not in wrath (cf. Exod 33:3 LXX). This certainly is exhibited in the episode where Jesus feeds the multitude as he leads the disciples and a large crowd to the mountain (6:1–14), teaches the people over the matter of the bread from heaven on the other side of the sea (6:22–40), and speaks to the Jews in the synagogue in Capernaum (6:41–59). According to the covenant, the presence (*charis*) of God is at work when this great nation of Israelites/Jews remains God's people (Exod 33:13, cf. 34:9 LXX). The miracle of feeding the multitude certainly confirms that Jews remain God's own flock.

According to the covenant, the presence (*charis*) of God is encountered when the Lord takes away the sins of the people (Exod 34:9 LXX). Similarly, Jesus offers himself as the bread from heaven to take away the sins of those who partake and believe so that they may have everlasting life (6:47–58). Otherwise, the people will die in their sins (8:21–24).

Covenantal Connotations of *doxa* in the Sign of Giving Sight to the Blind Man

According to the covenant, the presence (*charis*) of God is evinced when the Lord does glorious things (*endoxa*) that have not been done in all the earth or in any nation, and all the people see the marvelous (*thaumasta*) works (*erga*) of the Lord (Exod 34:10 LXX). Jesus passes by[212] a man blind from birth, and the disciples ask, "Rabbi, who sinned,

---

212. This may well be yet another pointer to the Sinaitic covenant. Compare Jesus passing by [*paragōn*] the man born blind with the account of the covenant made at Sinai, "I will pass by [*pareleusomai*] before thee with my glory [*doxē*] ... when my glory [*doxē*] shall pass by [*pareleusomai*] ... until I shall have passed by [*parelthō*].... And

this man or his parents, that he would be born blind?" Jesus points to the Sinaitic covenantal works of the Lord:[213] "*It was* neither *that* this man sinned, nor his parents; but *it was* so that the works [*ta erga*] of God might be displayed in him" (9:3). Hence, the sign is *designed* to witness to ratification of the covenant of *charis*. To this end Christ performs an *incomparable* miracle—giving sight to the man born blind (!). Its incomparability is explicitly confirmed by the one healed: "Since the beginning of time it has never been heard that anyone opened the eyes of a person born blind" (9:32).

According to the covenant, the incomparable *endoxa*, "glorious things," are to be attested by the Israelites (Exod 34:10). The incomparable sign of giving the sight to the man born blind is witnessed precisely by the covenantal nation of Jews: the man himself, his parents, "the neighbors," "those who previously saw him as a beggar," "others," "*still* others," "some of the Pharisees," "others of the Pharisees," "the Jews";[214] and it is eventually acknowledged by the Jewish community at large (cf. 11:36–37).

According to the covenant, the presence (*charis*) of God is attested when he reveals himself so that he may be known/seen (Exod 33:13; cf. Exod 33:18—34:7 LXX) and when he manifests his *doxa* (Exod 33:18—34:10 LXX). As the man receives sight, this allows him to see the visible appearance (*doxa*) and realize the intrinsic character (*doxa*) of God as Jesus (9:35-38). The Jews' charge "Give glory [*doxan*] to God" (9:24) might have been intended by them as a command to the man to confess his alleged sin of lying about the reason for his blindness and subsequent healing by Jesus. But the attentive audience of the Gospel realizes that the man actually gives glory to God by recognizing the presence—the visible appearance (*doxa*) and the intrinsic character (*doxa*)—of God as Jesus as attested by the miraculous splendor (*endoxa*). Noticeably, it is again[215] Jesus who takes the initiative to reveal himself to the man, so in

---

the Lord descended in a cloud [of glory?], and stood near [*parestē*] him . . . . And the Lord passed by [*parēlthen*] before his face" (Exod 33:19—34:6). Notice this pattern of "*par*. . ." with the reference to (the *doxa* of) God.

213. Cf. *hamartiai* . . . *anomiai* and *endoxa* . . . *ta erga kuriou* . . . *thaumasta* (Exod 34:9–10 LXX).

214. Notice *heōs*, "until" (9:18).

215. Just as in the episode of healing the cripple to whom Jesus takes the initiative to reveal himself later in the temple (5:14).

covenantal terms, "You have both seen [*heōrakas*[216]] Him, and He is the one who is talking with you" (9:37). In accordance with the covenant, not only is Jesus seen, but now also *known* by the formerly blind man. Before the revelation the man knew neither where his healer was (9:12), who his healer was (9:17), nor whether his healer was a sinner (9:25). After he is healed the man knows who Jesus is, addressing him as the Lord (9:35-38). Jesus demonstrates the graciousness—healing the man—and also the integrity of the divine character by acknowledging, "We must work the works of Him who sent Me" (9:4). As an exposure to God's *doxa* at Sinai makes one worship (*prosekunēsen*, Exod 34:8 LXX), so does its manifestation in the Son of God cause the formerly blind man to worship Jesus (*prosekunēsen*, 9:38).

According to the covenant, the presence (*charis*) of God is experienced when God leads his people (Exod 33:12; cf. 33:15 LXX) and gives them rest (Exod 33:14 LXX); God is present in grace, not in wrath (cf. Exod 33:3 LXX). Jesus leads the man born blind (9:7, 11) and gives him rest not only from the impairment in sight but also from the Jews persecuting him (9:34-35).

According to the covenant, the presence (*charis*) of God is encountered when the Lord takes away the sins and iniquities of the people (Exod 34:9 LXX). The blindness of the man was not caused by sin (9:2-3). But the attentive audience grasps yet another pointer to the Sinaitic covenant of *charis*, as the Jews (9:18, 22) and Pharisees (9:13, 15, 16) revile the man: "we are disciples of Moses. We know that God has spoken to Moses, but as for this man [, Jesus], we do not know where He is from." To this the formerly blind man responds exactly in terms of the miraculous splendor (*endoxa*) article of the covenant of *charis*: "here is a marvelous[217] thing [*to thaumaston estin*], that you do not know where He is from, and *yet* He opened my eyes. . . . Since the beginning of time it has never been heard that anyone opened the eyes of a person born blind." This brings into play the Sinaitic covenant link between taking away sins and performing incomparable works of the Lord (Exod 34:9-10 LXX). It is the discernment of the Jews and Pharisees that is at stake. They acknowledge that the Lord spoke to Moses (which happened exactly at Sinai in the originating of the covenant of *charis*!). They claim to

---

216. Cf. *heōrakas* here with *idō* of Exod 33:13 (cf. variants of reading).
217. NASB has "amazing."

be disciples of Moses themselves. Hence, they are supposed to know the articles of the covenant. They did see or hear of this incomparable work of God (9:3, 16, 30–32, 40), but failed to recognize the ratification of the covenant of the presence (*charis*) of God to which it witnesses. Jesus, therefore, is not obligated to keep his part of the covenant—to take their sins and iniquities away—either. Hence, Jesus says to the Pharisees, "If you were blind, you would have no sin [*hamartian*]; but since you say, 'We see,' your sin [*hamartia*] remains" (9:41). Of all those who remain in their sins due to their failure to recognize ratification of the covenant of *charis* behind the incomparable works of God, Jesus concludes, "If I had not come and spoken to them, they would not have sin [*hamartian*], but now they have no excuse for their sin [*hamartias*] . . . If I had not done among them the works [*erga*] which no one else did [![218]], they would not have sin [*hamartian*]; but now they have both seen and hated Me and My Father as well" (15:22–24).

Covenantal Connotations of *doxa* in the Sign of Raising Lazarus from the Dead

According to the covenant, the presence (*charis*) of God is evinced when the he does glorious things (*endoxa*) that have not been done in all the earth or in any nation, and all the people see the marvelous (*thaumasta*) works (*erga*) of the Lord (Exod 34:10 LXX). The sign of raising Lazarus from the dead is *designed* to witness to the ratification of the covenant of *charis*. Jesus explains this first to Mary and Martha's courier(s) and, perhaps, to the disciples (11:3) as well: "This sickness is not to end in death, but for the miraculous splendor[219] [*doxēs*] of God" (11:4, cf. 11:11–15). Then, Jesus explains the covenantal purpose of the sign also to Martha: "Did I not say to you that if you believe, you will see the miraculous splendor[220] [*doxan*] of God?" (11:40, cf. 11:3–4). Finally, he actually performs the incomparable—Lazarus has been dead in the tomb for four (!) days—sign (11:17, 39).

This sign is one of the covenantal glorious things (*endoxa*), which are marvelous (*thaumasta*). A cognate of *thaumastos* is not utilized in the episode, but there are two references to the term. First, some of the

---

218. A definite reference to the incomparability of works required by the covenant of presence (*charis*) of God (Exod 34:10 LXX).

219. NASB has "glory."

220. NASB has "glory."

witnesses to the raising of Lazarus from the dead say of Jesus, "Could not this man, who opened the eyes of the blind man, have kept this man also from dying?" (11:37). The sign of giving sight to the man born blind *is* recognized as a marvelous thing (*thaumaston*, 9:30–32). By comparison, the sign of raising Lazarus from the dead is also marvelous. Second, Jesus and Martha discuss the role of Jesus in the resurrection (11:21–27), the matter that is marvelous to the Jews (5:20–21).

According to the covenant, such incomparable *endoxa*, "glorious things," are to be attested by the Israelites. The incomparable sign of raising Lazarus from the dead is seen precisely by the covenantal nation of Jews: the disciples (1:7–16f.), Mary and Martha (11:28–32, 39), and the Jews (11:19, 31–33, 45). Hence, the incomparability of this marvelous sign witnessed by the people of God evinces the presence (*charis*) of God as Jesus.

According to the covenant, the presence (*charis*) of God is attested when God reveals himself so that he may be evidently known/seen (Exod 33:13; cf. Exod 33:18—34:7 LXX) and when he manifests his *doxa* (Exod 33:18—34:10 LXX). Jesus—the visible appearance (*doxa*) of God—is clearly *seen* by those around him. Jesus also exhibits the utmost graciousness and integrity of the *character* (*doxa*) of God. On the one hand, Jesus is gracious: even though "the resurrection on the last day" Martha is awaiting is not yet (11:24), he still raises Lazarus from the dead. He loves Lazarus, Martha, and Mary (11:3, 5, 36); he is full of compassion and even weeps over the matter (11:33–35, 38). On the other hand, Jesus's integrity is evident: he says, "I go, so that I may awaken him out of sleep." And he actually raises Lazarus from the dead, just as promised. He travels to Judea even though "the Jews were just now seeking to stone" him, going beyond mere duty. Hence, Jesus is depicted as being *plērēs charitos kai alētheias* in character.

According to the covenant, the presence (*charis*) of God is encountered when the Lord takes away the sins and iniquities of people (Exod 34:9 LXX). If one recalls that the *astheneia*, "sickness," of the cripple was definitely caused by sin (5:5, 14) then it become possible that the deadly[221] *astheneia* of Lazarus (11:4) is caused by sin as well. If this is the

---

221. Cf. Deut 28:15–46, especially 20, 22, 27, 35, 45. The Evangelist is well acquainted with the book of Deuteronomy; see NA[27], 770–806. Consider also our comments over the case of covenantal connotations of *doxa* in the sign of healing of the son of a royal official (with regard to deadly *puretos*, "fever," cf. Deut 4:52; 28:22).

case, then Jesus takes away the sin that had caused the deadly sickness of Lazarus. This, according to the covenant, is yet another evidence of an encounter with the presence (*charis*) of God as Jesus.

According to the covenant, the presence (*charis*) of God is experienced when God leads his people (Exod 33:12; cf. 33:15 LXX), gives them rest (Exod 33:14 LXX), and goes before (Exod 33:14; cf. 34:15 LXX) and with (Exod 33:16 LXX) them; God is present in grace, not in wrath (cf. Exod 33:3 LXX). And so Jesus directs the disciples (11:7) and the gathered around the tomb (11:39), giving rest to the sisters over their grief about their deceased brother. As an exposure to God's *doxa* at Sinai makes one worship (Exod 34:8 LXX), so its manifestation as Jesus causes the disciples, Martha, and many of the Jews to believe (11:15, 27, 45).

Jesus ensures that the covenantal purpose of the miracle is recognized. Not only does he allude to the miraculous splendor (*endoxa*) article of the covenant—"This sickness is not to end in death, but for the miraculous splendor[222] [*doxēs*] of God—but he also expounds, "so that the Son of God may be honored[223] [*doxasthē*] by it" (11:4). The divine passive of *doxasthē* indicates an allusion to the divine honor (*endoxasthēsomai*) article of the Sinaitic covenant (Exod 33:16 LXX) being ratified by God in Jesus. In the course of the event Jesus is glorified exactly from above as the Father approves the Son's miracle from the heavens (11:41–42).

Covenantal Connotations of *doxa* in the Sign of Jesus's Crucifixion and Resurrection

In the crucifixion, Christ is divinely honored by God, as the passive voice of *edoxasthē* (7:39; 12:16, 23; 13:31a, 31b; 13:32) indicates: "the Spirit was not yet *given*, because Jesus was not yet honored [*edoxasthē*]" (7:39); "The hour has come for the Son of Man to be honored [*doxasthē*]" (12:23); "Now is the Son of Man honored [*edoxasthē*], and God is honored [*edoxasthē*] in Him; if God is honored [*edoxasthē*[224]] in Him, God

---

222. NASB has "glory."

223. NASB has "glorified."

224. See n. 190. These two occurrences of *edoxasthē* (13:31b; 32a) may well also echo the miraculous splendor (*endoxa*) article of the covenant. Incomparable *endoxa* —Jesus's *sēmeia*, *erga*, *terata*, *thaumasta*—are required by the covenant to verify the presence of God. The crucifixion/resurrection of Christ is such *endoxon*—the ultimate incomparable glorious deed—which glorifies God.

will also honor Him [*doxasei*] in Himself, and will honor [*doxasei*] Him immediately" (13:31–32); and "when Jesus was honored [*edoxasthē*]" (12:16). According to the divine honor (*endoxasthēsomai*) article of the covenant, such divine honor confirms the presence of God as Jesus. Just as required by the covenantal article, Jesus on the cross is honored "beyond all the nations, as many as are upon the earth" (Exod 33:16 LXX): many of the Jews read the inscription written on the cross in Hebrew, Latin and Greek (19:20). This presence of God remains as Jesus, having been divinely honored on the cross, bestows the Spirit on believers.

According to the covenant, the presence (*charis*) of God is evinced when the Lord does glorious things (*endoxa*) that have not been done in all the earth or in any nation; and all the people see the marvelous works of the Lord (Exod 34:10 LXX). Jesus himself constitutes such *incomparable* glorious work of God seen by all the people (12:20; 19:20).

According to the covenant, the incomparable *endoxa*, "glorious things," are to be attested by the Israelites (Exod 34:10). So the incomparable sign of the resurrection of Jesus is seen exactly by the covenantal people: Mary Magdalene (20:1f.), Simon Peter and the other disciple whom Jesus loved (20:2f.), and the disciples (20:19f.).[225]

According to the covenant, the presence (*charis*) of God is attested when God reveals (*emphanizō*) himself so that he may be evidently known/seen (*gnōstōs (e)idō*) (Exod 33:13; cf. Exod 33:18—34:7 LXX), when he lets people know his ways so that they may know him (Exod 33:13 LXX), and when he manifests (*deiknumi*) his *doxa* (Exod 33:18—34:10 LXX). Jesus reveals himself to the disciples (*emphanisō*, 14:21, *emphanizein*, 14:22; 20:19f.). The Father is evidently known/seen by the disciples in the Son; Jesus lets people know his way, and in fact he is himself the way (14:5–10).[226]

According to the covenant, the presence (*charis*) of God is attested when God reveals (*deixon*) his glory (Exod 33:18 LXX). Also, Jesus reveals (*deixon*, 14:8, 9) the Father to the disciples; he reveals (*edeixen*, 20:20) his hands and his side pierced on the cross—just exactly where

---

225. The crucifixion of Jesus is also attested by the covenantal people: many of the Jews (19:20, 31), his mother and her sister, Mary the *wife* of Clopas, and Mary Magdalene (19:25), the disciple whom he loved (19:26f.), Joseph of Arimathea (19:38), and Nicodemus (19:39).

226. On the matter of the exact terminological correlation between 14:5-10 and Exod 33:13—34:10 LXX, see elsewhere in our study.

Jesus has been glorified—to the disciples; he reveals (*deiknueis*, 2:18f.) to the Jews the miraculous splendor of his crucifixion and resurrection. Not only does Jesus reveal the visible appearance (*doxa*) of God, he also demonstrates the intrinsic character (*doxa*) of God. Jesus is gracious: he turns the fear of the disciples into joy (15:11; 16:20–22; 20:19). The integrity of Jesus is obvious: he keeps the promise of coming back, of giving peace, and of pouring out the Spirit. Jesus grants the intrinsic character (*doxa*) of God to believers by bestowing the Holy Spirit *charitos kai alētheias* (1:32–33; 3:34, 20:22) onto them. Hence, Jesus is depicted as *plērēs charitos kai alētheias* in character. Just as the one exposed to the *doxa* of God at Sinai worships (Exod 34:8 LXX), so does Thomas confess Jesus as "My Lord and my God" (20:28).

According to the covenant, the presence (*charis*) of God is encountered when the Lord takes away the sins and iniquities of people (Exod 34:9 LXX). Jesus, by the crucifixion and resurrection, takes away the sin of the world (1:29, passim). The ability to take away the sin (as a witness to an encounter with the presence of God) is also given to the disciples (20:23); as those who have gained the character (*doxa*) of God (17:22; 20:22) they are now capable of conveying the presence of God.

According to the covenant, the presence (*charis*) of God is experienced when God leads his people (Exod 33:12; cf. 33:15 LXX) and gives them rest (Exod 33:14 LXX), and goes before (Exod 33:14; cf. 34:15 LXX) and with (Exod 33:16 LXX) them; God is present in grace, not in wrath (cf. Exod 33:3 LXX). Fulfilling all of this, Jesus himself comes (*ēlthen*, 20:19)[227] to believers and stands in their midst (*estē eis to meson*).[228]

According to the covenant, the presence (*charis*) of God is at work when the Israelites remain God's people (Exod 33:13, cf. 34:9 LXX). The resurrected Jesus comes to his Jewish disciples (20:19). Just as Jesus promised, he does not leave his own as orphans (14:18); on the contrary,

---

227. It may well be of significance that a cognate of *erchomai*, "come, go," (20:19) is utilized to describe the appearance of Jesus. Cf. the usage of cognates of *proporeuomai*, "go before, in front of" (Exod 33:14); *poreuomai*, "go" (Exod 33:15); and *sumporeuomai*, "go along with," (Exod 33:16; 34:9) applied to God in the course of the covenant at Sinai as a requirement to verify the presence of God. Notice also that a cognate of *parerchomai*, "go, pass by," (Exod 33:19–22) is utilized of God to depict the Sinaitic actualization of the presence of the Divine.

228. *estē eis to meson*; cf. *parestē* of God (Exod 34:5). Notice that according to Exodus God reveals himself in his *doxa* from the midst (*mesos*) of the cloud (Exod 24:16, 18; cf. Exod 25:22).

Jesus addresses them as *teknion* (13:33) and *paidion* (21:5. cf. 16:21). As his own receive Christ they gain "the right to become children of God" (1:12). Hence Jews remain God's people. Thus, in full accord with the article of the covenant, yet another evidence is provided to attest to the presence (*charis*) of God as Jesus.

Conclusion

Our study concludes that four Sinaitic *doxa* aspects of the presence of God—1) the visible appearance of God (*doxa*), 2) the intrinsic character of God (*doxa*), 3) the miraculous splendor verifying the presence of God (*endoxa*), and 4) the divine honor confirming the presence of God (*endoxasthēsomai*)—become evident in the course of the ratification of the covenant of the presence (*charis*) of God as Jesus.

Conclusion

This study has made the case that three key concepts—1) *hē charis kai hē alētheia*, 2) *charis*, and 3) *doxa*—of the Gospel's account of the revelation of God as Jesus (John 1:14–18ff.) allude to the covenant of God's presence originated in the revelation of God at Sinai (Exod 33:12—34:10 LXX). In *essence*, both revelations deal with the *same* matter of the presence of God. In *quality*, the revelation of God at Sinai is *surpassed* by the revelation of God as Jesus in all the three above aspects.

First, in the course of the revelation of God as Jesus, the concept of *(hē) charis kai (hē) alētheia* is first announced in the prologue (John 1:14, 17) and then unfolded throughout the whole of the Gospel in accordance with the covenant of God's presence (*charis*) originated at Sinai (Exod 33:12—34:10 LXX). The Gospel depicts the *bestowal* of the divine character *charitos kai alētheias* on believers.

To begin with, the phraseology *plērēs charitos kai alētheias* (John 1:14) and *hē charis kai hē alētheia* (John 1:17) *does* allude[1] to the Sinaitic phraseology *wərab-ḥesed weʾĕmet*[2] (Exod 34:6), which depicts the character of God. The major uncertainty in this case had been the discrepancy between *wərab-ḥesed weʾĕmet* (Exod 34:6 MT), *polueleos kai alēthinos* (Exod 34:6 LXX), and *plērēs charitos kai alētheias* (John 1:14).

---

1. Our study has established *allusions* of the revelation of God as Jesus to the revelation of God at Sinai (with the reference to *hē charis kai hē alētheia, charis*, and *doxa* as depicted in the Gospel). In our view, both notions—the presence of God (*ḥesed/charis*) and the qualities of the character of God (*ḥesed weʾĕmet/hē charis kai hē alētheia*)—may well have also been *echoed* throughout the Gospel. Cf. Jer 16:5; Isa 54:10 with John 14:27; 20:19, 21, 26. Cf. Mic 7:20; Hos 4:1; Pss 26:3; 36:6; 44:3 OG; 44:27/43:27 OG; 57:4, 11/56:4, 11 OG; 69:14; 88:12/87:12 OG; 89:3, 25; 103:11; 136:5, 26; Prov 10:32 OG; 14:22; 16:6/15:27 OG, 1 Kgs 8:23; Neh 1:5; 2 Chr 6:14. See our thoughts on their relevancy elsewhere in our study. Due to the time and volume constraint applicable to this study we did not intend to formally establish cases of this list. For the proper methodology with regard to establishing echoes see Bauckham, "Study of Gospel Traditions"; Davila, "Perils of Parallels"; Hays, *Echoes*; Michael Thompson, *Clothed with Christ*.

2. Likely to the whole creed *raḥûm wəḥannûn ʾerek ʾappayim wərab-ḥesed weʾĕmet* (Exod 34:6).

On the one hand, alleged objections to the case of the allusion[3] and previous attempts to positively account for the discrepancy[4] have been demonstrated as either invalid or inadequate. On the other hand, this study has utilized new approaches to make the case. The Evangelist *can* legitimately translate *rab* with *plērēs*[5], *ḥesed* with *charis*[6], and *ʾĕmet*[7] with *alētheia*;[8] he *does* translate from Hebrew (12:10, 40; 13:1) if there is a reason for it;[9] and he *does* have major[10] reasons to translate *wərab-ḥesed we'ĕmet* exactly with *plērēs charitos kai alētheias*: 1) Instead of the usual

3. Including a) Bultmann's (et al.) argument from the alleged incongruity in the meaning of *alētheia* and *ĕmet*, and b) Harris's (et al.) argument from the alleged unlikelihood of the recognition of *wərab-ḥesed we'ĕmet* behind *hē charis kai hē alētheia*.

4. Including a) Piper's argument from a stylistic variation, b) Hanson's argument from a hypothetical Greek non-LXX version of Exod 34:6, c) Montgomery's argument from the Syriac versions and Christian Palestinian dialect, d) Boismard's argument from modern comparative linguistics, e) Brown's argument from unfaithfulness of usage, f) Dodd's argument from Hellenistic Judaism, and g) Hanson's argument from feebleness of translation.

5. We have argued from the OT/LXX/OG practices, echoes of Exodus in the Gospel, the Evangelist's own tendency to use the excessive language while speaking of the Divine, the NT authors' usage of extraordinary degrees and the terminology different from the standard LXX's while speaking of the divine *charis*.

6. The study has identified numerous occurrences of *ḥesed* translated with *charis* (cognates) in the OG and recensions—Theodotion, Aquila, Symmachus, Quinta, Sexta—to the LXX/OG (we have established that findings in three latter recensions post-dating the Gospel should still be treated as independent and unbiased witnesses to practices of translating *ḥesed*, and can be legitimately projected onto the époque of the Gospel).

7. In the LXX/OG, when it comes to creedal pair *ḥesed and ĕmet* (*'ĕmûnāʰ*), the terms *ĕmet* and *'ĕmûnāʰ* are always translated with a cognate of *alētheia*.

8. The phraseology *plērēs charitos kai alētheias* reflects practices common to the époque of the Evangelist in alluding/echoing the OT creed; cf. Luke 1:50, 58, 72; Rom 2:4; 15:7-11, Eph 2:4-8 (notice the equivalency of *charis* and LXX/OG's *eleos*); Jas 5:11; 1 Pet 1:3; *Pr. Man.* 7; Sir 2:11; 5:4-6.

9. Menken, *Quotations*, 99–122, 123–38, 205.

10. The minor considerations being: 1) the irregular and excessive *plērēs* hints that all three creedal terms denoting "grace" linked by *w—raḥûm wəhannûn . . . wərab-ḥesed*—are conveyed with single *charis* (the three creedal terms denoting "grace" had lost their distinctiveness by the époque of the Evangelist and term *charis* is suitable for all the three); 2) the adjoined distinctive attribute *we'ĕmet* is communicated with *kai alētheias* (the Evangelist, with the importance of the notion of *alētheia* in the Gospel and its Christological significance for the writer, may well have wanted to bring out the sense of the Hebrew *rab-* . . . *'ĕmet* rather than the inadequate LXX's *alētheias*); and 3) the absence of creedal *'erek 'appayim/makrothumos* warns that God's longsuffering nature has come to an end (cf. 3:36).

LXX/OG's *polu/plēthos* for *rab*, the Evangelist chooses *plērēs* because the term *plērēs* with a following genitive is indeclinable.¹¹ This feature of *plērēs* allows the expression *plērēs charitos kai alētheias* to modify either *patēr*, *(monogenēs) logos*, or *doxa*. By utilizing *plērēs* the Evangelist emphasizes the sameness of the character (*doxa*) of God *plērēs charitos kai alētheias* inherent in the *patēr* and *(monogenēs) logos*. 2) Instead of the common LXX/OG's *eleos* for *ḥesed*, the Evangelist utilizes the legitimate option of *charis* because the term a) draws the attention of the reader to the sequence of the six (Exod 33:12; 33:13, 13, 16, 17; 34:9-10 LXX) Sinaitic requests to confirm the presence (*charis*) of God—the usage of *charis* in *plērēs charitos kai alētheias* defines the Sinaitic covenant of *charis* (Exod 33:12—34:10 LXX) as the definitive background for the Gospel—and b) reminds the reader that the Spirit poured out on the house of David and on the inhabitants of Jerusalem according to the prophecy quoted in the Gospel is the Spirit of *charis* (19:37 + Zech 12:10 LXX). Hence, the Gospel's qualities *plērēs charitos kai alētheias* of the Word match the requisites *hē charis kai hē alētheia . . . ek metrou* of the Spirit (3:34; 14:17; 15:26; 16:13; 19:37 + Zech 12:10 LXX).

Moreover, this study has shown that neither *wərab-ḥesed weʾĕmet* (Exod 34:6), *plērēs charitos kai alētheias* (John 1:14), nor *hē charis kai hē alētheia* (John 1:17) constitutes hendiadys in terms of "the coordination of two ideas, one of which is dependent on the other." On the one hand, the speculations¹² and arguments¹³ of proponents of treating *ḥesed weʾĕmet/(hē) charis kai (hē) alētheia* as hendiadys have been demonstrated as invalid. On the other hand, in the OT¹⁴ whenever

---

11. BDF, §137.

12. Unsubstantiated (Sakenfeld, Speiser), immune to criticism (Sakenfeld, Zobel), circular (Johnson), and associative (Kellenberger, Sakenfeld) attempts.

13. Including a) Williams's/Zobel's argument from a single preposition followed by two or more nouns joined by a conjunction (as in Proverb 16:6), and b) Zobel's contention from Hosea's phraseology projected onto the chain *kî ʾēn-ʾĕmet wəʾēn-ḥesed wəʾēn-daʿat ʾĕlōhîm*, "because there is no *ʾĕmet* or *ḥesed* or knowledge of God" (as in Hos 4:1).

14. See also our arguments from a) irrelevancy of the relatively late date of the construct state development in affinity to syndetic parataxis and the paucity of adjectives in Biblical Hebrew to the case of *ḥesed weʾĕmet*, b) parallelism of *ḥesed* and *ʾĕmet* (*ʾĕmûnāʰ*) in adjoining colons often without the terms paralleling each other, c) parting of *ḥesed* and *ʾĕmet* (*ʾĕmûnāʰ*) outside of parallel forms, d) *ḥesed* and *ʾĕmet* (*ʾĕmûnāʰ*) of God occurring in various modes of pairing in a literary unit, e) rendering of the word pair in both direct *ḥsd wʾmt* and reverse *ʾĕmûnāʰ wḥsd* order in the same literary

the word-pair ḥesed . . . ʾĕmet is the subject of a verb, the verb is always in third person plural (Prov 3:3; 20:28, Pss 40:12; 61:8; 85:11; 89:15). The LXX/OG's translators perceive the creedal ḥesed weʾĕmet as denoting two attributes.[15] The Evangelist conveys two attributes with *(hē) charis kai (hē) alētheia* because:[16] a) *(hē) charis kai (hē) alētheia* alludes to *wərab-ḥesed weʾĕmet*, which does not constitute hendiadys itself; b) in the Gospel, the construction "article-noun in singular-*kai*-article-noun in singular" always conveys two attributes (2:22; 6:42; 11:5, 25, 48; 13:13, 14; 14:6; 19:25, 26; 20:28); and c) in the LXX/OG/NT, the construction[17] "article-noun-*kai*-article-noun-verb in singular" (as in *hē charis kai hē alētheia . . . egeneto*) always conveys two attributes (Num 13:29; 1 Kgs 21:3a and, similarly, 1 Esd 8:61; Zeph 1:18, cf. Jas 5:3; 1 Esd 8:61; 1 Macc 2:12; 4 Macc 17:14; Prov 25:10; Zeph 1:18, cf. Jas 5:3; Ep Jer 1:71; Ezek 19:10; Dan 2:20, so also Dan (TH) 2:20; Dan (TH) 7:27, cf. Dan 7:27 OG; Matt 13:22; Acts 4:28; Acts 19:27; Rom 5:15; 2 Cor 8:2; 1 Thess 3:11; 2 Thess 2:16–17; Jas 5:3).[18] Hence, the terms of *(hē)*

---

unit, and f) characterization of God by an unaccompanied attribute of either one of the families *ḥsd, ʾmn*.

15. LXX/OG translators are capable of recognizing hendiadys in Hebrew and of expressing it by means of adjectival or genitival constructions. But neither one of the *ḥesed . . . ʾĕmet* (*ʾĕmûnāʰ*, cognates) constructions is conveyed with such adjectival or genitival construction in Greek. Particularly, the creedal *raḥûm wəḥannûn ʾerek ʾappayim wərab-ḥesed weʾĕmet*, a heterogeneous construction of nouns and adjectives, is conveyed by *oiktirmōn kai eleēmōn makrothumos kai polueleos kai alēthinos*, a homogeneous recurrence of adjectives only; adjectives may not constitute hendiadys in a way affecting our study. Whenever the word-pair *ḥesed . . . ʾĕmet* is the subject of a verb, the LXX/OG renders the verb in third person plural (Prov 3:3; 20:28; Pss 40:12; 85:11; for the case of Ps 89:15 see our invalidation of the BDF §135b rule).

16. Consider also the following factors: 1) The Evangelist is well aware of the usage of adjectival and genitival constructions expressing the idea of modification, but does not use them in *(hē) charis kai (hē) alētheia*. Notice, especially, the writer's favorite "true something" expressions *to phōs to alēthinon*, "the true Light" (1:9); *hoi alēthinoi proskunētai*, "the true worshipers" (4:23); *ton arton ek tou ouranou ton alēthinon*, "the true bread out of heaven" (6:32); *hē ampelos hē alēthinē*, "the true vine" (15:1); and *ton monon alēthinon Theon*, "the only true God" (17:3). Observe also that had the Evangelist wanted to express the idea of a "gift of *alētheia*" by *(hē) charis kai (hē) alētheia* he would have likely employed a familiar construction, such as *tēn dōrean tou Theou*, "the gift of God" (4:10). 2) Hendiadys is not listed as a feature of the style of the Evangelist. 3) The usage of construction "*plērēs*-noun-*kai*-noun" in the LXX/OG/NT discourages one from envisioning hendiadys in *plērēs charitos kai alētheias*.

17. See our comments on the case of Gen 9:2 elsewhere in the study.

18. Contra Harris, Schoneveld. These findings of our study invalidate the BDF §135

charis kai (hē) alētheia do not modify each other such that the expression means anything like either "true grace" or "gracious truth." Neither do they collapse into anything akin to either "the gracious gift of divine reality" or "the reality of the grace." The phraseology *(hē) charis kai (hē) alētheia* alluding to *ḥesed weʾĕmet* denotes graciousness and integrity, two qualities of the divine character *(doxa)*.

Furthermore, the Gospel depicts the *bestowal* of the divine character *charitos kai alētheias* on believers. The Word made flesh is *plērēs charitos kai alētheias* in the divine character *(doxa,* 1:14b). Jesus bestows God's character—*hē charis kai hē alētheia*—on the faithful *(egeneto,* 1:17). The Son gives the Father's "glory"—the intrinsic character of God—to the disciples (17:22). Christ manifests and makes God's "name"—the character of God—known to believers (17:6, 26). Jesus bestows God's character on believers by means of the Holy Spirit (1:33; 7:39; 20:22): the Holy Spirit is not only *to pneuma tēs alētheias* (14:17; 15:26; 16:13) but also *pneuma charitos* (19:37 + Zech 12:10). Both these qualities of the divine character are inherent in the Holy Spirit without measure *(ek metrou,* 3:34). Hence, the Holy Spirit is the Spirit *plērēs charitos kai alētheias*. The time when "the Spirit was not yet *given*, because Jesus was not yet glorified" is over. Jesus is glorified on the cross; believers receive the Spirit of *(hē) charis kai (hē) alētheia* (1:32–33; 3:34; 7:39; 20:22).[19]

Both the eyewitnesses and non-eyewitnesses receive the divine character via the Spirit of *(hē) charis kai (hē) alētheia ek metrou* (1:32–33; 3:34; 7:39; 20:22). The role of the Spirit in conveying the character *(doxa)* of God *plērēs charitos kai alētheias* to non-eyewitnesses[20] is conceptually introduced in the prologue: 1) the reference to the testimony of John[21] (1:15) invites the reader to consider exactly the day on which

---

(1)b rule on "agreement with two or more co-ordinate words connected by *kai (hē),*" which reads, "When the subject consists of sing. + sing. or sing. + plur. the verb agrees . . . (b) with both subjects taken together if the verb stands after the second subject." In addition to the listed examples, notice other LXX/OG/NT examples contrary to the rule—Judg (A) 19:19; Ps 144:4 OG; Sir 10:24; Hos 4:2; Isa 32:20; Jer 43:25; Matt 6:19.

19. The post-resurrection audience naturally envisions both qualities *hē charis kai hē alētheia* in other various references to the Spirit in the Gospel (4:23, 24; 14:17; 15:26; 16:13).

20. See elsewhere in our study.

21. The very name John *(Yôḥānān)* means "Yahweh is gracious." Hence, by mentioning the name "John" in 1:15 the Evangelist points out the revelation of God at Sinai as the background to 1:14–18 (where, in the exact terminology of Exod 33:12, 13; 13; 16; 17; and 34:9–10, Moses is represented as the one who found grace with Yahweh).

John the Baptist spoke of Jesus as "the One who baptizes in the Holy Spirit" (1:33), and 2) the distinction between *hēmeis*, "we," (1:14) and *hēmeis pantes*, "we all," (1:16) hints that even though the Word *plērēs charitos kai alētheias* in character dwells only among the eyewitnesses, *both* the eye-witnesses and non-eyewitnesses receive the presence (*charis*) of God. The non-eyewitnesses gain this presence through the Holy Spirit of *(hē) charis kai (hē) alētheia ek metrou* in character dwelling in them. Further in the Gospel, the role of the Spirit in conveying the character (*doxa*) of God *plērēs charitos kai alētheias* to non-eyewitnesses is implied in Jesus's statement, "the Spirit . . . will glorify [*doxasei*] Me, for He will take of Mine and will disclose *it* to you" (16:14).

Finally, *hē charis kai hē alētheia* (qualities of the divine character) and *ho nomos* (the divine legal corpus) belong to different dimensions (1:17, passim). As such, they cannot be either contrasted or compared; neither can they conceivably replace or fulfill one another. The two divine entities—*ho nomos* and *hē charis kai hē alētheia*—complement each other. The Gospel holds the Law in high regard. Jesus engages with the Decalogue. There are allusions to each of the Ten Commandments (Exod 20:1–17): you shall have no other gods before Me (10:30); you shall not make for yourself an idol (10:33); you shall not take the name of the Lord your God in vain (10:25); remember the Sabbath day (7:23; cf. 5:18); honor your father (8:49; cf. 5:23); you shall not murder (7:19, 8:40, 44; cf. 5:18); you shall not commit adultery (8:41); you shall not steal (10:1, 8, 10); you shall not bear false witness (8:14[22]); you shall not covet (8:44). There is also an allusion to the Shema (8:41b–42a).[23] By challenging, "Which one of you convicts Me of sin?" (8:46), Jesus makes himself a subject to the Law.[24] Jesus approves of the fact that believers have kept the Father's word (= the Law, 17:6). Jesus's saying, "do not sin anymore," only makes sense in the framework of the Law (5:14, cf. 8:11; 20:23). The Law is a revelation of the Divine (1:17). Jesus acknowledges that "the Scripture cannot be broken" (10:35). His new commandment provides the proper insight into the Law (13:34 cf. Lev 19:18). The risen Lord grants, "If you forgive the sins of any, *their sins* have been forgiven them; if you retain the *sins* of any, they have been retained" (20:23).

22. Motyer here adds also 8:44 (Motyer, *Your Father the Devil?* 130).

23. On the Decalogue and Shema in the Gospel see Brooke, "Christ and the Law," 103–8; Motyer, *Your Father the Devil?* 30, 42, 129–30, 193.

24. To say the opposite is to deny that Jesus was fully human.

Conclusion 249

These factors imply that observance of the relevant articles of the Law is expected even after Jesus's resurrection. The believers' possession of *hē charis kai hē alētheia* not only *illumines* in interpreting, but also *enables* the faithful to comply with *ho nomos*, as they are one with the Divine (14:22; 15:4–5; 17:11, 21–23). This *complementary* nature of *ho nomos* and *hē charis kai hē alētheia* fulfills the Scripture (10:35 cf. Jer 31:31–33; Ezek 36:26–28).

Second, in the course of the revelation of God as Jesus the concept of *charis* is first announced in the prologue (*charin anti charitos*, John 1:16) and then unfolded throughout the whole of the Gospel in accord with the covenant of God's presence (*charis*) originated at Sinai (Exod 33:12—34:10 LXX). The Gospel depicts the *ratification* of the Sinaitic covenant of God's presence (*charis*) as Jesus.

To begin with, the terminology and phraseology *charin anti charitos* (John 1:16) alludes to the covenant of God's presence (*charis*)[25] originated at Sinai (Exod 33:12—34:10 LXX). The message of the Sinaitic covenant—expressed by the six Sinaitic "*charis*" requests to confirm the presence of God (Exod 33:12; 33:13, 13, 16, 17; 34:9–10 LXX)—is clear: God's *charis is* the presence of God. In the Gospel, each occurrence of *charis* in *charin anti charitos* (John 1:16) denotes the presence (*charis*) of God; the presence of God as Jesus was granted over the presence of God experienced at Sinai.[26]

Moreover, this *charin anti charitos* concept is unfolded throughout the Gospel. The Gospel depicts the *ratification* of the covenant of God's presence (*charis*) as Jesus in accord with the "six requests for the confirmation of *charis*" scheme originated in the course of the revelation of God at Sinai:

25. Gracious presence, indeed. Notice the full extent of this *charis*; cf. *charis* of Exod 33:12—34:10 with the reference to the wrath of God of Exod 33:3.

26. This incessant—*charin anti charitos*—presence of God *results* from the character of God *plērēs charitos kai alētheias*—full of graciousness and integrity (Exod 34:6, cf. John 1:14, 17). To make sense within the intended—Sinaitic—frame of reference of the Gospel, the phrase *charin anti charitos* must have originally been intended to mean "the presence of God as Jesus over the presence of God at Sinai." Non-eyewitnesses who had first grasped this original meaning of *charin anti charitos* could then apply the typological meaning "the presence of God as the Spirit over the presence of God as Jesus" to the phrase. Both eyewitnesses and non-eyewitnesses would interpret *hēmeis pantes elabomen kai charin anti charitos* as "all believers, eyewitnesses and non-eyewitnesses bestowed with the Spirit, gained the grace of the presence of God over the grace of the presence of God the Israelites encountered at Sinai."

1) God's presence (*charis*) is encountered when God reveals[27] himself so he may be evidently seen/known; God lets people know his ways that people may know him.[28]

2) God's presence (*charis*) is attested when God manifests himself.[29]

3) God's presence (*charis*) is confirmed when God leads people and gives them rest, goes before and with them.[30]

4) God's presence (*charis*) is experienced when God's people are glorified beyond all the nations, as many as are upon the earth[31]; this great nation remains God's people.[32]

---

27. *emphanison* (Exod 33:13 LXX); cf. 14:21–22.

28. *hôdīʿēnî nāʾ ʾet-dərākekā wəʾēdāʿăkā*, "let me know Your ways that I may know You"; *emphanison moi seauton gnōstōs (e)idō se*, "reveal Yourself to me, that I may evidently know/see You" (Exod 33:13 MT; (G)RLXX; cf. Exod 33:18—34:7). Notice the Sinaitic *Deixon moi tēn seautou doxan*, "Manifest Your glory to me" (Exod 33:18). For *emphanison* see 14:21-22. For a blend of *hodos*, "way"; *ginōskō*, "know"; *oida*, "know"; *horaō*, "see"; and *deiknumi*, "manifest," suggesting that the Evangelist is aware of all the three variants, see 14:5-9. The prominence of actually seeing Jesus is enormous. It is evident in fundamental accounts of the Evangelist (1:14, 18), advice of Philip to Nathanael (1:46), wish of the Greeks (12:21), prophecy of Zechariah (19:37), anxious anticipation of believers (16:16, 17-19), resurrection announcement of Mary (20:18), and ultimate joy of the disciples (20:20, 25). It causes Christ to grieve, "you have seen Me, and yet do not believe" (6:36), but leads the man born blind (9:37-38) and Thomas to believe (20:27-29) and worship (just as the Sinaitic revelation of *doxa* causes one to worship; cf. Exod 34:9). The Evangelist emphatically concludes, *ho heōrakōs memarturēken*, "he who has seen has testified" (19:35). Cf. also the significance of seeing Jesus (18:26; 19:6; 19:33), the Son of Man (1:51), God (5:37), the Father (6:46; 8:38), the kingdom of God (3:3), the glory of God (11:40; 12:40-41), signs, wonders, works, and all the things that Jesus has done (1:50; 4:45, 48; 6:14, 30; 15:24). See our discussion elsewhere in this study on knowing/seeing God on Sinaitic terms in the Gospel.

29. *Deixon moi tēn seautou doxan*, the creed, etc. (Exod 33:18—34:7); cf. 1:14, 17; 2:18; 5:20; 10:32; 14:8-9; 17:22; 20:20.

30. Exod 33:12, 14, 15, 16; John 10:1-16; 14:2-28.

31. *endoxasthēsomai egō te kai ho laos sou para panta ta ethnē hosa epi tēs gēs estin* (Exod 33:16; cf. Isa 45:25 LXX); cf. 11:45–50; 18:14. Notice the usage of *laos* (8:2; 11:50; 18:14) and *ethnos* (11:48, 50, 51, 52; 18:35) exclusively of Jews. Moses *is* depicted in exalted terms (1:17; 1:45; 5:45, 46; 7:19, 22, 23; cf. 8:5; 9:29); "the serpent in the wilderness" (3:14ff) and "the bread out of heaven" (6:30-35) episodes narrate Moses as the predecessor of the saving activity of God as Jesus. The Jews *are* glorified in the Gospel (1:14; 2:11; 11:40; 12:41; 17:10, 22).

32. *laos sou to ethnos to mega touto* (Exod 33:13), *esometha soi* (Exod 34:9). It was Jews who first saw Jesus glorified after the resurrection, received the Spirit, and

5) God's presence (*charis*) is demonstrated when the Lord takes away the sins and iniquities of people.[33]

6) God's presence (*charis*) is evinced when the Lord ratifies the covenant of God's *charis* in the presence of all people by doing glorious things, which have not been done in all the earth or in any nation; all the people see the works of the Lord, that they are marvelous.[34] The Gospel depicts the incomparable miracles—*sēmeia, erga, terata, thaumasta*—principally[35] to evince the ratification of the covenant of God's presence (*charis*) as Jesus.[36]

Third, in the Gospel's account of the revelation of God as Jesus, the concept of *doxa* is first announced in the prologue (John 1:14a, 14b) and then unfolded throughout the whole of the Gospel in accord with the covenant of God's presence (*charis*) originated at Sinai (Exod 33:12—34:10 LXX).[37] At Sinai, Moses requests from God, *deixon*[38] *moi*

were privileged, "If you forgive the sins of any, *their sins* have been forgiven them; if you retain the *sins* of any, they have been retained" (20:23). The Jews *are* mediators of blessing for all the nations (4:22; 12:20). The true Light comes to his own (1:11); Jesus acknowledges that Galilee is his own country (4:44); the Jews are the Good Shepherd's own (10:3, 4, 12, 14, 27; 13:1; cf. 15:9).

33. *apheleis su tas hamartias hēmōn kai tas anomias hēmōn* (Exod 34:9); cf. 1:29, also 13:10–11; 15:3; 20:23.

34. *endoxa . . . ta erga kuriou . . . thaumasta* (Exod 34:10). Cf. cognates of *thaumazō* (3:7; 4:27; 5:20, 28; 7:15, 21; 9:30–32; cf. 2:10, 11:37). Notice the covenantal link alluded to in the Gospel between taking away sins and iniquities and doing glorious things, which have not been done in all the earth, or in any nation . . . the marvelous works of the Lord (Exod 34:9–10): the correlation of *astheneia*, "sickness"; *adikia*, "iniquity"; and *hamartia*, "sin," with cognates of *thaumastos*, "marvelous (act)"; *ergon*, "work, deed"; *teras*, "wonder"; and *sēmeion*, "sign," is evident in 5:1(5)–(14)15; 9:3, 41; 11:4; 15:22–24; etc.

35. Besides, Jesus *is* depicted as the Prophet in the Gospel.

36. The Sinaitic covenant of *charis* relates manifestations of God's self, name, glory, and deeds, and so does the covenant of *charis* ratified in Jesus (the Gospel reserves cognates of *phaneroō*, "reveal," exclusively for this purpose; cf. 1:5, 31; 2:11; 3:21; 7:4; 9:3; 17:6; 21:1, 14).

37. This explains the two peculiarities to the Johannine usage of *doxa*: 1) in the Gospel connotations of *doxa* are set alongside one another without restraint, and 2) whereas the vast majority of NT authors' statements concern the glorification of the risen Lord after Easter, the picture is rather different in the Gospel to the degree that one finds more references to the *doxa* of the earthly Jesus.

38. The Evangelist utilizes cognates of *deiknumi*, "manifest," exclusively while alluding to the covenant and so only with the reference to the Divine (2:18; 5:20; 10:32; 13:15; 14:8, 9; 20:20; cf. 2:18).

tēn seautou doxan "Manifest Your glory to me!" (Exod 33:18 LXX). In the description of the Sinaitic revelation, cognates of *doxa* are used in four ways: 1) the visible appearance of God (*doxa*, Exod 33:19 LXX); 2) the intrinsic character of God (*doxa*, Exod 33:19, 22 LXX); 3) the miraculous splendor verifying the presence of God (*endoxa*, Exod 34:10 LXX); and 4) the divine honor confirming the presence of God (*endoxasthēsomai*, Exod 33:16 LXX). According to the Gospel, all four Sinaitic covenant aspects of *doxa* are now evident to believers in Jesus Christ:

1) The visible appearance of God (*doxa*) is continuously seen in the Word made flesh (1:14a, 14:9). Christ has never given up the *doxa* inherent in him before (12:41; 17:5) and throughout (1:14, 17:10; 17:5) the incarnation.

2) The intrinsic character of God (*doxa*) is bestowed on believers: The only begotten from the Father is *plērēs charitos kai alētheias* in character (*doxa*) himself (1:14b). Jesus Christ bestows God's character (*doxa*) of *hē charis kai hē alētheia* onto believers (*egeneto*, 1:17, cf. 1:14). The Son gives the Father's intrinsic character (*doxa*) to the faithful (17:22).

3) The miraculous splendor verifying the presence of God (*endoxa*) is evident to believers in Jesus's signs, deeds, wonders, and marvelous acts.[39] *Endoxa* (*erga, thaumasta*) of a kind "which have not been done in all the earth, or in any nation" are required by the Sinaitic covenant to ratify the covenant of the presence (*charis*) of God. So does the Gospel depict the incomparable[40] *sēmeia, erga, terata, thaumasta*[41] in order to attest to the presence (*charis*) of God as Jesus. This Sinaitic covenant purpose of the Gospel's signs, works, wonders, and marvels with reference to *doxa* is confirmed by Christ (9:2–3; 11:4; 17:1–4), attested by the Evangelist (2:11; 20:31–32), and verified by their Sinaitic interrelatedness with the matter of taking away *hamartiai . . . anomiai*,[42]

---

39. And further in believers' greater works in the Spirit (14:12; cf. 14:16, 26; 15:26; 16:7).

40. This incomparability, as the requirement of the Sinaitic covenant of *charis* (Exod 34:10 LXX), explains the superior scale of miraculous deeds depicted in the Gospel compare to other Gospels, an issue much debated by scholars. See, for example, 9:32.

41. Cf. cognates.

42. The assumed *hamartia/anomia*, "sin/iniquity," of the son of the royal official (cf. *puretos*, "fever," in 4:52 and Deut 28:22); the evident *hamartia*, "sin," of the cripple (5:14); the *astheneia*, "sickness," of Lazarus (11:4); *tēn hamartian tou kosmou*, "the sin of the world" (1:29). Cf. *apheleis su tas hamartias hēmōn kai tas anomias hēmōn*, "Thou

by their causing partakers to believe and worship (2:11; 9:38; 12:37–41. cf. Exod 34:9 LXX), and by their being always witnessed by Jews as required by the articles of the covenant originated at Sinai.[43] As God's presence is incessant, so are *endoxa*. The Son accounts to the Father, "The glory [*doxan*] which You have given Me I have given to them" (17:22). This *doxa*—the divine character of the Father inherent in the Son—is given to the disciples; it is bestowed on believers with the Spirit of *hē charis kai hē alētheia . . . ek metrou* (1:17; 3:34; 14:17; 15:26; 16:13; 19:37 + Zech 12:10 LXX; 20:22). This conformity of the character of the faithful with God enables believers to continue performing covenantal *endoxa* (*erga, sēmeia*) in the Spirit (6:14; 14:12; 21:19) to glorify God after the resurrection of Jesus (14:12; cf. 5:19–20; 15:8; 21:19; notice 16:13–15; 17:10).

4) The divine honor confirming the presence of God (*endoxasthēsomai*) is evident to believers. The Sinaitic divine honor (*endoxasthēsomai*) attestation to the presence (*charis*) of God, "*endoxasthēsomai egō*[44] *te kai ho laos sou* beyond all the nations, as many as are upon the earth" (Exod 33:16 LXE), is now consummated in the glorification of Jesus and the children of God (cf. 19:20). Jesus is glorified by God and glorifies God throughout the Gospel, ultimately so by his death and resurrection (12:16, 23; 13:31–32; 17:1–5) but also beyond the resurrection through believers in the Spirit (16:13–15; 17:10). The children of God—those who recognize the presence (*charis*) of God as Jesus—are glorified accordingly. The "divine passive" form of the Sinaitic covenantal term *endoxasthēsomai* specifies that this glorification must come from God. Those who glorify themselves—receive glory from one another and do not seek the glory that is from the one and only God—labor in vain (5:44; 7:18; 8:50–54; 12:42–43).

The Sinaitic concepts of the covenant of God's presence (*charis*) with reference to *doxa* remarkably come together in the one and only

---

shalt take away our sins and our iniquities" (Exod 34:9–10 LXX). Notice the opposite effect depicted in 9:39–41.

43. Cf. *enōpion pantos tou laou sou poiēsō endoxa ha ou gegonen en pasē tē gē kai en panti ethnei kai opsetai pas ho laos en hois ei su ta erga kuriou hoti thaumasta estin ha egō poiēsō soi*, "in the presence of all thy people; I will do glorious things, which have not been done in all the earth, or in any nation; and all the people among whom thou art shalt see the works of the Lord, that they are wonderful, which I will do for thee" (Exod 34:10 LXE). In the Gospel the terms *ethnos* and *laos* are utilized exclusively of Jews.

44. Moses was glorified (Exod 34:29–35 LXX; Sir 45:1–3).

verbal conversation between the Son and the Father preserved in the Gospel. In response to the Son's appeal, "Father, glorify Your name," a voice comes out of heaven: "I have both glorified it, and will glorify it again" (12:28). When has God glorified his name? At Sinai, as God promised, "I will pass by before thee with my glory [*doxē*], and I will call by my name, the Lord, before thee" (Exod 33:19 LXE). When will God glorify his name again? In Jesus Christ and further in the Holy Spirit, as the Son prays, "Father, glorify Your name" (12:28); reports, "I have manifested Your name to the men . . . I have made Your name known to them, and will make it known" (17:6–26); accounts, "The glory which You have given Me I have given to them" (17:22); and predicts, "the Spirit . . . will glorify [*doxasei*] Me" (16:13–15). What is common to the revelations at Sinai and as Jesus? The presence (*charis*) of God—the visible appearance (*doxa*) and the intrinsic character (*doxa*) of God—described in terms of glory and name. Thus, in this sense, the Father's "I have both glorified it, and will glorify it again" in response to Jesus's "Father, glorify Your name" corresponds to the Evangelist's *charin anti charitos* (1:16). The covenant of the presence (*charis*) of God is now ratified in Jesus as it was earlier ratified at Sinai.[45]

The findings of this study allow one to make the following conclusion with regard to the revelations of God: in *essence*, the revelations of God at Sinai and as Jesus are the *same*; both deal with the presence (*charis*) of God, hence *charin anti charitos* (1:16). In *quality*, the revelation of God at Sinai is *surpassed* by the revelation of God as Jesus in all the three aspects—*doxa, charis,* and *hē charis kai hē alētheia*. To begin with, in the course of the former revelation only *one* man saw the visible appearance (*doxa*) of God, and only *from behind*; in the latter revelation *all* believers have seen the visible appearance (*doxa*) of God *face to face* (1:14a, passim). Moreover, at Sinai only *one* man merely *heard* God's word proclaiming that the divine character (*kābôd*) was *wərab-ḥesed we'ĕmet*. In Jesus, *all* believers in the Word—both eyewitnesses and non-eyewitnesses—have *become charitos kai alētheias* in the divine character (*doxa*) themselves (1:17; 17:22; 20:22). This conformity of the divine character allows believers to be one with God (14:22; 15:4–5; 17:11, 21–23); it also illumines believers in interpreting and enables them to comply with the divine Law (13:34; 14:15; 15:10; 20:23).

---

45. Isa 54:10; Jer 16:15; 31:31–33; Ezek 36:26–28. See Boismard, *St. John's Prologue*, 138–45.

Furthermore, as a result of the former revelation, only *the Israelites* gained the presence (*charis*) of God. As a result of the latter revelation, *all* believers—not only those with whom the Word dwelt (*hēmin*, 1:14), but also those who believe through the testimony of the Gospel and possess the divine character via the Holy Spirit (*hēmeis pantes*, 1:16)—have received the presence (*charis*) of God.

With the findings of the study listed above in mind, John 1:14–18, if paraphrased, means:

> 14 God became flesh; we, the eyewitnesses, perceived the visible appearance of God as God the Son who retained the intrinsic character of God the Father being full of graciousness and integrity. 15 As was attested by John the Baptist, this divine character was to be shared by the Father through the Son via the Spirit with all believers to allow the divine presence among humanity. 16 The Divine is inexhaustible; hence all believers, eyewitnesses and non-eyewitnesses bestowed with the Spirit, gained the grace of the presence of God over the grace of the presence of God the Israelites encountered at Sinai. 17 The divine Law was given by God to believers through Moses; the divine character—the graciousness and the integrity—God bestowed onto believers through Jesus Christ. 18 Prior, without this conformity of humans with the Divine, no one had been capable of dwelling in the presence of God; the Son abiding in the Father himself has now made dwelling in the presence of God a reality for humans as well.

Bibliography

Aalen, S. "'Truth', a Key Word in St John's Gospel." In *Studia evangelica II*, edited by F. L. Cross, 3–23. TUGAL 87. Berlin: Akademie-Verlag, 1964.

Abbott, Edwin Abbott. *Johannine Grammar*. Diatessarica 6. London: A. & C. Black, 1906.

Aland, Kurt, Barbara Aland, Johannes Karavidopoulos, Carlo M. Martini and Bruce M. Metzger, editors. *Novum Testamentum Graece*. 27th ed. Stuttgart: German Bible Society, 1993.

Alexander, Philip S. "Targum, Targumim." In *ABD*.

Allen, Leslie C. *Ezekiel 20–48*. Vol. 29 of *WBC* (1990).

———. *Psalms 101–150*. Vol. 21 of *WBC* (1983).

Allen, Ronald B. "What Is in a Name?" In *God: What Is He Like?*, edited by W. F. Kerr, 107–27. Wheaton, IL: Tyndale, 1977.

ANLEX GNTDICT. BibleWorks 7.0.019k.1, 1992–2007. Print ed.: Timothy Friberg, Barbara Friberg, and Neva F. Miller. *Analytical Lexicon of the Greek New Testament*. Grand Rapids: Baker, 2000. [*AnLex*]

Andersen, Francis I. "Yahweh, the Kind and Sensitive God." In *God Who Is Rich in Mercy: Essays Presented to D. B. Knox*, edited by Peter T. O'Brien and David G. Petersen, 41–88. Homebush West, NSW, Australia: Lancer, 1986.

The Anchor Bible Dictionary on CD-ROM. Logos Library System 2.0c, 1995, 1996. Print ed.: *Anchor Bible Dictionary*, edited by David Noel Freedman. 6 vols. New York: Doubleday, 1992. In *ABD*.

Anderson, A. A. *2 Samuel*. Vol. 11 of *WBC* (1998).

Anderson, Hugh. "Third Maccabees." In *ABD*.

Asensio, Félix. *Misericordia et Veritas, el ḥesed we'ĕmet divinos, su influjo religioso-social en la historia de Israel*. Analecta Gregoriana 48. Rome: Apud aedes Universitatis Gregorianae, 1949.

Attridge, Harold W. "Hebrews, Epistle to the." In *ABD*.

Aune, David E. *Revelation 1–5*. Vol. 52a of *WBC* (1997).

———. *Revelation 17–22*. Vol. 52c of *WBC* (1998).

———. *Revelation 6–16*. Vol. 52b of *WBC* (1998).

Avishur, Yitshak. *The Construct State of Synonyms in Biblical Rhetoric: Studies in the Stylistic Phenomenon of Synonymous Word Pairs in the Construct State*. Jerusalem: Kiryat Sepher, 1977.

———. "Pairs of Synonymous Words in the Construct State (and in Appositional Hendiadys) in Biblical Hebrew." *Semitics* 2 (1971–72) 17–81.

———. *Stylistic Studies of Word-Pairs in Biblical and Ancient Semitic Literatures*. Edited by Kurt Bergerhof, Manfried Dietrich, and Oswald Loretz. AOAT 210. Kevelaer, Ger.: Butzon & Bercker, 1984.

Barkhuizen, J. H. "A Short Note on John 1:17 in Patristic Exegesis." *Acta Patristica Et Byzantina* 8 (1997) 18–25.

Barr, James. "'Faith' and 'Truth'—an Examination of Some Linguistic Arguments." In *The Semantics of Biblical Language*, 161–205. London: Oxford University Press, 1961.

Barrett, C. K. *The Gospel According to St John: An Introduction with Commentary and Notes on the Greek Text*. 2nd ed. 1955. Reprint, London: SPCK, 1978.

Barthélemy, Dominique. *Les devanciers d'Aquila*. VTSup 10. Leiden: Brill, 1963.

———, and O. Rickenbacher. *Konkordanz zum Hebräischen Sirach: mit Syrisch-Hebräischem Index*. Göttingen: Vandenhoeck & Ruprecht, 1973.Barthélemy, Dominique. "Qui Est Symmaque?" *CBQ* 36 (1974) 451–65.

Bauckham, Richard. *God Crucified: Monotheism and Christology in the New Testament*. Didsbury Lectures 1996. 1998. Reprint, Grand Rapids: Eerdmans, 1999.

———. *The Gospels for All Christians: Rethinking the Gospel Audience*. Edinburgh: T&T Clark, 1998.

———. *Jesus and the Eyewitnesses: The Gospels as Eyewitness Testimony*. Grand Rapids: Eerdmans, 2006.

———. *Jude, 2 Peter*. Vol. 50 of *WBC* (1983).

———. "The Study of Gospel Traditions Outside the Canonical Gospels: Problems and Perspectives." In *Gospel Perspectives: The Jesus Tradition Outside the Gospels*, edited by David Wenham, 369–404. Sheffield, UK: JSOT Press, 1984.

Bauer, Walter, W. F. Arndt, F. W. Gingrich, and F. W. Danker. *A Greek-English Lexicon of the New Testament and Other Early Christian Literature: A Translation and Adaptation of the Fourth Revised and Augmented Edition of Walter Bauer's Griechisch-deutsches Wörterbuch zu den Schriften des Neuen Testaments und der übrigen urchristlichen Literatur*. 2nd ed. Chicago: University of Chicago Press, 1979. [BAGD].

Beasley-Murray, George Raymond. *John*. Vol. 36 of *WBC* (1989).

Bebb, Llewellyn J. M. "Versions (Georgian, Gothic, Slavonic)." In *Dictionary of the Bible Dealing with Its Language, Literature, and Contents, Including the Biblical Theology*, edited by James Hastings et al., 4:848–55. New York: Scribner, 1902.

Beentjes, Pancratius C. *The Book of Ben Sira in Hebrew: A Text Edition of All Extant Hebrew Manuscripts and a Synopsis of All Parallel Hebrew Ben Sira Texts*. Edited by J. A. Emerton. VTSup 68. Leiden: Brill, 1997.

Behm, Johannes. "*ametanoētos*." In *TDNT*.

Beker, J. Christiaan. *Paul the Apostle: The Triumph of God in Life and Thought*. Philadelphia: Fortress, 1980.

Belle, Gilbert van. *The Signs Source in the Fourth Gospel: Historical Survey and Critical Evaluation of the Semeia Hypothesis*. BETL 116. Leuven: Leuven University Press, 1994.

Ben-Hayyim, Zeev. spr bn sîrʾ hmqûr qûnqûrdnṣiyāʰ wnytwt ʾwṣr hmlîm (*The Book of Ben Sira: Text, Concordance and an Analysis of the Vocabulary*). Jerusalem: Academy of the Hebrew Language and the Shrine of the Book, 1973.

Bernard, J. H. *A Critical and Exegetical Commentary on the Gospel According to St. John*. Edited by A. H. McNeile. Vol. 1. Edinburgh: T. & T. Clark, 1928.

Bertram, Georg. "*paideuō, paideia, paideutēs, apaideutos, paidagōgos*." In *TDNT*.

Bichsel, M. Alfred. "Hymns, Early Christian." In *ABD*.

Bietenhard, Hans. "*onoma, onomazō, eponomazō, pseudōnumos*." In *TDNT*.

Birdsall, J. Neville. "Versions, Ancient (Introductory Survey)." In *ABD*.

Black, Matthew. "Does an Aramaic Tradition Underlie John 1.16?" *JTS* 42 (1941) 69–70.

Blass, F., A. Debrunner, and Robert W. Funk. *A Greek Grammar of the New Testament and Other Early Christian Literature: A Translation and Revision of the Ninth-Tenth German Edition Incorporating Supplementary Notes of A. Debrunner.* Translated by Robert W. Funk. 4th ed. Chicago: University of Chicago Press, 1970. Originally published as *Grammatik des neutestamentlichen Griechisch* (Göttingen: Vandenhoeck & Ruprecht, 1961). [BDF].

Blumenthal, Christian. "Charis anti charitos (John 1,16)." ZNW 92 (2001) 290–94.

Boadt, Lawrence. "Ezekiel, Book of." In *ABD*.

Boismard, Marie Émile. "Dans le sein du Père." *RB* 59 (1952) 23–39.

———. Lamouille, and Gérard Rochais. *L'Évangile de Jean: Commentaire.* Paris: Éditions du Cerf, 1977.

———. *Moses or Jesus: An Essay in Johannine Christology.* Translated by B. T. Viviano. BETL 84. Leuven: Leuven University Press, 1993. Originally published as *Moïse ou Jésus: Essai de christologie Johanniquei* (1988).

———. *St. John's Prologue.* Translated by Carisbrooke Dominicans. London: Blackfriars, 1957. Originally published as *Le Prologue de Saint Jean*, LD 11 (Paris: Éditions du Cerf, 1953).

Borbone, P. G., J. Cook, K. D. Jenner, and D. M. Walter. *The Pentateuch: Concordance.* Vol. 1, pt. 5 of *The Old Testament in Syriac According to the Peshitta Version*, edited by Borbone P. G., and K. D. Jenner. Leiden: Brill, 1977.

Borgen, Peder. *Bread from Heaven: An Exegetical Study of the Concept of Manna in the Gospel of John and the Writings of Philo.* NovTSup 10. Leiden: Brill, 1965.

———. "Some Jewish Exegetical Traditions as Background for Son of Man Sayings in John's Gospel (Jn 3,13–14 and Context)." In *L'Évangile de Jean: Sources, Rédaction, Théologie*, edited by M. De Longe, 243–58. Leuven: Leuven University Press, 1977.

Bover, J. M. "Charin anti charitos (Joh. 1, 16)." Biblica 6 (1925) 454–60.

Bowen, Boone A. "A Study of *ḥsd*." Ph.D. diss., Yale University, 1938.

Bowman, John. "Samaritan Studies." BJRL 40 (1958) 298–327.

Bratcher, Robert G. "What Does 'Glory' Mean in Relation to Jesus: Translating Doxa and Doxazo in John." *BT* 42, no. 4 (1991) 401–8.

Brock, S. P. "Versions, Ancient (Syriac)." In *ABD*.

Brongers, Hendrik Antonie. *Merismus, Synekdoche und Hendidys in der Bibel-Hebraïschen Sprache.* Edited by P. A. H. De Boer. Oudtestamentlich Werkgezelschap in Nederland 14. Leiden: Brill, 1965.

Brooke, George J. "Christ and the Law in John 7–10." In *Law and Religion: Essays on the Place of Law in Israel and Early Christianity*, edited by B. Lindars, 102–12, 180–84. Cambridge: James Clarke, 1988.

BDB-GESENIUS. BibleWorks 7.0.019k.1, 1992–2007. Print ed.: Francis Brown, S. R. Driver, and Charles A. Briggs. *A Hebrew and English Lexicon of the Old Testament, with an Appendix Containing the Biblical Aramaic.* Oxford: Clarendon, 1906. [BDB].

Brown, Raymond Edward. *The Birth of the Messiah: A Commentary on the Infancy Narratives in Matthew and Luke.* New York: Doubleday, 1977.

———. *The Gospel According to John (I–XII)*. Edited by William Foxwell Albright and David Noel Freedman. Vol. 1. AB 29. Garden City, NY: Doubleday, 1966.

———. "Gospel Infancy Narrative Research From 1976 to 1986." *CBQ* 48 (1986) 469–83, 661–80.

Bruce, F. F. *1 & 2 Thessalonians*. Vol. 45 of *WBC* (1982).

———. *The Gospel of John*. Basingstoke, UK: Pickering, 1983.

Brueggemann, Walter. *David's Truth in Israel's Imagination & Memory*. Philadelphia: Fortress, 1985.

Bultmann, Rudolf. "*alētheia, alēthēs, alēthinos, alētheuō*." In *TDNT*.

———. "*alēthinos*." In *TDNT*.

———. "*charis* (Special Developments in Hellenism)." In *TDNT*.

———. "*eleos, eleeō, eleēmōn, eleēmosunē, aneleos, aneleēmōn*." In *TDNT*.

———. *The Gospel of John: A Commentary*. Edited by R. W. N. Hoare and J. K. Riches, translated by George Raymond Beasley-Murray. Philadelphia: Westminster, 1971. Originally published as *Das Evangelium Des Johannes*, KEK 2 (Göttingen: Vandenhoeck & Ruprecht, 1964).

———. "*katakauchaomai*." In *TDNT*.

———. "*oiktirō, oiktirmos, oiktirmōn*." In *TDNT*.

———. *Theology of the New Testament*. Translated by Kendrick Grobel. Vol. 1. London: SCM, 1952.

Calvin, John. *The Gospel of St. John, 11–21, and the First Epistle of John*. Edited by David W. Torrance and Thomas F. Torrance, translated by T. H. L. Parker. Vol. 5 of *Calvin's Commentaries*. Edinburgh: Oliver and Boyd, 1959–72.

Carson, D. A. *The Gospel According to John*. Grand Rapids: Eerdmans, 1991.

Carter, Warren. "The Prologue and John's Gospel: Function, Symbol and the Definitive Word." *JSNT* 39 (January 1990) 35–58.

Catchpole, David R. "The Son of Man's Search for Faith (Luke xviii 8b)." *NovT* 19 (1977) 81–104.

Charles, R. H. "Ecclesiasticus." In *The Apocrypha and Pseudepigrapha of the Old Testament in English: With Introductions and Critical Explanatory Notes to the Several Books*, edited by R. H. Charles. Oxford: Clarendon, 1913.

Charlesworth, James H. "Manasseh, Prayer of." In *ABD*.

———. "Prayer of Manasseh." In *The Old Testament Pseudepigrapha*, edited by James H. Charlesworth, 2:625–38. Garden City, NY: Doubleday, 1985.

Christensen, Duane L. *Deuteronomy 1–11*. Vol. 6a of *WBC* (1991).

Chrysostom, St. John. *Homilies on St. John 14*. PG 51:93; *NPNF*[1] 14:126.

Clines, David J. A. *Job 1–20*. Vol. 17 of *WBC* (1989).

Conzelmann, Hans. "*charis, charizomai, charitoō, acharistōs*." In *TDNT*.

———. "*charis, charizomai, charitoō, acharistōs* (NT)." In *TDNT*.

———. "*charisma*." In *TDNT*.

Cook, W. Robert. "The 'Glory' Motif in the Johannine Corpus." *JETS* 27, no. 3 (1984) 291–97.

Craigie, Peter C. *Psalms 1–50*. Vol. 19 of *WBC* (1983).

———, Page H. Kelly, and Joel F. Drinkard Jr. *Jeremiah 1–25*. Vol. 26 of *WBC* (1991).

Crüsemann, Frank. *Studien zur Formgeschichte von Hymnus und Danklied in Israel*. WMANT 32. Neukirchen-Vluyn: Neukirchener, 1969.

Cyril of Alexandria, St. *In Jo. Ev. Lib.* I.101. PG 73:172–73.

D'Alès, Adhémar. "Charin anti charitos (Ioan. 1, 16)." RSR 9 (1919) 384–86.
Daly-Denton, Margaret. *David in the Fourth Gospel: The Johannine Reception of the Psalms*. Edited by Martin Hengel. AGJU 47. Leiden: Brill, 2000.
Dancy, J. C., W. J. Fuerst, and R. J. Hammer. *The Shorter Books of the Apocrypha: Tobit, Judith, Rest of Esther, Baruch, Letter of Jeremiah, Additions to Daniel and Prayer of Manasseh*. Edited by P. R. Ackroyd, A. R. Leaney, and J. W. Packer. CBC. Cambridge: Cambridge University Press, 1972.
Davids, Peter H. *Commentary on James*. NIGTC. Grand Rapids: Eerdmans, 1982.
Davila, James R. "The Perils of Parallels: 'Parallelomania' Revisited." Draft for discussion, St. Andrews, Scotland, 2001.
Delling, Gerhard. "*plērēs, plēroō, plērōma, anaplēroō, antanaplēroō, ekplēroō, ekplērōsis, sumplēroō, plērophoreō, plērophoria*." In *TDNT*.
DeVries, Simon J. *1 Kings*. Vol. 12 of *WBC* (1985).
Dewailly, Louis-Marie. "Finns det menga hendiadys i Nya Testamentet?" *Svensk Exegetisk Ersbok* 51–52 (1986) 50–56.
Dickie, Matthew W. "Envy." In *ABD*.
Díez Macho, Alejandro. *Éxodo*. Vol. 2 of *Neophyti 1: Targum Palestinense ms. de la Biblioteca Vaticana*, edited by Federico Pérez Castro. Edición príncipe. Seminario Filológico Cardenal Cisneros del Instituto Arias Montano, Textos y estudios 8. Madrid: Consejo Superior de Investigaciones Científicas, 1970.
———. "The Recently Discovered Palestinian Targum: Its Antiquity and Relationship with the Other Targums." *Vetus Testamentum Supplements* 7 (1959) 222–45.
Dodd, Charles H. *The Interpretation of the Fourth Gospel*. Cambridge: Cambridge University Press, 1953.
Dumbrell, William J. "Grace and Truth: The Progress of the Argument of the Prologue of John's Gospel." In *Doing Theology for the People of God: Studies in Honor of J. I. Packer*, edited by Donald M. Lewis and Alister E. McGrath, 105–21. Downers Grove, IL: InterVarsity, 1996.
Dunn, James D. G. *Baptism in the Holy Spirit: A Re-Examination of the New Testament Teaching on the Gift of the Spirit in Relation to Pentecostalism Today*. SBT, 2nd ser., 15. London: SCM, 1970.
———. "Let John Be John: A Gospel for Its Time." In *Das Evangelium und die Evangelien: Vorträge vom Tübinger Symposium 1982*, edited by Peter Stuhlmacher, 309–39. Tübingen: Mohr, 1983.
———. *Romans 1–8*. Vol. 38a of *WBC* (1988).
———. *Romans 9–16*. Vol. 38b of *WBC* (1988).
Durham, John I. *Exodus*. Vol. 3 of *WBC* (1987).
Edwards, Ruth B. "*Charin anti charitos* (John 1.16) Grace and the Law in the Johannine Prologue." *JSNT* 32 (1988) 3–15.
Eerdmans, B. D. "The Chasidim." *OtSt* 1 (1942) 176–257.
Eichrodt, Walther. *Theology of the Old Testament*. Translated by J. A. Baker. Philadelphia: Westminster, 1961. Originally published as *Theologie des Alten Testaments*, 6th ed. (Leipzig: J. C. Hinrichs, 1939).
Evans, Craig A. *Word and Glory: On the Exegetical and Theological Background of John's Prologue*. Edited by Stanley E. Porter. JSNTSup 89. Sheffield: JSOT Press, 1992.
Fichtner, Johannes. "*orgē, orgizomai, orgilos, parorgizō, parorgismos*." In *TDNT*.

Field, Fridericus, editor. *Jobus–Malachias*. Vol. 2 of *Origenis Hexaplorum quae supersunt*. Oxonii [Oxford]: Typgrapheo Clarendoniano, 1875.
Foerster, Werner. "*sebomai, sebozomai, sebasma, Sebastos, eusebēs, eusebia, eusebeō, asebēs, asebia, asebeō, semnos, semnotēs.*" In *TDNT*.
Fortna, Robert T. Review of *The Gospel of John and the Sociology of Light: Language and Characterization in the Fourth Gospel*, by Norman R. Petersen. JBL 116 (Fall 1997) 562–64.
Glasson, Thomas Francis. *Moses in the Fourth Gospel*. SBT 40. London: SCM, 1963.
Glueck, Nelson. *ḥesed in the Bible*. Edited by Elias L. Epstein, translated by Alfred Gottschalk. 2nd ed. Cincinnati: Hebrew Union College Press, 1967. Originally published as *Das Wort hesed im alttestamentlichen Sprachgebrauche als menschliche und göttliche gemeinschaftsgemässe Verhaltungsweise* (Giessen: Töpelmann, 1927).
Gnilka, Joachim. *Johannesevangelium*. Neue Echter Bibel. Würzburg: Echter Verlag, 1983.
Goldingay, John E. *Daniel*. Vol. 30 of *WBC* (1989).
Good, E. M. "Love in the Old Testament." Vol. 3 of *The Interpreter's Dictionary of the Bible*, 164–68. Nashville: Abingdon, 1962.
Goodwin, Charles. "How Did John Treat His Sources?" *JBL* 73, no. 2 (1954) 61–75.
Goshen-Gottstein, M. H. "The 'Third Targum' on Esther and MS Neofiti 1." *Biblica* 56 (1975) 301–29.
Greenspoon, Leonard J. "Aquila's Version." In *ABD*.
———. "Symmachus, Symmachus's Version." In *ABD*.
———. "Versions, Ancient (Greek)." In *ABD*.
Guelich, Robert A. *Mark 1–8:26*. Vol. 34a of *WBC* (1989).
Guilding, Aileen. *The Fourth Gospel and Jewish Worship: A Study of the Relation of St. John's Gospel to the Ancient Jewish Lectionary System*. Oxford: Clarendon, 1960.
Guillet, Jaques. *Themes of the Bible*. Translated by Albert J. LaMothe Jr. Notre Dame: Fides Pub. Assoc., 1960. Originally published as *Thèmes bibliques: études sur l'expression et le développement de la revelation* (Paris: Aubier, 1954).
Gurzon-Siggers, W. S. "Grace and Truth." *ExpTim* 4 (1892–93).
Haenchen, Ernst. *John: A Commentary on the Gospel of John*. Edited and translated by Robert W. Funk. 2 vols. Hermeneia. Philadelphia: Fortress, 1984. Originally published as *Das Johannesevangelium: ein Kommentar* (Tübingen: Mohr, 1980).
Hafemann, Scott J. "The Ministry of Moses: Exodus 32–34 in Canonical Tradition." In *Paul, Moses, and the History of Israel: The Letter/Spirit Contrast and the Argument from Scripture in 2 Corinthians 3*, 189–254. WUNT 81. Tübingen: Mohr, 1995.
Hagner, Donald A. *Matthew 1–13*. Vol. 33a of *WBC* (1993).
Hanson, Anthony Tyrrell. *Grace and Truth: A Study in the Doctrine of the Incarnation*. London: SPCK, 1975.
———. "John I. 14–18 and Exodus XXXIV." *NTS* 23 (1977) 90–101.
———. *The Prophetic Gospel: A Study of John and the Old Testament*. Edinburgh: T. & T. Clark, 1991.
Harris, Elizabeth. *Prologue and Gospel: The Theology of the Fourth Evangelist*. Edited by Stanley E. Porter. JSNTSup 107. Sheffield, England: Sheffield Academic, 1994.
Hartley, John E. *Leviticus*. Vol. 4 of *WBC* (1992).

Hauck, Friedrich. "*koinōnos, koinōneō, koinōnia, sunkoinōnos, sunkoinōneō*." In *TDNT*.
Hawthorne, Gerald F. *Philippians*. Vol. 43 of *WBC* (1983).
Hays, Richard B. *Echoes of Scripture in the Letters of Paul*. Binghampton, NY: Vail-Ballou, 1989.
Healey, Joseph P. "Faith (Old Testament)." In *ABD*.
HALOT. BibleWorks 7.0.019k.1, 1992–2007. Print ed.: L. Köhler, W. Baumgartner, and J. J. Stamm. *The Hebrew and Aramaic Lexicon of the Old Testament*. Translated and edited under the supervision of M. E. J. Richardson. 5 vols. Leiden: Brill, 1994–2000. [*HALOT*]
Heitmüller, W. *Das Evangelium des Johannes*. Die Schriften des NT 2. Göttingen: Vandenhoeck & Ruprecht, 1908.
Hiebert, Theodore. "Theophany in the OT." In *ABD*.
Hodges, Zane C. "Grace after Grace—John 1:16." *BSac* 135 (January–March 1978) 34–45.
Hooker, Morna D. "The Johannine Prologue and the Messianic Secret [a paper read at the meeting of S.N.T.S. at Southhampton, 31 August 1973]." *NTS* 21 (1975) 40–58.
Horst, Johannes. "*makrothumia, makrothumeō, makrothumos, makrothumōs*." In *TDNT*.
Hoskyns, Edwyn Clement, Sir. *The Fourth Gospel*. Edited by Francis Noel Davey. London: Faber, 1947.
Houtman, Cornelis. *Exodus*. Translated by Johan Rebel and Sierd Woudstra. Vol. 3. Historical Commentary on the Old Testament 3. Leuven: Peeters, 2000. Originally published as *Exodus*, 3 vols., Commentaar op het Oude Testament (Kampen: Kok, 1986).
Hyatt, J. Philip. "The God of Love in the Old Testament." In *To Do and To Teach: Essays in Honor of Charles Lynn Pyatt, Presented by His Friends upon his Retirement from the College of the Bible, June, 1953*, edited by Roscoe M. Pierson, 15–26. Lexington, KY: 1953.
An Introduction to Biblical Hebrew Syntax. By Bruce K. Waltke and M. O'Connor. Winona Lake, IN: Eisenbrauns, 1990. [*IBHS*]
Jacob, Edmond. *Theology of the Old Testament*. Translated by Arthur W. Heathcote, and Philip J. Allcock. New York:, 1958. Originally published as *Theologie de l'Ancien Testament* (Neuchatel: Delachaux & Niestle, 1955).
Jepsen, Alfred. "*'ĕmet 'āmēn 'ĕmûnāʰ 'āman*." In *TDOT*, 1:292–323.
———. "Gnade und Barmherzigkeit im Alten Testament." *KD* 7 (1961) 261–71.
———. "*ḥesed* and *ḥāsîd*." In *Interpretationes ad Vetus Testamentum pertinentes Sigmundo Mowinckel septuagenario missae*, 100–112. Oslo: Land og Kirke (Fabritius and Sønner), 1955.
Jeremias, Joachim. "*Mōusēs*." In *TDNT*.
Johnson, Aubrey R. *The Cultic Prophet and Israel's Psalmody*. Cardiff: University of Wales Press, 1979.
Joüon, P. "Jean 1,16: *kai charin anti charitos*." *RSR* 22 (1932).
Kaufman, Stephen A. "Languages (Aramaic)." In *ABD*.

Kellenberger, Edgar. *Häsäd wa'uämät als Ausdruck einer Glaubenserfahrung: Gottes Offen-Werden und Bleiben als Voraussetzung des Leben*. ATANT 69. Zurich: Theolgischer Verlag, 1982.

Keown, Gerald L., Pamela J. Scalise, and Thomas G. Smothers. *Jeremiah 26–52*. Vol 27 of *WBC* (1995).

King, J. S. "The Prologue to the Fourth Gospel: Some Unsolved Problems." *ExpTim* 86 (1975) 372–75.

Kiraz, George Anton. *Lexical Tools to the Syriac New Testament*. JSOT Manuals. 7 ed. Sheffield, England: JSOT Press, 1994.

Kittel, Gerhard. "*akouō*." In *TDNT*.

———. "*alētheia* (B. *'ĕmet* in Rabbinic Judaism)." In *TDNT*.

———. "*doxa* (F. The NT Use of *doxa*, II)." In *TDNT*.

———. "*legō, logos, rhēma, laleō, logios, alogos, logikos, logomacheō, logomachia, eklegomai, eklogē, eklektos* (D. Word and Speech in the NT)." In *TDNT*.

König, E. *Stilistik, Rhetorik, Poetik in Bezug auf die biblische Literatur komparativisch*. Leipzig: Dieterich, 1900.

Köster, Helmut. "*splanchnon, splanchnizomai, eusplanchnos, polusplanchnos, asplanchnos*." In *TDNT*.

Krasovec, Jože. *Antithetic Structure in Biblical Hebrew Poetry*. VTSup 35. Leiden: Brill, 1984.

Krentz, Edgar M. "2 Thessalonians." In *ABD*.

Kselman, John S. "Forgiveness (Old Testament)." In *ABD*.

———. "Grace (Old Testament)." In *ABD*.

Kuyper, Lester J. "Grace and Truth: An Old Testament Description of God, and Its Use in the Johannine Gospel." *Int* 18 (October 1964) 3–19.

Kysar, Robert. "John, the Gospel of." In *ABD*.

La Croix, Paul Marie de. *L'Évangile de Jean et son témoignage spirituel*. Paris: Desclée De Brouwer, 1959.

La Potterie, Ignace de. "*Charis* paulinienne et *Charis* johannique." In *Jesus und Paulus: Festschrift für Werner Georg Kümmel zum 70. Geburstag*, edited by E. Earle Ellis and Erich Grässer, 256–82. 2nd ed. Göttingen: Vandenhoeck & Ruprecht, 1978.

———. "L'arrière-fond du thème johannique de vérité." In *Studia evangelica I*, edited by Kurt Aland, 285–92. TUGAL 87. Berlin: Akademie-Verlag, 1959.

———. *La Vérité dans Saint Jean*. 2 vols. AnBib 73–74. Rome: Pontificio instituto Biblico, 1977.

Lacan, M.-F. "Le prologue de Saint Jean. Ses thémes, sa structure, son mouvement." *Lumiure et vie* 33 (1957) 91–110.

Lagrange, Marie Joseph. *Évangile selon Saint Jean*. 7th ed. EBib. Paris: Gabalda, 1948.

Lane, William L. *Hebrews 1–8*. Vol. 47a of *WBC* (1991).

Larue, Gerald A. "Recent Studies in *ḥesed*." In *Ḥesed in the Bible*, edited by Elias L. Epstein, translated by Alfred Gottschalk, 1–32. 2nd ed. Cincinnati: Hebrew Union College Press, 1967.

Le Déaut, R. "Targumic Literature and New Testament Interpretation." *BTB* 4 (1974) 243–89.

Lee, Edwin Kenneth. *The Religious Thought of St. John*. London: SPCK, 1950.

Lévi, Israel. *The Hebrew Text of the Book of Ecclesiasticus*. Edited by Richard J. H. Gottheil, and Morris Jastrow Jr. SSS 3. Leiden: Brill, 1951.
Levy, B. Barry. *Targum Neophyti 1: A Textual Study*. Vol 1. Studies in Judaism. Lanham, MD: University Press of America, 1986.
Lincoln, Andrew T. *Ephesians*. Vol. 42 of *WBC* (1990).
———. *Truth on Trial: The Lawsuit Motif in the Fourth Gospel*. Peabody, MA Hendrickson, 2000.
Lindars, Barnabas. *The Gospel of John*. Edited by Ronald E. Clements and Matthew Black. New Century Bible. London: Oliphants, 1972.
Loisy, Alfred Firmin. *Le quatrième Évangile*. Paris: Alphonse Picard et fils, 1903.
Longenecker, Richard N. *Galatians*. Vol. 41 of *WBC* (1990).
LNLEX. BibleWorks 7.0.019k.1, 1992–2007. Print ed.: Johannes P. Louw and Eugene A. Nida. *Greek-English Lexicon of the New Testament: Based on Semantic Domains*. 2nd ed. New York: United Bible Societies, 1989. [L&N].
Mafico, Temba L. J. "Ethics (Old Testament)." In *ABD*.
Manns, Frédéric. *John and Jamnia: How the Break Occured Between Jews and Christians c. 80–100 A.D.* Translated by Mildred Duel and Marina Riadi. Jerusalem: Franciscan Printing Press, 1988.
———. "L'Évangile de Jean, réponse chrétienne aux décisions de Jamnia." *LASBF* 30 (1980) 47–92.
Martin-Achard, Robert, and Terrence Prendergast. "Resurrection (Old Testament)." In *ABD*.
Martin, Ralph P. "Gifts, Spiritual." In *ABD*.
———. *James*. Vol. 48 of *WBC* (1988).
———. *2 Corinthians*. Vol. 40 of *WBC* (1986).
Martyn, J. Louis. *History and Theology in the Fourth Gospel*. Rev. ed. Nashville: Abingdon, 1979.
Masing, Uku. "Der Begriff ḥesed im Alttestamentlichen Sprachgebrauch." In *Charisteria Iohanni Kõpp: Octogenario Oblata*, 27–63. Papers of the Estonian Theological Society in Exile 7. Holmiae: Estonian Theological Society in Exile, 1954.
Maurer, Christian. "*tithēmi, atheteō, athetēsis, epitithēmi, epithesis, metatithēmi, metathesis, paratithēmi, parathēkē, [parakatathēkē], protithēmi, prothesis, prostithēmi*." In *TDNT*.
McCarter, P. Kyle. *II Samuel: A New Translation with Introduction, Notes and Commentary*. Edited by William Foxwell Albright and David Noel Freedman. AB 9. Garden City, NY: Doubleday, 1984.
Meeks, Wayne A. *The Prophet-King: Moses Traditions and the Johannine Christology*. NovTSup 14. Leiden: Brill, 1967.
Melamed, Ezra Zion. "Hendiadys in the Bible." *Tarbiz* 16 (1945) 173–89.
Mendenhall, George E., and Gary A. Herion. "Covenant." In *ABD*.
Menken, Maarten F. F. *Old Testament Quotations in the Fourth Gospel: Studies in Textual Form*. CBET 15. Kampen: Kok, 1996.
Meyer, Ben F. "Jesus (PERSON)." In *ABD*.
Michaelis, Wilhelm. "*kakopatheō, sunkakopatheō, kakopatheia*." In *TDNT*.
Michaels, J. Ramsey. *1 Peter*. Vol. 49 of *WBC* (1988).

Michel, Otto. *Der Brief an die Römer*. 13th ed. KEK. Göttingen: Vandenhoeck & Ruprecht, 1966.

Milgrom, Jacob. *Numbers = [Ba-midbar]: The Traditional Hebrew Text with the New JPS Translation*. JPS Torah Commentary. Philadelphia: Jewish Publication Society, 1990.

Montgomery, James A. "Hebrew *Hesed* and Greek *Charis*." *HTR* 32, no. 2 (1939) 97–102.

Moore, Carey A. "Judith, Book of." In *ABD*.

Morris, Leon. *The Gospel According to John: The English Text with Introduction, Exposition and Notes*. Edited by F. F. Bruce. NICNT. London: Marshall, Morgan & Scott, 1972.

Motyer, Stephen. *Your Father the Devil? A New Approach to John and 'the Jews.'* Paternoster Biblical and Theological Monographs. Carlisle: Paternoster, 1997.

Mowley, Henry. "John 1:14–18 in the Light of Exodus 33:7—34:35." *ExpTim* 95 (October 1983–September 1984) 135–37.

MRD. BibleWorks 7.0.019k.1, 1992–2007. Print ed.: James Murdock. *The New Testament, A Literal Translation from the Syriac Peshito Version*. New York: Carter & Bros., 1851.

Murphy, Roland E. *Ecclesiastes*. Vol. 23a of *WBC* (1992).

———. "Grace in the Old Testament." In *Grace upon Grace: Essays in Honor of Thomas A. Langford*, edited by Robert K. Johnston, L. Gregory Jones, and Jonathan R. Wilson, 63–71. Nashville: Abingdon, 1999.

———. *Proverbs*. Vol. 22 of *WBC* (1998).

Myers, Edward P. "Interpreting Figurative Language: Simile, Metaphor, Metonymy, Synecdoche, Hyperbole, Personification, Irony, Apostrophe, Litotes, Aposiopesis, Proverb, Hendiadys, Euphemism, Allegory, and Parable." In *Biblical Interpretation: Principles and Practice*. Edited by F. Furman Kearley, Edward P. Myers, and Timothy D. Hadley, 91–100. Grand Rapids: Baker, 1986.

Neirynck, F. *Jean et les synoptiques: Examen critique de l'exégèse de M.-E. Boismard*. BETL 49. Leuven: Leuven University Press, 1979.

Neubauer, Karl Wilhelm. "Der Stamm *Ch n n* im Sprachgebrauch des Alten Testaments." Ph.D. diss., Berlin Kirchliche Hochschule, 1964.

Newman, Barclay M. *A Concise Greek-English Dictionary of the New Testament*. 1971. Reprint, Stuttgart: German Bible Society, 1993. [UBSDict]

The Nicene and Post-Nicene Fathers, Series 1. AGES Software 1.0, 1997. Print ed.: Edited by Philip Schaff. 14 vols. 1886–89. Reprint, Peabody, MA: Hendrickson, 1994. [*NPNF[1]*].

Nicol, W. *The Semeia in the Fourth Gospel: Tradition and Redaction*. NovTSup 32. Leiden: Brill, 1972.

Nolland, John. *Luke 9:21—18:34*. Vol. 35b of *WBC* (1993).

———. *Luke 1:1—9:20*. Vol. 35a of *WBC* (1989).

O'Brien, Peter T. *Colossians, Philemon*. Vol. 44 of *WBC* (1982).

O'Grady, John F. "Jesus the Revelation of God in the Fourth Gospel." *BTB* 25 (Winter 1995) 161–65.

Odeberg, Hugo. *The Fourth Gospel: Interpreted in Its Relation to Contemporaneous Religious Currents in Palestine and the Hellenistic-Oriental World*. Chicago: Argonaut, 1968.

———. *3 Enoch: Or, the Hebrew Book of Enoch.* 1928. Reprint, New York: Ktav, 1973.
Origen. *Commentary on the Gospel of John.* In *The Ante-Nicene Fathers.* AGES Software 1.0, 1997. Print ed.: Edited by Alexander Roberts and James Donaldson. Vol. 10. 1885–87. Reprint, Peabody, MA: Hendrickson, 1995. [*ANF*].
Pancaro, Severino. *The Law in the Fourth Gospel: The Torah and the Gospel, Moses and Jesus, Judaism and Christianity According to John.* NovTSup 42. Leiden: Brill, 1975.
Panimolle, Salvatore A. *Il dono della legge e la grazia della verita (gv 1,17).* Teologia oggi 21. Rome: Veritas, 1973.
Parker, D. C. "Hexapla of Origen, The." In *ABD.*
Patrologia graeca. Edited by J.-P. Migne. 162 vols. Paris, 1857–1886. [PG].
Peters, Melvin K. H. "Septuagint." In *ABD.*
Petersen, Norman R. *The Gospel of John and the Sociology of Light: Language and Characterization in the Fourth Gospel.* Valley Forge, PA: Trinity Press International, 1993.
Petersen, William L. "Diatessaron." In *ABD.*
Piper, John F., Jr. *The Justification of God: An Exegetical and Theological Study of Romans 9:1–23.* Grand Rapids: Baker, 1983.
Pope, Marvin H. "Bible, Euphemism and Dysphemism in the." In *ABD.*
Quell, Gottfried. "*agapaō, agapē, agapētos* (A. Love in the OT)." In *TDNT.*
———. "*alētheia* (A. The OT Term ʾĕmet)." In *TDNT.*
———. "*dikē, dikaios, dikaiosunē, dikaioō, dikaiōma, dikaiōsis, dikaiokrisia.*" In *TDNT.*
Reed, William L. "Some Implications of *ḥēn* for Old Testament Religion." *JBL* 73 (1954) 36–41.
Reim, Günter. *Studien zum altestamentlichen Hintergrund des Johannesevangeliums.* SNTSMS 22. Cambridge: Cambridge University Press, 1974.
Reumann, John. "Righteousness (New Testament)." In *ABD.*
Richardson, Alan. *An Introduction to the Theology of the New Testament.* London: SCM, 1958.
Robichaux, Kerry S. "Christ, the Spirit, and Glory." *Affirmation & Critique* January (1997) 5–14.
Robinson, H. Wheeler. *Inspiration and Revelation in the Old Testament.* Oxford: Clarendon, 1964.
Robinson, John A. T. *Redating the New Testament.* London: SCM, 1976.
Robinson, J. Armitage. *St. Paul's Epistle to the Ephesians: A Revised Text and Translation with Exposition and Notes.* London: Macmillan, 1903.
Rochais, Gérard. "La formation du Prologue (Jn 1,1–18)." *ScEs* 37 (January–April 1985) 5–44.
Rose, Martin. "Names of God in the OT." In *ABD.*
Ruckstuhl, Eugen. "Johannine Language and Style: The Question of Their Unity." In *L'Évangile de Jean: Sources, Rédaction, Théologie,* edited by M. de Longe, 125–47. Leuven: Leuven University Press, 1977.
———. *Die literarische Einheit des Johannesevangeliums.* Edited by Max Küchler. NTOA 5. Göttingen: Vandenhoeck & Ruprecht, 1987. Originally published as *Die literarische Einheit des Johannesevangeliums* (Freiburg: Paulus, 1951).

———, and Peter Dschulnigg. *Stilkritik und Verfasserfrage im Johannesevangelium: die johanneischen Sprachmerkmale auf dem Hintergrund des Neuen Testaments und des zeitgenössischen hellenistischen.* NTOA 17. Göttingen: Vandenhoeck & Ruprecht, 1991.

Sakenfeld, Katharine Doob. *Faithfulness in Action: Loyalty in Biblical Perspective.* OBT 16. Philadelphia: Fortress, 1985.

———. "Love (Old Testament)." In *ABD*.

———. *The Meaning of ḥesed in the Hebrew Bible: A New Inquiry.* HSM 17. Missoula, MT: Scholars, 1978.

Sanders, Joseph Newbould. *A Commentary on the Gospel According to St. John.* Edited by B. A. Mastin. BNTC. London: A. & C. Black, 1968.

Sarna, Nahum M. "Exodus, Book of." In *ABD*.

Schlatter, Adolf von. *Das Evangelium nach Johannes: Ausgelegt für Bibelleser.* 4th ed. Erläuterungen zum Neuen Testament 3. Stuttgart: Calwer, 1928.

———. *Der Evangelist Johannes: Wie er spricht, denkt und glaubt: Ein Kommentar.* 2nd ed. Stuttgart: Calwer, 1948.

Schlier, Heinrich. "*aleiphō*." In *TDNT*.

———. "*bebaios, bebaioō, bebaiōsis*." In *TDNT*.

Schmidt, Karl Ludwig. "*basileus, basileia, basilissa, basileuō, sumbasileuō, basileios, basilikos* (E. The Word Group *basileus ktl.* in the NT)." In *TDNT*.

Schnackenburg, Rudolf. *The Gospel According to St. John.* Translated by Kevin Smyth, Cecily Hastings et al. 3 vols. Herder's Theological Commentary on the New Testament. London: Burns & Oates, 1968-82. Originally published as *Das Johannesevangelium*, 3 vols., HTKNT 4 (Freiburg: Herder, 1965-75).

———. "Zur johanneischen Forschung." *BZ* 18 (1974) 272-87.

Schneider, Johannes. "*omnuō*." In *TDNT*.

Schoeps, Hans Joachim. "Symmachusstudien." In *Aus frühchristlicher Zeit: religionsgeschichtliche Untersuchungen*, 82-119. Tübingen: Mohr, 1950.

Schoneveld, Jacobus. "Torah in the Flesh: A New Reading of the Prologue of the Gospel of John As a Contribution to a Christology Without Anti-Judaism." *Immanuel* 24-25 (1990) 77-94.

Schrenk, Gottlob. "*dikē, dikaios, dikaiosunē, dikaioō, dikaiōma, dikaiōsis, dikaiokrisia*." In *TDNT*.

Schweizer, Eduard. *Ego Eimi. Die religionsgeschichtliche Herkunft und theologische Bedeutung der johanneischen Bildreden, zugleich ein Beitrag zur Quellenfrage des vierten Evangeliums.* 2nd ed. FRLANT 38. Göttingen: Vandenhoeck & Ruprecht, 1939.

———. "*pneuma, pneumatikos, pneō, empneō, pnoē, ekpneō, theopneustos* (IV. John)." In *TDNT*.

Scott, Ernest Findlay. *The Fourth Gospel: Its Purpose and Theology.* Edinburgh: T. & T. Clark, 1906.

Scullion, John J. "God (God in the OT)." In *ABD*.

———. "Righteousness (OT)." In *ABD*.

Segal, M. Z. (H). *An Introduction to the Old Testament.* Jerusalem: n.p., 1960.

Seow, C. L. "Hosea, Book of." In *ABD*.

Skehan, Patrick W. *The Wisdom of Ben Sira: A New Translation with Notes*. Edited by William Foxwell Albright and David Noel Freedman. AB 39. Garden City, NY: Doubleday, 1987.
Smith, C. Ryder. *The Bible Doctrine of Grace and Related Doctrines*. London: Epworth, 1956.
Smith, Dwight Moody. "Grace upon Grace in the Gospel of John." In *Grace upon Grace: Essays in Honor of Thomas A. Langford*, edited by Robert K. Johnston, L. Gregory Jones, and Jonathan R. Wilson, 25–32. Nashville: Abingdon, 1999.
Smith, Ralph L. *Micah–Malachi*. Vol. 32 of *WBC* (1984).
Snaith, Norman H. *The Distinctive Ideas of the Old Testament*. Fernley-Hartley Lecture 1944. London: Epworth, 1944.
———. "Loving-kindness." In *A Theological Word Book of the Bible*, edited by Alan Richardson, 136–67. New York: Macmillan, 1951.
Sorg, Dom Rembert. *Hesed and Hasid in the Psalms*. St. Louis: Pio Decimo, 1953.
Speiser, E. A. *Genesis: Introduction, Translation and Notes*. Edited by William Foxwell Albright and David Noel Freedman. 2nd ed. AB 1. Garden City, NY: Doubleday, 1964.
Stauffer, Ethelbert. "*agapaō, agapē, agapētos* (C. Love in Judaism)." In *TDNT*.
Stoebe, Hans Joachim. "Die Bedeutung des Wortes *Häsäd* im Alten Testament." *VT* 2 (1952) 244–54.
Strachan, Robert Harvey. *The Fourth Gospel: Its Significance and Environment*. 3rd ed. London: SCM, 1941.
Stuart, Douglas. "Exegesis." In *ABD*.
———. *Hosea–Jonah*. Vol. 31 of *WBC* (1987).
Swete, Henry Barclay, editor. *1 Chronicles–Tobit*. Vol 2 of *The Old Testament in Greek According to the Septuagint*. Cambridge: Cambridge University Press, 1896.
Tate, Marvin E. *Psalms 51–100*. Vol. 20 of *WBC* (1986).
Theobald, Michael. *Die Fleischwerdung des Logos: Studien zum Verhältnis des Johannesprologs zum Corpus des Evangeliums und zu 1 Joh*. NTAbh 20. Münster: Aschendorff, 1988.
TDNT. Libronix Digital Library System 2.1c, 2000–2004. Print ed.: *Theological Dictionary of the New Testament*. Edited by Gerhard Kittel and Gerhard Friedrich, translated by Geoffrey W. Bromiley. Grand Rapids: Eerdmans, 1964–76). [*TDNT*]
Theological Dictionary of the Old Testament. Edited by G. Johannes Botterweck and Helmer Ringgren. Translated by John T. Willis, Geoffrey W. Bromiley, and D. E. Green. 8 vols. Grand Rapids: Eerdmans, 1977. [*TDOT*].
TWOT. BibleWorks 7.0.019k.1, 1992–2007. Print ed.: *Theological Wordbook of the Old Testament*. Edited by R. Laird Harris, Gleason L. Archer Jr., and Bruce K. Waltke. 2 vols. Chicago: Moody, 1980. [*TWOT*].
Theophylact. *Enarr. in Jo.* I.518f. PG 123:1164.
Thompson, Marianne Meye. "'God's Voice You Have Never Heard, God's Form You Have Never Seen': The Characterization of God in the Gospel of John." *Semeia* 63 (1993) 177–204.
———. *The God of the Gospel of John*. Grand Rapids: Eerdmans, 2001.

Thompson, Michael. *Clothed with Christ: The Example and Teaching of Jesus in Romans 12.1—15:13*. Edited by Stanley E. Porter. JSNTSup 59. Sheffield: JSOT Press, 1991.

Thüsing, Wilhelm. *Die Erhöhung und Verherrlichung Jesu in Johannesevangelium*. NTAbh 21/1-2. Münster: Aschendorff, 1960.

Thyen, Hartwig. "Das Heil commt von den Juden." In *Kirche: Festschrift für Günther Bornkamm zum 75, Geburstag*, edited by D. Lührmann and G. Strecker, 163-83. Tübingen: Mohr, 1980.

Tov, Emanuel. *The Greek and Hebrew Bible: Collected Essays on the Septuagint*. Edited by H. M. Barstad et al. VTSup 72. Leiden: Brill, 1999.

Trilling, Wolfgang. *Untersuchungen zum zweiten Thessalonicherbrief*. ETS 27. Leipzig: St. Benno, 1972.

Turner, Max. *The Holy Spirit and Spiritual Gifts: Then and Now*. Carlisle: Paternoster, 1996.

Turner, Nigel. "The Style of John." In *Style*, by Nigel Turner and James Hope Moutlon, 64-79. Vol. 3 of *A Grammar of New Testament Greek*. Edinburgh: T. & T. Clark, 1976.

———, and James Hope Moulton. *Syntax*. Vol. 3 of *A Grammar of New Testament Greek*. Edinburgh: T. & T. Clark, 1963.

Urbrock, William J. "Blessings and Curses." In *ABD*.

Von Rad, Gerhard. "*doxa* (C. *kābôd* in the OT)." In *TDNT*.

Westhuizen, J. P. van der. "Hendiadys in Biblical Hymns of Praise." *Semitics* 6 (1978) 50–57.

Walters (Katz), Peter. *The Text of the Septuagint: Its Corruptions and Their Emendation*. Edited by D. W. Gooding. Cambridge: Cambridge University Press, 1973.

Watts, John D. W. *Isaiah 34–66*. Vol. 25 of *WBC* (1987).

Weiser, Artur. "*pisteuō, pistis, pistos, pistoō, apistos, apisteō, apistia, oligopistos, oligopistia* (B. The OT Concept)." In *TDNT*.

Weiss, Konrad. "*chrēstos, chrēstotēs, chrēsteuomai, chrēstologia*." In *TDNT*.

Wenham, Gordon J. *Genesis 1–15*. Vol. 1 of *WBC* (1987).

———. *Genesis 16–50*. Vol. 2 of *WBC* (1994).

Westcott, Brooke Foss. *The Gospel According to St. John: The Greek Text with Introduction and Notes*. 2 vols. London: John Murray, 1908.

Wetter, Gillis Petersson. *Charis ein Beitrag zur Geschichte des ältesten Christentums*. Edited by Hans Windisch. UNT 5. Leipzig: J. C. Hinrichs, 1913.

Wevers, John William. *Notes on the Greek Text of Exodus*. Edited by Claude E. Cox. SCS 30. Atlanta: Scholars, 1990.

———. *Text History of the Greek Exodus*. MSU 21. Göttingen: Vandenhoeck & Ruprecht, 1992.

Whitaker, Richard. *Revised BDB Hebrew-English Lexicon*. CD-ROM. Big Fork, MT: BibleWorks, 1998. Print ed.: 1995.

Williams, Ronald J. *Hebrew Syntax: An Outline*. 2nd ed. Toronto: University of Toronto Press, 1976.

Williamson, H. G. M. *Ezra, Nehemiah*. Vol. 16 of *WBC* (1985).

Windisch, Hans. "*Hellēn, Hellas, Hellēnikos, Hellēnis, Hellēnistēs, Hellēnisti* (B. *Hellēnes* among the Jews, C. *Hellēnes* in the NT)." In *TDNT*.

Witherington, Ben, III. "Dorcas." In *ABD*.

———. *John's Wisdom: A Commentary on the Fourth Gospel*. Cambridge: Lutterworth, 1995.
———. *Women in the Earliest Churches*. Edited by G. N. Stanton. SNTSMS 59. Cambridge: Cambridge University Press, 1988.
Word Biblical Commentaries on CD-ROM. Logos Library System 2.1f, 1998. Print ed.: *Word Biblical Commentaries*, edited by David A. Hubbard, Glenn W. Baker, John D. Watts, and Ralph P. Martin. 54 vols. Dallas: Word, 1982–. [*WBC*]
Wright, Benjamin G. *No Small Difference: Sirach's Relationship to Its Hebrew Parent Text*. Edited by Claude E. Cox. SCS 26. Atlanta, Georgia: Scholars Press, 1989.
Zimmerli, Walther. "*charis* (OT)." In *TDNT*.
———. "*ḥsd* im Schrifttum von Qumran." In *Hommages à André Dupont-Sommer*, 439–49. Paris: Adrien-Maisonneuve, 1971.
———. "*pais Theou*." In *TDNT*.
Zobel, Hans J. "*ḥesed*." In *TDOT*, 3:44–64.

www.ingramcontent.com/pod-product-compliance
Lightning Source LLC
Chambersburg PA
CBHW070239230426

43664CB00014B/2357